Visions of Modernity

Visions of Modernity

Representation, Memory, Time and Space in the Age of the Camera

Scott McQuire

SAGE Publications
London • Thousand Oaks • New Delhi

First published 1998

 SAGE Publications Ltd
6 Bonhill Street
London EC2A 4PU

SAGE Publications Inc
2455 Teller Road
Thousand Oaks, California 91320

SAGE Publications India Pvt Ltd
32, M-Block Market
Greater Kailash – I
New Delhi 110 048

British Library Cataloguing in Publication data

A catalogue record for this book is available from
the British Library.

ISBN 0 7619 5300 0
ISBN 0 7619 5301 9 (pbk)

Library of Congress catalog card number 97–069468

Typeset by Photoprint, Torquay, Devon
Printed in Great Britain by Redwood Books, Trowbridge, Wiltshire

Contents

Acknowledgments

Many people have contributed to the shaping of this text. It began as a doctoral dissertation and I thank my supervisors, Don Miller and Fiona Mackie, for their endless encouragement and friendship. Nikos Papastergiadis provided many sparks of inspiration, and always turned up at the right time to prove the other side of the world is not so far away. I also extend my thanks to Peter Lyssiotis, whose wonderful photographs first tempted me to write about television. John Hutnyk and Peter Phipps have seen this text through many twists and turns, and I am grateful for all our discussions. Philippa Rothfield, Lyndal Jones and Kate Latimer all offered generous support at crucial times. Katharine Grimshaw has been a clear sighted and generous reader as deadlines approached. I would also like to thank the many students I have taught at different universities in the last four or five years – many of these ideas were first worked out with you! My deepest gratitude goes to Shari Leigh and Lex, who shared many of the emotions of this project. To Stuart, Wendy, Kendal and Alex, whose home has been a haven for writing, and to the rest of my family – Lisa, David, Cameron, Alison, David and Atsuko – I am especially grateful for all their support. Above all, I want to thank my parents for the way they have always encouraged us in whatever we do. I would like to dedicate this book to them.

you could never envisage all the camera has seen, countless images scattered at random in time and space like the fragments of a vast and ancient mosaic, the remnants of a visual holocaust, the ruins of representation . . . colossal . . . a unique map, a phantom topography coiling the entire globe, an endless collage which in the end forms . . . another world, the true surrealist universe . . . you will never know a limit to all the stories, plots, parables, histories, myths and fictions spawned in this oneiric archive – assuming it can exist – the truths it could tell if only we knew how to read its languages, interpret its codes, translate its evidence . . . and the other narratives, the impossible, forbidden, illegitimate or illegible narratives, the swings across the void between madness and negentropy? . . . within this tableau, amongst myriad-faceted shifts of light and shadow, you could never hope to locate a centre, an origin, an end . . . you will never comprehend the totality of such a fabulous and excessive montage . . . or be able to decide if it intensifies and magnifies identity or instead annihilates all possible selves, reducing them to insignificant specks amongst its specular grandeur . . . you will never know if it brings the gift of foresight or the curse of blindness, if it weaves the tapestry of history or forms the crypt of memory . . .
you (but, who, you?) will never know . . .

Introduction

I know of few things in the range of science more surprising than the gradual appearance of the picture on the blank sheet of paper, especially the first time the experiment is witnessed.

William Henry Fox Talbot

In the one and a half centuries since rays of light reflected from an object were first passed through a lens and brought into contact with a sensitive emulsion capable of preserving their different intensities, camera technologies have profoundly transformed the world we inhabit. Approaching this transformation is fraught with difficulty. The diverse practices, institutions, knowledges and pleasures generated by the camera have been integral to the uneven process of modernization, helping to define the global reach of capitalism and the colonial ambitions of the West, while facilitating the instrumental reorganization of social and political life 'at home'. The shift to secular, urban–industrial, bureaucratic societies, which has forged the distinct horizons of modernity, is not only unimaginable but practically inoperable in the camera's absence.

Beyond any question of empirical inadequacy raised by the extreme dispersion of photographic effects, a more intractable concern is the camera's profound influence on modes of perception, forms of cognition and systems of knowledge which were previously considered to be fundamental. In transforming the basic means through which we encounter the world, the camera has shifted the grounding of both 'the world' and the 'we' who might pose the question of this encounter. The uncanny equivalence between 'direct' and 'indirect' perceptions – which spreads from the first still photographs to the moving image of cinema and the live image of television, and is today entering new dimensions with virtual reality technologies – presents a radical challenge to traditional formations of identity and subjectivity. By decentring the authority of embodied perception and destabilizing the customary relationship between presence and absence, the camera has induced a crisis at the border between 'representation' and 'reality', affecting all contemporary experiences of time, space and memory.

How might these different trajectories be represented so as to respect their diversity and dispersion while acknowledging the common forces which condition their emergence? Applying established frameworks of analysis to

References for all quotes at the beginning of parts or sections are given in Sources for Epigraphs. References for all quotes used within the text are provided in footnotes on the page.

new phenomena is always problematic. Insofar as the camera's effect has been precisely to transgress previous perceptual limits and to unseat a host of prior conceptual allegiances, the potential gap between theory and its constructed object is greatly accentuated. Writing 'about' the camera must take into account the manner in which camera technologies have redefined the rhythms of representation and the horizons of knowledge. A strategic aim of this text is to cross-hatch accounts of technical innovation and socio-political change with analyses of conceptual and epistemological rupture, thereby relating the camera to major paradigm shifts in modern thought.

The other side of this equation is the manner in which so many theories of modernity have been, explicitly or implicitly, informed by the metaphor of the camera, bound up with the possibilities of disembodied vision that it provides, the spatio-temporal distances it spans, the claims to objectivity it authorizes. Take, for example, what Freud termed 'primal scene' fantasies, the most extreme case being the fantasy of observing parental intercourse while still an unborn baby in the womb.[1] Negotiating the complexity of origins and formulating an account of the time before 'I' existed are crucial determinants of identity. If we accept that such accounts vary culturally and historically, what significance should we give to the fact that Freud's description of an unborn observer so closely resembles the out of body perceptual experience provided by the camera?

Does this resemblance 'explain' our enduring fascination with camera images? (This is the standpoint adopted by much film theory, which has found comparisons between the scene of cinema and Freud's keyhole scenario so fertile and compelling.) Or should explanation proceed in more than one direction? Is it only coincidence that the text usually offered as the origin of psychoanalysis (the *Studies on Hysteria* that Freud co-authored with Breuer) appeared in 1895, virtually alongside the first public demon-stration of the *cinématographe*?

In attempting to plot the convergence between the camera and psycho-analysis, there is a need to go beyond simply interpreting the former in terms of the theory provided by the latter. The camera's capacity to reproduce the primal scene doesn't so much make the fantasy 'real' as alter its conditions of existence. What of all those children growing up in the present who can observe, if not the 'decisive moment' of their own conception, the video record of their own birth? Or the ultrasound image of themselves in the womb? Or simply the faces of their parents as children, before they themselves were born? The ability to witness things *outside all previous limits of time and space* highlights the fact that the camera doesn't only give us a new means to represent experience: it changes the nature of experience and redefines our processes of understanding.

*

1 See S. Freud, 'The paths to the formation of symptoms', in *The Standard Edition of the Complete Psychological Works of Sigmund Freud*, vol. 16 (translated under the general editorship of J. Strachey), London, Hogarth Press, 1963, p. 370.

Most accounts of photography begin by determining an origin with respect to François Arago's famous announcement unveiling the Daguerreotype at the *Académie des Sciences* on 7 January 1839. In similar vein, cinema is usually defined with reference to the celebrated screenings held by the Lumière brothers at the *Grand Café* in Paris on 28 December 1895. However, the security of these co-ordinates tends to be immediately undercut by a certain wavering over precisely who invented what we now call photography or cinema. Was it in fact Louis Daguerre, who gave his name to the Daguerreotype which dominated the early years of photography but proved to be a technical dead end and was little used even two decades from its inception? Or was it the Englishman, William Henry Fox Talbot, whose process of 'photogenic drawing' (publicly demonstrated almost contemporaneously with Daguerre's announcement) became the basis for making multiple positive prints from a single negative plate? Or had the origin occurred earlier? The names of Niepce, Bayard, Wedgewood and Herschel are occasionally thrown into the ring, while the history of cinema recites its own alternative honour roll, with Muybridge and Marey, Edison and Skladanowsky cropping up most often.

While these arguments are of interest, many of the assumptions on which they are based seem dubious. Instead of seeking to resolve the confusion with reference to significant individuals and decisive moments, it is perhaps more productive to question the common orientation of these received accounts. The 'history of photography', like 'the history of cinema', is, in fact, a relatively recent invention. Most arguments as to whether Daguerre, Talbot, Niepce or someone else 'invented' photography depend upon the unspoken assumption that we know exactly what photography is and what taking a photograph involves. Yet perhaps nothing is less certain.

On the one hand, different aspects of the photographic process clearly had a lengthy gestation. The principle of the camera obscura was discussed by a chain of writers, including Euclid, Aristotle, Alhazen, Bacon, Leonardo and Kepler, and had been known for at least 2,000 years prior to its photographic application. The key nineteenth-century breakthrough lay in chemistry rather than optics, in the stabilization of images rather than in their production or projection. On the other hand, it is equally evident that the practices we today designate by the name 'photography', especially the proliferation of cheap, portable cameras and the mass circulation of photographic images in the media, were not possible until much later than 1839. Yet, most photographic histories have been content to narrate a more or less unbroken lineage stretching from Daguerre to the present day. Such an assumption is both revealing and problematic.

Under the influence of evolutionary accounts of technological progress, image production is understood to have become steadily cheaper, faster, more responsive and more versatile, with its social and political effects following a similar democratic continuum. In these narratives, the camera is to representation what parliament is to representative democracy: the idealization of neutrality itself. Against such heroic accounts one could easily oppose accounts which narrate the history of the camera as a continuous despotism: the extension of technological surveillance, the emergence of societies of spectacle, the internalization of the objectifying gaze. What tends to remain constant is precisely the presumption of a continuous historical trajectory and a unified subject-effect. To question this presumption is not to advocate replacing narratives of continuity with those privileging discontinuity. Rather, it is a matter of examining, as patiently and rigorously as possible, the means by which certain unities and continuities have been established and consolidated in and as the camera's history, while potential breaks, ruptures and differences have been discounted or truncated in the name of that history.

*

In his famous discussion of technology, Heidegger argued that any technology involves the establishment of a particular relation to the world. As such, it forms a mechanism of enframing, which, far from being a mere technique of performance, constitutes an essential part of the definition of the task to be performed.[2] The aptness of the metaphor of enframing for thinking about the camera – the ubiquitous technology which literally frames the world – is significant. If camera technology has never merely 'improved' or 'evolved', as if in some neutral space, today the camera stands as symptomatic of the coupling of the technological to the socio-political in contemporary culture. More to the point, it is a strategic symptom, insofar as it throws contemporary relations between power and representation – including the dialectic between the politicization of aesthetics and the aestheticization of politics which has dominated this century – into the most acute relief.

Yet critical theory has rarely treated the camera in a manner adequate to the complexity of the questions it raises. Despite the early example of those such as Siegfried Kracauer and Walter Benjamin, analysis has frequently suffered by hastily assembling an overly unified concept of 'the image', or by arbitrarily isolating the domains of photography, cinema and television in order to define 'proper' objects of study. Cutting across these categories is the silent paralysis caused by the split between analysis of cultural–aesthetic formations on the one hand and scientific–industrial applications on the other. The fact that camera technologies have been an integral part of the process of industrialization has been as much neglected in social theory as the camera's dependence on a whole network of industrial practices and production techniques has been excluded from art history. This concatenation of absences skews our perceptions of history, and limits our ability to respond to change in the present.

Even the most cursory scan reveals the immense diversity of zones, functions and practices that camera technologies span in contemporary life:

2 M. Heidegger, 'The question concerning technology', in *The Question Concerning Technology and Other Essays* (trans. W. Lovitt), New York, Harper and Row, 1977, pp. 3–35.

network television news, X-rays, passport photos, experimental film, astro-photography, photojournalism, photomicrography, military observation, tele-conferencing, family snapshots, police surveillance, Hollywood cinema, pornography, photocopying, documentary film, postcards, music video – an unimaginable and perhaps unmanageable heterogeneity of categories, genres, images and imagery. Yet, for a variety of reasons, a decisive absence still structures the dominant routes of politics, sociology and social theory: a paucity of reference to the camera and a lack of consideration of the scope of its social and political effects, which are regularly consigned either to the margins and footnotes, or the implicitly narrower domain of 'media studies'. While 'postmodern' thought has given a new prominence to the media as an object of analysis, it has rarely posed its own emergence in relation to the spread of media technologies.

To make these observations is not to advance the claims of a new discourse which might be capable of totalizing its object. The sense of mastery generated by the desire for panoramic vision to which camera technologies have frequently been attached is itself a key effect to scrutinize. But remaining blind to the exclusions promoted by rigid disciplinary boundaries risks allowing the camera to ground its own history as the uninterrupted history of technological progress. To dislodge this teleology – to displace teleology as such – demands the importation of insights from a variety of disciplines and attention to the dissonance masked by conventional theoretical positions. There is a double injunction here: the refusal of points of departure which acknowledge no parentage must be balanced with respect for the uniqueness of the camera's historical thresholds in their distinctive emergence and irreducible singularity. Approaching the camera by moving between the contradictions it detonates offers neither the consolation of an absolute origin, nor the safety of a stable centre which could regulate and order the entire problematic. But, suspended in the orphic space between the discourse of art and the discourse of science, there is a greater possibility of engaging with some of the most critical cultural and political mutations of the late twentieth century.

*

The ubiquity of migration has made cultural displacement integral to the experience of modernity. John Berger has observed: 'Never before our time have so many people been uprooted. Emigration, forced or chosen, across national frontiers or from the village to the metropolis, is the quintessential experience of our time.'[3] For those who leave home, the rupture is not only spatial, but temporal. In the new country, the migrant is often split between nostalgia for the past and investment in the promise of the future: the present is mortgaged to garnering opportunities for the next generation.

3 J. Berger, *And Our Faces, My Heart, Brief as Photos*, London, Writers and Readers, 1984, p. 55.

As the twentieth century draws to a close, it has become increasingly evident that aspects of 'the migrant experience' extend well beyond the parameters conventionally ascribed to migration. 'Modernization' has been synonymous with the disintegration of tradition and the destabilization of links between locality and identity. This has been particularly acute for those excluded from the narrative of modernity, the so-called 'primitives' whose lands were expropriated in the name of progress, indigenous peoples who have been made foreigners within their own countries. But even those embraced as citizens of the modern nation state have found themselves exposed to intense pressures of estrangement, as the rapidity of social change has exacerbated social tensions and outstripped capacity for adaptation. It is from this perspective that Nikos Papastergiadis has suggested: '. . . migration with all its asymmetrical contours and uneven times is a metaphor for the modern condition.'[4]

If modern migration has been driven by the development of a global economy and the consolidation of a global division of labour, these processes have been inseparable from the emergence of transnational cultural flows. Rapid circulation of people and products is today counterpointed by the rapid circulation of images and representations. Like the proliferation of new vehicles of transportation, the new vectors of communication have redefined the centres of lived existence. The ubiquity of rupture to the co-ordinates of the familiar, and the generalization of displacement to plant it at the heart of contemporary experience, has profoundly altered the meaning of home, and of the unknown which lies beyond its increasingly uncertain bounds. 'Home' – in all its senses from physical shelter to existential dwelling place – is no longer inextricably bound to a particular place, synonymous with a single language, homogeneous people, or unified culture. Under pressure of new forms of circulation and new demands for social mobility, home has increasingly become a relation one must seek to establish wherever one finds oneself, amongst a crowd of others at the juncture of a diversity of cultures.

Mircea Eliade once defined home as the heart of the real. The crisis of the real generated by the camera's capacity to hijack visual appearances, cross borders and redefine boundaries belongs to modernity's lingering sense of existential homelessness. The political ambivalence of this condition is mirrored by the double-edged role of the camera in its formation. While modernity has always promised liberation from the bonds of immediacy and relief from the strictures of parochialism, possibilities of cultural and political reinvention have often been accompanied by social dislocation and cultural dispossession. It is to this legacy of cultural trauma, which is not simply modernity's unfortunate accident but an intractable part of its bloodstained progress, that one must look to understand the intensity of the modern desire to transcend time and space.

4 N. Papastergiadis, *Modernity as Exile: The Stranger in John Berger's Writing*, Manchester, Manchester University Press, 1993, p. 1.

If the camera has opened new horizons to the gaze of colonizer and tourist, it has also offered the diasporic and displaced a powerful means to overcome distance and absence, to sew together the poles which life has split asunder. As much as the photograph marks a site of irreducible absence, it is frequently the talisman signalling the possibility of return. Similarly, the seduction of cinema has often depended upon the camera's promise to reassemble the shattered fragments of modern existence. And, in a bombed out cultural landscape, television has increasingly become the lifeline between the bunkers. These historically new means of linking representation to memory and identity cannot be interpreted simply as 'inauthentic', nor yet accepted uncritically on their own terms. Nostalgia for the lost past has frequently been the correlate of modernity's heroic quest to invent the future, and the camera has often been asked to carry a double burden on this journey, 'preserving' what went before, while reconstructing the borders of self, home and community in the process.

Despite the fact that it often seems as if no further acceleration is possible – what could exceed the light speed of television? – it would be rash to believe that the modern desire to annihilate space and time is drawing to a close. Acceleration remains the dominant frame of current technological development, most notably in the computer industry which is increasingly merging with camera and telephone technologies in the multi-purpose screen. Yet, all these techniques of rapid communication – especially broadcast television whose economy has been so driven by the lure of instantaneity – perhaps also serve to affirm the existence of something quite *other*. An insubstantial something which traces a certain void at the heart of time; a zone of indetermination circling the paradox of the *now* which confounds every attempt at precise definition.

Traditional understandings of space and time have been under challenge for most of this century. If the modernist attack on classical discourses presuming temporal continuity and spatial homogeneity has always been comprehended by meta-narratives promising restoration of the whole, what must be attempted today is the rather different task of rethinking concepts such as home, nation, community and identity in conjunction with the values to which they have always been systematically opposed: foreignness, difference, dispersion, alterity. The camera offers a strategic point of departure for this project. Insofar as it opens a new type of relation to the scene of the other – the elsewhere, the outside – it demands that we approach what has been most strenuously repressed in Western thought: the heterogeneity of time and the heteronomy of identity which eludes the thought of being determined as presence.

*

My own point of departure can be stated quite simply: I belong to the first generation in Australia born into a world in which television already existed.[5] I wanted to reflect on this experience by situating the historical development of what is commonly called 'media culture'. In writing a political anatomy of the camera I have sought to explore the tension between the need to represent history, and the necessity to historicize representation. The text is divided into three main parts: the first concerning representation, the second memory and history, and the third space and time. Clearly, these themes are not mutually exclusive. On the contrary, I perceive them to be fundamentally interrelated. The most difficult part of writing has undoubtedly been the task of ordering a final text while acknowledging the limits of finalizing and the politics of ordering. The need to conceptualize, to narrate, to theorize 'about' the camera must constantly be measured against the different patterns of explanation and novel configurations of power and knowledge that camera technologies have generated and legitimated.

In seeking to formulate connections which don't necessarily conform to the model of linear narrative, there is a temptation to say everything at once. Since this proves impossible, other means must be found. What follows can certainly be read from beginning to end, but this is not the only legitimate way to proceed. The text is structured less as the unwinding of a single path than the intertwining of a series of spirals. The three major parts, and the sections into which they are divided, each have their own concerns and coherences. At the same time, it is my hope that they inform each other and deepen certain insights developed over the course of the whole.

While the bulk of this text has been written in Melbourne, Australia, my primary concerns have been neither local nor national, nor yet universal or global, but emerge rather from the instability that affects co-ordinates of proximity and place in the present. My theoretical location has also been necessarily hybrid. In cross-hatching various modes of writing about the camera with deconstructive and postcolonial critiques of the privilege of 'the West', I have attempted to articulate the strategic importance of engaging with modernity and postmodernity as political and cultural formations whose thresholds of emergence, bound up with the rupture and realignment of traditional borders, are intertwined with the emergence of photography, cinema and television as vital social relations in themselves.

If this work nevertheless obeys the dictates of what Blanchot has called the imperious centre – that centre which displaces itself while remaining the same, always becoming more central, more hidden, more uncertain – the place to which it seems directed here is the question of identity and the transformation of subjectivity. Comparisons between the camera and the eye of God have often been made, although usually with scant consideration as to what 'God' can mean in cultures whose ostensibly secular horizons have been redefined by the camera. But, assuming that one could ever write a 'history of subjectivity' in the manner Kristeva once proposed, it seems to me that the camera's influence is today comparable in scope and depth to

5 My parents bought their first TV set in 1956, the year television arrived in Australia for the Melbourne Olympics. I was born in 1962.

that of the great religious formations (Judaism, Christianity) she takes as her exemplars.[6]

Doubtless different readers will plot their own paths through this work according to itineraries which bear little or no resemblance to mine. For some, what follows will be too elliptical and allusive, for others it may not be nearly fragmentary or aphoristic enough. In adopting a shuttling motion between different positions, I have sought less to transcend existing antinomies than to occupy their enigmatic intervals. It is in these interstices that resonances, patterns and relations which resist more conventional approaches to this domain might imperceptibly allow themselves to be seen or silently make themselves heard.

6 See her *Tales of Love* (trans. L.S. Roudiez), New York, Columbia University Press, 1987, p. 16.

PART 1
THE RUINS OF REPRESENTATION

During long periods of history, the mode of human sense perception changes with humanity's entire mode of existence.

Walter Benjamin

You know exactly what I think about photography. I would like to see it make people despise painting until something else will make photography unbearable.

Marcel Duchamp

1

Photomimesis

The objective nature of photography confers on it a credibility absent from all other picture making. In spite of any objections our critical spirit may offer, we are forced to accept as real the existence of the object reproduced, actually *re*-presented, set before us, that is to say, in time and space.

André Bazin

From its inception the camera has been an object of intense fascination. What first astonished viewers was the unprecedented realism of the photographic process, and, while this astonishment has in some ways abated, its effects have continued to spread. The symbiotic connection perceived between camera images and the objects they depict has consistently been used to draw the most diverse photo-technologies towards a single horizon. 'Realism' forms the lynchpin on which the heterogeneous array of images produced in different eras with vastly differing camera equipment and processes can be integrated into an ostensibly homogeneous field.

And yet, beneath this ideal of perfect imitation, there has always been another awareness: namely, that the invention of the camera marks a threshold beyond which representation is itself irreversibly transformed. It was there in Daguerre's first appeal to investors in 1839:

> The DAGUERREOTYPE is not merely an instrument which serves to draw nature; on the contrary it is a chemical and physical process which gives her the power to reproduce itself.[1]

And, in various guises, it has remained there ever since. Whether the image is photographic, cinematic, or televisual, belief in a mimetic power *beyond all previous jurisdiction* constitutes the camera's codex.

Because photography has become synonymous with fidelity in representation, it is easy to forget the extraordinary impact the first photographs made on eyes accustomed to painting, drawing, etching and engraving. One reviewer in England noted:

> . . . the effects produced are perfectly magical. The most fleeting of all things – a shadow, is fixed and made permanent; and the minute truths of the many objects, the exquisite delicacy of the pencilling, if we may be allowed the phrase, can only be discovered with a magnifying glass.[2]

1 Broadsheet for Subscription 15 January 1839, reprinted in H. and A. Gernsheim, *L.J.M. Daguerre: The History of the Diorama and Daguerreotype*, London, Dover, 1968, p. 81.

2 *The Athenaeum*, 2 February 1839, quoted in G. Buckland, *Fox Talbot and the Invention of Photography*, Boston, David R. Godine, 1980, p. 44.

Another in New York enthused:

> Talk no more of 'holding the mirror up to nature' – she will hold it up to herself
> . . . What would you say to looking in a mirror and having the image
> fastened?[3]

Photography was widely applauded for surpassing the greatest achieve-
ments in painting. If the most celebrated remark was that attributed to
painter Paul Delaroche ('From today, painting is dead'), more perceptive
was the sentiment expressed by Elizabeth Barrett:

> [I]t is not at all monstrous in me to say . . . that I would rather have such a
> [photographic] memorial of one I loved dearly than the noblest artist's work ever
> produced . . . it is not merely the likeness which is precious in such cases but the
> association and sense of nearness involved in the thing . . . the fact of the *very
> shadow of the person* lying there fixed forever.[4]

What is noteworthy in all these statements is their recognition of the
extent to which photography exceeded established paradigms of representation. A new era was to be ushered in on the wings of objectivity spread by
the camera's technique of faithful recording. Photography's potential value
to science was never in doubt (this being the prime reason for Fox Talbot's
experiments). The eminent scientist F.F. Statham gave the camera its
characteristic stamp of neutrality in 1860, declaring: 'Photography is never
imaginative, and is never in danger of arranging its records by the light of a
preconceived theory.'[5] Equally significant was the manner in which a similar
perception came to inform the adoption of the camera as a social scientific
tool. In 1917 Paul Strand gave photography its characteristic modernist
tenor: 'Photography finds its *raison d'être*, like all media, in a complete
uniqueness of means. This is an absolute and unqualified objectivity.'[6] This
valorization of objective vision was more than an aesthetic strategy (the shift
to ultra-sharp focus, high quality glossy prints, and the new range of subject
matter pioneered by Stieglitz and Photo-Secession); it also took on the force
of a moral stance. Strand's contemporary, Edward Weston, declared:

> Only with effort can the camera be forced to lie: basically it is an honest medium:
> so the photographer is much more likely to approach nature in a spirit of inquiry,
> of communion, instead of with the saucy swagger of self-dubbed 'artists'. And
> contemporary vision, the new life, is based on an honest approach to all problems,
> be they morals or art. False fronts to buildings, false standards in morals,
> subterfuges and mummery of all kinds, must be, will be scrapped.[7]

An immense gulf stretches between the desire to remake the world for the
'New Man', shared by so many artists, visionaries and revolutionaries in the

3 *Corsair*, 13 April 1839, quoted in G. Buckland, *Fox Talbot and the Invention of
Photography*, p. 53.
4 Letter to Mary Russell Mitford quoted in M. Haworth-Booth (ed.), *The Golden Age of
British Photography 1839–1900*, New York, Aperture, 1984, p. 22.
5 Quoted in J. Darius, *Beyond Vision*, Oxford, Oxford University Press, 1984, p. 11.
6 'Photography', *Seven Arts*, August 1917, quoted in M. Hambourg (ed.), *The New Vision
(Photography Between the Wars)*, New York, Metropolitan Museum of Art, 1989, p. 24.
7 S. Sontag, *On Photography*, Harmondsworth, Penguin, 1979, p. 186.

first decades of this century – a project in which the camera was often given a leading role – and the world we inhabit today. Faith in the capacity of what Moholy-Nagy termed 'the hygiene of the optical' to enable people to 'see things as they really are' has been shaken. Today, under the ubiquitous eyes of global media machines, it is more difficult to believe in photographic crusades to change the world – even though this is precisely what the collective impact of photography, cinema and television has achieved.

The arrival of the digital threshold has ensured that photo-realism finds itself in increasing dispute, especially with regard to the extravagant claims of 'objectivity' once made in its name. Yet, despite the rash of declarations heralding the death of photography, it seems premature to dismiss the power of photographic testimony. Barthes suggested such power has an ontological charge:

> Now, in the Photograph, what I posit is not only the absence of the object; it is also, by one and the same movement, on equal terms, the fact that this object has indeed existed and that it has been there where I see it. Here is where the madness is, for until this day no representation could assure me of the past of a thing except by intermediaries; but with the Photograph, my certainty is immediate: no one in the world can undeceive me.[8]

If there is a unique power belonging to the camera, it always returns to the invisible umbilicus joining image and referent, the link which commands, often beyond reason (is it merely coincidence that Elizabeth Barrett speaks of 'monstrous' feelings, Bazin of compulsion, Barthes of madness?) a belief that the scene *did* exist, that it *was* photographed. Here it is opportune to recall a few of the vast litany of similar declarations which have studded the history of cinema: from Louis Lumière who avowed 'I only wished to reproduce life', to Hollywood pioneer D.W. Griffith who envisaged the historical film as a 'properly adjusted window' through which the viewer could 'actually see what happened . . . There will be no opinions expressed', to the doyen of British documentarists John Grierson who proposed 'opening up the screen on the real world' to fulfil cinema's 'natural destiny of discovering mankind', to the great Soviet proponent of *cinéma vérité* Dziga Vertov, who stated his goal of 'observing and recording *life as it is*'.[9]

Confronted with this pervasive faith in photo-mimesis, one needs to pause and ask: what is the itinerary of desire that has so insistently positioned the camera upon the throne of truth in representation? For clearly, the symbiosis between the camera and realism offers a point of departure rather than a final destination. 'Realism' is a vexed concept and suffers repeated identity crises insofar as it harbours different and often warring tendencies within its embrace. The division between 'essence' and 'appearance', which has

8 R. Barthes, *Camera Lucida* (trans. R. Howard), London, Fontana, 1984, p. 115.

9 Lumière quoted in S. Heath, *Questions of Cinema*, London, Macmillan Press, 1981, p. 4; Griffith quoted in T. Elsaesser (ed.), *Early Cinema: Space, Frame, Narrative*, London, British Film Institute, 1990, p. 327; J. Grierson, *Grierson on Documentary* (ed.) Forsyth Hardy, London and Boston, Faber and Faber, 1979, pp. 36 and 70; Dziga Vertov quoted in S. Mamber, *Cinema Verite in America: Studies in Uncontrolled Cinema*, Massachusetts, MIT Press, 1974, p. 6.

proved so durable in philosophy, has often been echoed in aesthetics in the recurrent gap between 'expressionist' and 'straight' realisms. The fact that both sides of this argument claim to exert unique power over reality – depending on whether realism is conceived as a reconstruction of appearances which penetrates the 'mere surface' of things, or as an absolute fidelity to appearances which itself reveals essential truths – is less a sign of confusion within the concept than the conflictual space of its emergence.

The camera's placement in this terrain is instructive. Although photography is most readily associated with 'straight' realism to distinguish it from painting, drawing and other visual media, a similar division between 'art' and 'documentary' photography has frequently structured its own domain. This curious relationship in which the photographic part – the most common standard of realism used to regulate the entire field of representation – is itself internally partitioned by the very measure it seeks to establish, is indicative of the abyssal structure destabilizing 'realism' at its core.[10]

In this regard, it is important to recognize that any homogeneity pertaining to the concept of realism in the age of the camera has never been constituted simply by the exclusion of differences within its field. Rather, it has depended upon the systematic regulation of such differences, and the limitation of their play, above all in the conceptual space marked out by the separation of the realm of images from that of reality. It is this division, determining the task of representation as the expression of the real (or, as Heidegger might say, the adequation of its presence), which defined the nineteenth-century economy of representation into which the camera was first inserted. Yet the camera's integration within this economy has always been uneasy. Despite consistent attempts to embrace new camera technologies as successive stages in the steady progress towards the complete reproducibility of 'life itself', the camera has finally stretched and perhaps irreparably torn the concept of mimesis which first authorized its privilege.

Because the photograph fuses sign and referent in a new way, the line separating image and reality has become far more equivocal, and the arrival of cinema and television have greatly heightened this effect. As Deleuze observed (echoing Merleau-Ponty), cinema is not the same as other arts which aim at something unreal: it is that unique art which begins to render the world itself unreal.[11] With television, realism is no longer a function of

10 This instability is revealed in the long-running arguments over whether or not photography is 'art'. Initially the camera's hyper-realism was treated as an impediment to photography being accorded the status of 'art'. But these debates gradually took other tracks. One of photography's proudest, and quintessentially *modernist* claims has been that it makes people perceive the 'art' in the reality of daily life. As Walter Benjamin pointed out, art, as much as realism and nature, enters a period of rapid transformation under the eye of the camera.

11 'With the cinema, it is the world which becomes its own image, and not an image which becomes the world.' G. Deleuze, *Cinema 1: The Movement-Image* (trans. H. Tomlinson and B. Hammerjam), London, Athlone Press, 1986, p. 37. See M. Merleau-Ponty, 'The film and the new psychology' (1945), in *Sense and Non-Sense* (trans. H.L. and P.A. Dreyfus), Evanston, IL, Northwestern University Press, 1964.

space (perspective, framing, depth) so much as time. The elision of the time of the 're' in re-presentation lays the traditional terrain of mimesis wide open and susceptible to mutation. If, as Derrida has argued, the history of the interpretation of mimesis has been decisive with regard to the 'Western concept of reality', one can grasp the enormity of the stakes here.[12]

An analysis which seeks to explore these cracks in the edifice of realism needs firstly to understand its foundations. Posing the question of a politics of realism in relation to camera technologies today is above all to probe the pulse or beat, which has established a certain rhythm of representation: the formal priority of reality over its images, the 'thing itself' over the representation, the precedence of original over copy, the switching back and forth which orchestrates all distinctions between true and counterfeit images, as well as the preference for the former over the latter as the horizon of meaning. For it is this rhythm which is interrupted in the regularity of its tempo by the click of the camera's shutter.

---

12 J. Derrida, *Dissemination* (trans. B. Johnson), Chicago, University of Chicago Press, 1981, pp. 184–94.

2

The Geometric Universe

In antiquity the conquest of illusion by art was such a recent achievement that the discussion of painting and sculpture inevitably centred on imitation, *mimesis*. Indeed, it may be said that the progress of art towards that goal was to the ancient world what the progress of technics is to the modern: the model of progress as such.

E.H. Gombrich

One of the most striking features of photographic history is the immediacy of the camera's public acceptance. Photography seemed to fulfil a deeply rooted desire for realism, even as it translated this longing into the uncertain conditions of the industrial age. To appreciate this technological grafting, which links something very old to the irruptive force of the new, it is vital to consider the legacy that European oil painting bequeathed to photography. If the camera seemed miraculous in the nineteenth century, if its images were so quickly able to saturate consciousness and common sense as an unrivalled means of manufacturing lifelike resemblances, this acclaim was crucially underpinned by the dominance that geometric perspective had already achieved in visual representation.[1]

This heritage, which finds its genesis in the Renaissance, must itself be understood as more than a modification of artistic style. Rather, it was part of a far-reaching transformation of knowledge and social practices in which visual representation played a critical role. The 'quattrocento' system, which involves the depiction of three-dimensional objects upon a plane surface so that the picture may affect the eye of the observer similarly to the objects themselves, formed a crucial prototype for a new mode of subjectivity: the subject figured as distant observer. It was this matrix of identity, predicated on the separation of the interiority of the observer from the exteriority of the object world, which the camera intersected and began to transform in the mid-nineteenth century.

In his famous treatise on art and architecture, Leon Battista Alberti (arguably the first theoretician of geometric perspective) proposed that the picture should be envisaged as a 'window' through which the world could be

1 As will become apparent, I am not arguing that the photographic camera simply extended 'perspective' painting. But, while I agree with Jonathan Crary that it is vital to displace the teleology of technological progress which has dominated histories of the camera, I disagree with his contention that continuities with the classical system of the camera obscura are 'insignificant'. See J. Crary, *Techniques of the Observer: On Vision and Modernity in the Nineteenth Century*, Cambridge, MA, October/MIT Press, 1990, p. 13.

viewed.[2] His concept of an optical system structured around symmetrical visual pyramids, with the apex of one forming the vanishing point in the picture and the other stretching to the eye of the beholder, eventually became the most influential model of visual representation across Europe. This was not because the subsequent history of painting demonstrates a universal adherence to its law – it doesn't – but because it constituted a powerful formula for visual standardization; a mathematical vision which could be continually projected onto the real in a social context in which mathematics was increasingly offered as the universal measure of knowledge.

The quattrocento system constructed a new representational space: a scenographic space enabling artists to transcribe real appearances by figuring depth, proportion, texture and density so as to 'place' objects in the scene for the eye of the spectator. Literally a space for putting *things* into perspective.[3] German art historian Erwin Panofsky characterized this new spatiality in terms of its presupposing both continuity and infinity: pictorial space metamorphosed into 'a homogeneous system within which every point, regardless of whether it happens to be located in a solid or a void, is uniquely determined by three co-ordinates perpendicular to each other and extending *in infinitum* from a given "point of origin" '.[4] This marked a significant departure from the conventions of medieval painting in Europe, where object size had been determined not according to the rectilinear propagation of visual rays and the optical effect of recession in depth, but by each object's place in a symbolic hierarchy.[5]

Displacing evolutionary accounts which represent the history of painting as a history of progress towards greater verisimilitude suggests that the significance of geometric perspective must be located less in its perfection of an abstract 'realism' than in its proposal of a new world picture.[6] What was involved was a new manner of situating an observer *in* the world, with effects which resonated far beyond the confines of the painted surface. As French art historian Pierre Francastel wrote in his important study of the period:

2 Alberti wrote: 'Painters should know that they move on a plane surface with their lines and that, in filling in the areas defined with colours, the only thing they seek to accomplish is that the forms of the things seen appear on this plane surface as if it were made of transparent glass.' Quoted in E. Panofsky, *Renaissance and Renascences in Western Art*, New York, Harper and Row, 1969, p. 120.

3 John Berger has emphasized this materialism: 'Oil painting, before it was anything else was a celebration of private property. As an art form it derived from the principle that *you are what you have.*' *Ways of Seeing*, London, BBC and Harmondsworth, Penguin, 1972, p. 139.

4 Panofsky, *Renaissance and Renascences in Western Art*, p. 122.

5 See M. Baxandall, *Painting and Experience in Fifteenth Century Italy*, Oxford, Oxford University Press, 1972, p. 82.

6 Barfield suggests: 'Before the scientific revolution the world was more like a garment men wore about them than a stage on which they moved. In such a world the convention of perspective was unnecessary . . . It was as if the observers themselves were in the picture.' O. Barfield, *Saving the Appearance: A Study in Idolatry*, New York, Harcourt Brace Jovanovich, 1965, pp. 94–5.

It was a question for a society in process of total transformation of a space in accordance with its actions and its dreams . . . Spaces are born and die like societies; they live, they have a history. In the fifteenth century, the human societies of Western Europe organized, in the material and intellectual senses of the term, a space completely different from that of the preceding generations; with their technical superiority they progressively imposed that space over the planet.[7]

The camera obscura constituted a vital relay in normalizing the new spatial arrangement. Firstly, it offered a practical system for image-making according to mathematical principles. But, more than this, the camera obscura provided a distinct *social* architecture, setting in place a functional model of subject–object relations in which the interiority of the viewing subject could be held apart from the exteriority of the object world. This division was itself both premised on, and embedded within, a much larger reorganization of knowledge which culminated in the emergence of modern science. While the principle of the camera had been known for some 2,000 years, Crary argues that by the late 1500s the camera obscura had become 'hegemonic', both as a practical tool and a (scientific, philosophical) metaphor describing the status and possibilities of an observer.[8]

The growing popularity of the camera occurred during a period in which the proficiency of natural vision was itself being challenged by an increasing emphasis on submitting sensory experience to normative principles of reason. This profound transformation of knowledge and subjectivity spanned several major upheavals to Europe's epistemological centre of gravity in the fifteenth and sixteenth centuries. The Reformation, and the explicit questioning of the absolute authority of doctrine by Luther and Calvin, stripped religion of its veneer of unity. The rapid discovery of distant lands brought increased contact with other cultures, especially China.[9] But perhaps the most disorienting shift was the unsettling effect of the heliocentric universe proposed by Copernicus and popularized by Galileo.[10] This de-centring, which displaced the earth itself, radically undermined the solidity of the ground on which 'Man' had long imagined himself to stand in the cosmos. The organic enclosure of the old universe no longer held firm; as Moussau points out, in the Copernican universe 'there is no reason for a straight line

7 P. Francastel, quoted in Heath, *Questions of Cinema*, p. 29.

8 See J. Crary, 'Modernizing vision', in H. Foster (ed.), *Vision and Visuality*, Seattle, Bay Press, 1988, pp. 30–1; 'The camera obscura and its subject', in Crary, *Techniques of the Observer*, pp. 26–66.

9 In 1490 the world known to the Europeans was essentially the same as that described by Ptolemy some 1200 years earlier. By 1521 the globe had been circumnavigated and a ship had sailed in every ocean. By the end of the sixteenth century, the world map was not all that different to that which persists today. See E.R. Chamberlain, *Everyday Life in Renaissance Times*, New York, Capricorn, 1965, p. 23.

10 Paul Virilio suggests that 'by upsetting geocentric cosmogony, this reverberation of the human look called perceptual faith into question, and "remote anticipation" anticipated the grave philosophical problems that have recently been posed by electro-optical television . . .' *War and Cinema: The Logistics of Perception* (trans. P. Camiller), London and New York, Verso, 1989, p. 3.

to stop at any given point and so it does not stop at all'.[11] Straight lines extending to infinity shattered the spheres of the medieval universe.

*

It is in this context of the crumbling medieval symbolic order that the revolutionary ordering of pictorial space emerged in the Renaissance. Geometric perspective created a representational space that was simultaneously aesthetic and analytical, a space organized around the growing separation between the external world and a psychic interiority thought proper to the mind's eye. The significance of geometric perspective can be grasped in the fact that it not only colonized the visual arts, but coalesced into an enduring paradigm capable of representing the relation between subject and object across a wide variety of discourses.

A crucial index of this shift was the emergence of art and science as secular activities increasingly independent of religion. For Heidegger, the transformation of art into 'aesthetics' corresponded precisely to the separation of art from 'life' and opened the way for the modern determination of the role of art as the expression of life.[12] The leaching away of the sacred quality of art by the secular cult of the beautiful also transformed the work's implied viewer, displacing the omnipresent eye of God with the lidless eye of reason. This introduced a different aesthetic problem – that of reference between the ostensibly divorced domains of art and life – and opened the duel between mimesis and reality which formed the matrix of aesthetics up to this century.

The emergence of science from theology and religious cosmology equally depended on transformations in representation, as Heidegger makes clear:

> We first arrive at science as truth when, and only when, truth has been transformed into the certainty of representation. What it is to be is for the first time defined as the objectiveness of representing and truth is first defined as the certainty of representing in the metaphysics of Descartes.[13]

It is significant that the telescope – the first technological overturning of the primacy of human perception – was a vital relay for Descartes (as it had

11 M. Moussau, 'Infinite space, perspective space', quoted in S. Bordo, *The Flight to Objectivity*, Albany, State University of New York, 1987, p. 123.

12 See especially his 'The origin of the work of art' in *Poetry, Language, Thought* (trans. A. Hofstadter), New York, Harper and Row, 1971; Heidegger, 'The age of the world picture', in *Technology and Other Essays*, pp. 115–54. It is important to grasp Heidegger's analysis in relation to its context of production: lectures for 'The origin of the work of art' were first presented in 1935–6, while 'The age of the world picture' was delivered on 9 June 1938, in a Nazi Germany transformed by the emergence of perhaps the first *media culture*, radically dependent on spectacle. In the wake of his 'commitment' to the Party, Heidegger later (1945) argued these texts developed his critique of the headlong rush of science into 'technicism': 'What is essential is that we are caught up in the consummation of Nihilism, that "God is Dead" and every time–space for the Godhead covered up.' 'The Rectorate 1933/34: facts and thoughts' (trans. K. Harries), *Review of Metaphysics*, 38, 3, issue 151 (March 1985), p. 498.

13 Heidegger, 'Age of the world picture', p. 127.

been for Galileo before him).[14] What Rorty has aptly termed the 'invention of the mind' encapsulates the manner in which the Cartesian search for truth and new foundations is posed as the problem of relating the external world to the interiority of a pure mind divested of all traces of emotion, sensuality and corporeality.[15] Formulating the problem in this way levies new demands upon representation. As Heidegger puts it: 'Through Descartes, realism is first put in the position of having to *prove* the reality of the outer world, of having to save that which is as such.'[16]

Cartesian doubt, that radical doubt which wants to shut its eyes and stop its ears, deny feeling and imagination, even the very existence of the senses, is born in the fallout of cosmological dislocation and epistemological crisis. Descartes's audacious declaration that the subject is indisputably present to 'himself' in thought finally enables 'Man' to grasp himself as the unshakeable foundation of the cosmos. Heidegger posited this act as the inauguration of the modern age, clearing the way for the rational–scientific interpretation of nature to establish a 'ground plan' which regulates knowledge according to homogeneous dimensions of time and space.[17] It is not simply that such a 'ground plan' mirrors the pictorial space of geometric perspective, thus enabling the world to be represented as a unified field. For Heidegger, the fundamental event of the modern age is precisely the conquest of the world *as perspective*, determining a new relation between representation and subjectivity.

> Man becomes that being upon which all that is, is grounded as regards the manner of its Being and its truth. Man becomes the relational centre of that which is as such.[18]

What the Cartesian text formalizes is the new sense of enclosure belonging to the self. Rather than approaching the problem of knowledge from the point of view of existence within the natural world, for Descartes it is precisely the alien and impersonal nature of this world which lets it be known objectively. It is because the world has been made distinct from the mind that it can be submitted to the principles of mathematics and geometry, which will henceforth provide the dominant matrix for scientific knowledge and visual representation.

None of this is to suggest that Descartes marks the end, or even the beginning of the end, of religious interpretations of the world. If the sacred

14 Descartes credited the telescope with stimulating his work on optics, teaching him that it is 'the mind which sees, not the eye'. R. Descartes, *Discourse on Method* (1637) (trans. P.J. Olscamp), Indianapolis, Bobbs-Merril, 1965, p. 108.

15 Rorty writes of the philosophical orientation of Descartes and Locke: 'The novelty was of a single inner space in which bodily and perceptual sensations . . . were objects of quasi-observation.' *Philosophy and the Mirror of Nature*, Oxford, Blackwell, 1980, pp. 49–50.

16 Heidegger, 'Age of the world picture', p. 139 (my italics).

17 'Into this ground plan of nature, as supplied with its prior stipulation, the following definitions among others have been incorporated: Motion means change of place. No motion or direction of motion is superior to any other. Every place is equal to every other. No point in time has preference over any other.' Heidegger, 'Age of the world picture', p. 119.

18 Heidegger, 'Age of the world picture', p. 128.

world had already begun its long, slow bow before the secular forces of mathematics and science at least a century prior to Cartesianism, Descartes himself always sought to ground reason in the existence of God.[19] However, as Cassirer points out, the Cartesian notion of a truth revealed not in God's word but in his work still threatened the established foundations of the Church. As empirical science increasingly came into open conflict with religion (notably with Voltaire's denigration of 'Biblical physics' and Hume's scepticism which finally withdrew the support of the concept of God from the understanding of nature), it became apparent that the reconciliation between theology and science sought by both Galileo and Descartes would not be achieved. By the end of the eighteenth century it was no longer religion which grounded science by virtue of its 'higher' truth, but science which drew religion into its magic circle.[20]

Nor did Descartes's mechanistic philosophy rule unchallenged, even in France. Its method was in fact completely reversed by Newton and his followers in the course of the next century, who replaced the 'eternal verities' with an emphatic declaration of the importance of empirical investigation. Reason was transformed from a natural heritage into a process of discovery determined by the analysis of experimental data, and science assumed the hypothetico-deductive form which it carried into this century.

Nor did the ascendancy of geometric perspective, whose mathematical and philosophical rules were most fully systematized by Descartes, operate unchallenged in the realm of art. The parodic use of anamorphosis, which developed alongside geometric perspective (to the annoyance of some of its practitioners including Leonardo), and subsequent counter-traditions, such as Mannerism and the Baroque, all departed from the quattrocento model of painting as a 'mirror to nature'. However, as John Berger has pointed out, it was not until the twentieth century that the incendiary impact of Cubism finally destroyed the primacy of the representational space established in the quattrocento.[21] Similarly, despite the Newtonian reversal of Cartesian method, there was little questioning of the fundamental framework of

19 This point cannot pass without a brief remark on the question of God's *double*, the 'Evil Genius' whose appearance in the Cartesian text is by no means accidental. It seems the shadow of the double is destined to fall across the subject of certainty whenever it attempts to ground representation in truth. As Lacan observed: 'But the true remains so much outside that Descartes then has to reassure himself – of what, if not an Other that is not deceptive, and which shall, into the bargain, guarantee him that there are in his own objective reason the necessary foundations for the very real, about whose existence he has just reassured himself, to find the dimension of truth.' J. Lacan, *The Four Fundamental Concepts of Psycho-analysis* (trans. A. Sheridan), Harmondsworth, Penguin, 1979, p. 36. Truth *demands* a detour through the other: in the Cartesian splitting between the beneficent other (God) and his malevolent double (the Evil Genius), we find the polarization of true and counterfeit images which frames the scene of representation that the camera enters.

20 E. Cassirer, *The Philosophy of the Enlightenment* (1932) (trans. F.C.A. Koelln and J.P. Pettegrove), Boston, Beacon Press, 1951, pp. 42–64.

21 J. Berger, 'The moment of cubism', in *The Moment of Cubism and Other Essays*, London, Weidenfeld and Nicolson, 1969.

scientific knowledge until the ripples of relativity began to make themselves felt with Maxwell and Einstein.

In fact, Newton's universal law of gravitation seemed to finish the project that Kepler and Galileo had begun. The discovery of a – or rather *the* – cosmic law promised the final victory of science over nature, the long-awaited arrival on the shore of certainty after a voyage of doubt inaugurated several centuries earlier. Newton's towering stature in the eighteenth and nineteenth centuries derived not simply from his discoveries in the field of physics, but from the prestige they were able to claim as the philosophical underpinning of all fields of knowledge. As Cassirer observed: 'Thanks to Newton [the eighteenth century] believed it stood finally on firm ground which could never again be shaken by any future revolution of natural science.'[22]

Despite certain challenges, reversals, and departures, the conceptual force of the Cartesian–Newtonian universe extended well into the nineteenth century. In this universe, 'Man' became the 'relational centre of what is' (Heidegger): a subject granted dominion over a natural world in which all objects could be compared and related to each other as a single, homogeneous system. The positioning of 'Man' as the centre of representation inscribed a stable relation between knowing subject and known world, held in place by the structured distance of dispassionate observation that enabled the one to master the other.[23] While various means have been employed to describe the detached observer of modern thought, the optical metaphor has consistently retained pride of place.[24] It was this fertile and receptive soil into which the seed of the photographic camera dropped in the nineteenth century.

*

This excursion through quattrocento perspective and Cartesian philosophy helps to situate the ready-made acceptance of photographic vision in the nineteenth century. Put simply, the camera is a machine designed so that, in its 'normal' functioning, it will reproduce the geometrical perspective of quattrocento painting.[25] According to art historian William Ivins:

22 Cassirer, *Philosophy of the Enlightenment*, p. 44.

23 If there is a sense in which this subject is radically *disembodied* by its ideal of bypassing the human sensory apparatus, it was nevertheless systematically *gendered*, according to the separation of mind and body which remains active in defining 'masculine' and 'feminine'. See E.F. Keller, *Reflections on Gender and Science*, New Haven, Yale University Press, 1985, p. 79.

24 Crary argues: 'If at the core of Descartes's method was the need to escape the uncertainties of mere human vision and the confusion of the senses, the camera obscura is congruent with his quest to found human knowledge as a purely objective view of the world.' Crary, *Techniques of the Observer*, p. 48.

25 It is important to acknowledge the role that photographic *convention*, including specific choices of lens and exposure time, plays in the reproduction of geometric perspective as photographic 'realism'.

Strong as the mathematical convention of perspective had become in picture making before the pervasion of photography, that event definitely clamped it on our vision and our beliefs about 'real' shapes, etc. The public has come to believe that geometrical perspective, so long as it does not involve unfamiliar points of view, is 'true', just as a long time ago it believed the old geometry of Euclid was 'the truth'.[26]

The camera's precision and minuteness of detail, coupled with its instantaneous action, ensured its decisive victory over existing visual media: Walter Benjamin often cited the fate of the portrait miniaturist, who either became a photographer or went out of business altogether.[27] But as well as forcing a reappraisal of the hand's capacity, the camera also altered its entire heritage. From the time of Daguerre, it became feasible to add another chapter to the history of art. In this coda, the steady progression from 'primitive' forms to the 'realism' of the quattrocento culminates in photography, which 'frees' painting from the burden of resemblance to enable it to pursue its true – modernist – vocation: abstraction. André Breton's introduction to Max Ernst's first exhibition in Paris in 1920 proposed what has today become a new orthodoxy:

> The invention of photography has dealt a mortal blow to the old modes of expression . . . Since a blind instrument now assured artists of the aim they had set themselves up to that time, they now aspired, not without recklessness, to break with the imitation of appearances . . .[28]

Although appealing, such an account is scarcely troubled by history. As Scharf has argued, the interaction between camera and canvas has been far more complex.[29] And yet there is a sense in which Breton's declaration is more poetic and more correct. In rejecting the 'progression to abstraction' thesis, Scharf argues that the camera has established a climate in which an unprecedented heterodoxy of artistic forms can proliferate, because different styles can be compared and contrasted more easily.[30] However, this Utopian vision of artistic freedom (resembling Malraux's famous 'Museum Without Walls'), ignores the fact that the camera can only be thought to sustain a plurality of styles if one has already made a prior determination that photography itself is not a style.[31] This role as meta-medium was in fact

26 W.M. Ivins, *Art and Geometry*, New York, Dover, 1964, p. 108.

27 W. Benjamin, *One Way Street and Other Writings* (trans. E. Jephcott and K. Shorter), London, Verso, 1985, p. 246.

28 A. Breton, 'Max Ernst', in F. Rosemount (ed.), *What is Surrealism?*, London, Pluto Press, 1978, p. 7.

29 A. Scharf, *Art and Photography*, London, Penguin, 1979, pp. 227–48.

30 Scharf, *Art and Photography*, p. 312.

31 Douglas Crimp's comments on Malraux are apposite: 'But Malraux makes a fatal error near the end of his *Museum*: he admits within its pages the very thing that had constituted its homogeneity; that thing is, of course, photography. So long as photography was merely a *vehicle* by which art objects entered the imaginary museum, a certain coherence obtained. But once photography itself enters, an object among others, heterogeneity is re-established at the heart of the museum; its pretensions of knowledge are doomed. Even photography cannot hypostatize style from a photograph.' See 'On the museum's ruins', in H. Foster (ed.), *Postmodern Culture*, London, Pluto Press, 1983, p. 51.

envisaged at the camera's birth: one of Fox Talbot's first proposals was the photographing of great works of art from museums and galleries all over the world. Today, an enduring legacy of the camera is that, whether a painting is labelled abstract, neo-expressionist, hyper-realist or whatever, its appearance is inevitably measured in relation to an implicit photographic standard. It is this reflex comparison, which extends beyond the realm of art into the domain of 'life itself', that constitutes the camera's most indelible water-mark on contemporary vision.

What remains to be further explored is the extent to which this mark is also a site of ambivalence. Even as photography emerged as the central pillar of the modern hierarchy of realism, it disturbed the paradigm it sought to inhabit. By combining the directness of embodied perception with a freely transportable image which could be multiplied at will and viewed in a multiplicity of contexts, the camera intersected the configurations of know-ledge and formations of subjectivity which had dominated European thought for several centuries, only to set them adrift in new ways.

3

Writing with Light

I have seized the light.

Louis Daguerre

And thus we say writing for all that gives rise to an inscription in general, whether it is literal or not and even if what it distributes in space is alien to the order of the voice.

Jacques Derrida

As Moholy-Nagy observed succinctly in 1928, 'Photography is creation with light'.[1] This fact, while ever-present in the name the process eventually assumed (*photo*-graphy succeeding appellations including Daguerreotype, Talbotype, Heliotype and Calotype), often seems curiously forgotten, at least in comparison to the attention given to the camera as a system of perspective and framing. But the seduction of the photograph has never been purely a matter of geometry or visual resemblance. Photography has also drawn immense authority – bordering on faith – from the fact that it is solar-powered.

Even though early photographic images were often unable to live up to the demands made of them, due to poor resolution or tonal contrast, these inadequacies paled in face of the excitement generated by the discovery of the photographic *process*.[2] If photographs used in nineteenth-century atlases of natural history and anatomy (such as J.B.L. Foucault's famous *Cours de Microscopie* of 1844) disappointed some observers with their lack of verisimilitude in comparison to drawings, such controversies scarcely hampered the extravagant claims made by eminent scientists such as François Arago and Sir John Herschel for the camera's dominion in the field of science.[3] This suggests that, as much as its images actually achieved immediate practical results, the acclamation of photography in the nineteenth century was related to cultural changes which had produced the need

1 L. Moholy-Nagy, 'Photography is creation with light', *Bauhaus*, 1 (1928), reprinted in K. Passuth, *Moholy-Nagy* (trans. E. Grusz et al.), London, Thames and Hudson, 1985, p. 320.

2 The level of detail achieved by the Daguerreotype was markedly greater than other early processes, whose images were often blurry and indistinct. But even the Daguerreotype could initially function optimally only in a limited range of conditions, under strong light with a still object to enable long exposure. Hence the recourse to head supports for early portraits.

3 Arago (Director of the Paris Observatory and Permanent Secretary of the *Académie des Sciences*) commended Daguerre's process to the *Académie* in the strongest terms. The English astronomer Sir John Herschel was not only an enthusiastic public advocate of the camera, but was himself a photographic pioneer of some note. He was also first to apply the terms 'negative' and 'positive' to Fox Talbot's process.

for a new language of truth. This was a position the camera proved uniquely able to fill.

Even a poor photograph carried a force and conviction that other representations lacked. Fox Talbot's early speculations that 'the picture, divested of the ideas which accompany it, and considered only in its ultimate nature, is but a succession or variety of stronger lights thrown upon one part of the paper and of deeper shadows upon another' led him to assert an intimate exchange in which light itself left a deposit in the bank of representation.[4] Despite numerous attempts to 'demystify' photography, this commerce remains central to photographic authority. Writing one and a half centuries after Fox Talbot, Roland Barthes declared:

> What matters to me is not the photograph's 'life' (a purely ideological notion) but the certainty that the photographed body touches me with its own rays . . . light, though impalpable, is here a carnal medium, a skin I share with anyone who has been photographed.[5]

This unique relation between object and image (Susan Sontag memorably describes the photographic image as the object's death mask) has determined two related avenues along which photographic credibility has since flowed. One is the sense of independence from any human operator that the photographic process is able to claim. I want to defer consideration of this automatism for the moment, in order to place it in the context of the transformation of the scientific ideal of 'truth to nature' into a mechanical objectivity.[6] The other path, which concerns me here, is the significance of the camera's intersection with the privilege that light and vision have long enjoyed as metaphors for truthful understanding. Clear sightedness, clarity, enlightenment, and the ubiquity of the 'I see' find themselves opposed to the shadows of doubt, blindness and obscurity with a consistency that is frequently offered as that of nature itself. Yet to collapse these metaphors into a continuous history is misleading. If the same terms persist, it is insofar as they can be inserted into different formations of knowledge and attached to new configurations of power.

Like many other religions, the Christian cosmology of creation emphasizes the importance of light as a form of origin in itself. Cartesian philosophy still held God's own light to be truthful beyond question, as the pinnacle of that *natural* light essential to good understanding. It was natural light which was decisive for Descartes in overcoming radical doubt: 'for I cannot doubt that which the natural light causes me to believe to be true, as,

---

4 Fox Talbot added: 'The variegated source of light or shade might leave its image or impression behind, stronger or weaker on different parts of the paper according to the strength or weakness of the light which had acted there.' Notebook entry 1834 quoted in G. Buckland, *Fox Talbot and the Invention of Photography*, p. 26.

5 Barthes, *Camera Lucida*, p. 81.

6 See 'The mechanical eye of reason' below.

for example, it has shown me that I am from the fact that I doubt'.[7] Modern subjectivity focuses itself in this exemption of natural light from the exigencies of doubt.

However, around this time the whole manner of relating to light began to change. Walter Benjamin pointed to the 'exclusive emphasis on an optical connection to the universe' initiated in the astronomy of Kepler and Copernicus as a significant threshold.[8] The publication of Newton's *Opticks*, which, among other things, proved that 'natural' light was less an originary or pure form than an amalgam of different colours, prefaced a proliferation of theories of light. The fierce arguments which developed in the nineteenth century over particle and wave models of light (symptomatic of major fissures in scientific thought) seem a long way from the story of Genesis.

And yet, as Crary points out, the scientific understanding of light as a radiant is itself deeply theological. Crary argues that only when light becomes part of the broader electro-magnetic spectrum in the work of Faraday and Maxwell does it finally lose its ontological privilege.[9] In contrast, Virilio contends that, far from being dethroned, light has assumed a new supremacy in the twentieth century. Light is not only something to see by, it has become something to measure with.[10] In our new solar cult we seem strangely proximate to the heliocentrism first proposed by the Egyptian Pharaoh Akhenaten. With the difference that light today radiates not from a single orb but from an infinite number of artificial suns.

*

Light is only one term we need to consider here. The unique evidential force of the photograph depended equally on the belief that here, for the first time, representation achieved parity with direct perception. Yet there are powerful historical currents which might have opposed this understanding. As its name also suggests, photo-*graphy* constitutes a species of writing. For this reason, one might expect it to be marred by the subordinate status consistently accorded technologies of representation – or the technological in

7 R. Descartes, *The Philosophical Works of Descartes*, vol. 1 (trans. E. Haldane and G.R.T. Ross), Cambridge, Cambridge University Press, 1970, p. 160. Descartes, who so violently distrusted sensory perception, pronounced sight to be the 'noblest' sense: 'All the management of our lives depends upon the senses and since that of sight is the most comprehensive and noblest of these, *there is no doubt the inventions which augment its power are among the most useful there can be.*' Descartes, *Discourse on Method*, p. 65 (my italics).

8 Benjamin, *One Way Street*, p. 103.

9 Crary, *Techniques of the Observer*, pp. 86–7.

10 After 1972, the metre was defined as 'the length crossed by light in a vacuum in 1/299 792 458th of a second'. Light-energy also forms the standard means of measuring time (atomic decay) and the 'speed of light' stands as the absolute marker of the universe's physical limits.

general – in comparison to the living presence against which technics has traditionally been comprehended.[11]

How does photography install itself as that which transcends representation to constitute the apparent equal of direct perception?[12] Tracing the curious nature of the representation of truth sheds some light on this matter. For truth has always been thought according to an idealization of pure thought itself. To conform to its own dictates, truth must be that which is somehow beyond representation, without allegiance to style, form, medium, material or technical support of any kind. To assume absolute and unconditional value, truth can only belong to the realm of the pure idea, the ideal meaning, the unadulterated concept which floats beyond language, beyond any context of time, space, or culture. Carrying this ideality to its logical end culminates in the enigmatic imperative of a transcendental signified which necessarily eschews fealty to any signifier as such. A truth which surrenders either its immateriality or unconditionality can no longer properly conform to the economy it has historically named.

If truth is necessarily 'outside' representation, how can it ever be grasped? Of course, the need to efface the density and materiality of the signifier has always been truth's peculiar problem. The privileged form of solution, whose privilege is registered precisely to the extent that it escapes the imprint of form, has historically been the realm of language. Or rather, as Derrida has pointed out, it is not language in general, but spoken language which has alone been accorded the aura of transparency enabling that pure expression of thought on which the thought of truth depends. This privilege of the speaking voice, which has been decisive in ordering a certain hierarchy of truth and representation over a long period, helps to situate the ready acceptance of photographic truth.[13]

From the perspective that would indissolubly wed the voice to pure thought, any form of writing is necessarily derivative, a second order representation, the sign of a sign. Nevertheless, at its inception the camera largely avoided this stigma, and was instead acclaimed as vision without mediation, a medium in which the signifier effaced itself before the force of the signified. (If this evaluation was stronger in the nineteenth century, it still lingers in the present. When we look at photographs, we tend not to see them as 'signs', but to see only their 'referents'.) Such an accord is not without

11 See Derrida's discussion of the anti-technological bias of phonocentrism and logocentrism in which: 'All signifiers, and first and foremost the written signifier, are *derivative* . . .' J. Derrida, *Of Grammatology* (trans. G.C. Spivak), Baltimore, Johns Hopkins University Press, 1976, p. 11 and pp. 6–26 (my italics).

12 In fact, Platonic denigrations of the photograph as 'mere image' have always accompanied its history. What I am more interested in here is the manner in which the camera inserted itself into a novel conceptual space.

13 The relationship between speech and writing as the inscription of the logocentric order of truth was a major theme of Derrida's early work. See, for example, *Of Grammatology*, pp. 11–12.

tension. In fact, it effectively undercuts a major support of the entire tradition of mimesis: namely, the opposition between *physis* and *techne* as one dividing natural self-presence from the technological and mediated mastery of absence. How did photography find such ready acceptance? To answer this question, we need to return to the conceptual system which originally elevated speech over writing. For the place of writing within this equation is itself duplicitous. As Derrida has pointed out, what is involved in the historical subordination of the written to the spoken is less the total condemnation of writing than the declaration of *a preference for one form of writing over another*. Even as writing in general was occulted, *natural writing* – that writing discussed by Socrates which forms the inscription of truth in the soul, that writing which belongs to God and which has repeatedly produced the idea of the Book of Nature – has been celebrated and renowned.[14]

It is at this point that we can bring together the two paths we have been tracing – those of writing and light – which is in fact the historic junction at which the camera stands in the nineteenth century. It is as a species of natural writing, writing by God's own hand with the very fingers of his light, that photography was able to claim its unique proximity to truth in representation. The ingenuous tone of Fox Talbot's celebrated remark while sketching with a camera obscura ('How charming it would be if it were possible to cause these natural images to imprint themselves durably and remain fixed on the paper') sets the scene in which the development of the process of 'photogenic drawing by the power of the sun's rays' (as he later put it) seemed to place the fidelity of God's hand within human grasp.[15]

In this manner the camera entered nineteenth-century consciousness, not simply as a new mode of representation, but as a new language of truth, at a time when the natural claims of language as a vehicle for truth were themselves being tested. This situates a vital historical cleft. Belief in the transparency of language had been disturbed by the invention of the printing press, and the spread of written 'vernacular' languages, including the first translations of sacred texts such as the Bible and the Koran. By the nineteenth century, the potential gap between sign and meaning had become an object of theoretical concern, culminating in the work of Saussure, Nietzsche and Freud. But, even as the concept of the sign within which logocentrism had maintained its coherence became increasingly problematic, photography (and later cinematography) became new repositories for the old

14 Derrida, *Of Grammatology*, pp. 15–18. For Derrida, it is the insistent emergence of this 'good writing' which ruins the possibility that the relation between speech and writing could ever be governed by a simple opposition of mutual exclusivity. See also Derrida, *Dissemination*, pp. 103 and 149.

15 Fox Talbot quoted in B. Coe et al., *Techniques of the World's Great Photographers*, New Jersey, Chartwell, 1981, p. 25.

dream of a universal language. In fact, such a transference raised as many problems as it solved. Because of its extreme reproducibility and transportability, the photographic sign began to threaten truth's stable dominion in new ways. What the camera finally exposes is the instability of meaning and the paradoxical concept of the sign on which logocentrism depends.[16]

16 See 'Promiscuous meanings' below.

4

The Mechanical Eye of Reason

Before drawing conclusions from our observations, we shall let nature reproduce herself; we shall fix her on a daguerreotype plate with all her details and infinite nuances . . . We are determined to support each observational fact on a rigorous representation safe from any illusions or preconceived ideas.

Alfred Donné

The camera was invented and found its footing in an era in which positivism held sway. It is difficult to overstate the importance of this conjunction which not only had a lasting effect on the photographic imagination, but also decisively influenced the project of positivism, and from more than one direction. If, in the long term, the camera has contributed to the corruption of positivist certitudes by exposing investment in the neutrality of representation to the uncomfortable drift of perspective, this stands in marked contrast to its inception when photography seemed the ultimate confirmation of the positivist universe. At the historic moment in which positivism subjugated virtually the entire field of Western knowledge, the camera was able to fuse the realism of geometric perspective and the theological investment in light as the origin of truth with the scientific valorization of the objective eye. In an age in which machines held the promise of the future, the development of photography perfectly fulfilled the desire to invest truth in the disinterested gaze of an optical machine.

Like all durable *philosophemes*, the concept of 'objectivity' is conglomerate rather than unitary. What is distinctive to the nineteenth century is the emergence of an objectivity conceived not simply as the truthful imitation of nature, but in terms of the ideal of *letting nature speak for itself*.[1] This epistemological shift, which intensified desire for a mode of representation capable of bypassing the human observer to seize nature directly, was vital to the camera's appeal. As Fox Talbot put it when attempting to distinguish

---

1 This was exemplified in the work of French biologist and photographic pioneer Etienne-Jules Marey. From the 1850s, Marey invented numerous pneumatic machines for analysing internal bodily functions (such as the sphygmograph, which would lead to the cardiograph), but later turned to the photographic sensor for recording more elusive external movements (the flight of birds, the beating of insect wings). Marey's famous chronophotographic rifle (a high speed camera capable of taking one hundred images per second) was the crowning achievement of his advocacy of a 'wordless' science which spoke in the 'language of the phenomena'. See F. Dagognet, *A Passion for the Trace* (trans. R. Galeta and J. Herman), New York, Zone Books, 1992.

his photographic process from previous devices such as the camera obscura and camera lucida:

> From all these prior ones, the present invention differs totally in this respect (which may be explained in a single sentence) viz., that by means of this contrivance, it is not the artist who makes the picture, but the picture which makes ITSELF.[2]

The sense of a unique objectivity which belongs to the camera – Strysky's avant-garde slogan proclaiming 'PHOTOGRAPHY: objective truth and documentary clarity above all doubts' succinctly evokes the Cartesian lineage – has been both pervasive and enduring.[3] Often it has seemed to remove the camera from the sphere of art, or has demanded a redefinition of art's domain. Peter Henry Emerson, one of the first great photographers of nature, declared in 1891:

> I believe that there is no true realism or naturalism in the arts proper, but only in *Photography*: for TRUE realism and naturalism are IMPERSONAL – the results of a mechanical process which photography logically is because under the same physical conditions the same results will always follow . . .[4]

But if the photograph was not quite art, it was already more than the existing forms of science. The manner in which the photographic process promised to replace the human operator with the universal laws of optics and chemistry was itself instrumental in the emergence of mechanical objectivity as the goal of nineteenth-century science. If positivism formed the social environment in which photographic images were first read, the camera also helped to shape positivism in its own image. By 1888, the astronomer P.J.C. Janssen was able to pronounce:

> The sensitive photographic film is the true retina of the scientist . . . for it possesses all the properties science could want: it faithfully preserves the images which depict themselves upon it, and reproduces and multiplies them indefinitely on request; in the radiative spectrum it covers a range more than double that which the eye can perceive, and soon perhaps will cover it all; finally it takes advantage of that admirable property which allows the accumulation of events, and whereas the retina erases all impressions more than one tenth of a second old, the photographic retina preserves them . . .[5]

As subjectivity was increasingly identified as a dangerous and polluting attribute, the pursuit of mechanical objectivity assumed the status of a moral quest. The machine was valued not simply because it was labour-saving, but

2 Letter to the *Literary Gazette* 2 February 1839, quoted in G. Buckland, *Fox Talbot and the Invention of Photography*, p. 43. This echoes Daguerre's boast that 'the Daguerreotype is not merely an instrument which serves to draw nature; on the contrary it . . . gives her the power to reproduce herself.'

3 *Disk* (Prague 1923), quoted in S. Bann (ed.), *The Tradition of Constructivism*, New York, Viking, 1974, p. 101.

4 Quoted in M. Haworth-Booth (ed.), *Golden Age of British Photography*, p. 154.

5 Quoted in Darius, *Beyond Vision*, p. 11.

because it was seen to surpass the capacities of the fallible human observer.[6] Unstinting, methodical, uniform, durable, ever alert, incapable of being swayed by emotion or passion, the machine was invested as a paragon of Victorian virtues. Insulation from the spectre of individual judgement provided by all kinds of machines of measurement and recording con- solidated the empirical orientation of the positivist project, in which physical appearances investigated by the armature of reason were increasingly treated as unambiguous facts. As John Berger has pointed out, positivism is in effect a proposition concerning the nature of the material world: 'The proposal was (and is) that when something is visible, it is a fact, and that facts contain the only truth.'[7] It is no accident that the camera, which combined the primacy of vision with the promise of automatism, held pride of place in this universe.

Rejection of ambiguity and the hardening of the split between art and science corresponded to the systematic denial of the importance of sub- jectivity across broad swathes of social life. In the name of Reason, much was occulted as superstition, folklore, mysticism, primitivism or madness, or routinely stigmatized as irrational and emotive – often simply 'feminine' – and thus disqualified from the threshold of legitimate knowledge. At the same time, and as part of the same process, positivism increasingly sought to manage subjective differences by inscribing them within new formations of knowledge, distributing social variance along the statistical bell-curve, and dividing all phenomena between the poles of the normal and the pathological.

Under the sway of positivist ideals, all sensory experience, including vision itself, was increasingly submitted to normalizing principles. Jonathan Crary notes that a renewed concern with embodied vision emerged in the 1820s to constitute the eye as a specific zone of scientific inquiry. For Crary, this reintroduction of the body into the discourse around vision marked an important break with classical optics. Where the latter had been dominated by the model of the camera obscura which ignored individual variance in perception, the new paradigm made vision less a privileged form of knowing than an object of knowledge itself.[8] Yet, what is most apparent in this research is not so much the desire to recognize the claims of subjectivity, but the urge to contain its perils; to evaluate subjective experience quantitatively and validate it theoretically, thus confining it within the bounds of reason.

---

6 It remains significant that one of the most oft-repeated stories in the history of the camera concerns Eadweard Muybridge's use of photography to settle a wager about galloping horses – a movement which lay beyond the threshold of human perception.

7 J. Berger and J. Mohr, *Another Way of Telling*, New York, Pantheon, 1982, p. 100.

8 Crary comments: 'What begins in the 1820s and 1830s is a repositioning of the observer, outside of the fixed relations of interior/exterior presupposed by the camera obscura, and into an undemarcated terrain in which the distinction between internal sensation and external sign is irrevocably blurred.' See Crary, *Techniques of the Observer*, p. 24. This is the crux of Crary's contention that the subjectivity of the 'classical observer' was in fact reconstructed *prior* to the emergence of photography.

The need to account for the vagaries of individual subjectivity situates the immense epistemological passage between the classical dioptrics of Descartes and Locke in the seventeenth century, and Goethe's famous *Theory of Colours* published in 1810. In the latter, vision is no longer the prerogative of a stable observer but has itself become radically temporalized.[9] What Foucault termed the replacement of the memorable man by the *calculable* man conditions the explosion of physiological research into afterimages, persistence of vision and other optical phenomena pioneered by those such as David Brewster (inventor of the kaleidoscope), Joseph Plateau and Gustav Fechner from the 1820s.[10] In the space of some 20 to 30 years, the eye was converted into a field of statistical information, as researchers timed how long it took to become fatigued and to recover, measured the size of the dilation and contraction of the pupil, the strength of eye movements, and so on. In the process the eye was colonized as a scientific territory, mapped according to various zones of efficiency and aptitude, with specific parameters of normal and pathological vision. A startling feature of this early physiological research was its obsessive nature. Often it involved staring directly into the sun for long periods of time to study the incandescent colours of after-images. Brewster, Plateau and Fechner – the most celebrated students of vision of the period – all went blind or permanently damaged their eyesight in this fashion. What were they staring at with such intensity? What wonders were they hoping to see? It is this image of three men trying desperately to see inside the workings of the eye until their own eyes no longer see that remains longest with me.

*

How does photography intersect this transformation of knowledge, subjectivity and vision in the nineteenth century? Its immediate and dominant effect was to confirm the authority of the objective eye by providing a mechanical vision capable of transcending the suspicions directed towards the 'merely human'. In this respect, the valorization of photographic objectivity moved in concert with, rather than in opposition to, the new concern for embodied perception. Photography became the standard against which the variations of the mortal body could be measured. Acceptance that the camera's images represented an 'absolute truth' beyond human perception was fundamental to the positivist reorganization of knowledge. To many, the camera seemed the ideal mechanism for realizing the Comtean dream that the collection of scientific data would eventually provide such comprehensive knowledge about nature and society that the workings of both could be planned to construct a technological utopia on earth.

9 Crary notes: 'Once vision became located in the empirical immediacy of the observer's body, it belonged to time, to flux, to death. The guarantee of authority, identity and universality supplied by the camera obscura belonged to another epoch.' Crary, *Techniques of the Observer*, p. 24.

10 M. Foucault, *Discipline and Punish: The Birth of the Prison* (trans. A. Sheridan), Harmondsworth, Penguin, 1977, p. 193.

As much as the camera became a privileged metaphor for the hierarchical split between subjectivity and objectivity that positivism sought to enshrine *as* reality, photography also became a practical tool of enormous importance to the growth of industrial culture. Machine production and industrial capitalism depended not only on the wholesale objectification of the natural world, its conversion to what Heidegger termed a 'standing reserve' of resources and raw materials; they also demanded the systematic reorganization of human bodies into a productive labour force. As Foucault has argued, the aggregation of large-scale workforces into dense urban centres of population and the desire to utilize workers' bodies more 'efficiently' necessitated a significant transformation in techniques of power. As the nineteenth century progressed, it was no longer practical to regulate the social body as an undifferentiated mass; instead it was increasingly constituted as a mass individuality.

Instrumental in constructing this new social order was the formation of what Foucault has aptly termed 'the disciplines': psychology, physiology, biology, anatomy, criminology and sociology all emerged or were significantly transformed in the nineteenth century, taking the 'natural sciences' as their matrix. This ideological–intellectual shift provided the practical means for the deployment and exercise of qualitatively new relations of power, facilitating a dispersed and flexible constellation of techniques predicated upon precise observation, recording, and analysis of social phenomena. These methods provided the instruments for that 'government of individuality' which Foucault posited as a key factor in the modern exercise of power:

> For a long time ordinary individuality – the everyday individuality of everybody – remained below the threshold of description. To be looked at, observed, described in detail, followed from day to day by an uninterrupted account of writing was a privilege . . . The disciplinary methods reversed this relation, lowered the threshold of describable individuality and made of this description a means of control and a method of domination. It is no longer a monument for future memory, but a document for possible use . . . The disciplines mark the moment when the reversal of the political axis of individualization – as one might call it – takes place.[11]

A decisive factor in the construction of the disciplines was the transformation of habitual ways of seeing. The crux was the creation of an instrumental relation between vision and power in which the scrutinizing gaze of empiricism could be transposed from the realm of natural science and systematically applied to the organization of social spaces in which human bodies were positioned, studied and analysed as the objects of a scientific discourse. Throughout Foucault's work on the disciplines this systematic realignment of vision and power is prominent. In *Madness and Civilization*, the insertion of insanity into the discourse of psychology is intrinsically linked to the development of new asymmetrical techniques of observation; the intimacy of a gaze that constantly approaches in order to see better, but

11 Foucault, *Discipline and Punish*, pp. 191–2.

at the same time recedes, holds itself aloof, remains ever distant.[12] In *The Birth of the Clinic*, what opens the space for clinical discourse to mobilize the authority of the rational expert, and to deploy the opposition between the normal and the pathological which will prove so decisive, is precisely a transformation of space; the establishment of a new theoretical dimensionality in which the human body was to be made exhaustively legible.[13] *The Order of Things* begins with the famous discussion of Velasquez's *Las Meninas*, which Foucault describes as 'the representation, as it were, of Classical representation, and the definition of space it opens up to us'.[14] But it is in *Discipline and Punish*, with Bentham's Penitentiary Panopticon, that Foucault found his most compelling optical metaphor for situating the threshold of modernity.

The Panopticon was intended as a reform of prison design which would enable the supervision and scrutiny of prisoners in the most humane, efficient and cost-effective manner possible. (The convergence perceived between these values in the nineteenth century is an integral part of the transformation in question.) Its operating principle was simple. In a prison building with a central observation tower ringed by back-lit cells, a single supervisor placed in the central position is able to observe the behaviour of a multiplicity of prisoners, each silhouetted in their respective cells. The same light which exposes the prisoners enables the observer to remain shadowed and unseen. Even if supervision is discontinuous, the dis-symmetry of the mechanism ensures that a constant state of potential visibility can be induced in each prisoner.

With panopticism, visibility has become a trap. The mechanism not only enabled secure observation but constituted a living laboratory, an analytic machine in which different methods of training and punishment could be tested, results obtained, statistics tabulated and fed back into the operation of the system. Panoptic power resides not so much in the specific individuals or groups who occupy the central observation point, but in the structure of the mechanism itself, in its systematic distribution of relations between bodies, light and the right of inspection. For Foucault, the full significance of panopticism lay in the fact that it did not remain confined to the prison, but was destined to spread throughout the entire social body, remaking the

12 Foucault describes this in terms of 'a passage from a world of Censure to a universe of Judgement. But thereby a psychology of madness becomes possible, for under observation madness is constantly required, at the surface of itself, to deny its dissimulation. It is judged only by its acts; it is not accused of intentions, nor are its secrets to be fathomed. Madness is responsible only for that part of itself which is visible. All the rest is reduced to silence. Madness no longer exists except as *seen*.' M. Foucault, *Madness and Civilization*, New York, Vintage, 1973, p. 250.

13 Medical practice in the clinic privileges sight rather than touch and depends upon 'a fundamental redistribution of the visible and the invisible insofar as it is linked with the division between what is stated and what remains unsaid'. M. Foucault, *The Birth of the Clinic* (trans. A.M. Sheridan Smith), New York, Vintage, 1975, p. xi.

14 M. Foucault, *The Order of Things*, New York, Random House, 1973, p. 17.

hospital, the army barracks, the reformatory, the factory, the asylum, the school, in its image.[15]

Given his attention to the role of the discriminating gaze as a fundamental technique of disciplinary power, it remains a striking lacuna in Foucault's work that he didn't concern himself with the camera. His suggestion that the new 'political anatomy' demanded 'instruments that render visible, record, differentiate and compare' seems as directly applicable to the camera's transportable optics as to Benthamite panoptics.[16] Moreover, the two systems emerge more or less simultaneously: the birth of the technology of the modern prison coincides with the birth of photography in the 1830s, and the integration of the camera with key institutions of disciplinary society was both rapid and pervasive.[17] Photography was quickly adopted by the newly established police forces, both as a method of criminal identification and a means of recording evidence. It was also used in the burgeoning files kept on inmates and patients in the hospitals, asylums, children's homes, work houses and prisons which spread at this time. Psychiatrist Dr Hugh Diamond, whose photographs taken at the Surrey County Asylum constituted one of the earliest applications of this kind, saw the camera as a boon to the nineteenth-century predilection for physiognomy:

> [T]he photographer secures with unerring accuracy the external phenomena of each passion, as the really certain indication of internal derangement, and exhibits to the eye the well known sympathy which exists between the diseased brain and the organ and features of the body.[18]

Photography was equally instrumental in representing different bodies elsewhere, constructing a typology of racial and cultural 'others' in anthropology and ethnography, and redefining the sexual other through its capacity to expose the female body for pornographic consumption.[19] The camera also found broad military, industrial and scientific applications. Taylorist principles for the scientific management of labour, dependent on the minute observation and precise timing of movement to establish minimum 'unit times' for the performance of particular tasks, found a corollary in Frank Gilbreth's chronocyclographs, which adapted the serial image format of Marey's chronophotographic method to the analysis of industrial produc-

15 Foucault notes: 'Whenever one is dealing with a multiplicity of individuals on whom a task or a particular form of behaviour must be imposed, the panoptic schema may be used.' Foucault, *Discipline and Punish*, p. 205.

16 Foucault, *Discipline and Punish*, p. 205.

17 Foucault comments: 'In the 1830s the Panopticon became the architectural plan of most prison projects.' *Discipline and Punish*, p. 249.

18 Quoted in S.L. Gilman (ed.), *The Face of Madness: Hugh W. Diamond and the Origin of Psychiatric Photography*, New Jersey, Brunner Mazel, 1976, p. 20.

19 On the use of photography in nineteenth-century anthropology, see 'The crisis of memory' below. Linda Williams relates the emergence of a distinct modern pornography to the obsessive investigation of the body practised by those such as Muybridge and Marey. See her *Hardcore: Power, Pleasure and the 'Frenzy of the Visible'*, Berkeley, University of California Press, 1989, ch. 2.

tion.[20] From the 1850s, regiments of the Royal Engineers throughout the British Empire began to employ photographers in surveying and mapping teams, presaging the decisive role camera technologies would assume in modern military strategy. And across the whole spectrum of science, from photomicrography to astrophotography, the camera reigned with untrammelled authority.[21] In short, photographic 'facts' fed directly into every major social and political regulatory system which developed at this time. As Tagg has argued, it is within these conceptual frameworks that the truth value of the photographic image was consolidated, as a practical technique functioning within an institutional paradigm of research, surveillance and control.

*

As much as the camera was deployed as a tool of observation, it also offered new social pleasures. The invention of photography immediately broadened the range of people to whom individual representation was both economically and ideologically accessible. Where the painted portrait had been the preserve of the very wealthy, it rapidly became a sign of status for the ascendant middle classes to have their photographs taken. It was here that the first battles for the popularity of the camera were won; it is estimated that more than 90 per cent of the daguerreotypes taken (in vogue from 1839 to around 1854) were portraits.[22] However, while this 'democratization' of portraiture can be read as prefiguring the political trajectory towards universal suffrage, it also carries other connotations. If the photographic portrait conferred the status of subjectivity, it equally enforced a new inscription of social identity capable of intervening at just that threshold of 'describable individuality' which Foucault posited as a principal axis of disciplinary power. Photography transforms the practice of self-identity and amplifies the duplicity of the term 'subject', pointing on the one hand towards the sovereignty of the individual, and on the other to the possibility of being subjected to the rule of a normalizing discourse. Opened to the vicissitudes of an other eye, whose snapshot could not become an identity

20 Gilbreth, one of Taylor's most fervent disciples, boasted that chronocyclography enabled records of 'the time and path of individual motions to the 1/1000th of a minute'. 'Motion study in a household', *Scientific American*, 13 April 1912, quoted in S. Kern, *The Culture of Time and Space 1880–1918*, Cambridge, MA, Harvard University Press, 1983, p. 115. Marey was himself enlisted as an adviser on military training in the 1880s. See Dagognet, *A Passion for the Trace*, pp. 170–1.

21 Much scientific data is now produced by the camera: for example, every major astronomical discovery this century has occurred through photographic images of various kinds. See Darius, *Beyond Vision*, pp. 12–19.

22 J. Tagg, *The Burden of Representation*, London, Macmillan, 1988, p. 41. Photographic visiting cards also became hugely popular; in the late 1850s some 300 to 400 million were sold annually in England alone. See H. and A. Gernsheim, *A Concise History of Photography*, London, Thames and Hudson, 1965, p. 118.

card, or part of a discourse of social engineering such as physiognomy?[23] If the popularization of photography marked a broadening of the social terrain of representation, it also formed the historic threshold beyond which surveillance would no longer originate from above – whether the vigilant eye belonged to God, Monarch, or State – but was increasingly dispersed within the populace at large.

The extent to which surveillance from above – literally from above with the proliferation of aerial reconnaissance, multispectral earth resource satellites and remote sensing devices – is today complemented by the self-surveillance of private image production reflects the extraordinary degree to which contemporary culture has been shaped by the internalization of panopticism. John F. Kennedy's observation that 'the camera has become our best inspector' finds ominous echoes in the advertising slogan, 'Nothing escapes Agfa.'[24] If, in Orwell's wake, this dream of an omniscient sight machine seems less than benign, one should not be too hasty to assume that it is the camera's only possibility. Nevertheless, institutionalized surveillance has become such an indelible point of reference in the present that it is frequently the lack of the camera – rather than the lack of escape – which today makes itself felt. Whether taking photographs at a wedding, or videoing a child's first steps, or seeing ourselves on a screen while standing in a bank queue, or simply watching television, we have learnt the importance, and, perhaps more tellingly, the pleasure of surveying ourselves in a world in which the consciousness of one's constant visibility has never been more intense.

*

The swings between narcissism and voyeurism shaping the modern spectacle are undoubtedly conditioned by the manner in which the camera has hardened resistance to belief in the invisible. What cannot be seen, photographed or filmed often assumes an anxious and fluctuating existence in the present, a tendency which has been accentuated by the development of imaging techniques which extend the reach of photographic proof far beyond the range of the human eye. Few inventions have produced the explosive effect of the X-ray, publicly unveiled (alongside the *cinématographe*) in 1895. Roentgen's discovery, which exposed the body's internal organs to an uncanny light capable of negating the opacity of flesh, galvanized public and scientist alike, dramatically confirming the camera's capacity to reveal a new reality. Equally startling was the cine-camera's ability to reproduce bodily functions in 'real time', graphically demonstrated

23 While it is today common to dismiss physiognomy as outmoded, the emphasis that contemporary media culture places on close-ups of the face bears consideration. For an interesting visual commentary, see Robert Heinecken's *A Case Study in Finding an Appropriate TV Newswoman* (*A CBS Docudrama in Words and Pictures*) (self published), 1984. I am grateful to Peter Lyssiotis for drawing my attention to this book.

24 Kennedy cited in P. Virilio, *The Lost Dimension* (trans. D. Moshenberg), New York, Semiotext(e), 1991, p. 18.

in Ludwig Braun's 1898 film of a dog's beating heart. These experiments prefigured the extraordinary proliferation of devices for visualizing physiological processes which have completely reconstructed the frontiers of the body in the present.

Contemporary imaging techniques often seem to have completed the Enlightenment project of conquering the body – if not the entire universe – by enhancing the observer's perceptual prowess. Fantastic voyages into the body have proved infectious: while of practical use to experts, their images have also converted the body into a pleasurable spectacle for lay observers. But here the nature of the image – and the entire concept of an image which is 'true to nature' – is being radically redefined. Many contemporary medical techniques such as ultrasound, computerized tomography, positron emission tomography, and magnetic resonance imaging are not themselves 'visual', but depend upon the construction of an image from non-optical data, such as mass, density, or heat.[25] The disjunction between visible images and perceptible referents is widening further with the spread of digital technology. Crary has argued:

> Most of the historically important functions of the human eye are being supplanted by practices in which visual images no longer have any reference to the position of an observer in a 'real', optically perceived world. If these images can be said to refer to anything, it is to millions of bits of electronic mathematical data.[26]

This threshold is arguably comparable to the break the photographic camera made with classical optics in the nineteenth century. To understand better the increasing abstraction of vision in opto-electronics, we need to recognize that, while the camera initially lent itself to the encyclopaedic dreams of positivism, it never simply confirmed that paradigm. The pursuit of certainty through the objective eye of the photographic apparatus found itself opened to new uncertainties in the course of the twentieth century: the prospect of technotopia receded in the face of global war and global capitalism, each of which produced an onslaught of images. Moreover, even within the domain of scientific photography, there was never absolute agreement on photographic realism. Once images were no longer timeless, but carried time directly into the scene of representation, the fixed relation between observer and object which had dominated the paradigm of the camera obscura no longer held firm. Both observer and object found their

---

25 This is also the case for many other imaging techniques; astrophotography utilizes the extremes of ultra-violet and infra-red spectra to reconstruct images with the aid of sophisticated computer algorithms. Military surveillance uses radar, remote sensing, thermal and light intensifying cameras. Computer animation, synthetic holography, robotic image recognition, virtual environment helmets and multispectral sensors all employ images that are no longer 'referential' in a traditional photographic sense. See L. Cartwright, ' "Experiments of destruction": cinematic inscriptions of physiology', *Representations*, 40 (Fall 1992), p. 133.

26 Crary, *Techniques of the Observer*, p. 2.

stability dissolved by a new visual order in which 'direct' and 'indirect' perceptions achieved a radical equivalence. While a certain relationship between optics, realism and reason undoubtedly crystallized with the invention of the camera, it found only an unstable equilibrium in a social environment increasingly subject to movement and change.

5

Promiscuous Meanings

Above all, look to the things around you, the immediate world around you. If you are alive, it will mean something to you, and if you know how to use it [the camera], you will want to photograph that meaningness.

Paul Strand

All of Western faith and good faith was engaged in this wager on representation: that a sign could refer to a depth of meaning, that a sign could *exchange* for meaning and that something could guarantee this exchange . . .

Jean Baudrillard

The positivist interpretation of photography took it as axiomatic that the question of meaning no longer remained to be asked of the photographic image. Yet this arrest of meaning in the name of self-evidence, entailing the submission of appearances to the absolute jurisdiction of mechanical reproduction, has remained strikingly insecure. Despite the camera's intimate association with truth in representation, photographs have never been entirely exempt from the Platonic denigration of 'mere images', signs which are too easily orphaned from their origins and original meanings.

Even within the domain of nineteenth-century science, where the camera was received so enthusiastically, disputes over the use of photographic evidence disclosed an unsettling halo of semantic indeterminacy. If something as infinitely variable as the angle of the camera could significantly affect the image, transforming its appearance and sometimes 'distorting' it beyond recognition, where did this leave photographic objectivity?[1] Such questions revealed a significant – and still unresolved – tension between the irreducible perspectivism of the camera, and the claim to transcend the limits of perspective which has been integral to the concept of objectivity.

One means advocated to ward off the perils of 'subjectivism' was standardization in framing, particularly in photographs of the body which gave rise to the genre of anthropometric photography.[2] This approach, which

1 See, for example, the arguments over the use of X-rays described in L. Daston and P. Galison, 'The image of objectivity', *Representations*, 40 (Fall 1992), pp. 110–11.

2 In 1869, Thomas Henry Huxley put a proposal to the British Colonial Office for taking 'a systematic series of photographs of the various races of men comprehended within the British Empire', stressing the need to make these photographed bodies measurable in relation to one another by posing them in view of a measuring scale (anthropometer). See F. Spencer, 'Some notes on the attempt to apply photography to anthropometry in the second half of the nineteenth century', in E. Edwards (ed.), *Anthropology and Photography*, New Haven, Yale University Press and London, Royal Anthropological Institute, 1992, p. 99.

extended from anthropology to state bureaucracy, was used to map racial identity in one domain and civil identity in the other.[3] However, this strategy can be readily applied only in controlled situations such as the prison, laboratory or studio. Elsewhere, more versatile methods for securing meaning had to be found.

To understand the problem, it is important to recognize the extent to which photography altered the status of the image in scientific discourse. Before the photograph, scientific illustration was dominated by hand-drawn images whose function was to synthesize a multiplicity of possible examples into an 'ideal' representation. The camera gradually tipped the balance in favour of images taken directly from 'nature herself', bypassing the increasingly suspect mediation of human hand and judgement. But the advantage of reproducing 'real' cases – for example, Darwin's use of photographs alongside engravings for *The Expression of the Emotions in Man and Animals*[4] – also proved a disadvantage: excessive particularity made it more difficult for photographs to exemplify. As a consequence, scientific photography increasingly found itself propelled towards seriality as a structure of meaning. Instead of creating a single ideal image able to gather diversity within itself, the aim increasingly became one of aggregating a multiplicity of 'real' images and thereby securing meaning by exhausting the totality of the field.[5]

Of course, one never actually reaches the limit of possible images. (Not even Muybridge's monumental treatises could make such a claim.) In fact, a new means of extrapolating meaning from multiplicity had to be found. The proximity between serial reproduction and statistics was long ago remarked on by Walter Benjamin, who at one point defined film and photography as techniques of 'reality-testing'.[6] Statistics, which transfers the burden of cause and effect to a threshold of probability, presages the dawn of the information society. Yet, despite the expansion of statistical projects to interpret the real through sheer weight of numbers – from the insurance

3 Alphonse Bertillon, a Parisian police official who established a photographic system of criminal identification widely used in Europe and the United States from the 1890s, stressed the need to standardize pose, focal length and lighting. See A. Sekula, 'The body and the archive', *October*, 39 (1986), p. 26.

4 Darwin included seven sets of photographic plates to illustrate Suffering, Grief, Joy, Sneering and Defiance, Contempt, Helplessness, and Fear. In the first edition he included the following note: 'Several of the figures in these seven Heliotype Plates have been reproduced from photographs, instead of from the original negatives; and they are in consequence somewhat indistinct. Nevertheless they are faithful copies, and are much superior for my purpose to any drawing, however carefully executed.' *The Expression of the Emotions in Man and Animals*, London, John Murray, 1872, p. vi.

5 A counter-tendency can be found in the work of Francis Galton (cousin of Charles Darwin and founder of eugenics), who used photographic superimposition to create generic images of social and racial 'types' (one was the frontispiece of Havelock Ellis's *The Criminal*). See Sekula, 'The body and the archive', pp. 40–6.

6 Mechanical reproduction 'manifests in the field of perception what in the theoretical sphere is noticeable in the increasing importance of statistics'. W. Benjamin, *Illuminations* (trans. H. Zohn), London, Fontana, 1973, p. 225.

industry and opinion polls to quantum physics – the uncertainty surrounding meaning in the present has not been quelled. It has merely been displaced onto new technologies such as the computer. Accelerating the capacity to produce and process data in the hope of encompassing 'life' creates the conditions for what Paul Virilio has termed 'a generalized delirium of interpretation'.[7]

Of late, hermeneutics has found its way back into the domain of scientific photography – and even science itself – where, of course, it was never absent but was only believed to be. Darius's observation that '[i]nterpretation is the key. Photographs, and *a fortiori* scientific photographs, utter sterling truths no more than do galvanometer readings' is far removed from the unqualified enthusiasm for the camera displayed by so many nineteenth-century scientists.[8] However, if the need to learn to 'read' images is today more widely acknowledged, the horizon within which such readings are conducted remains limited. Even outside scientific usage, photographic interpretation is still dominated by a lingering positivism which assumes that ambiguity is contingent and ultimately reducible, by patient application of the correct protocols, to a core of certainty. It is precisely this assumption that the camera brings most radically into question.

Sekula argues that positivism has historically attempted to define and regulate social deviance through photography by distributing photographic meaning along two methodological axes: that of generalization which converts photographic contingency into typicality by making the photograph into an 'example'; and that of individualization which depends on a 'machine' (a filing system and clerical apparatus) to retrieve the particular instance from the archive's infinite bounds.[9] But permeating these official currents has always been another current: what might be termed the irreducible drift of photographic meaning. Alexander Rodchenko, one of the first photographers to appreciate the implications of the camera for the notion of a static and eternal truth, asserted: 'With photography we can refute the idea that one set [of characteristics] exists for a given subject.'[10] Unlike the projects of Galton or Bertillon, Rodchenko's advocacy of portraits assembled from diverse 'photo-moments' conforms less to statistical attempts to totalize the subject than to a profound questioning of the very notion of identity.

---

7 Virilio, *Lost Dimension*, p. 53. In fact, the relation between accelerated production of information and increasing problems of interpretation had been recognized by Bertillon as early as 1891: 'The collection of criminal portraits has already attained a size so considerable that it has become physically impossible to discover among them the likeness of an individual who has assumed a false name.' Quoted in Sekula, 'The body and the archive', p. 26.

8 Darius, *Beyond Vision*, p. 19.

9 Sekula associates the first approach with Galton, and the second with Bertillon, arguing: 'These two semantic paths are so fundamental to the culture of photographic realism that their very existence is usually ignored.' Sekula, 'The body and the archive', p. 18.

10 Quoted in S.O. Khan Magomedov, *Rodchenko: The Complete Work* (trans. H. Evans), London, Thames and Hudson, 1986, p. 9.

Extending this line of thought, I would argue that the issues the camera raises for the social relations of meaning – perspectivism, seriality, the mobility of signs and the proliferation of centres of representation – go beyond simply disappointing certainty of meaning according to a regulated polyvalency which would leave unity of meaning untouched as the ultimate goal. In displacing the centre of gravity which previously regulated concepts such as intentionality, context and totality, the camera entrains a profound epistemological shift in which the meaning of meaning has itself been irreversibly transformed. This transformation involves both a shortfall and a beyond of meaning. In so closely approaching, and yet failing, the ideal of an objective system of signification capable of indissolubly binding sign and significance to a referent in the real, the camera has been instrumental in opening this entire orientation – which has also been that of the modern West – to other headings.

*

The desire to append a name, a text, a context to the image, to give an explanation of what is (supposedly) already there, reveals the thorns of doubt embedded in the positivist evaluation of photography. Despite acclamation of the photograph as the embodiment of natural language, there remains a mistrust of the visual; not so much a dispute as to the camera's veracity, but a suspicion that it gives too much veracity. Or rather, that the weight of information lacks order, direction, focus.

A principal fascination of the first Daguerreotypes was the level of detail they captured; viewers pored over them for hours with the aid of magnifying glasses, seduced by a veritable incitement to decipher.[11] The flatness of the photographic surface seemed to nurture investment in the depth of photographic meaning. But this meaning remains enigmatic, resistant to being pinned down. Difficulty in defining the significance of a particular image from *within* (perhaps a face; but whose, where, when?) dictates the importance of the series of hermeneutic frames, ranging from the caption to the establishment of generic boundaries and distinct avenues of publication and display, which have developed as means of regulating photographic meaning. Most commonly the image is thought to be anchored by the word: Barthes was dismissive of press photography because 'it is not the image which comes to elucidate or "realize" the text, but the latter which comes to sublimate, patheticize, or rationalize the image'.[12] Yet, even illustrative photographs presumed to obey the common hermeneutic loop in which the photograph guarantees the truth of the text by affirming 'this really hap-

11 Edgar Allen Poe declared: 'If we examine the work of ordinary art, by means of a powerful microscope, all traces of resemblance to nature will disappear – but the closest scrutiny of the photographic drawing discloses only a more absolute truth, more perfect identity of aspect with the thing represented.' Quoted in Daston and Galison, 'Image of objectivity', p. 111.

12 'The photographic message', in R. Barthes, *Barthes: Selected Writings*, London, Fontana, 1983, p. 204.

pened', while the text selects and directs a 'preferred reading' of the photograph, often point elsewhere. Is the image really under the complete jurisdiction of the word? Or might the image ventriloquize, seduce the word, and lure it away from its common sense?

Part of the problem is that a photograph will always show more than its caption states. (Imagine trying to name all the objects in even the simplest photograph, to describe their appearances and catalogue their relations to all other objects. This was the impossible project that Alain Robbe-Grillet pursued in his early novels: to write with photographic or cinematographic precision, thereby pushing descriptive language over the edge. It is no accident that he moved to writing for cinema and then to making films.) But this 'more' marks something other than mere quantity. It is not that the photograph is inherently richer in meaning than the word, rather that the two orders are in some way discontinuous. The tradition of linearity which has formed the privileged order of the word (often posing as order itself) seems incommensurable with the domain of the image, which conforms to its dictates only with difficulty.

To recognize this is not to assert, with McLuhan or Ong, that the camera's challenge to the primacy of the book necessarily leads to the restoration of 'oral' culture.[13] The technological immediacy of television (McLuhan's prime example) constitutes a far more complex 'return' than his generally uncritical investiture allows. For the moment, it will suffice to suggest that the camera marks less the end of 'writing' than the opening of the traditional concept of writing to elements which were always present within it, but were suppressed *in the name of meaning*. Nor can it be assumed that current challenges to linearity offer an indisputable path to freedom. The displacement of linearity belongs to a transition in which formations of knowledge and techniques of power, long regulated by the model of the line, are themselves mutating.[14]

This double trajectory situates the political ambivalence of the camera's interruption of traditional patterns of meaning. The printing press is an important point of reference. The mechanical reproduction of the book not only changed its material characteristics, but significantly altered the social relations of meaning, engendering the new mobility of signs that Baudrillard

13 McLuhan suggested: 'Our old industrialized areas, having eroded their oral traditions automatically, are in the position of having to rediscover them in order to cope with the electric age.' M. McLuhan, *Understanding Media: The Extensions of Man*, London, Abacus, 1974, p. 36. Ong proposes a notion of 'secondary orality' in which new technologies such as telephone, radio and television are able to 'maintain' oral cultures without the disruptive shifts which marked the transition to literacy. See his *Orality and Literacy: The Technologising of the Word*, London, Methuen, 1982.

14 Derrida argues that linearity has been intimately connected to a certain determination of writing, technics, and time, which has consolidated the matrix of capital and science. This formation begins to give way 'at the moment when linearity – which is not loss or absence but the repression of pluri-dimensional thought – relaxes its oppression because it begins to sterilize the technical and scientific economy it has long favoured', Derrida, *Of Grammatology*, p. 86.

described as a new level of abstraction.[15] If this new mobility of signs and meanings constitutes a vital threshold of modernity, the camera has vastly accentuated this condition by producing a multitude of signs without anchorage or home. If the printed book was one of the first serial objects of a nascent capitalism, the photograph corresponds to the maturing logic of commodity production in a world remade by machines.[16] As social life has increasingly been defined by mass production and the rapid circulation of identical objects, photography stands as the very sign of the industrial proliferation of signs.

*

The demand for 'context' which is constantly levied on the photographic image undoubtedly stems from the unprecedented speed of its process. Looking at a photograph or film, we are invited to re-enter the world it projects. But it is a gift given and received across an abyss. John Berger suggests:

> Photographs preserve instant appearances. Habit now protects us against the shock involved in such preservation. Compare the exposure time of a film with the life of the print made, and let us assume the print only lasts for ten years: the ratio for an average modern photograph would be approximately 20 000 000 to 1. Perhaps that can serve as a reminder of the violence of the fission whereby appearances are separated by the camera from their function.[17]

This ability to split life open using what Benjamin called 'the dynamite of the tenth of a second' lies at the heart of the camera's distinctive vision.[18] Because it offers a radically disembodied vision – vision seized not only in the absence of the viewer's body but, potentially, *any* body – the camera is often accused of opening a gap in which significance can be attenuated, fractured, or even annihilated. Where evaluations of the photograph as 'objective reproduction' tend to paper over this disjunction, Susan Sontag poses it as an insurmountable problem: 'A photograph is only a fragment, and with the passage of time its moorings come unstuck. It drifts away into a soft abstract pastness, open to any kind of reading.'[19] This fluidity of

---

15 Baudrillard linked the abstraction of the modern sign to changing class relations: 'In caste societies, feudal or archaic, *cruel* societies, the signs are limited in number, and are not widely diffused, each one functions with its full value as interdiction, each is a reciprocal obligation between castes, clans or persons. The signs therefore are anything but arbitrary. The arbitrary sign begins when, instead of linking two persons in an unbreakable reciprocity, the signifier starts referring back to the disenchanted universe of the signified . . . The modern sign dreams of the signs of the past and would well appreciate finding again, in its reference to the real, an *obligation*: but what it finds again is only a *reason* . . .', J. Baudrillard, *Simulations* (trans. P. Foss et al.), New York, Semiotext(e), 1983, pp. 84–6.

16 Benedict Anderson describes the book as 'the first modern style mass produced industrial commodity'. *Imagined Communities: Reflections on the Origins and Spread of Nationalism*, London, Verso, 1983, p. 38.

17 In Berger and Mohr, *Another Way of Telling*, p. 51.

18 Benjamin, *Illuminations*, p. 238.

19 Sontag, *On Photography*, p. 71.

meaning has undoubtedly increased in an era in which industrialized optics has made the accelerated circulation of images integral to economic, political and cultural life. But the question also seems more complex than Sontag allows.

This complexity can be registered in the ambivalence the camera displays to the order of intentionality (which has often posed as *the* order of meaning). Both its speed of operation and air of independence from a human operator initially seemed to divorce photographic meaning from the photographer's intentionality. However, despite the attractions of automatism, photography only briefly dispensed with intention. Disqualified in the name of science, it re-entered through the door of art. If the photograph was denied the status of art in the nineteenth century because of its machine-like qualities – only the staged images of the Pictorialist movement gained admittance – modernism decisively reversed this judgement. At least since the time of Stieglitz and the reappraisal of Atget, the photographer's 'personal vision' has been saluted as an integral part of a transformed field of aesthetics.[20]

More significant than the victory of one side or the other in this rivalry as to whether photography is art, less than art, or beyond art, is the manner in which the camera has forced a reassessment of the relation between intentionality and meaning. According to the traditional analysis in which the camera is merely a 'blind instrument', there can be no question of intentionality. The order of meaning merely corresponds to the order of 'nature herself' objectively mirrored in the photographic image. If, on the other hand, photography is validated as art, legitimate meaning is supposed to centre around the artist's intentions. So far, so good. But – and this is the crux of the matter – the camera has consistently proved to be neither properly objective, nor yet properly subjective, at least as these terms have been conventionally understood.

Despite Ansell Adams's assertion (quintessential to one line of modernist aesthetics) that '[a] photograph is not an accident – it is a concept', the field of photography abounds with stories of the lucky photograph: that chance encounter or fortuitous snap which reveals aspects of a scene about which the photographer was unaware at the moment of taking. The combination of speed and mechanization – 'instamatics' as the advertisements say – make the camera the perfect scene for a Duchampian rendezvous (to evoke a counter-current of modernism). Even the most rigorously 'staged' photo-

---

20 With the emergence of Photo-Secession around Stieglitz in New York from 1902, 'art' photography began to turn its gaze from the studio to the street. By the time Atget's *Photographes de Paris* (1930) became the first monograph on a photographer to be published in both Europe and the United States, the terrain of photography had shifted considerably. In his review of the book, Walker Evans expressed respect for Atget as an 'artist' who projected his own person through photography. While this has since become a stock evaluation of the art photographer, it also needs to be remembered that fluctuations between celebration of the photographer and celebration of the photograph have continued to punctuate the history of the camera.

graph exudes the power of contingency, offering delight in the unexpected and inexplicable stab of significance that Barthes termed *punctum*.[21] Benjamin saw this as the unique fascination of the medium:

> No matter how artful the photographer, no matter how carefully posed his subject, the beholder feels an irresistible urge to search such a picture for the tiny spark of contingency, of the Here and Now, with which reality has seared the subject . . .[22]

To the lasting chagrin of aspiring *photo-auteurs*, the camera has never simply given itself to the system treating consciousness and intentionality as the authoritative guidelines for the determination of a work's meaning. Even as the professional photographer has achieved a heightened stature, the cultural frame in which this heroism of vision is embedded has shifted significantly.

This shift has depended not only on the camera's division of time into instants, but on its ability to dissect space in new ways. The close-up exemplifies the new mode of vision that Moholy-Nagy aptly dubbed *intensive seeing*. The capacity to approach objects and isolate details offered a new frame of perception with far-reaching consequences. As Benjamin observed: 'The enlargement of a snapshot does not simply render more precise what in any case was visible, though unclear: it reveals entirely new structural formations of the subject.'[23] He made the nature of the shift clearer by adding: 'The camera introduces us to unconscious optics as does psychoanalysis to unconscious impulses.'[24]

This comparison between photography and psychoanalysis is perhaps even more suggestive – or suggestive in another way – than Benjamin thought.[25] Both photography and psychoanalysis lavish unprecedented attention on the detail, the part-object, the fragment; especially the fragmented body as a structure of deep psychic meaning. To this might be added their mutual concern with ephemera and all sorts of marginal phenomena: what psychoanalysis collects in the form of slips, lapses and insignificant babble, photography finds in its devotion to trivia, junk and the residues of daily life. Finally, as Derrida points out, the process of deciphering the photograph via microscopic examination closely resembles the psychoanalytic 'blow-up' of

---

21 Barthes writes: 'Hence the detail which interests me is not, or at least is not strictly, intentional, and probably must not be so; it occurs in the field of the photographed thing like a supplement that is at once inevitable and delightful . . .'. Barthes, *Camera Lucida*, p. 47.

22 Benjamin, *One Way Street*, p. 243.

23 Benjamin, *Illuminations*, p. 238.

24 Benjamin, *Illuminations*, p. 238. See also Benjamin, *One Way Street*, p. 243.

25 Benjamin was largely content to leave the analogy in terms of the camera's capacity to part the veils of perceptual habit: 'Even if one has a general knowledge of the way people walk, one knows nothing of a person's posture during the fractional second of a stride. The act of reaching for a lighter or a spoon is a familiar routine, yet we hardly know what really goes on between hand and metal, not to mention how this fluctuates with our moods. Here the camera intervenes with the resources of its lowerings and liftings, its interruptions and isolations, its extensions and accelerations, its enlargements and reductions.' Benjamin, *Illuminations*, pp. 238–9.

the (apparently) trivial symptom as the basis of its narrative order.[26] To recognize these parallels is not to advocate simply submitting photographic images to psychoanalytic 'decoding', but to underline the fact that both techniques emerged in an historical conjuncture in which older semantic structures were breaking down in the face of new experiences (urban–industrial acceleration, mechanized warfare). And in both, the role given to context in the production of meaning had to be radicalized.

Freud was one of the first to touch on this situation. In *The Interpretation of Dreams*, he situates his departure from traditional hermeneutics with specific reference to context:

> My procedure is not so convenient as the popular decoding method which translates any given piece of a dream's content by a fixed key. I, on the contrary, am prepared to find that the same piece of content may conceal a different meaning when it occurs in various people or different contexts.[27]

What if this indeterminacy extends beyond the dream, affecting the word, the image, the sign itself, as the general condition of signification? This is certainly how Derrida reads Freud, arguing that Freud effectively undermines the traditional concept of the sign.[28] Elsewhere Derrida has pointed out that the minimum determinant for a sign to function is that it must be capable of being repeated or re-iterated. This quite innocent and obvious requirement has complex ramifications. If a sign, in order to *be* a sign, must always be capable of being re-presented in a new context, it can never be fully present in any one context. Some 'part' must always remain in reserve, deferred, waiting to be presented elsewhere. This structural partition of the sign opens any and every possible space of communication, but simultaneously prevents it conforming to the unified semantic horizon which governs the conventional notion of meaning.[29] This line of thought is particularly fruitful in thinking about the effect of photography on meaning. If the context of a sign, as much as its content, determines its meaning, but, at the

26 Derrida suggests that photography and psychoanalysis constitute 'two religions, or two cultures of the "detail", namely two that amounts to one, and which are also techniques or systems of knowledge, as well as fine arts, magnificent arts, arts of magnification. By means of them it becomes possible to enlarge the minute or discrete element. Thus, whether deliberately or not, it is in fact possible to idealize it, to dematerialize or spiritualize it, to charge it with significance.' J. Derrida, 'Right of inspection' (trans. D. Wills), *Art & Text*, 32 (Autumn 1989), p. 73.

27 S. Freud, *The Interpretation of Dreams* (1900), vol. 4 of *The Standard Edition of the Complete Psychological Works of Sigmund Freud* (translated under the general editorship of J. Strachey), London, Hogarth Press, 1953, p. 105. Later in the same text, he rejects exhaustive codification of dream symbols, insofar as 'they frequently have more than one, or even several meanings, and, as with Chinese script, the correct interpretation can only be arrived at on each occasion from the context' (*Standard Edition*, vol. 5, p. 353). Despite this insistence, Freud will continue to propose readings of great generality.

28 See his discussion of Freud's recourse to a 'psychical script' which is never exterior and posterior to the spoken word in 'Freud and the scene of writing', *Writing and Difference* (trans. A. Bass), London and Henley, Routledge and Kegan Paul, 1978, pp. 199, 209–10.

29 See J. Derrida, 'Signature, event, context', *Margins of Philosophy* (trans. A Bass), Brighton, Harvester Press, 1982, pp. 307–30.

same time, the very nature of the sign (its ability to be repeated) *prevents the saturation of context*, meaning necessarily becomes subject to a radical drift. This goes beyond the assertion that signs can assume a 'plurality' of meanings, but rather asserts an irreducible polysemy which challenges the very notion of meaning conceived as a process of gathering, collecting, or unifying. The historical significance of the camera is, in part, to have exposed this condition while accentuating its effects. If problematizing the fixity of meaning has become a prominent theme of recent theory, this threshold seems unimaginable without the proliferation of cameras, and the mediatization of culture in the second half of this century.

*

Like psychoanalysis, photographic dissection of the real has often promised to unlock the hidden secrets of existence. Because the photographic image appears to offer a natural language rather than a signifier, photographic signs have often been (mis)taken for the wonders of nature itself. But there has always been a tension between the purity of photographic recording and photography's capacity for revelation. The camera's ability to frame images in unorthodox ways disturbed what were previously thought to be the natural frames of representation, such as painting's window or theatre's proscenium arch. For those such as Moholy-Nagy and Rodchenko, this fluidity offered the means to shatter past traditions of realism. Manipulating point of view to charge familiar objects with their latent unfamiliarity held great possibilities for political intervention.[30]

But as much as photographic surgery is capable of conferring new significance, it has also been charged with threatening coherence and undermining meaning 'as such'. Sontag, for whom photography represents the ultimate realization of the surrealist dream, comments: 'In a world ruled by photographic images, all borders ("framing") seem arbitrary', adding that this 'contributes to the erosion of the very notion of meaning'.[31] Because of the tendency for one image to meld into another, Sontag warns that photography produces a state of paralysis in which political change is replaced by a change in the repertoire of images.

Such a condition is undoubtedly serious. But what is the 'very notion of meaning' to which Sontag appeals in delineating this threshold? Throughout her text, her analysis of the image slides towards a spirited defence of the word. Her most damning criticism of photography is that it cannot narrate: having made this determination, Sontag is able to reduce photographs to

30 Rodchenko proclaimed: 'We . . . must unlock the world of the visible. We have to revolutionize our visual thinking. We must draw back the curtains from eyes.' *Novy LEF*, 9 (1928), quoted in Hambourg, *New Vision*, p. 86. For Moholy-Nagy, abandoning traditional laws of perspective promised to bring 'to light phenomena imperceptible to the human eye and made visible by the photographic apparatus, thus perfecting the eye by means of photography'. See 'Light – a medium of plastic expression', *Broom*, 4 (1923), reprinted in Passuth, *Moholy-Nagy*, p. 292.
31 Sontag, *On Photography*, p. 22, p. 106.

offering only a semblance of understanding.[32] Disappointment with the lack of fixity in the meaning of images pushes her into arguing that 'print seems a less treacherous form of leaching out the world, of turning it into a mental object', and leaves her finally lamenting that '[t]here is a rancorous suspicion in America of whatever seems literary, not to mention a growing reluctance on the part of young people to read anything . . .'.[33] What this standpoint occludes, with its constant recourse to simple oppositions between word and image, narrative and non-narrative, semblance and substance, is whether the security of the book and the ideal of completeness it once nurtured is still a sufficient horizon from which to pose the question of meaning in the age of the camera.

Stability of meaning is inevitably linked to the capacity of representation to totalize its field of play. Photography is 'difficult' in this regard. Despite the proliferation of cameras and images, what has emerged from the photographic diaspora is less a complete picture of the world than a mobile army of representations. If this accentuates the importance of seriality as a structure of photographic meaning, it has also diminished the claim of any single image to completely capture its subject. In this light, what does it mean to describe a photograph as 'only a fragment'? Is the image less than whole only when it represents a part-object, perhaps the close-up of the hand which Fox Talbot included in the first photographic book (*The Pencil of Nature*, 1844)?[34] But what photograph would not be a 'part-object', a fragment of a larger, more inclusive whole? (This touches the paradox of set theory.) Or is the photograph fragmentary only when the image is internally fractured, along the lines practised by *monteurs* such as John Heartfield and Hannah Höch? Yet isn't every photograph already the result of selection and framing; in short, of montage?

Difficulty in resolving these questions points to another problem: in the absence of the whole, can one still speak meaningfully of the fragment? How does the fragment maintain an identity save by referring to the hallucinatory completeness of an other's spectral body? (The Lacanian 'mirror-stage' and the formation of identity via specular misrecognition is not far away.) Pertinent to Sontag's dismissal of the photograph as 'only a fragment' is Derrida's observation (made in another context) that: 'The concept of the fragment, however, since its fracturedness is itself an appeal to some totalizing complement, is no longer sufficient here.'[35] Can the

32 Sontag, *On Photography*, p. 23.

33 Sontag, *On Photography*, pp. 4 and 74.

34 André Breton's remark that 'if one were to displace a hand by severing it from an arm, that hand becomes more wonderful as a hand' highlights the profound surrealist sympathies bound up with photographic vision. Quoted in D. Ades, *Photomontage*, London, Thames and Hudson, 1976, p. 22.

35 J. Derrida, *Spurs: Nietzsche's Styles* (trans. B. Harlow), Chicago and London, University of Chicago Press, 1979, p. 125. Derrida writes elsewhere that this 'leads one to think that, since the time of photography a whole has been neither promised nor given, that the whole begins by being withdrawn, by appearing to retreat without being seen'. 'Right of inspection', pp. 74–5.

radical elasticity of photographic framing in fact be mastered by an opposition between the fragment and the whole? What would be the scale or register which could hope to secure a stable relation between a micro which extends to the sub-atomic and a macro which can encompass an entire galaxy? And what order of meaning can be sustained when every whole is revealed as merely another fragment? When there are only fragments, fragments which overlap and envelop other fragments without thereby becoming 'complete'?[36]

The profound *deterritorialization* of image and meaning produced by the camera corresponds to an industrial dynamism of people, objects and signs which has transformed the mimetic tradition. The conventional logic of the whole demands the stability of a fixed centre of representation. But this ideal, enshrined in the classical model of the camera obscura which dominated European thought for around two centuries, proved inadequate to the emerging capitalist environment dependent on rapid circulation and exchange. In the proliferation of disembodied visions and the wholesale portability of images, the photographic camera offers the modern subject not an image of totality, but an image of its own ambivalence, suspended between the silken promise of liberation and nostalgia at loss of anchorage.

*

Increase in the volume and velocity of image circulation resulting from the industrialization of the camera has undoubtedly heightened the volatility of photographic meaning. The introduction of mass-produced cameras by Kodak in 1888, and the manufacture of pre-packaged roll film a year later, vastly expanded both the number of cameras and the number of photographs they could take.[37] Around the same time, the invention of the half-tone bloc brought photographic reproduction into the print media. By the turn of the century, people had come to expect to have news stories illustrated photographically. This marked the end of the time when it was remarkable to possess an image of something or someone well-known. The modern era of disposable images had begun.

Benjamin's seminal analysis of the impact of technical reproducibility on the 'aura' of the work of art proclaimed an immense shattering of the bonds of tradition.

36 Lacan offers another image for this abyssal relation of part and whole in his description of the structure of the 'signifying chain' as 'rings of a necklace that is a ring in another necklace made of rings'. J. Lacan, *Écrits: A Selection* (trans. A. Sheridan), London, Tavistock, 1977, p. 153.

37 George Eastman was the first to apply the principles of mass production to the camera. As well as marketing the Kodak camera and roll film, Eastman founded a network of developing centres which inspired great increases in the number of photographers. By 1900, one in ten people in Britain owned a camera. The Eastman Co. rapidly dominated both camera and film sales: by 1902 they were producing 80–90 per cent of the world's output of film and their famous advertising slogan, 'You Press the Button, We Do The Rest', still defines the territory for domestic photography.

> To an ever greater degree the work of art reproduced becomes the work of art designed for reproducibility. From a photographic negative, for example, one can make any number of prints; to ask for the 'authentic' print no longer makes sense. But the instant the criterion of authenticity ceases to be applicable to artistic production, the total function of art is reversed. Instead of being based on ritual, it begins to be based on another practice – politics.[38]

Six decades later these hopes appear somewhat quixotic. The concept of authenticity remains alive and marketable, not least in the realm of photography where limited editions, signed copies and 'original' prints abound with a vigour that marks the return of the repressed. Yet, the terrain staked out by Benjamin's analysis remains critical. The crux of the matter is still the multiparous nature of the camera; no-one has yet devised a social protocol equal to the rupture opened by the possibility of infinite reproduction. The extent to which the effects of reproduction now condition the entire framework of perception can perhaps be grasped in the reversal to which travel has been subjected: instead of journeying to see the unseen, travellers often find themselves viewing the already seen and comparing it with its images.[39]

In one of his short stories, Italo Calvino described a photographer's journey from naivety to obsession, as his search for the perfect photograph was overwhelmed by the profusion and increasing autonomy of the images he created. Antonino's desperate final solution was to abandon the world he once believed to be real and instead immerse himself in the world of images. In this, he prefigured 1980s fashion: 'photographing photographs was the only course that he had left, or rather, the one course that he had obscurely sought all this time.'[40] Calvino's allegory, written over three decades ago, remains instructive reading. But today the effacement of the real by its images has moved from the realm of 'fiction' to become a central theme of social theory. In this vein, one could easily find many lives which rival that of Calvino's photographer. What of Jacques-Henri Lartigue who, as a small boy experimenting with a crude camera, exclaimed: 'It's marvellous, marvellous! Nothing will ever be as much fun. I'm going to photograph everything, everything!' and proceeded to do so, accumulating some 40,000 negatives on file?[41] Or Garry Weinogrand who shot 300,000 negatives in the last six years of his life, developing few and printing even less?[42] Photographic obsession has a long history, from Muybridge's 60,000-strong encyclopaedia to that doyen of American photographers, Edward Steichen, whose immense and varied career included portraiture, documentary, military reconnaissance in two world wars and a period as America's

---

38 Benjamin, *Illuminations*, p. 226.

39 As early as the 1930s, Kodak's marketing strategy involved signposting towns in the USA with lists of what to photograph. Markers were also placed in national parks directing visitors to the best vantage points.

40 I. Calvino, 'The adventure of a photographer', *Difficult Loves* (trans. W. Weaver), London, Picador, 1985, p. 52.

41 Quoted in *The Camera*, New York, Time-Life International, 1970–1, p. 13.

42 See H. Bishop, 'Looking for Mr. Weinogrand', *Aperture*, 112 (Fall 1988).

highest-paid magazine photographer. At the end of his life, Steichen's gaze came to rest on a single tree in front of his house, which he photographed countless times.

It is the disarming ease of photographic repetition which fans these lives lurching somewhere between meditation and monomania. Where art traditionally focused on the sacred, the heroic, the scenic, and the monumental, the camera immediately swallowed these categories and went hungrily searching for more. Such an expansion in the reach of representation brought many previously hidden, forgotten or neglected subjects before the public eye. The work of reformist photographers such as Jacob Riis and Lewis Hine lent photography an ethical reputation which still lingers.[43] However, the project of unlimited photography long ago passed the point where images revealing 'unseen' cultural recesses can be assumed to challenge the dominant political order. Unlimited photography has itself emerged as a new kind of dominant order. (As Robert Frank recognized in the 1960s when he gave up photography: 'You can photograph anything now.') Supplying the appetite of the image apparatus without challenging its conditions of production merely conforms to the 'arty journalism' Benjamin satirized:

> *The world is beautiful* – that is its watchword. Therein is unmasked the posture of a photography that can endow any soup can with significance but cannot grasp a single one of the human connections in which it exists . . .[44]

When everything is a potential photograph simply because it can be so easily taken, there no longer seems any reason to stop taking. If the camera has produced a crisis in meaning and a crisis in the real, it is perhaps because (as Calvino suggested) we now find ourselves suspended between the desire to consider every moment of life photographable, and the necessity to live in the most photographable way possible. Where photographs were once thought to belong to an order of reference in which images depended on reality, the growing autonomy of the image-world has complicated this trajectory. It is the uncertainty of this transition – from an order of reference binding image to reality to a vertigo of referentiality in which the priority of the real as the final guarantor of meaning is withdrawn – which conditions our relation to the camera today.

*

As the number of photographs has multiplied, far from simply increasing the sum of available knowledge and disseminating it more widely to enable a reassessment of political and cultural heritage (the modern democratic dream), they often seem to have emptied themselves of meaning. Or rather,

43 John Berger argues that the period between the two world wars was the moment in which photography posed the sharpest challenge to existing forms of perception and power. J. Berger, *About Looking*, London, Writers and Readers, 1984, p. 48.

44 Benjamin, *One Way Street*, p. 255. Benjamin's immediate target here was photographer Albert Renger-Patsch whose famous *The World is Beautiful* had been published in 1928.

their values and meanings have been dispersed in the ubiquity of their circulation. John Berger's distinction between photographs which belong to private experience and those which are used publicly offers one means of avoiding this impasse.[45] This is not because the distinction is flawless, but because it affords valuable insights into the processes by which photographic meaning is created and enforced in the present. Berger understands the private photograph – perhaps a photograph taken by the viewer, or which represents people or places familiar to the viewer – as one which is read within the context of the life nurturing its testimony. If its image is a selective 'quote from appearances', it nevertheless re-enters the flow of time: not by effacing the disjunction between the photographed instant and the moment of viewing, but by making this gap the subject of stories bridging the time inbetween. Looking at our own photographs or those of friends is always an incitement to storytelling. In this context, the image is not overburdened with the demand to inform and explain, but functions more as a touchstone for remembering and recounting.[46]

By contrast, the contemporary public image often comes from so far outside the experience of those who view it that the gulf separating appearance from significance defies imagination. This doesn't mean it therefore has no meaning; rather, that its meaning is easily channelled in particular directions. Because most public images depend on minimizing whatever might compromise belief in their directness and transparency, their meaning tends to be confined to a rhetoric of the obvious. This creates a paradox: in an image-dominated culture, images are asked to do so little. This state of affairs is most evident on 'the news', which finds its authority in the promise to extend the eye of each 'eye-witness' along the vector of reality itself. Every night, a vast heterogeneity of images are brought together and juxtaposed to great effect, but the price is a profound levelling of their specificities and differences. The result is that the camera's potential to redistribute cultural and experiential horizons becomes less an interruption to daily life than the confirmation of its present order. This conservatism is bolstered by the basic stance of the news media. Although the credibility of journalistic detachment (another trope of scientific 'objectivity') has lost some of its sheen, it is still presumed that a camera operator's first duty is to report to an anonymous and abstract audience, rather than to represent those involved in the events being filmed or photographed. (As Jean Mohr has observed: 'There are many reasons for not taking images. But if you are a press photographer your employers will recognize none as

45 See his 'Uses of photography', in Berger, *About Looking*, pp. 48–63.
46 This is not a function of the image but of the context of reading. In discussing an 'anthropological' photograph, Anne Salmond writes: 'It is when a photograph such as this comes face to face with descendants of those depicted, the inheritors of the traditions and ancestral names, that it most truly speaks. Then alienation may end in recognition, in greeting, or quite often, as I have seen, in tears.' Edwards, *Anthropology and Photography*, p. 228.

valid.')[47] In this way media images too often exploit or patronize the very people on whose behalf they should speak.[48]

Photographed, filmed or televised images are always discontinuous with the contexts in which they are viewed. This is not the problem. But when discontinuity is denied in the name of the simple 'truth' of the image; when the histories and desires of those represented are habitually passed over in silence; when no time or attention is given to the need to reconstruct its context, the function of the image inevitably shifts. It loses specificity and becomes emblematic, contributing to a media environment in which all images slide towards radical interchangeability. All peoples affected by famine can be made into the same archetypal victim who will never be self-sufficient. To avoid reducing the camera to an impassive and impotent witness, a minimum condition is acknowledgment of the disjunctions – including disparities of power – between event, image and the dispersed community of viewers.

Acknowledging the importance of 'context' in the production of meaning is not to argue that images suffer simply from 'lack of context'. As much as there is a general repression of context in the use of images in the contemporary media, there can also be a fetishization of context as a critical response. But context is not a finite quality which could ever be completely preserved or fully restored. Instead of placing the recovery of a lost origin and the stability of meaning as the most desirable goals, what is required is a redefinition of the problem. Entertaining the plurality of origins and the complexity of meaning demands recognition of the limits of any one interpretative frame. Compounding this necessity is the fact that meaning never resides in one time or place, but traverses a circuit linking the event to the recording apparatus and the scene of viewing. Slippage between the moments of 'reality', 'representation' and 'reception' indicates the potential for immense fluctuations in different readings of the same image.

Berger's distinction between public and private images is not watertight. Elsewhere he discusses how some public photographs can nevertheless produce the emotional resonance he attributes to private images.[49] For Berger, 'expressive' photographs are those which are able to extend the 'length' of their 'quotation from appearances', not in terms of their exposure time, but as narrative time.[50] This belief that the photograph is potentially a

---

47 In Berger and Mohr, *Another Way of Telling*, p. 78.

48 Occasionally such *systemic* disjunctions catch up with the system, often to the bewilderment of its functionaries. In his account of the 1976 Soweto massacre, Alf Khumalo wrote: 'I began taking pictures of the little boy who was dying next to me. Blood poured from his mouth and some children knelt next to him and tried to stop the flow of blood. Then some children shouted they were going to kill me . . . I begged them to leave me alone. I said I was a reporter and there to record what happened.' *The Observer* (London), 20 June 1976, quoted in Sontag, *On Photography*, p. 192.

49 See 'Appearances' in Berger and Mohr, *Another Way of Telling*, pp. 111–22.

50 Berger writes: 'An instant photographed can only acquire meaning insofar as the viewer can read into it a duration extending beyond itself. When we find a photograph meaningful we are lending it a past and a future.' Berger, *About Looking*, p. 89.

narrative seed rather than simply a narrative shard is Berger's most significant departure from Sontag's more pessimistic evaluation of photographic culture. It also suggests that the photograph able to speak to us from outside our own experience will not be the fabled mirror-image which resembles the real absolutely, but will be that image which reassembles visual appearances in order to tell a story. For Berger, any alternative use of photography must aim to construct a context 'which replaces [the image] in time – not its own original time for that is impossible – but in narrated time'.[51] Displacing the goal of finding the original meaning fosters respect for ambiguity and multiplicity as forms of meaning in themselves.

Berger's notion of 'expressive' images cuts across his distinction between public and private images. One characteristic of the private image would be its lower threshold to function 'expressively', because the viewer already knows its story. But the distinction between public and private is also blurred from the other side. Rituals with cameras have become an integral part of family life over this century, especially on ceremonial occasions such as weddings and birthdays. Bourdieu has suggested that the family photograph is simultaneously an index of family unity and a tool to achieve that unity: 'Photographic practice only exists and subsists for most of the time by virtue of its *family function* of reinforcing the integration of the family group by reasserting the sense it has both of itself and its unity.'[52] But, as much as it symbolizes unity, the family photograph also functions as a sign of the family's dispersion. The camera belongs to the era of mass migrations in which the experience of separation has been generalized, and the family photograph assumes its full – fetishistic – force only when it represents a family unit which has all but disappeared. (As Sontag has observed: 'A family's photograph album is generally about the extended family – and often is all that remains of it.')[53]

Berger likens the effect of the contemporary public photograph to the bewilderment of being exposed to the memory of a stranger: 'It records an instant in which this stranger has shouted: "Look!".'[54] Treating the world as spectacle produces a lack of specificity and an attenuation of significance for which the mass media is now notorious. But the private photograph can also be drained of meaning in this way, simply by a transposition of the context in which it is seen. Snapshots from the family album are regularly used by the media to flesh out celebrity stories, while personal photographs are frequently used to give 'ordinary people' their 15 minutes (or 15 seconds) of limelight or notoriety.

These oscillations between public and private spheres are scarcely unusual: as Barthes noted, an ascendant cultural dynamic since the invention

51 Berger, *About Looking*, p. 81.

52 P. Bourdieu, R. Castel, J.-C. Shambouredon and D. Schapper, *Photography: A Middle Brow Art* (1965) (trans. S. Whiteside), Cambridge, Polity Press, 1990, p. 19. His quintessential example is the rural peasant community.

53 Sontag, *On Photography*, p. 9.

54 Berger, *About Looking*, p. 52.

of the camera has been precisely the *publicity* of the private.[55] This highlights the fact that there are no essential differences which could be formalized to distinguish rigorously between public and private images. Every exposure is at least a double exposure, offering one face to intimates and a different visage to strangers.[56] Which is another way of saying that images have no essential meaning. Their significance is relational, their meanings are always partly determined by context, or rather, by the intersection of multiple contexts. Perhaps this has always been the case. But growing consciousness of this semantic fragility marks a significant historic threshold which can be defined by the intersection of two apparently contradictory discourses. On the one hand, the production of meaning has become a political issue in a new way, while, on another, lack of meaning has emerged as a privileged image of camera culture.

*

Sergei Eisenstein's incisive observation about the 'trouble' of montage – 'no matter how unrelated [two shots] might be, and frequently despite themselves, they engendered a "third something" and became correlated when juxtaposed according to the will of an editor'[57] – expresses the general condition image and meaning enter in this century. Since the meaning of an image is indelibly shaped by what comes before and after, this structural openness is vastly accentuated by the emergence of texts comprised entirely of chains of moving images. Commenting on early modes of exhibition in Russia, Yuri Tsivian notes:

> A torrent of films would be shown without intervals, and the selection of scenes was generally a matter of chance. . . . the impressions from one picture were involuntarily transferred to the next, to which it was connected only by random adjacence . . .[58]

Alarmed by this unpredictability, the Tsar banned projections of his image, lifting the prohibition only when these images were framed differently (separated from the general flow by the cessation of musical accom-

---

55 Barthes, *Camera Lucida*, p. 98.

56 In his work on an archive of mining photographs, Allan Sekula stressed the variety of positions which could be taken in relation to the images, contrasting the gaze of a miner to that of a stockholder in the mining company. See his 'Reading an archive', in B. Wallis (ed.), *Blasted Allegories: An Anthology of Contemporary Artists' Writings*, New York, New Museum of Contemporary Art and Cambridge, MA, MIT Press, 1987, p. 117. Similarly, Barthes refused to reproduce the photograph of his mother which was the subject of a long meditation: 'For you it would be nothing but an indifferent picture, one of the thousands of manifestations of the "ordinary" . . . at most it would interest your *studium*: period, clothes, photogeny; but in it, for you, no wound.' Barthes, *Camera Lucida*, p. 73.

57 S. Eisenstein, *The Film Sense* (trans. J. Leyda), London, Faber and Faber, 1963, pp. 17–18.

58 Y. Tsivian, 'Some historical footnotes to the Kuleshov experiment', in Elsaesser, *Early Cinema: Space, Frame, Narrative*, p. 248.

paniment and the lowering and raising of a special curtain).[59] This scene proved prophetic. The narrative strategies developed in feature films in the first decades of this century were directed precisely against the chance effects of montage (which retreated to the closet of 'experimental' film).[60] But, beyond cinema's planned economy for producing textual closure, a strikingly similar effect has re-emerged in contemporary television. With its multiple channels and the development of remote control 'grazing' (viewers flicking among programmes, not to choose one, but to view several at the same time, recalling André Breton's desire for immersion in a flow of anonymous images, which he indulged by serial film watching, arriving in the middle of one film and leaving before the end to view another)[61], television has become the ubiquitous scene for the enigmatic and bizarre encounters which so delighted the surrealists.

Barthes once suggested: 'The West moistens everything with meaning, like an authoritarian religion which imposes baptism on entire peoples.'[62] Since its invention the camera has proved a versatile tool for realizing this project, which today reaches a certain zenith when television takes 'the world' in its entirety as its legitimate sphere of interest. But here the dream of natural language – of transparent signs, stable frames and certain meanings – that the camera was once thought to offer has stumbled into a new crisis of its own making. If meaning is found everywhere, its coinage may be debased. Throughout this century, a growing suspicion has emerged that, as much as everything is 'meaningful', meaning resides nowhere. Watching television epitomizes this semantic promiscuity, in which meaning seems radically withdrawn even as it is promised at every turn.[63]

Overdetermination of meaning should not be too hastily equated with the rejection of reason, nor with the advocacy of 'anything goes'. As Homi Bhabha notes, indeterminism is also the conflictual conceptual space from which new languages of cultural intervention will emerge.[64] What remains significant is that the camera, which once offered to complete the positivist project by eliminating uncertainty, has increasingly found itself overtaken by

59 Elsaesser, *Early Cinema: Space, Frame, Narrative*, p. 248.

60 See 'Flickering in eclipses' below.

61 See A. Breton, 'As in a wood', in P. Hammond (ed.), *The Shadow and its Shadow: Surrealist Writings in Cinema*, London, British Film Institute, 1978, p. 81.

62 R. Barthes, *Empire of Signs* (trans. R. Howard), New York, Hill and Wang, 1982, p. 70.

63 I am not arguing that the industrialized image 'caused' this condition, rather that it necessitated its recognition by exposing an indeterminacy inhabiting meaning and context as they had long been thought. Lacan's comment on metaphor reminds us of the linguistic basis often given to this phenomenon: 'It should be said that modern poetry and especially the Surrealist school have taken us a long way in this direction by showing that *any conjunction of two signifiers would be equally sufficient to constitute a metaphor . . .*', Lacan, *Écrits*, p. 156 (my italics). Eisenstein, who was fond of analysing montage in literature, would doubtless agree.

64 H. Bhabha, 'Freedom's basis in the indeterminate', *October*, 61 (Summer 1992), pp. 46–57.

positivism's worst enemy: ambiguity.[65] If we turn our attention to the productive conflicts of this ambivalence, we may yet find it akin to the shift that Benjamin had in mind when suggesting that art based on ritual (the realm of natural signs, fixed obligations and stable meanings) would give way to a new practice: *politics*.

65 This situation was highlighted by the arguments over one of the most widely watched sequences of images this century: George Holliday's video recording of the Rodney King beating. Judge John Davies, who presided over the second trial, commented: 'It's becoming clear that the video tape is a very ambiguous view.' Interview on *Lateline*, ABC Television (Australia), 26 October 1993.

6

The Mobile Frame

If there is an aesthetics of cinema, it can be summarised in one word: movement.

René Clair

From the first moment its moving images hit the screen, cinema generated a certain *disturbance*. Legion are the (perhaps apocryphal) stories of the screams and pandemonium which greeted the arrival of the train at the pioneering public screenings of the Lumière brothers' *cinématographe* at the Grand Café in Paris in 1895.[1] Such reports form one of the most enduring and stable elements of the 'history of cinema', simultaneously distinguishing the naivety of these early spectators from the sophistication of their modern successors, as well as confirming the hyper-realism of the medium even in its infancy. If this simple distinction between the naive and the knowing spectator, as well as the continuum of 'realism' it presupposes, appears increasingly problematic, the story at least preserves the sense of rupture integral to the new apparatus.[2]

At the heart of this rupture was movement. The cinematograph's unprecedented ability to reconstitute motion through the projection of a calibrated series of still images ushered representation onto a radically new terrain. While its apparatus drew together the technical thresholds crossed in a variety of nineteenth-century mechanical–optical devices, the nature of cinematic movement differed fundamentally from all previous attempts to animate images.[3] Where earlier contrivances had enabled the simple juxtaposition of a moving figure against a static background (or vice versa), the

1 The first programme included the now famous short film, *L'arrivée d'un train en Gare La Ciotat*. Typical is Erik Barnouw's description of the audience response: 'The arrival of the train – virtually "on-camera" – made spectators scream and dodge.' E. Barnouw, *Documentary: A History of the Non-Fiction Film*, Oxford, Oxford University Press, 1983, p. 8.

2 Locating cinema within a broader spectrum of contemporary entertainment such as the fairground and amusement park, Tom Gunning has argued that 'the first spectator's experience reveals not a childlike belief but an undisguised awareness of (and delight in) film's illusionistic capacity.' T. Gunning, 'An aesthetic of astonishment: early film and the (in)credulous spectator', *Art & Text*, 34 (Spring 1989), p. 43.

3 Like the genesis of photography, the origin of cinema was less the work of one genius than the intersection of a variety of practical–theoretical thresholds. Investigation of 'persistence of vision' (Plateau's *Phenakistiscope* and Stampfer's *Stroboscope*, both of 1832), the projection of images (magic lanterns), the invention of photography, and the development of techniques of rapid exposure (Marey's chronophotographic rifle, Muybridge's *Zoopraxiscope*) were the major arms of the cinematograph. See C.W. Ceram, *Archaeology of the Cinema* (trans. R. Winston), London, Thames and Hudson, 1965.

cinematic image produced a complex, articulated movement in which all parts of each image could vary in relation to all other parts. Moreover, movement was no longer restricted to a lateral plane, but objects could approach and recede relative to the viewer. Echoing the fascination with detail created by the first photographs, early films transfixed audiences with minute gradations of movement – rising smoke, breaking waves, fluttering leaves, the settling dust of a demolished wall.

The phenomenological *thereness* of cinema belongs to this historic conjunction of movement and image. However, the conditions of cinematic realism remain enigmatic. As Hollis Frampton points out:

> It is remarkable that cinema depends from [*sic*] a philosophical fiction that we have from the paradoxes of Zeno, and that informs the infinitesimal calculus of Newton: namely, that it is possible to view the indivisible flow of time as if it were composed of an infinite succession of discrete and perfectly static instants.[4]

Logic dictates that this approach must inevitably miss the actual movement. Yet cinema seems to confirm the trick we would otherwise like to reject. Of course, as Henri Bergson points out, Zeno's paradox itself depends upon a particular understanding of time.[5] Nevertheless, the question remains: how do we perceive continuous motion from a series of still images? Even prior to cinema, this effect was explained by theories of 'retinal persistence', positing the eye's capacity to retain images as a necessary part of the illusion. However, recent studies in the physiology of perception have tended to discredit this rationale without offering a firm alternative.[6] Instead of using physiological research to comprehend the perception of movement in cinema as a 'trick', perhaps we need to use the experience of cinema – especially the manner in which the concept of 'retinal retention' implicates memory in immediate perception – as the means to open up traditional assumptions concerning vision, space and time.[7]

*

4 H. Frampton, *Circles of Confusion*, New York, Visual Studies Workshop Press, 1983, p. 74.

5 Bergson argued that in order to reconstitute movement from immobile spatial sections ('instants'), one has to add the abstract idea of succession. Against this model, Bergson opposes a model in which movement is not *added* to its apprehension as image, but the two are fused as *movement-image*. See H. Bergson, *Matter and Memory* (trans. N.M. Paul and W.S. Palmer), New York, Zone Books, 1988, pp. 188–97.

6 See J. and B. Anderson, 'Motion perception in motion pictures', in S. Heath and T. De Lauretis (eds), *The Cinematic Apparatus*, London, Macmillan, 1980.

7 See P. Virilio, 'A topographical amnesia', in *The Vision Machine*, Bloomington and Indianapolis, Indiana University Press and London, British Film Intitute Publishing, 1994. While Bergson dismissed cinema as 'false movement', he later suggested that 'the mechanism of our *ordinary* knowledge is of a cinematographical kind.' See *Creative Evolution* (trans. A. Mitchell), London, Macmillan, 1912 (my italics). Deleuze reads Bergson against himself to situate the radical phenomenological and epistemological changes that the image undergoes in cinema. See Deleuze, *Cinema 1*, chs 1 and 4.

If movement was decisive to cinema's capacity to mime reality, cinematic movement also transformed the nature of visual representation. The ambiguous formulation 'living photographs' (as early cinema was often dubbed) situates the uncanny resurrection that the image underwent. Representation emerged from the crypt, abandoning the role of mummification to which it had been confined for millennia, to instil the sensation that 'life itself' might burst through the screen at any moment.

The fact that cinema emerged alongside the most radical redefinition of Western art for four centuries can scarcely be overstated.[8] But cinematic images not only depicted motion in new ways, along the lines of Duchamp's nude, Boccioni's dynamic sculptures or Balla's dog; they combined 'realism' with a unique immateriality and mutability.[9] This shift, from a regime of stable, fixed or monumental images to images which are transitory, immaterial and incessantly labile, marks a fundamental threshold of modern experience.

As much as it perfected an older dream of mimesis, cinema completely reoriented the mimetic project. The reproduction of spatial relations (perspective, form, composition) was henceforth indissolubly meshed with the reproduction of temporal relations (duration, rhythm, sequence).[10] The power to strictly control the *length* as well as the direction of the spectator's look – André Bazin writes that where photography takes the cast of an object, cinema takes the imprint of its duration as well – distinguishes the cine-image from all others.[11] While time undoubtedly sears the photograph, opening the image to the vicissitudes of contingency, cinema marks the first occasion in which the *time of watching* is directly incorporated into the image. This unique capacity to express duration, to reproduce change and movement over the course of time, often creates the impression that time itself is caught in the nets of representation. Andrei Tarkovsky suggested:

> The image becomes authentically cinematic when (amongst other things) not only does it live within time but time lives within it . . . The dominant, all powerful factor of the film image is *rhythm*, expressing the course of time within the frame. . . . Although the assembly of shots is responsible for the structure of a film, it

8 The critical importance of cinema to the new art was most eloquently argued by Fernand Léger. See, for example, 'The spectacle: light, colour, moving image, object spectacle', in F. Léger, *Functions of Painting* (trans. A. Anderson), New York, Viking Press, 1973.

9 Christian Metz's pioneering work stressed the perceptual imbalance of the cinematic signifier. For Metz: 'More than the other arts, or in a more unique way, the cinema involves us in the imaginary: it draws upon all perception, but to switch it immediately over into its own absence, which is nonetheless the only signifier present.' C. Metz, *Psychoanalysis and the Cinema: The Imaginary Signifier* (trans. B. Brewster et al.), London, Macmillan, 1982, p. 45.

10 Merleau-Ponty (surprisingly the only major phenomenologist to concern himself with cinema) suggests that, for this reason, a film cannot be 'summarized': 'The meaning of a film is incorporated into its rhythm just as the meaning of a gesture may be read in that gesture: the film does not mean anything but itself.' M. Merleau-Ponty, 'The film and the new psychology', *Sense and Non-Sense*, p. 57.

11 A. Bazin, *What is Cinema?*, vol. 1, (trans. H. Gray), Berkeley, University of California Press, 1967, pp. 96–7.

does not, as is generally assumed, create its rhythm. The distinctive time running through the shots makes the *rhythm*; and rhythm is determined not by the length of the edited pieces, but by the pressure of the time that runs through them.[12]

This rather Proustian aesthetic, which takes patina – Tarkovsky used the Japanese word *sabi*, the rust of time – as the essential cinematic phenomenon, touches a vital chord. But in so diminishing the significance of montage, one suspects Tarkovksy was as much concerned with demarcating himself from the most influential cinema theory associated with his former homeland as with addressing broader questions of cinema.[13] While film uniquely expresses the pressure of time within the frame (manifested in the movement of objects and the duration of shots), cinema's other decisive visual innovation was to enable movement of the frame itself. Whether movement is continuous (tracking shots, pans, zooms, rolls and tilts) or discontinuous (cuts, fades, or dissolves), for the first time the image was free to shift with eye and look.[14]

Treating the axes of camera movement and montage as interrelated rather than opposed allows better recognition of the fact that cinema's most radical break was not simply projecting moving images but producing *moving fields of perception*. While critics such as Jean-Louis Commolli have observed a certain lineage linking the stable rectangular proportions of painting's easel to cinema and television screens, it is important to recognize that the operation and function of the frame has been continually redefined. Historically, the frame first appeared in Renaissance oil painting in order to separate the image from the building it adorned. Specialized frames emerged when visual images were no longer constrained by architectural features such as walls, domes, arches, ceilings, nor limited to altar pieces and door panels, but were assuming a new portability. As each painting came to function more as a 'window' opening onto a scenographic world, the frame secured this vision by demarcating scene from surrounds. Frames exerted an organizing function (embellished and legitimated in the discourse of Aesthetics, according to principles of composition, balance and symmetry) which formalized the centring of the viewer's eye.

---

12 A. Tarkovsky, *Sculpting in Time: Reflections on the Cinema* (trans. K. Hunter-Blair), London, Bodley Head, 1986, pp. 68, 113 and 117.

13 One might contrast Pudovkin's assertion that 'editing is the basic creative force, by power of which the soulless photographs (the separate shots) are engineered into living, cinematographic form' with Tarkovsky's ambition for *Stalker*, 'I wanted it to be as if the whole film had been made in a single shot.' See V. Pudovkin, *Film Technique and Film Acting* (1933), quoted in J. Leyda (ed.), *Voices of Film Experience 1894 to the Present*, New York, Macmillan, 1977, pp. 371–2; Tarkovsky, *Sculpting in Time*, p. 194.

14 Continuous and discontinuous camera movements have frequently been treated as different 'ethical' poles of filmmaking, with Bazin's eloquent advocacy of deep-focus and the continuous shot influencing movements from neo-realism to *cinéma vérité*. But the usefulness of this opposition, which always tended to marginalize decisions made prior to, during, and after filming, in favour of a realist ontology of the cine-image, is itself becoming marginal in an age of digital imagery.

Despite its pervasiveness, the frame was always a problematic notion for classical aesthetics. Neither properly inside, nor yet wholly outside, the frame is paradoxically both essential and extrinsic to the image.[15] This liminality has been vastly accentuated by the camera. The proliferation of images which followed the industrialization of photography fatally disturbed the neutrality of the frame: as each act of framing came to seem increasingly arbitrary, a growing air of contingency threatened the coherence of images which had previously sought anchorage in the careful deliberation of their composition. However, it was moving images which definitively ruptured the stability of the frame, as painting's 'window' became a screen crossed by a multiplicity of transient appearances and rapid disappearances.

With cinema, the frame lost all semblance of its former passivity. The edges of the frame/screen immediately became active, as actors could leave the scene, or conversely, emerge from the blind field always lying beyond.[16] These possibilities disrupted established principles of centred composition, and also destabilized the viewer's accustomed place of mastery. As cinema developed its own narrative forms, the act of framing was foregrounded to such an extent that the play of the frame – the rhythm of its enlargement and contraction, the shifting distance between spectator and object, the alternation of space in-frame and out-of-frame – emerged as the decisive element of cinematic textuality.

Montage enabled the intertwining of distinct visual fields, creating *mise-en-abyme* effects capable of projecting the spectator into the picture.[17] It also opened the possibility for the abrupt interruption of continuous time within this domain. Cuts and breaks could be assembled into distinctive rhythms of their own, counterpointing the duration of the shot and the 'pressure of time' (Tarkovsky) within it. As Griffith, Gance, Eisenstein and others were to demonstrate, narrative time could be accelerated or decelerated, intensified and concentrated by trimming away 'dead' time, or dilated and rarefied by multiplying actions and reactions to suspend the moment of arrival.

Augmenting these developments was the liberation of the fixed and static camera which was replaced by a camera not only able to pan, tilt and roll, but capable of itself becoming a mobile field of vision. While initial experiments concentrated on placing the fixed camera on moving vehicles

15 Derrida notes: 'That which produces and manipulates the frame sets everything in motion to efface its effect, most often by naturalizing it to infinity . . .' 'The Parergon' (trans C. Owens), *October*, 9 (1979), p. 33. As I will argue in 'Flickering in eclipses' below, 'naturalizing' the cinematic frame proved crucial to the development of narrative cinema.

16 Exploitation of the outside of the frame distinguishes the emergence of narrative cinema from Marey's use of the multi-image camera. Whereas Marey sought to record movement for analysis by a static observer, narrative cinema increasingly sought to construct a mobile observer. (On Marey's disdain for cinematic illusion, see Dagognet, *A Passion for the Trace*, p. 157.)

17 This counterpointed the desire of the Futurist painters: ' We shall henceforward put the spectator in the centre of the picture.' See U. Boccioni et al., 'Futurist painting: technical manifesto 1910', reprinted in U. Apollonio (ed.), *Futurist Manifestos* (trans. R. Brain et al.), London, Thames and Hudson, 1973, p. 28.

(most frequently trains), this soon went beyond the merely 'scenographic' narrative.[18] Karl Freund's path-breaking camera work in Murnau's *The Last Laugh* (1924) and Dupont's *Variety* (1925), where the camera variously graces a wobbling bicycle, an ascending and descending elevator, a swinging trapeze, and a revolving door, exemplified the new awareness of ways in which camera movement could itself be used to explore space and to inflect vision with particular sensibilities.

In effect, cinema inaugurated a mimetic economy in which movement rather than stasis was paramount. Watching a film, the eye soon tires of even the most 'painterly' image, and modern tableau compositions (Pasolini, Greenaway, Paradjanov) remain exceptions. The lure of cinema rapidly shifted from the single shot and composition within a stable frame to dependence upon movement within the frame and transition between frames. It is not simply what we see but the movement from one scene to the next, not the shot but the displacement of one shot by another, which has emerged as the fundamental cinematic 'problem'. (For Godard: 'It seems to me that the sole great problem of film in each movie is where and why to begin a shot and why to complete it.')[19] In the same process, various means of structuring the play of vision by 'motivating' shot transition to twine knowledge and desire in the bed of narrative have emerged as the favoured 'solution'. Ricouer's observation that 'the activity of the narrative consists in constructing coherent temporal ensembles' situates the stakes in this transition to narrative cinema: the *time* of meaning itself.[20] But, as much as film reflected new spatial and temporal relations, it also created them. Drifting between the chaos of the modern world and its infinite possible orderings as narrative, cinema wandered on the cusp of a reality which was itself rapidly mutating.

18 The affinity between cinema and moving vehicles was underlined by the early popularity of the Hale's Tours cinema circuit, which simulated scenic rail journeys by projecting scenes shot from moving trains to audiences seated in mock carriages which rocked and tilted. See R. Fielding, 'Hale's tours: ultra-realism in the pre-1910 motion picture', in J. Fell (ed.), *Film Before Griffith*, Berkeley, University of California Press, 1983. Charles Musser identifies the train film as an important transitional moment in the development of narrative cinema: 'The railroad which projected its passengers through the countryside was ideally suited to move the narrative through time and space.' See T. Elsaesser (ed.), *Early Cinema: Space, Frame, Narrative*, p. 127.

19 J.-L. Godard, *Godard on Godard* (trans. and ed. T. Milne), London, Martin Secker and Warburg, 1972, p. 214.

20 Ricouer quoted in Virilio, *Lost Dimension*, p. 103. See 'Flickering in eclipses' below.

7

Flickering in Eclipses

My head is here inside the machine and I carry it in my hand.

Luigi Pirandello

[A]t the very moment I was sure I had captured life, it escaped me for this very reason, and here I fall on my feet again and those of William Wilson who thought he had seen his double in the street, followed him, killed him, realized he was himself and that he, who remained alive, was only his double. Wilson, as they say, was making himself a film. Taken literally, this expression gives us a pretty good idea, or definition by reel, of the problems of the cinema, where the real and the imaginary are clearly distinct and yet are one, like the Moebius curve which has at the same time one side and two, like the technique of *cinéma vérité* which is also a technique of lying. It's pretty disconcerting, to say the least.

Jean-Luc Godard

With cinema, mimesis seemed to find its home. Lumière's assertion that 'I only wished to reproduce life' sets a lasting tone: perspective and depth of field, movement and duration, gradations of light and shadow, and eventually sound and colour, all submit to cinematic representation with a facility and facticity exceeding any previous medium.[1] Yet, the luminous perfection of the image is also stained by an unsettling shadow: the profound de-realization of appearances engineered by the dynamism of cinematic discourse. Because movement subverts the repose of the viewer, cinema necessarily interrupted the lines of recognition which placed the subject at the centre of geometric representation. This tension clearly emerged in the first decades of this century as film was moulded into discursive forms in which the cine-spectator was increasingly called upon to negotiate the dispersion of a stable and unified perspective into a plurality of mobile 'points of view'. Finally, the spectator's placement at the centre of things does not disappear in cinema, so much as find itself reformulated on a new plane: that of narrative. Cine-realism amounts less to the extension of an unbroken tradition than to a reformulation of realism's conceptual space, as narrative continuity becomes the effect of radical discontinuity at the level of the signifier.

It is worth accenting this shift in light of a significant historical divergence in attempts to theorize the cinematic scene. Where many early critics stressed cinema's disjunctive impact on human perception, more recent accounts have tended to emphasize cinema's role in the production of a

1 Lumière quoted in Heath, *Questions of Cinema*, p. 4.

unified spectator–subject.[2] To a certain extent, this gap is the result of differing focus. Where the earlier writers were struck by the potency of the cinematic displacement of the embodied eye, later analyses have concentrated more on the systematic structuring of this 'primary' identification as the means to achieving a particular form of narrative closure.[3]

But these differences also testify to a marked reassessment of cinema's potential for catalysing social and political change. From being acclaimed as a tool of cultural subversion and political awakening, cinema has come to be frequently castigated as a mechanism of social conservatism and political narcosis. This transformation is both complex and significant. On one level, it belongs to the gradual naturalization of cinematic perception over the course of this century: where it once shocked, cinema now saturates habitual ways of seeing. Cutting across this re-evaluation is cinema's imbrication in the emergent culture of mass spectacle, symbolized on the one hand by the rise of Hollywood, and, on another, by the experience of fascism. Without collapsing these two poles, it is important to recognize that they are less easily separated than is often thought. While it has always been a serious mistake to assume that Nazism was simply an 'exception' to the political culture and political rationality of the twentieth century, this error is magnified when relating social and political transformations to transformations in technologies of representation. What emerges in the first decades of the twentieth century – and not only in Nazi Germany – is the invention of a radically new political constituency in which 'the media' (particularly radio and cinema) assume a dramatically heightened role in defining the collective space of the nation state, and in recruiting and integrating individual citizens into its dispersed 'community'.[4] The shift to narrative cinema formed a crucial part of this trajectory.

What was at stake was the emergence of a cinema capable of utilizing the dynamic possibilities of camera movement and montage while still providing viewers with axes of identification and structures of coherence. The consolidation of 'classical narrative cinema' (particularly in Hollywood)

2 The 'early critics' I am thinking of include Benjamin, Kracauer, Balázs, Breton, Vertov, and Eisenstein, while the 'more recent accounts' follow the turn to semiotics and psychoanalysis by those such as Metz, Commolli, Bellour, Baudry and the writers associated with *Screen* (Heath, Mulvey, Brewster, McCabe, Rose, etc.).

3 For example, both Benjamin and Metz stress the primacy of identification with the camera, but with different emphases and to different ends. Benjamin focuses on the rupture with traditional aesthetic experience: 'The audience's identification with the actor is really an identification with the camera. Consequently the audience takes the position of the camera; its approach is that of testing. This is not the approach to which cult values may be exposed.' Benjamin, *Illuminations*, pp. 230–1. In contrast, Metz sees spectatorial identification arising from a *prior* psychical structure, in which desire is canalized by the camera: 'as he identifies with himself as look, the spectator can do no other than identify with the camera.' Metz, *Psychoanalysis and Cinema*, p. 49. I am less interested in elevating one of these analyses over the other than in juxtaposing Benjamin's evocation of a potentially *liberated spectator* with Metz's description of a subject produced under *compulsion*.

4 This will be further discussed in 'Unstable architectures' below.

produced a powerful new mode of representation which sought to establish the cine-spectator as an enhanced centre of perception inhabiting an auto-nomous screen world.[5] This is not to suggest that all films aimed at what is, often reductively, termed 'realism'; cinema has more often been the avowed realm of the fantastic, the extraordinary, the astonishing. But, for even the most fantastic stories, orienting the spectator in narrative dimensions of time and space has come to constitute the most important cinematic task, with shot matching and continuity coalescing into a model analogous to the ideal and idealizing logic of geometric perspective which governed notions of realism in painting for some four centuries.

What still demands emphasis is the extent to which cine-realism remains endlessly uncertain. The movement of the image, the insistence of the cut, the ex-centricity of the frame, all ensure that cinema not only departed the shores of painting, but unmoored the traditional co-ordinates of mimesis itself, inscribing a new instability in the relation between representation and reality. Cinema increasingly withdraws a perceptible reality as the referent of its discourse, presaging the wholesale dematerialization of the physical world which televisual culture generalizes. 'Cheating' with the relative position of props, objects, people, architecture and geographies, or with the relative times in which actions and reactions occur, is second nature to anyone involved in film production. In the well-finished product, one cannot tell the difference between a fictive room, landscape or even person and the 'real thing': as Noël Burch points out 'everything on the film screen has exactly the same intrinsic "reality", the same "presence".'[6] Far from shoring up the real, cinema accentuates its ambiguity. Opting for neither one nor the other, cinema finally cannot choose between faking reality and the reality of its own fakes.

This undecidability entrains a vortex of referentiality which confounds traditional distinctions in this domain. The convergence between simulating the real by filming it, and simulating simulations of the real by filming them, is precisely what opens cinema's unique capacity to re-vision the world around us, to represent meticulously the time, space and causality of an *other* reality; the double which remains apart in its difference and yet comes disturbingly close, touching us in our most secret places, its voice in our ears, its visions in our eyes. Because cinema offers 'real perceptions' unburdened by the necessarily real referents that Barthes posited as the

5 I am using 'classical narrative cinema' as a convenient shorthand for the main heading cinema took from around 1914 when Hollywood emerged as the centre of global film production. But such a heading has been neither exclusive nor monolithic, and, as I will argue, its borders are increasingly uncertain in the present. Insofar as one can talk of 'rules' in relation to narrative cinema, they are always subject to transgression and reinvention. In fact, one of cinema's most noticeable qualities is the speed at which it consumes its own children, as the conventions of the past become points of departure for the films of the present.

6 N. Burch, *Theory of Film Practice* (trans. H.R. Lane), London, Secker and Warburg, 1973, p. 33.

corollary of the photograph, its mimetic aspect resides far less in plotting direct correspondences between images and objects or events than in the structure of its viewing experience. This has engendered effects which can justly be termed extra-ordinary: drawing up the reservoir of faith in the camera's mimetic destiny but directing it elsewhere, cinema does not merely produce other perceptions, but the *other* of embodied perception.

*

From the first, cinema exhibited a marked ambivalence to realism. As much as 'actualities' and 'scenes from life' were in vogue, it was the cine-camera's capacity to destructure space and time which drew its initial crowds. Reversals, distensions and compressions of time, magical tricks and staged disappearances were all popular early cinematic fare. Audiences were fascinated by sequences projected backwards – a wall rebuilding itself; a diver exiting the water and landing precisely on the tip of the board he sprang from; a collapsed building defying gravity to magically reassemble itself, rising skywards like a primitive rocket. Slow motion (what Pudovkin later dubbed 'close-ups in time') and rapid motion were other common devices, utilized to good effect in the ubiquitous chase scenario which satirized the motor functions and dysfunctions of the modern city.[7] The trick film, with its substitutions and dissolves, used the camera to replace the stage trapdoor as the means to open a wrinkle in time or a fold in the fabric of space.[8] And the close-up – most audaciously Edwin S. Porter's famous outlaw shooting directly along the camera–audience axis – expanded the sense cinema was able to give its spectators of not only seeing the real world differently, but of *really seeing a different world*.[9]

But, over a period of time, an important inversion took place in this theatre of doubles. While Méliès saw his invention of stop-motion photography as a means 'to make visible the supernatural, the imaginary, even the impossible', such tricks became integral to narrative cinema as it developed

7 Like the train film, the chase film had a broader significance as a narrative prototype. Gunning suggests: 'The chase [was] the original truly narrative genre of the cinema, providing a model for causality and linearity as well as a basic editing continuity.' 'The cinema of attractions', in T. Elsaesser (ed.), *Early Cinema: Space, Frame, Narrative*, p. 60.

8 The magician George Méliès was the most renowned practitioner of this genre, famous for films in which he confronted his own double, or made his cast, and finally himself, disappear with the wave of his wand.

9 Porter's *The Great Train Robbery* (1903) featured a medium shot of a cowboy bandit pointing his gun straight at the camera. The fact that the shot could be placed at either the beginning or end of the film, depending on the exhibitor's preference, reveals the looseness of the narrative economy at this time.

its own laws of realism.[10] In this regard, a crucial threshold was crossed in the first decades of this century as film makers progressively fragmented both the proscenium space and the continuity of action which characterized early cinema.[11] Instead of a fixed camera recording a single, continuous shot with all action taking place centre 'stage', enabling the screen to form a stable 'theatrical' space from which actors made entrances and exits in real time, a more complex orchestration of shots, camera positions and film sequences emerged. Even though the initial strangeness of this new organization has undoubtedly been tempered by its subsequent generalization, something of the disjunction in both visual and narrative coherence can be felt in Lillian Gish's account of working with legendary Hollywood director D.W. Griffith:

> Mr. Griffith turned to a young actor . . . 'Let's see some distrust on your face.'
> The actor obliged.
> 'That's good', Griffith exclaimed. 'Everyone will understand it.' Billy Bitzer objected, as he was to do often when Griffith attempted something new. 'But he's too far away from the camera. His expression won't show up on the film.'
> 'Let's get closer to him then.'
> 'Mr. Griffith, that's impossible! Believe me, you can't move the camera. You'll cut his feet off – and the background will be out of focus.'
> 'Get it, Billy', Griffith ordered . . .
> After the rushes were viewed, Griffith was summoned to the front office. Henry Marvin was furious.
> 'We pay for the whole actor Mr. Griffith. We want to see *all* of him.'[12]

The significance of this anecdote is less its mendacity concerning the invention of the close-up (most of Griffith's 'inventions' have since been shown to have been borrowed from other film makers), than its illustration

10 Méliès quoted in P. Virilio, *The Aesthetics of Disappearance* (trans. P. Beitchmann), New York, Semiotext(e), 1991, p. 15. Like many important modernist innovations, Méliès's invention was less than fully planned: 'One day, when I was prosaically filming the Place de l'Opéra, an obstruction of the apparatus I was using produced an unexpected effect. I had to stop a minute to free the film and started up the machine again. During this time passersby, omnibuses, cars had all changed places. When I later projected the reattached film, I suddenly saw the Madeleine–Bastille bus changed into a hearse, men changed into women. The trick-by-substitution, soon called the stop-trick, had been invented . . .' Virilio, *Aesthetics of Disappearance*, p. 15.

11 Barry Salt notes that about half the surviving pre-1906 films are single shot/one scene films. See his 'Film form 1900–1906' in Elsaesser, *Early Cinema: Space, Frame, Narrative*, p. 35.

12 L. Gish, *The Movies, Mr. Griffith and Me*, London, W.H. Allen, 1969, pp. 59–60. There are many similar stories dotting the history of cinema. Tarkovsky reports that early audiences screamed in horror at the close-up face, believing it to be the image of a severed head. See Tarkovsky, *Sculpting in Time*, p. 105. Kevin Brownlow cites Abel Gance being told by a producer: 'Don't take your camera too close. You know you're supposed to show the whole of your actors so you can see their gestures' and again, 'What are these huge pictures supposed to mean? They'll show up all the faults in a face. You'll have people panicking in the cinema.' Quoted in K. Brownlow, *The Parade's Gone By . . .* , London, Abacus, 1968, pp. 603 and 607. The repetition of these stories suggests their function lies not only in describing the rupture but in *negotiating* its threat – even in the present.

of the extent to which this innovation was not so much a logical progression of film aesthetics as the progression of film making to an entirely different logic. While the close-up already had a long history as a photographic technique, what was new was its utilization as an integrated element of a multi-shot scene. The logic of montage – assembling separate shots to construct a representational economy based upon fragmentation and the mobility of perspective – gave cinematic perception a new historic significance.

Extreme plasticity of the cinematic frame opened new possibilities for representing modern experience. Both Kracauer and Benjamin noted cinema's affinity for the scope of emergent social phenomena such as the mass event. Benjamin suggested: 'Mass movements are usually discerned more clearly by a camera than a naked eye. A bird's eye view best captures gatherings of hundreds of thousands.'[13] At the other end of the scale, Fritz Lang declared: 'The first important gift for which we have film to thank was in a certain sense the rediscovery of the human face.'[14] But, apart from rare exceptions such as Dreyer's *Jeanne d'Arc* (1928), cinematic discourse developed by privileging neither the wide angle nor the close-up. Instead, films 'moved' by interlacing them. If the camera could effortlessly encompass the mass assembly, it could equally distinguish an individual face within the crowd.

This capacity to relate the one and the many has not only provided a flexible and enduring narrative matrix, but constitutes a key political technology in a period in which the primary social dynamics have been framed between the poles of 'individual' and 'society'. Leni Riefenstahl's *Triumph of the Will* (1935) stands at the threshold of the cinematic reinvention of the scene of politics. Close-ups brought Hitler 'face to face' with his thronging supporters in the film's narrative space, as well as the audience's viewing space. Intimate shots of the Führer were continually juxtaposed with shots of the adoring crowds taken from his implied point of view. (As Riefenstahl commented in a 1993 interview: 'There was nothing else. Just Hitler and the people.')[15] Montage enabled multiple points of identification: spectators could align themselves with the crowd as partici-pant, but also enjoy looking at the crowd as spectacle. In cinema's capacity to switch between different points of view – Hitler is seen everywhere but also shown to see everywhere – we can find the basis for the profound

13 Benjamin, *Illuminations*, p. 253. Kracauer made a similar point in his essay, 'The mass ornament' (1927), reprinted in *New German Critique*, 5 (Spring 1975), pp. 67–76.

14 'The feature film in Germany' (1926) (trans. D. Reneau), reprinted in A. Kaes, M. Jay and E. Dimendberg (eds), *The Weimar Republic Sourcebook*, Berkeley, University of California Press, 1994, p. 623.

15 Interview in Ray Müller's *Die Macht der Bilder (The Wonderful, Horrible Life of Leni Riefenstahl)*, 1993.

convergence between the leader principle and the star principle which dominates the contemporary mediascape.[16]

*

The transformation of film language to enable fluid transitions from longshot to mid-shot or close-up as part of an integrated narrative system was well underway prior to the Great War.[17] The synchronicity of this development with the immense socio-political disturbances and technological ruptures of this period – from cubism to the theory of relativity, the march of machine culture and the industrialization of warfare – can scarcely be overstated. The whole concept of how representation could and should 'imitate' the real underwent a decisive mutation as life was subjected to exponential acceleration. Writing in 1923, Fernand Léger recognized that film embodied a logic which saturated modern culture:

> The war had thrust me as a soldier into the heart of the mechanical atmosphere. Here I discovered the beauty of the fragment. I sensed a new reality in the detail of a machine, in the common object. I tried to find the plastic value in these fragments of modern life. I rediscovered them on the screen in the close-ups of objects which impressed and influenced me.[18]

By the end of the First World War, cinema had completely departed the province of the photographic mirror. With the photograph, one can still dream of locating the image within lived space and time, of referring it to a single 'real' instant which occurred at a determinate place. With cinema, even though individual shots may retain this aura of referentiality, the textual system of the multi-shot scene no longer functions with reference to a single, ostensibly real event. Cinematic credibility shifted from emphasis on the geometrical plane of perspective to planes of fictive and narrative logic, a change Commolli aptly described as the movement from optical to psychological realism.[19] Narrative action in cinema was no longer contained within discrete shots, but would increasingly move across and between them.

The development of these new narrative forms belonged to a period in which both the experience of watching a film, and the scene of watching itself, underwent significant modification. Until around 1905, film screenings had generally formed only one component of a live stage show. Over the next ten years, the collective relation previously sustained between an audience joining in sing-alongs and other participatory actions was increasingly transferred onto the screen itself, reformulated in terms of the

16 The prevalence of the 'cult of personality' – dictator, Führer, president, star – will be taken up in 'Unstable architectures' below.

17 Tom Gunning argues: 'the period 1907–1913 represents the true narrativization of the cinema, culminating in the appearance of feature films.' 'The cinema of attractions', *Wide Angle*, 8, 3/4 (1986), p. 68.

18 Léger quoted in Scharf, *Art and Photography*, p. 314. See also 'In the neon forest' below.

19 'Machines of the visible' in Heath and De Lauretis, *Cinematic Apparatus*, p. 130.

identification between the individual spectator and an autonomous screen world. What Gunning has termed the 'cinema of attractions' – that form of cinema which exploited the allure of the cinematic apparatus itself and its capacity to show, to surprise and to shock, rather than its ability to develop a plot or tell a story – was displaced by a narrative cinema whose parameters and orientations remain familiar today.[20] By around 1914, film programmes involving the serial screening of multiple short films (one or two reel narratives, travelogues, culturally significant or bizarre events) were giving way to longer, more self-contained narratives. While there are many arguments over the origin of the feature film, D.W. Griffith's *Birth of a Nation* (1915) remains the most commonly cited point beyond which multi-reel films began to assume the shape, length and dynamics which have dominated cinematic production and exhibition ever since.

Fundamental to the new narrative cinema was the development of a mode of address capable of absorbing viewers within a film's fictive world. This demanded the suppression of all 'extra-textual' elements, such as reliance on spectatorial foreknowledge (for example, the familiarity of the bible story) or an explanatory lecturer to provide narrative coherence. Intertitles were the first solution to the need to situate individual scenes and connect them into a whole story. Far more significant was the growing desire to 'justify' camera movement, framing and shot sequencing. As narrative cinema discovered what became its classical form, shot transitions were no longer directed solely by the need to centre the action, but increasingly depended upon 'internal' motivations provided by character look or character knowledge. Optical point of view and narrative point of view, while retaining a degree of separation, were increasingly intertwined to create the textual space for the omniscient spectator who forms the lynchpin of identification in 'classical narrative cinema'. The look *at* the camera, establishing direct eye contact between actor and spectator, became taboo. What Metz termed cinema's fundamental disavowal – 'I look at it but it does not look at me looking' – emerged as a crucial feature of the dominant cinematic imaginary.[21]

---

20 Gunning contrasts the exhibitionism of the 'cinema attractions' to the conventional classification of classical narrative cinema as voyeuristic. But clearly any contrast between exhibitionism and voyeurism is relative rather than fixed. The proximity between the 'cinema of attractions' and the manner in which contemporary television exploits direct spectatorial address and a fascination with the (televisual) apparatus will be taken up in 'The ends of representation' below.

21 C. Metz, 'History/discourse: a note on two voyeurisms', *Edinburgh '76 Magazine*, p. 14. The importance of this disavowal to the cinematic imaginary has been the subject of much debate within film theory. Barthes's assertion 'If a single gaze from the screen came to rest on me the whole film would be lost' typifies the emphasis often placed on this manner of positioning the spectator. See his 'Right in the eyes', in *The Responsibility of Forms* (trans. R. Howard), New York, Hill and Wang, 1985, p. 242. However, disavowal of the spectator's presence belongs to a specific type of cinema. There has always been that form of cinema which takes pleasure in making the presence of the camera *felt* (as Pasolini once put it). If this other cinema has historically been confined to the margins of representation, these margins are themselves shifting under the influence of television.

In addition, other elements of the 'cinema of attractions', such as unmotivated or overly long displays, were jettisoned or at least submerged.[22] In their place developed a new logic of spatial cues, eye-line match (co-ordinating the direction of looks between characters or from character to object), and a point of view structure interweaving on-frame and off-frame space. This new spatial organization was supported by the temporal logic of ellipsis, contraction and abbreviation, designed to structure scenes according to the selection of what Deleuze terms 'privileged instants' while avoiding jump cuts. Over time, these conventions assumed a regulative character, in some contexts bordering on the sacrosanct.[23]

A litmus test of this new narrative structure is the manner in which successive shots in films came to be read. In the first multi-shot films, shot sequences were read (virtually without exception) as signifying a simple temporal succession, often overlapping on action while conveying it to a new but proximate location. The development of parallel editing demanded that an alternate reading be entertained, in which two shots might signify spatially disjunctive sites of simultaneous action. The most influential moves in this direction were made by Griffith in his Biograph films from around 1908. Alternation between two shots/sites was used to create suspense – such as the cutting between rescuers and victim which structures *The Fatal Hour* (1908) and culminates in the ambitious montage in the final sequence of *Intolerance* (1916) – or to underline a contrast of opposites, such as that between rich and poor in the scenes of feast and famine in *A Corner in Wheat* (1909).[24]

Almost imperceptibly, the narrative organization of space and time through montage assumed a growing autonomy. The mere juxtaposition of two shots proved capable of creating 'causal' connections independent of any pro-filmic event, and ambiguity as to whether the second shot should be read as successive or simultaneous came to be resolved in the text itself, measured as an effect of narrative coherence. This layering of knowledge

22 As Gunning points out, this submersion is less than total: 'In fact, the cinema of attractions does not disappear with the dominance of narrative, but rather goes underground, both into certain avant-garde practices and as a component of narrative films, more evident in some genres (e.g. in musicals) than in others.' 'The cinema of attractions', in Elsaesser, *Early Cinema: Space, Frame, Narrative*, p. 57.

23 Recalling some of the reviews which greeted Godard's *Les Carabiniers* (1963) illustrates this cinematic doxa: 'Scenes shot at random, edited any old how, stuffed with continuity errors' (*La Croix*). 'A film shot wild, where each image reveals the director's supreme contempt for the audience' (*Candide*). 'A badly made, badly lit, badly everything film' (*L'Express*). Quoted in Godard, *Godard on Godard*, pp. 198–200.

24 Eisenstein, who greatly admired Griffith and always acknowledged his influence, was nevertheless critical of the manner in which he limited his montage (and his narrative structures) to merely confirming the two sides of a dichotomy (good/bad, rich/poor, black/white), rather than exploring the dialectical relation between them. Eisenstein contended that the privileged form of American cinema (parallel montage) was intrinsically related to the self-image of American bourgeois society. See his essay 'Dickens, Griffith and film today', in *Film Form: Essays in Film Theory* (trans. J. Leyda), London, Harcourt Brace Jovanovich, 1949, pp. 195–256.

between different characters, and between characters and spectators, provided a powerful new matrix for conferring spectatorial omniscience, creating effects which would be felt far beyond the bounds of the 'fiction' film.

*

What began as a 'trick effect' gravitated to constitute the very fabric of cine-realism – at least when performed within certain parameters. Cinema took the industrial logic of fragmentation as its own: filmic continuity became entirely dependent on the recombination of fragments to construct wholes exceeding the sum of their individual parts. If this new mode of discourse demanded an enhanced awareness of film's plastic potential on the part of film makers, it also required a loosening of the referential tie binding image to reality for film audiences. While cinema has never abandoned the real, its reality-effects increasingly belonged to the camera-reality established in the organization of the viewing experience. This threshold serves as an index of the profound transformation of experiences of space and time in this period; in a sense, the 'pleasure' and 'meaning' of narrative cinema belong precisely to its capacity to produce new spatio-temporal experiences for its audience to consume.[25]

Kuleshov's famous experiment – intercutting a single close-up of the actor Mozhukin's face with a series of different images (a bowl of soup, a coffin, a little girl with a toy bear) to incite the audience to read different expressions from the same shot – alerted film makers to some of the possibilities of the extreme plasticity of the new medium.[26] Even more radical was the realization that entirely fictive landscapes could be composed in a manner that carried all the conviction of the new cine-realism. Reflecting on an early work (*The Project of Engineer Prite*, 1917), Kuleshov noted:

> Let us suppose that in a certain place we are photographing a certain object. Then, in a quite different place, we film people looking at this object. We edit the whole thing, alternating the image of the object and the image of the people looking at it. In *The Project of Engineer Prite*, I show people looking at electric pylons in this way. It was thus that I made an accidental discovery: thanks to montage, it is possible to create, so to speak, a new geography, a new place of action. It is

25 The suggestion by French director Marcel L'Herbier that cinema became necessary when real time and space became too expensive for people to afford assumes a new irony today when cinematic time and space has become even more expensive than that which it sought to replace. L'Herbier quoted in G. Deleuze, *Cinema 2: The Time-Image* (trans. H. Tomlinson and R. Galeta), London, Athlone Press, 1989, p. 78.

26 See his description in his 1929 essay, 'Art of the cinema', *Kuleshov on Film: Writings of Lev Kuleshov* (trans. R. Levaco), Berkeley, University of California Press, 1974, pp. 53–4. Kuleshov was less the originator of the montage effect which bears his name than one of its earliest theorists. The tendency to theorize which marks early Soviet cinema was undoubtedly sharpened by shortages of film stock: unable to make films, the best recourse for aspiring directors was to write about making them.

possible to create in this way new relations between the objects, the nature, the people and the progress of the film.[27]

This principle of 'creative geography' could be – and was – pushed even further. Kuleshov adds:

> What I think was more interesting was the creation of a woman who had never existed. I did this experiment with my students. I shot a scene of a woman at her toilette: she did her hair, made up, put on her stockings and shoes and dress . . . I filmed the face, the head, the hair, the legs, the feet of different women, but I edited them as if it was all one woman, and, thanks to the montage, I succeeded in creating a woman who did not exist in reality but only in the cinema.[28]

These examples situate what Virilio has termed cinema's new 'logistics of perception': the move to a cine-realism in which the articulation of multiple shots formed a potentially infinite series of perceptual frames.[29] Once the 'Kuleshov effect' became a cornerstone of narrative technique, the nature of cinematic simulation irrevocably departed the project which had long oriented photography. If the realist photograph sought to hypostatize the real, to withdraw meaning and appearance from flux and to fix time and space forever, cinema became a machine for the wholesale reinvention of these co-ordinates. The editing desk increasingly functions as the laboratory of a twentieth-century Dr Frankenstein, that exemplary technician who cuts and sews celluloid parts to construct a virtual body.

Montage also implied an entirely different approach to film making, as the method of fragmenting and reassembling the camera's 'separate frames of truth' (Vertov) saturated the production process. By the 1930s, Walter Benjamin was able to observe the full extent of the divorce from theatrical representation:

> The shooting of a film, especially of a sound film, affords a spectacle unimaginable anywhere at any time before this. It presents a process in which it is impossible to assign a spectator a viewpoint which would exclude from the scene being enacted such extraneous accessories as camera equipment, lighting machinery, crew, etc. – unless the position of his eye were identical with that of the lens. This circumstance, more than any other, renders superficial and insignificant any possible similarity between a scene in the studio and one on the stage. In the theatre one is well aware of the place from which the play cannot be immediately detected as illusionary. There is no such place for the movie scene being shot. Its

27 Kuleshov in Leyda, *Voices of Film Experience*, p. 249.

28 J. Leyda (ed.), *Voices of Film Experience*, pp. 249–50. It is worth noting that the image which bears the weight of this creative imagination is one which has been so important to narrative cinema: the image of the ideal Woman, composed from a heterogeneity of real women. Laura Mulvey's comment: 'The determining male gaze projects its phantasy onto the female figure which is styled accordingly', and her emphasis on the function of the close-up in constituting woman as a series of body parts, are appropriate to recall here. See her 'Visual pleasure and narrative cinema', *Screen*, 16, 3 (Autumn 1975), pp. 11 and 13.

29 Virilio links the emergence of the pin-up girl at this time and the subsequent eroticization of female body parts (face, legs, breasts) to the perceptual fragmentation imposed by the First World War, suggesting that the pin-up constitutes a new kind of 'map' for which body measurements ('vital statistics') form the code or key. See his *War and Cinema*, pp. 21–3.

illusionary nature is that of the second degree, the result of editing. That is to say, in the studio the mechanical equipment has penetrated so deeply into reality that its pure aspect, freed from the foreign substance of equipment, is the result of a special procedure, namely, shooting from a particular camera set-up and linking the shot with other similar ones. The equipment-free aspect of reality has become the height of artifice; the sight of immediate reality has become the 'blue flower' in the land of technology.[30]

For Benjamin, changes in film production counterpointed profound changes in social experience as the commodity culture of the industrial city displaced 'nature' as the primary lived environment. His emphasis on the alignment between eye and lens in facilitating a 'second degree' realism remains crucial to understanding classical cinema's dominant imaginary. As much as the actual scene of film making exposed the 'illusion' to those present by the constant visibility of 'extraneous accessories', the finished product came to be constructed so as to place the spectator precisely in the blind spot from which its illusionism cannot be detected. Such constructions, embodied in the logic of continuity and shot matching, have so dominated the history of film making that anything outside their guidelines still risks being dismissed simply as a 'poorly made' film.

*

Jean-Pierre Oudart was perhaps the first to analyse the organization of cinematic discourse in terms of the psychoanalytic concept of suture.[31] What is important to grasp in understanding the term is its dependence on the ambivalence of the subject's placement in the visual field. For Lacan, this ambivalence is fundamentally conditioned by the alterity of the gaze – an experience he immediately relates to the camera:

> What determines me, at the most profound level in the visible, is the gaze that is outside. It is through the gaze that I enter light and it is from the gaze that I receive its effects. Hence it comes about that the gaze is the instrument through which light is embodied and through which – if you will allow me to use a word, as I often do, in a fragmented form – I am *photo-graphed*.[32]

Lacan's analysis explores the tension between what the subject can see and the fact of its existence in a visual field which exceeds it. Because 'I see only from one point but in my existence I am looked at from all sides', the security of any self-centred visual mastery is always at risk.[33] This split between eye and gaze ensures our experience of the visible is not that of the

30 Benjamin, *Illuminations*, pp. 234–5. This translation is modified in accordance with Miriam Hansen's rendering of the passage, which brings out the ambivalent connotations of Benjamin's final reference to 'immediate reality'. See her 'Benjamin, cinema and experience: "The blue flower in the land of technology" ', *New German Critique*, 40 (Winter 1987), pp. 203–4.

31 J.-P. Oudart, 'Cinema and suture' (trans. K. Hanet), *Screen*, 18, 4 (Winter 1977–8), pp. 35–47.

32 Lacan, *Four Fundamental Concepts of Psycho-analysis*, p. 106.

33 Lacan, *Four Fundamental Concepts of Psycho-analysis*, p. 72.

stable and unified subject posited by geometric perspective, but instead obeys the vicissitudes of the de-centred subject of desire. For Lacan, the fact that I am *where* I see from, but I am not *in* what I see carries particular consequences for representation and desire.[34] He reads the system of geometric perspective (which the camera took as its own) as a response to the visual 'hunger' of the subject. The function of the picture is to constitute a lure for the gaze; an invitation for it to lay down its 'weapons' while providing the subject with a means of mapping itself within its terrain.[35]

Lacan's analysis is helpful in situating the historic importance of cinema as a system of representation which explicitly addresses the tensions between eye and gaze. The strength of geometric perspective manifested in the still image lies in its ability to arrest the visible, according to practices of composition and framing which place the viewer at the centre of things. But, as I have argued earlier, photography's industrialized optics compromised the authority of these practices, firstly by eroding the uniqueness and permanence of the image, but also by opening the stability of the frame to new uncertainties. Walter Benjamin quoted the recollection of the poet Dauthenday on seeing the first photographs:

> We were abashed by the distinctness of these human images, and believed that the tiny little faces in the picture could see *us*, so powerfully was everyone affected by the unaccustomed clarity, and the unaccustomed truth to nature of the first daguerreotypes.[36]

These anxious fantasies inspired by the reversibility of the look have not so much disappeared as settled down elsewhere; notably in the shot/reverse shot cutting of cinema, but also in television, where – even though we *know* they can't – it is often customary for 'the tiny little faces in the picture' to act as if they *can* see us. These displacements reveal the intractability of a deeply ingrained desire. As Derrida has pointed out, the 'intersubjective look' constitutes a limit case for photography. While a photograph can certainly 'look back' at me, two gazes meeting 'face to face' necessarily escapes photographic representation – the camera would have to occupy both lines of sight at once.[37] Recognizing this limit of the still image as the target of desire in classical narrative cinema reveals the stakes at play in the system of suture.

Drawing on the Lacanian 'logic of the signifier', Oudart sketched a

---

34 'The picture is certainly in my eye. But I am not in the picture.' Lacan, *Four Fundamental Concepts of Psycho-analysis*, p. 96.

35 Here Lacan follows the lead of phenomenology, but is closer to Sartre than Merleau-Ponty in understanding the de-centring of visual mastery largely in terms of negativity and lack. Sartre's reading of the other's look ('suddenly an object has appeared which has stolen the world from me') in *Being and Nothingness* can be contrasted to Merleau-Ponty's evocation of the capacity of sight literally to transport the subject to the perceptual horizon. J.-P. Sartre, *Being and Nothingness* (trans. H.E. Barnes), London, Methuen, 1969, p. 253; M. Merleau-Ponty, 'Eye and mind' (trans. C. Dallery), in *The Primacy of Perception* (trans. J.M. Edie et al.), Evanston, IL, Northwestern University Press, 1964, p. 187.

36 Quoted in Benjamin, *One Way Street*, p. 244.

37 Derrida, 'Right of inspection', pp. 80–1.

'fictive' scenario in which the spectator's initial expansive relation to the screen is broken by an intruding awareness of the finitude of the image, and of the screen's framing function in determining an 'absent field'.[38] For Oudart: 'The revelation of this absence is the key moment in the fate of the image, since it introduces the image into the order of the signifier and cinema into the order of discourse.'[39] Oudart's basic contention is that (classical narrative) cinema developed by reappropriating the 'absent field' within its own narrative space. Unlike the still image, where the stability of the frame serves to guard the seen from the unseen, cinema does not deny the discontinuity of its signifier, but instead mobilizes that discontinuity by regulating its resurgence. What is outside the frame in one shot (perhaps implied by a character look) is subsequently revealed and placed in frame in a succeeding shot. The desire of the cine-spectator to look *at* the scene of the other, but also to look *from* the place of the other, is taken up as the basic filmic movement. The pleasure of the cinematic text depends upon rhythmically bringing these gaps and absences into play, employing the out-of-frame and the off-screen to blend the satisfaction of revelation with the enjoyment of hesitation and withholding. For Oudart, it is this process of reappropriation that 'sutures' the subject, securing its relation to its chain of discourse by filling the 'holes in consciousness' which might otherwise disturb the production of meaning and identity. This process does not take a linear path, but works to and fro, shuttling between proactive and retroactive effects of the image in the paradoxical figure of an asymmetrical circle.[40]

The concept of suture has been subject to many disputes.[41] Here I find it helpful insofar as it allows 'classical narrative cinema' to be related to a particular organization of space and time as a primary matrix of desire, identity and meaning. If 'cinema' names a key social institution which takes the ambivalence of the subject's placement in the visual field, and the

38 I use the term 'fictive' to signal the limits of linear chronology in this description. If, as Miller argues, linear time is an *effect* of subject production, its logical priority – its priority as logic itself – must be particularly suspect here. (See footnote 40 below.)

39 Oudart, 'Cinema and suture', p. 42. Here Oudart evokes Lacan's account of the passage from imaginary to symbolic (which, as Heath points out, is 'not one of a simple progression'). See S. Heath, 'Difference', *Screen*, 19, 3 (Autumn 1978), p. 77.

40 Miller echoes Lacan's description of the procuration of the subject in the dual processes of alienation–separation: 'The time of engendering can only be circular – which is why both these propositions are true at one and the same time, that subject is anterior to the signifier and that signifier is anterior to subject – but only appears as such after the introduction of the signifier. The retroaction consists essentially of this: the birth of linear time. We must hold together the definitions which make the subject the effect of the signifier and the signifier the representative of the subject: it is a circular, though non-reciprocal, relation.' J.-A. Miller, 'Suture' (trans. J. Rose), *Screen*, 18, 4 (Winter 1977–8), p. 33.

41 Heath notes a slippage, firstly in Oudart's appropriation of the term from Jacques-Alain Miller, and in later uses by Daniel Dayan and William Rothman. Where Miller posits suture as a general logic ('Suture names the relation of the subject to its chain of discourse'), Oudart (at times), and Dayan and Rothman (generally), identify suture with specific cinematic figures, such as shot/reverse shot editing. See S. Heath, 'On suture', *Questions of Cinema*, pp. 76–112.

uncertain pleasures of looking/being looked at as the basis for its operation, 'classical narrative cinema' describes an institutional–textual organization which resolves this scene in favour of the subject as sovereign identity.[42] It is the veiled self-presence of the sovereign subject which has governed the hierarchical play of looks dominating the cinematic institution: the camera looking at the scene, the actors looking within the scene, the spectators always arriving late on the scene, but armed with the expectation and assurance, the fundamental social contract on which narrative cinema has been based, that all remains to be revealed.

Classical structures of editing work to ensure that (as Noël Burch put it) when watching most films 'we still get the impression we recognize spatial relationships pre-existing the successive impressions conveyed on the screen'.[43] No matter how disjunctive individual shots (particularly close-ups) may appear when removed from the flow, the conventions of cinematic textuality which hardened in the first decades of the century have consistently functioned to orient viewers within what Heath aptly termed 'narrative space'.[44] This new logic of spatial continuity – the industrial continuity dependent on the aggregation of fragments of space into points of view – has been counterpointed by a cinematic temporality in which most films confirm a linear continuum as their primary matrix of narrative reference. Flashbacks, or inverted narratives which unfold from end to origin, are only simple modulations of this linear model.[45] Rhythm is vital to this economy: as Antonioni demonstrated in the final scenes of *L'Éclisse* (1962), once a shot is held beyond the duration of its narrative logic, the spectator's relation to the screen shifts: the linear pulsion of 'and then' is displaced by a radial drift of contemplation and speculation.

Sound also plays a crucial (if often unremarked) role in the system of suture. While films were never 'silent', and even synchronized sound had a longer history than many accounts of the 'miracle' of *The Jazz Singer* (1927) would suggest, the transition to a *talking* cinema only underlined film's claim to reproduce 'life itself'.[46] Warner Brothers' 1929 advertisement

42 Or at least attempts to. As I will argue below, mastery is always an effect to be achieved.

43 N. Burch, 'Sergei Eisenstein', in R. Roud (ed.), *Cinema: A Critical Dictionary*, New York, Viking Press, 1980, p. 318.

44 See Heath, *Questions of Cinema*, pp. 19–75.

45 It remains intriguing that cinema (even Gance, Eisenstein, L'Herbier) was slower to explore narrative regions stratified by time rather than space. Alain Resnais (in collaboration with Marguerite Duras) was one of the first to take this path. The fluid intermingling of past and present by which the persistence of memory and the stubbornness of history mark the limits of consciousness in *Hiroshima, Mon Amour* (1959) created a *mise-en-scène* in which repetition, rupture and duration, rather than location, object and character became the narrative forces, with an effect reminiscent of Proust's avowed aim: to dispel the illusion that events occur primarily in space.

46 Brownlow criticizes homage to *The Jazz Singer*, arguing that 'talking pictures have as long a history as motion pictures themselves.' Brownlow, *Parade's Gone By . . . ,* pp. 655–67.

proclaiming, 'At last "PICTURES that TALK like LIVING PEOPLE!"' bursts with the historical privilege that the voice has assumed in the logocentric economy of representation.[47] While Doane goes so far as to argue that 'what sound adds to cinema is not so much intelligibility as the *presence of speech*', it seems difficult to divorce 'the presence of speech' from the way that talk came to govern meaning in film.[48] The effect of synchronized sound on narrative structures was exacerbated by the need to insulate the camera from noise, which reduced camera mobility and confined film production to the studio. During the 1930s, continuity of speech became (and to a large extent remains) the principal means of sewing together cinematic narrative. In the process, the disjunctive use of sound forcefully advocated by Pudovkin, Alexandrov and Eisenstein in their manifesto of 1928 was marginalized in favour of employing synchronized sound to thicken the realism of the image. For Burch: 'The introduction of sound brought an increased emphasis on film as an essentially "realistic" medium that soon resulted in what might be called the "zero point" of cinematic style.'[49]

*

The value of what is inevitably a schematic description of 'classical narrative cinema' lies in its capacity to provide a reference point for a broader historical dynamic. Despite all the attempts to secure the spectator's relation to the moving image – *to naturalize its frame to infinity* (Derrida) – the experience of cinema has remained intensely ambivalent. Hailed as the repository of 'life itself', cinema has found equal acclamation as life's *other*, the waking dream of a world whose boundaries, surfaces and dimensions have become increasingly unstable. The recurrent fascination of 'film within film' structures – especially those in which 'real people' enter the film world or characters jump out of the screen to enter 'real life' – registers an equivocality that should not be dismissed or hastily resolved.[50] Usurping the speculative space of Alice's looking glass, the liminality of the screen stands

47 On the privilege of speech in a logocentric economy of representation, see 'Writing with Light' above. The ad from *Photoplay* for Warner's Vitaphone system is cited in Brownlow, *Parade's Gone By . . .* , p. 663.

48 See M.A. Doane, 'Ideology and the practice of sound editing and mixing', in Heath and de Lauretis, *Cinematic Apparatus*, p. 49 (my italics).

49 Burch, *Theory of Film Practice*, p. 11. This 'zero point' involved centring the shot on the speaker (or the listener) and motivating all sounds from within the image, so as to confirm its transparency.

50 Heath notes a 1902 Biograph film, *Uncle Josh at the Moving Picture Show*, which deployed the scenario of the credulous viewer seeking to enter the film world by jumping through the screen. See *Questions of Cinema*, pp. 4–5. This scene has been mirrored in numerous films, such as Godard's *Les Carabiniers* (1963), or reversed in others such as *The Last Action Hero* (1993) in which a film character comes to life. Recently, a new generation of films in which 'real people' inhabit virtual spaces (*TRON* (1982), *The Lawn Mower Man* (1992)), or virtual characters enter the real world (*Virtuosity* (1995)), have revealed a similar anxious fascination with 'cyberspace'.

as a powerful metaphor for the uncertain passage between representation and reality in the present. If film 'works' by facilitating a certain forgetting of our own bodies, inviting us to depart their fleshy bounds and wander into an *other* world, it also loosens those most secret and indefinable fibres which bind the self-presence of the sovereign subject. The commonplace of 'losing oneself' when watching a film puts into play all the ambiguity overloading a cliché. It is an experience everyone knows, or thinks they can recognize; and yet who could be certain of knowing precisely what is at stake, what stakes are risked in this oneiric scene?

In the absence of a necessary referent, cinema exposes us to the deep psychic uncertainties of experiencing 'real perceptions' which don't really exist. We see things which never happened. Or rather, we see them according to a temporality and spatiality which cannot be lived. This experience has today become so commonplace that it passes unremarked – at least until another threshold of simulation such as *Jurassic Park* (1993) is reached. But if cinema's potential to transform perception has generally been channelled along narrative lines promoting the sovereignty of spectatorial consciousness, this orientation has by no means been exclusive.

Dziga Vertov provided perhaps the most renowned manifesto for the disjunctive potential of the relation between human eye and camera lens. Vertov proposed less the anthropomorphization of the camera than the mechanization of the body, announcing the perpetual motion of a cinematic vehicle: the 'kino-eye' which was to revolutionize sight:

> I – the cinema eye. I – the mechanical eye. I, as a machine, am able to show you a world as only I can see it.
> I free myself now and forever from human immobility. I am in perpetual motion, I go toward and away from things, I sneak up on them, I climb on them, I move alongside the nose of a running horse, I charge at full speed into the masses, I run before fleeing troops, I fall on my back, I take off with airplanes, I rise and fall with the motion of moving bodies. Here am I, a camera, pushed about by resultant force, positioning myself amid the chaos of motions, fixing motion after motion in the most complex possible combinations.
> Freed from the restraint of 16–17 frames per second, freed from temporal and spatial constraints, I construct any points in the universe, wherever I wish to place them.
> My way – to the creation of a fresh perception of the world. Here I am deciphering a new world unknown to you.[51]

Like many of his contemporaries, Vertov posited the camera's de-centring of embodied perception as a crucial threshold of modernity. Identification with the machine, the projection of the self into its other dimensions of time and space, offered immense possibilities for a liberation from immediacy. In contrast to earlier visual prostheses such as the telescope and microscope, Vertov saw the promise of cinema as a far more radical merging of eye and

51 'Kinoki: Perevorot', *Lef*, 3 (June/July 1923), p. 137. Reprinted in S.R. Feldman, *Dziga Vertov: A Guide To References and Sources*, Boston, MA, G.K. Hall, 1978, p. 34. Vertov's famous *The Man with the Movie Camera* (1929) provides a visual compendium of this manifesto.

machine. Accepting, or being subjected to, this uncanny identity between 'direct' and 'indirect' perceptions – real perceptions which properly belong to human absence – is the unique inheritance of the modern observer whose migratory eye inhabits the heart of the optical machine.

Cinema's power to overthrow the subject's traditional place of visual mastery has frequently proved unnerving. In his analysis of the famous Odessa Steps sequence in Eisenstein's *Battleship Potemkin* (1925), Burch notes that the 'sense of a pre-existent space from which close-ups could have been extracted is severely shaken, perhaps for the first time in cinema over such a lengthy sequence, which doubtless explains the extraordinary shock effect it had at the time'.[52] Eisenstein's refusal to match shots according to the forms of analytical editing already well established by the mid-1920s stemmed from his desire to direct cinema elsewhere. His bold understanding of montage ('the juxtaposition of two separate shots by splicing them together represents not so much a simple sum of one shot plus another shot – as it does a *creation*')[53] led to film sequences composed of visual disjunctions, desynchronized movements, differential rhythms and strategic repetitions. Eisenstein was not interested in the deconstruction of appearances for its own sake, but instead sought the means to engineer a new map of reality, or rather the map of a hitherto unexpressed (and perhaps inexpressible) reality.

> Instead of a static 'reflection' of an event with all the possibilities for activity within the limit of the event's logical action, we advance to a new plane – free montage of arbitrarily selected, independent . . . attractions.[54]

If the montage of attractions is still directed towards 'final thematic effects', these no longer depend on the spectator regulating a totality of visual appearances. Shot transitions are no longer primarily oriented towards establishing the spatial and temporal continuity of narrative action. Instead, Eisenstein explored cinema's potential to represent a heterogeneous spatiality coursing with irregular, variably pulsing times. Discrepant perspectives and disjunctive movements were reassembled, not to inspire the panoptic effect of a totalizing vision, but to produce a text in which juxtaposed

---

52 Burch, 'Sergei Eisenstein' in Roud, *Cinema: A Critical Dictionary*, p. 318.

53 Eisenstein, *Film Sense*, pp. 16–17.

54 S. Eisenstein, 'Montage of attractions', *Lef*, 3 (1923), reprinted in Eisenstein, *Film Sense*, pp. 182–3. While this statement was made in relation to theatre, in a 1924 text Eisenstein asserted the method was 'even more applicable to the cinema'. See 'The montage of film attractions' (trans. E. Henderson), reprinted in J. Leyda and Z. Voynow, *Eisenstein at Work*, London, Methuen, 1982, p. 17. The theory of the montage of attractions formulates the basic principles of films such as *Strike* (1924), *Potemkin*, and (most notably) *October* (1927–8). Eisenstein's eventual reassessment of montage (in the 1938 essay 'Word and image', written at the time of completing *Alexander Nevsky*) occurred at the culmination of an extremely difficult period. Not only had he become one of the principal targets of the Stalin–Zhdanov critique of formalism, but the previous decade had seen the failure of his US and Mexican projects, and the destruction of his film *Bezhin Meadow*.

images enter a dialectical logic.[55] As Burch notes, in the Odessa Steps sequence:

> . . . not only do we never at any moment see the steps as a whole, not only do the soldiers seem to be descending an endless flight of steps, but the entire sequence is splintered into detail shots, some of which 'match' with others – are extracted from the same space, in other words – but most of which are linked together only by the movement traversing the screen . . . The perambulator running away from the dead nurse falls not so much down a flight of stone steps *as from one image to the next*.[56]

Such a system is not without order, but (perhaps even today) it lacks conventional order. A pram which falls from image to image rather than step to step offers itself less as a concrete object than as a signifier. A dead horse suspended on an iron bridge – but also suspended outside the classical unity of plot, place and time – invites the spectator to move beyond the immediacy of the image toward dialectics and allegory.[57] This conception of cinema is a long way from its initial acclamation as life's perfect match. Just how far can be appreciated by retracing the series of thresholds which signal transformations in the space–time matrix of the mimetic project. From the Renaissance virtually until the twentieth century, the continuity and uniformity of space and time formed a fixed background to representation, organizing narrative and aesthetic coherence as much as scientific explanation. In pictorial terms, this logic corresponded to the static frame of geometric perspective which dominated painting across this period. While this system continued in still photography in some respects, the increased mobility of the frame and the exponential expansion in the number of pictures surrounded the image with a new uncertainty. As Walter Benjamin recognized, the advent of cinema finally lifted representation out of its 'first degree' fidelity to appearances and began to establish a 'second degree' fidelity dependent on the new logic of montage. Eisenstein's move amounted to treating montage, not as the means of reproducing 'life with the dull bits cut out' (as Hitchcock once quipped), but as a lever for prising open the space–time grid of the Cartesian–Newtonian universe. This went beyond challenging the stability and fixity of a frontal point of view by placing the viewer at the centre of the picture – Griffith had already done much to realize this slogan of the Futurist painters – but demanded a radically different conception of film as text.

For Eisenstein, it is the collision of heteroclite images which produces 'meaning': the referential illusion, while never discounted, is neither paramount nor directed towards the same ends. Perhaps this was something that

55 Eisenstein placed great philosophical significance in the relation between montage and dialectics, describing the dialectical method as 'the *ne plus ultra* of philosophy and the method of film [as] the *ne plus ultra* in today's stage of the development of art'. Quoted in Leyda and Voynow, *Eisenstein at Work*, p. xi.

56 Burch, 'Sergei Eisenstein' in Roud, *Cinema: A Critical Dictionary*, p. 318 (my italics).

57 Eisenstein pushed his concept of 'intellectual' montage furthest in *October* (where the horse scene occurs).

cinema had always promised from the moment it opened a fault line between perception and identity. As Breton had pointed out as early as 1920:

> Today, thanks to the cinema, we know how to make a locomotive *arrive* in a picture. As the use of slow and fast motion cameras becomes more general, as we grow accustomed to see oaks spring up and antelopes floating through the air, we begin to foresee with extreme emotion what this time–space of which people are talking might be. Soon the expression 'as far as the eye can reach' will seem to us devoid of meaning; that is, we shall perceive the passage from birth to death without so much as blinking, and we shall observe infinitesimal variations. As it is easy to see by applying this method to the study of a boxing match, the only mechanism it can possibly paralyse in us is that of suffering. Who knows whether we may not thus be preparing to escape one day from the principle of identity?[58]

*

Yet any such escape remains ambiguous. On the one hand, cinema's decentring of embodied perception arising from the cine-spectator's identification with the camera's incessantly mobile frame has injected a new fluidity into contemporary experiences of space and time, breaking up the established unities, suspending and displacing accustomed causal relations, and modifying the presumed contours of identity (the unity of the subject, the permanence of objects, the fixity of point of view). On the other hand, this decentring has consistently been tempered by various forms of 're-centring' according to the practice of shot matching and the logic of suture as the means to achieving narrative closure. How should we understand this tension?

Clearly, it cannot be a matter of simply opposing films which 'centre' the subject to those which transgress this mode of subjectivity and proceed otherwise. While there are many differences one can point to, there is no final line of demarcation between 'classical narrative cinema' and that of Eisenstein, between mainstream and experimental film, between narrative and non-narrative, or whatever other couples one might pose. Over-reliance on the fixity of such distinctions tends to obscure the friction of cinematic experience, confining the ambivalence of the cinematic scene to so-called 'limit texts'. This creates the risk of fetishizing particular transgressive strategies, as if they could apply in all cultural and historical conjunctures. In this regard, it must be acknowledged that the sort of 'reflexivity' which once defined the space of an 'alternative' cinema has now clearly spread across a wider domain. Throughout this century the experimental has rapidly become the conventional: the innovations of Eisenstein lay the basis for the hyper-montage of the fifteen-second spot ad and the 'non-narrative' flow of *MTV*; the exposure of the cinematic apparatus by film makers from Vertov to

58 A. Breton, 'Max Ernst', in F. Rosemount (ed.), *What is Surrealism?*, London, Pluto Press, 1978, p. 8.

Godard has become the very symbol of street credibility for TV news and current affairs shows.[59]

Given the manner in which cinema engages the ambivalent placement of the subject in the field of vision, it seems more productive to regard the tensions of cinematic experience as irreducible rather than accidental. Even when positions of unity and effects of totality are established, it is only temporarily, defensively as it were, in the face of the perpetual resurgence of otherness and difference. While it is a particular type of cinema which works to expose its own discursive operations, there is a sense in which *every* cinematic text remains subject to forces which disrupt its smooth functioning and resist its totalizing tendencies. The danger in not respecting this deconstructive insight has often been rather reductive analyses of cinema's 'ideological effect'.[60] Eliding the ambivalence of identification renders the stereotype all too certain and subject-positioning all too secure. By contrast, Lacan's analysis of the subject's relation to the visual field suggests such certainty is permanently deferred: the other is 'there where I am not, because I cannot situate myself there'.[61]

Clearly, it is not a matter of simply resolving these tensions so much as situating them in relation to the historical stakes bound up in cinematic representation. If the cinematic scene has become a powerful metaphor for the exigencies of modern identity – the oscillation of real and imaginary, the displacement of stable centres of existence, the dislocation of fixed boundaries, the interruption of the continuous horizon of self-presence – it must be recognized as a metaphor which extends beyond the *re*-presentation of a reality centred elsewhere. Cinema has also been formative of modern experience, caught between the loss of primacy of the embodied eye and the desire to relocate the desiring subject as a stable figure within a narrative economy.

Stories have always been critical in constructing identity and negotiating a relation to death and the other by ordering the dimensions of time and space. The historical import of cinema – which, as John Berger points out, is this

59 This is not to consign these film makers to the past – on the contrary – but to recognize that replacing one filmic canon with another produces dubious consequences. Colin McCabe recently remarked: 'The positions elaborated by *Screen* in the mid-70s now seem in retrospect to be a terribly belated gasp of modernism in which a figure like Godard promised to articulate the relation between art and politics prefigured by Mayakovsky and the Formalists in the Soviet 20s or Brecht and Benjamin in the German 30s.' 'Preface' to F. Jameson, *The Geopolitical Aesthetic: Cinema and Space in the World System*, Bloomington, Indiana University Press; London, British Film Institute, 1992, p. xv.

60 For example, Dayan's Althusserian formulation of 'suture' leaves next to no room to question the process by which the textual system produces closure. See his 'The tutor code of classical cinema', *Film Quarterly* (Fall 1974), pp. 22–31. Homi Bhabha's comment is apposite: 'They operate a passive and unitary notion of suture which simplifies the politics and "aesthetics" of spectator-positioning by ignoring the ambivalent, psychical process of identification which is crucial to the argument.' H. Bhabha, *The Location of Culture*, London, Routledge, 1994, p. 70.

61 Lacan, *Écrits*, p. 166.

century's own form of storytelling – perhaps finally resides in the unique manner in which it exposes individual identity to the contingency of visions which arrive from outside and elsewhere. If this often confirms a sense of specular omniscience, at its furthest reaches it has also unsettled the stable space of the modern observer's self-identity. Liberated from immediacy, the cine-spectator is free to roam many worlds, unmoored in time and space (as Vertov dreamed), but perhaps at risk of losing all homes, as the here and now is set adrift in the infinite migrations of the nowhere.

8

The Ends of Representation

The television screen is the retina of the mind's eye. Therefore the
television screen is part of the physical structure of the brain. Therefore
whatever happens on the television screen emerges as raw experience for
those who watch it.

Videodrome

From the moment we are outside ourselves – in that ecstasy which is the
image – the 'real' enters an equivocal realm . . .

Maurice Blanchot

In one of his short stories, Borges fantasized a rebellion of the 'mirror
people' which freed those specular beings from the servitude of their shadow
existence. No longer dependent upon imitating every move and motion of
their corporeal masters, they began to initiate actions of their own. This
enigmatic uncoupling of the natural law of reflection registers something of
the vertigo engendered by the contemporary image-world as it assumes
unprecedented autonomy. Under the ubiquitous light of television, it has
often been asserted that images operate in dimensions which resemble
nothing 'real', which refer to nothing but themselves. The priority of the
real, its status as the ground or referent of which an image could be only a
copy, has never seemed less assured. The spectre of the wholesale supplanta-
tion of the order of reality by something *other* has gripped contemporary
imagination, resulting in a profusion of texts positing this transformation as
the very threshold of 'postmodernity'. Jean Baudrillard is perhaps the most
renowned prophet of this shift:

> The secret of the image (we are still speaking of contemporary, technical images)
> must not be sought in its differentiation from reality, and hence its representative
> value (aesthetic, critical or dialectical), but on the contrary in its 'telescoping' into
> reality, its short-circuit with reality, and finally the implosion of image and reality.
> For us there is an increasingly definitive lack of differentiation between image and
> reality which no longer leaves room for representation as such.[1]

As suggestive as Baudrillard's analysis is the breadth of the audience it
has found. The absolute confusion of the spheres of life and representation
which Artaud once sought on pain of madness has become a commonplace

1 J. Baudrillard, *The Evil Demon of Images* (trans. P. Patton and P. Foss), Sydney, Power
Institute, 1984, pp. 25–6. Elsewhere Baudrillard argues that once it has become 'a question of
substituting signs of the real for the real itself', '[t]he very definition of the real becomes: *that
of which it is possible to give an equivalent reproduction.*' Baudrillard, *Simulations*, pp. 4 and
146.

evaluation of the present which places itself under the sign of television. But, if TV is our own theatre of cruelty, it is one which disturbs the cultural frame.

To better understand the nature of this disturbance, it is instructive to return to what I earlier termed the rhythm of representation. For Baudrillard, the 'diabolical' nature of the contemporary image lies in its inversion of the traditional order according to which image necessarily follows reality. According to this schema, first there is the world, and into it images are born as its re-presentations. It is this order of truth, or rather, the truth of this ordering, in which the final point of reference – reference itself – is the unequivocal presence of the real, which is put at risk in the age of the camera. But what is the nature of this risk? Even without departing the conceptual space laid out by what Derrida has called the 'Platonic inter-pretation' of mimesis, it is apparent that this logic harbours the seeds of a madness which deforms its conceptual rigour from within.[2] Let us rehearse the problem. On the one hand, if an imitation is perfect, if it produces a faithful copy without deviating in any respect from what it copies, the copy will be identical to the original, and may in fact replace it. On the other hand, if the imitation differs in some way and therefore departs from the real because its resemblance is not absolute, it would no longer be a perfectly truthful representation (at least according to its own logic), but would become necessarily inferior, parasitical or tainted.[3]

It may be argued that, outside philosophy, such extremes of success and failure are unnecessary. Yet the problem cannot be dismissed so easily, particularly when the same switching between perfection and ruin is precisely what regulates so many critiques of camera technologies. There is a consistent pattern in which the camera is found wanting insofar as it is unable properly to represent the real, yet is also condemned because it represents too well and so threatens to replace it. For instance, early in her influential *On Photography*, Sontag declares: 'Although there is a sense in which the camera does indeed capture reality, not just interpret it, photo-graphs are as much an interpretation of the world as paintings and drawings

2 Derrida argues that the 'Platonic interpretation' of mimesis has persisted in, and posed as, an entire history of Western thought: 'First there is what is, "reality", the thing itself, in flesh and blood as the phenomenologists say; then there is, imitating these, the painting, the portrait, the zographeme, the inscription or transcription of the thing itself. Discernibility, at least numerical discernibility between the imitator and imitated is what constitutes order. And obviously, according to "logic" itself, according to a profound synonymy what is imitated is more real, more essential, more true, etc., than what imitates.' Derrida, *Dissemination*, p. 191.

3 Descartes clearly recognizes this problem: 'there are no images that must resemble in every respect the objects they represent – for otherwise there would be no distinction between the image and its object.' Descartes, *Discourse on Method*, pp. 89–90. But rather than draw the full consequences, he instead splits representation between good and bad resemblances, according to the oscillation of faithful images and faithless counterfeits which has consistently formed the conceptual poles of the mimetic tradition.

are.'[4] Yet elsewhere she asserts: 'The consequences of lying have to be more central for photography than they ever can be for painting . . . A fake painting . . . falsifies the history of art. A fake photograph (one which has been retouched, or tampered with, or whose caption is false) falsifies reality.'[5] Finally, Sontag suggests: '[photographic] images are indeed able to usurp reality because first of all a photograph is not only an image (as a painting is an image), an interpretation of the real; it is also a trace, something directly stencilled off the real, like a footprint or death mask.'[6] What is most significant is not simply the fact that Sontag switches between these positions, but her lack of acknowledgment of the tension it reveals.

Similar polarities have consistently defined the space of film analysis. One need go no further than André Bazin's renowned 'myth of total cinema' which proposes the existence of a guiding desire for 'an integral realism, a recreation of the world in its own image'.[7] In this way, Bazin is able to explain film's immediate acceptance as the complete imitation of 'life itself', despite the obvious deficiencies of early films in this regard (the images were jerky, black and white, silent). Ascribing these problems to purely 'technical' defects allows Bazin to posit the 'Platonic interpretation' of mimesis as both origin and end: it is because 'the concept men had of [cinema] existed . . . fully armed in their minds, as if in some Platonic heaven', that later supplements such as colour and sound can be seen as merely successive phases of a continuous trajectory stretching from the *cinématographe* to the present.[8] The obverse face of this acclamation of cinema as the perfection of mimesis can be found (among other places) in Lukács's critique of cinema as *pseudo-physis*. In Lukács's analysis, cinema does not reflect the real so much as dissolve it: 'Everything is true and real, everything is equally true and real: this is what a sequence of images in the cinema teaches us.'[9] He adds: 'because its technique expresses at every moment the absolute (even if only empirical) reality of this moment, "virtuality" no longer functions as a category opposed to "reality": both

---

4 Sontag, *On Photography*, p. 6.

5 Sontag, *On Photography*, p. 86.

6 Sontag, *On Photography*, p. 154.

7 See Bazin, 'The myth of total cinema', in *What is Cinema?*, vol. 1, p. 21.

8 A. Bazin, *What is Cinema?*, vol. 1, p. 17. To his credit, Bazin carries this logic to its enigmatic conclusion. He argues: 'Every new development added to the cinema must, paradoxically, take it nearer and nearer to its origins. In short, cinema has not yet been invented!' ('The myth of total cinema', p. 21). A strikingly similar 'myth' operates in many contemporary discussions of Virtual Reality. Simon Penny has observed: 'At the time of writing, virtual reality in the civilian domain is a rudimentary technology, as anyone who has worn a pair of eyephones will attest. That the technology is advancing rapidly is perhaps less interesting than the fact that nearly all commentators discuss it as if it was a fully realised technology. There is a desire for virtual reality in our culture that one can quite fairly characterise as a *yearning*.' 'Virtual bodybuilding', *Media Information Australia*, 69 (1993), p. 18.

9 Quoted in T. Elsaesser, 'Cinema – the irresponsible signifier or "the gamble with history": film theory or cinema theory', *New German Critique*, 40 (Winter 1987), p. 89.

categories become equivalent, identical.'[10] Baudrillard's thesis of the pure simulacrum is not far away.

If one remains faithful to the 'Platonic interpretation', imitation obeys an aberrant logic in which *perfection is ruin*. Representation approaches reality only to de-present it by coming too close. There is simultaneously deficit and excess in its economy – either too little or too much truth contaminates representation. It is no accident that this paradox has been thrown into stark relief in the age of the camera. From its inception, when the photograph was enthusiastically hailed as the writing of 'nature herself', the spread of camera technologies has been counterpointed by a crisis in the traditional definition of the sign. As Derrida points out, the Saussurean concept of the sign always turned on an unstable distinction between 'natural' and 'arbitrary' signs.[11] The generalization of photographic signs has made the network of alliances which historically secured this division between the 'natural' and the 'arbitrary' newly contentious. While the photograph originally appeared to conform, and even overconform, to the definition of the 'natural' sign, its susceptibility to the interminable drift of meaning which supposedly affects the 'arbitrary' sign more easily has confused its identity. In this confusion, what might be called the 'photo-effect' has brought the whole concept of the sign into question.[12]

The possibility of a sign which is neither 'natural' nor 'arbitrary', which no longer corresponds to one side or the other of this divide, which would no longer simply be a modified form of presence, or a strategy for mastering absence according to the prior dictates of *what is* (real) – this is precisely what has not been thought, what *could* not have been thought, within the logocentric tradition. In giving us more realism than we can cope with, and yet less than we impossibly desire, this is the uncertain terrain the camera asks us to occupy.

*

If the invention of the camera first inscribed a new question mark on the border between representation and reality, television radically accentuated this condition. Unlike the relationship of photography to painting in the nineteenth century, the attraction of television stems less from its higher

10 Quoted in Elsaesser, 'Cinema – the irresponsible signifier', p. 88. Here Lukács's analysis is close to that of Kracauer: it is the transformation of reality under capitalism, rather than the technological perfection of the image stressed by Bazin, which is active in the realignment of virtual and real.

11 Derrida analyses the distinction between the natural and the arbitrary sign as a critical limit of contemporary thought. In his critique of the Saussurean concept of the sign, Derrida notes a family of concepts 'clustering around the concept of arbitrariness' (such as nature/culture, *physis/techne*) 'whose ultimate function is perhaps to *derive* historicity; and paradoxically, not to recognize the rights of history, production, institutions, etc., except in the form of the arbitrary and in the substance of naturalism'. Derrida, *Of Grammatology*, p. 33.

12 See my analysis in 'Promiscuous meanings' above. In contrast to his reading of Saussure, Derrida offers a reading of Peirce's semiotics which posits an irreducible 'becoming-unmotivated' affecting every sign. See Derrida, *Of Grammatology*, pp. 48–50.

quality image than its higher velocity. The fundamental difference is not one of detail and resolution but speed. Elision of the time in between sending and receiving effectively removes the television image from the photographic or cinematic order. The extent of the gap this opens in the traditional terrain of representation can be grasped firstly in television's departures from the mode of address routinized in cinema. Most notably, the centrepiece of classical narrative cinema's voyeuristic economy – the prohibition placed on actors looking directly along the camera–audience axis – has been substantially overturned. Instead, television promotes a mode of direct address adapted from radio in which presenters look viewers straight in the eye, even speaking to us as if they could see into our living rooms. If this relationship is always a 'production' which plays on the spectator's ambivalent placement in the visual field, it is also the central feature of television's current imaginary.[13]

Direct address determines numerous other differences from cinematic spectatorship. Where cinema came to privilege the self-contained feature film, television is characterized by open-ended serial narratives such as soap operas or the news. In the former, the same characters are seen nightly in different situations, while, in the latter, the same situations are populated nightly with different characters. The individual segments of these programmes are usually less causally connected to each other than are those of a cinematic text. Or rather, interconnections are more dispersed, located on more abstract levels. News offers a paradigmatic example: following the fragmented logic of newspaper layout, the relation between the discrete items of any one bulletin depends less on linking events as a continuous plot than on a network of assumptions concerning immediacy and proximity (this happened *today*, or this happened *here*). A vital framing role is played by the presenter (the anchor or host).[14] Even in an age of pre-recording, the primary televisual fantasy is that everything is 'live', is occurring right now – or, at least, is being seen right now, even if only by the imaginary dyad of host and viewer. Pre-taped shows frequently begin with an introduction from the host who then turns to look at a monitor and, following their look, we 'zoom' into the show. Rather than the projective space hollowed out by the powerful presence of the cinematic signifier, identification on television belongs more to a regime of co-presence in which viewers and host converge in a novel experience of simultaneity.

This shift toward a mode of spectatorship which fuses individual viewers at home to the collective body of a geographically dispersed audience

13 Derrida argues: '[W]e should never forget what this entails: whenever a journalist or politician appears to be speaking to us directly, in our homes, and looking us straight in the eye, he or she is actually reading from a screen, at the dictation of a "prompter", and reading a text which was produced elsewhere, on a different occasion, possibly by other people, or by a whole network of nameless writers and editors.' J. Derrida, 'The deconstruction of actuality' (trans. J. Rée), *Radical Philosophy*, 68 (Autumn 1994), p. 28.

14 It is revealing that 'host' embraces both the one who entertains and the many who are massed together, while 'anchor' evokes the role of the presenter in securing meaning.

situates the heightened importance that television places on mechanisms of audience interaction and textual reflexivity. Audience participation has a long tradition on television, particularly in its staple diet of quiz shows, talent quests and variety programmes, where contestants and studio audiences function as shifting points of audience identification. Recently, participation has assumed new forms, including the structuring of feedback via viewer response segments, the inclusion of telephone talkback in on-air programming, and the much-heralded (if still incremental) moves towards television home shopping via 'smart terminals'.[15] The explosion of 'home video' programmes represents another avenue of 'participation' in which viewers not only appear in the show, but take on the role of production themselves.[16]

How should we read this trajectory, which was clearly discernible before the take-off of the Internet in 1993 made 'interactivity' such a buzz-word? Part of the answer is indicated by television's growing tendency to include its own technical apparatus in the scene of representation. From brief inserts showing the camera operator shooting news footage to the popularity of 'behind-the-scenes' programmes of all kinds, contemporary television displays a boundless fascination with its own techniques of production. The cinematic edict against revealing the process of enunciation in order to facilitate the transparency of the enounced – which for a time stood as *the* 'ideological effect' of cinema – has been renounced in favour of an expanded economy which appears to embrace all that was once thought most antagonistic to 'realism'.

But this reflexive turn is less the victory of the avant-garde than the appropriation of its techniques and the reinscription of its designs.[17] In a media-conscious environment, the allure of writing in the language of 'nature herself' (which inspired the first photographers), or the possibility of seizing 'life itself' (which enthused so many film makers), has been forced to assume another guise. Far from denying its mediation of the real, television celebrates it. Where classical narrative cinema might be compared to the magician who uses sleight of hand to deceive the eye, television increasingly styles itself as a conjurer who can expose the workings of the

---

15 Confessional talkshows such as *Donahue* and *Oprah* – where the audience is the show – use talkback to merge the visible studio audience with the home audience. Similarly, telecasts of sports events, where spectators perform to the cameras by holding up messages and banners, enable the direct integration of the audience into the televised spectacle of the game.

16 Home video programmes situate a fundamental difference between the cinematic and televisual imaginaries. Apart from historic exceptions, such as the Zapruder film of John F. Kennedy's assassination, home movies have never found a place in mainstream cinema, which has secured its identity precisely by centring itself around production values which home movies cannot attain. Where cinema usually represents the extraordinary other, television displays a fascination with the very ordinary other.

17 Fascination with the apparatus once defined the genre of avant-garde film which Commolli termed 'direct cinema'. Vertov's *The Man with a Movie Camera* (1929) was the most influential early example of a film focusing on 'the representation of representation'.

trick, and appear all the more seductive for doing so. *Nothing need be hidden* – this is television's slogan for an era which equates democracy and freedom with total global visibility. While such a claim is illusory – we see the cameras, but not the balance sheets – a level of formal reflexivity is critical to this contract. By revealing the workings of its own apparatus, contemporary television claims not only to show us 'the world', but also to show its own process of showing.[18]

Insofar as 'interactivity' has become a key term, it should be read less as a line dividing active viewers from passive spectators than as a new strategy to account for the placement of the observer's body in the scene of representation. This can be appreciated by briefly tracing a series of changes in this relation over the course of the camera's history. For several centuries, the camera obscura figured the observer as a stable and centred subject, external to the scene represented and therefore invisible *within* its picture.[19] The photographic camera maintained both the externality and invisibility of the classical observer, but introduced other tensions which have never been resolved. Because photographs could be uncoupled in time and space from the scenes they represented, image and observer found themselves exposed to an implacable drift of meaning and perspective. Cinema heightened this volatility by introducing a very different representational economy based on movement and montage. Yet, its classical narrative form also sought to maintain both the invisibility and the exteriority proper to the nineteenth-century observer: it is the spectator's absence from the screen which underwrites the voyeuristic fantasy of an all-seeing eye which is not itself subject to representation.[20]

In contrast to classical cinema, which worked to deny the existence of the gaze by regulating the reversibility of the look, television parries this moment differently. This reflects the fact that it was not the destruction of the existing spatial order, but the new pressure of time which necessitated another reconfiguration of the scene of watching. The collective imaginary of instant broadcasting and simultaneous viewing demands that the observer enter the scene as an integral part of its dynamic. If the tele-observer remains invisible – is not yet 'in' the picture – he or she is continually acknowledged

18 Recalling the avant-gardist advocacy of 'a filmic practice in which one watches oneself watching'. P. Gidal (ed.), *Structural Film Anthology*, London, British Film Institute, 1976, p. 10.

19 Crary argues that the camera obscura was a means of *decorporealizing* vision, separating the act of seeing from the physical body of the observer: 'The body . . . is a problem the camera could never solve except by marginalizing it into a phantom in order to establish a space of reason.' *Techniques of the Observer*, p. 41.

20 Metz relates this structure of spectating to Lacan's emphasis on the formative role of the mirror in constructing identity: '. . . what *makes possible* the spectator's absence from the screen – or rather the intelligible unfolding of the film despite that absence – is the fact that the spectator has already known the experience of the mirror (the true mirror) and is thus able to constitute a world of objects *without first having to recognize himself in it.*' Metz, *Psychoanalysis and the Cinema*, p. 46 (last italics mine).

as an active participant at the edge of its frame.[21] It is from this perspective that television's heightened reliance on showing its own mechanisms of production may be understood: as an attempt to construct a spectating position for a subject which desires to see, and to see itself seeing at the same time.

The ambivalence of this position can be registered by returning to Lacan's account of the gaze. Lacan correlates the dream experience in which 'I saw myself seeing myself' with the Cartesian *cogito* by which the subject apprehends itself as pure thought. But he argues that this apprehension remains a fundamental misapprehension.

> That in which the consciousness may turn back on itself – grasp itself, like Valery's Young Parque as *seeing oneself seeing oneself* – represents mere sleight of hand. An avoidance of the function of the gaze is at work here.[22]

What elides the gaze is precisely belief in the possibility 'of *seeing oneself seeing oneself*'.[23] Such a perfectly self-reflecting perception, like its corre- late of a perfectly self-reflexive consciousness, is a 'fiction' predicated on denial of the claims of the other. This analysis is useful in approaching the contemporary ambition to structure the world as a global TV studio. The proliferation of 'live' presentations of events 'even as they occur', like the explosion of 'reality television' which fuses *cinéma vérité* with the portability of new video technologies, registers the extraordinary extent to which television now claims dominion over the real, spreading a blanket over life through the universal distribution of points of recording, broad- casting and viewing. In the drive towards 24-hour programming, and the mobilization of all possible tactics to compel the real to submit itself to us – its anonymous witnesses – can be read a powerful desire to cut the scene of the other to the measure of the viewing self. The impulse to eliminate all gaps – the time in which representation once slept, or the space beyond the camera's reach – reveals a compulsion to subject the totality of experience to representation's frame. If neither photography nor cinema ever made quite so delirious a promise to contain the world, this seems less an accident of technology than the very space of television's current identity.[24]

*

21 Here one can situate the break made by Virtual Reality technologies, not as the complete fusion of reality and representation which has been so often announced, but as an overturning of Lacan's dictum: 'The picture certainly is in my eye. But I am not in the picture.' What is distinctive to VR technologies is the ability for the observer to be both witness *and* participant, visibly situating his or her own body in the picture via head sets, data gloves, and the like. (This trajectory had already been sketched by experimental video, such as certain works by Nam Jun Paik which used audience speech or movement to generate sounds or images within the video text.)

22 Lacan, *Four Fundamental Concepts of Psycho-analysis*, p. 74.

23 Lacan, *Four Fundamental Concepts of Psycho-analysis*, p. 83.

24 Kristeva describes the delirious discourse as one which acknowledges no outside: 'no other exists, no object survives in its irreducible alterity.' T. Moi (ed.), *The Kristeva Reader*, Oxford, Basil Blackwell, 1987, p. 308.

In 1927, Siegfried Kracauer published a remarkable essay in which he described the 'turn to photography' as *'the-go-for-broke game* of history'.[25] Kracauer arrived at this bold prognosis through his understanding that the age of the camera implied a significant structural transformation of consciousness. His description of the impact of the flood of photographic images remains instructive (one need only substitute 'television' for 'illustrated magazines'):

> The aim of the illustrated magazine is the complete reproduction of the world accessible to the photographic apparatus. They record the spatial impressions of people, conditions and events from every possible perspective. . . . Never before has an age been so informed about itself, if being informed means having an image of objects that resemble them in a photographic sense.[26]

However, Kracauer argues that the consequences of this proliferation of images remain uncertain: 'The blizzard of photographs betrays an indifference towards what the things mean.'[27] On the one hand this 'indifference', which results from the destruction of traditional relations of meaning, reflects a state of alienation from the world in which the images themselves destroy the possibility of contact with their 'originals' (the situations and events that they depict). Visibility produces a paradoxical state of blindness:

> In the illustrated magazines, people see the very world that the illustrated magazines prevent them from perceiving. . . . Never before has a period known so little about itself. In the hands of the ruling society, the invention of the illustrated magazines is one of the most powerful means of organizing a strike against understanding.[28]

But this 'indifference' created by the fragmented nature of the image-world could also become the basis for a new consciousness by exposing its own arbitrary organization.

> This ghost-like reality is *unredeemed.* It consists of elements in space whose configuration is so far from necessary that one could just as well imagine a different organization of these elements.[29]

Because photography provides a 'warehouse' of the appearances of social life under industrial capitalism, it holds unique potential for penetrating this new 'nature'.

> This warehousing of nature promotes the confrontation of consciousness with nature. Just as consciousness finds itself confronting the unabashedly displayed mechanics of industrial society, it also faces, thanks to photographic technology, the reflection of the reality that has slipped away from it.[30]

25 S. Kracauer, 'Photography', *The Mass Ornament* (trans. and ed. T.Y. Levin), Cambridge, MA and London, Harvard University Press, 1995, p. 61.

26 Kracauer, 'Photography', pp. 57–8.

27 Kracauer, 'Photography', p. 58.

28 Kracauer, 'Photography', p. 58.

29 Kracauer, 'Photography', p. 56.

30 Kracauer, 'Photography', p. 62.

Kracauer believed that the historical conjuncture was rapidly sharpening these contradictions. If capitalism were to endure, 'the nature that [photography] failed to penetrate would sit down at the very table consciousness had abandoned', presaging the victory of commodity culture and a spectacular society in which images become the ultimate commodity. But if capitalism were overthrown, 'then liberated consciousness would be given an incomparable opportunity. Less enmeshed in natural bonds than ever before, it could prove its power in dealing with them. The turn to photography is the *go-for-broke game* of history.'[31]

Kracauer's analysis, which was extended and politicized by Walter Benjamin a decade later in his 'Artwork' essay, remains pertinent to our current dilemma. If the image-world has today swallowed the 'real world' to produce a mutant state of being which is neither real, nor yet simply imaginary (at least as those terms have been customarily understood), it is naive to envisage a political critique which could be located entirely *outside* the world of images. Moreover, it suggests that transformations of contemporary culture will depend critically – which is not to say wholly – on the success of interventions in and transformations of 'the media'.

Sontag, who shared Kracauer's perception of the epochal change sparked by the camera, interpreted it in a more pessimistic light:

> What defines the originality of photography is that, at the very moment in the long, increasingly secular history of painting when secularism is entirely triumphant, it revives – in wholly secular terms – something like the primitive status of images.[32]

If this formulation owes a debt to Kracauer and Benjamin, Sontag's evaluation of the consequences of this paradoxical 'revival' differ. She argues that, where the potency of images in so-called 'primitive' cultures rested on the fact that they partook in the qualities of the real, capitalism reverses this relation. As the world is converted into an ensemble of potential photographs (*that* would make a nice picture), people begin to experience themselves as 'mere images' made real by cameras. In this argument one can recognize the echoes of numerous others from Marx to Debord to Baudrillard and beyond: representation is no longer shaped to fit what is real; instead, the world is called on to live up to its images.

Evidence of this shift proliferates in many places, from the role of advertising in machining desire to the measure of commodities, to the insertion of cameras into the micro-practices of daily life, to the radical primacy that 'the media' have assumed in the current distribution of cultural capital and political power. Given the force of these currents, one can never do enough to insist on the manufactured and produced nature of what is often passed off as 'reality' on our screens. But, in attending to this trajectory, it is important not to ignore all others. Many criticisms of 'media culture' are content simply to repeat a mantra of neo-Platonic angst which

31 Kracauer, 'Photography', p. 61.
32 Sontag, *On Photography*, p. 155.

declares a preference for 'reality' over images. Before mourning the loss of reality in the present, we need to re-examine our investment in that underlying, ever-present bedrock of the real to which 'images' have traditionally been opposed.

Why do many people so readily associate the destabilization of the order of reference with profound danger? What is the necessity of the divorce between real and imaginary which has cut so deeply through the cultural heritage of 'the West', especially in the age of reason? What is the source of the particular scorn still reserved for those 'primitives' who can't tell reality from images, dreams and imagination? So powerful is the hold of the binary opposition between image and reality (forming a matrix for other conceptual pairings such as ideology and truth, art and science, subjective and objective) that envisioning a world where this dividing line might itself be questioned often seems a frightening undertaking. One of the virtues of Borges's story with which I began this section is the manner in which his sightless eyes restore a sense of what might exist outside these polarities.

As Maurice Blanchot reminds us in his rich and suggestive analysis, there are (at least) two versions of the imaginary.[33] There is the ordinary analysis, according to which the image is secondary, derivative, referential; it supervenes on or follows the order of reality, and is thus made to serve the world's truth.[34] But there is also another aspect of the image which points not to the absent thing by means of a strategy of mastery, but evokes its absence as presence.[35] This evocation of *absence as presence* – are we not precisely in the terrain of the camera? – constitutes an ambiguity which is 'not such as to be mastered by the discernment of an either–or in that it could authorize a choice and lift from the choosing the ambiguity that makes choice possible'.[36] The ambiguity remains. Should we admit that sometimes we believe in the camera's truth, while sometimes we dispute it as mere pretence? That sometimes we understand the image as the expression of a 'subjective' vision and sometimes we experience its image as an 'objectification'? But, of course, as Blanchot reminds us, 'What we distinguish by saying "sometimes, sometimes", ambiguity introduces by "always", at least to a certain extent, saying both one and the other.'[37]

Blanchot's recognition of the claims of ambiguity, not as the failing of a leaky logic, but as an irreducible effect of representation, provides a valuable counterweight here. For it is precisely ambiguity which has been most

33 See 'Two versions of the imaginary' in his *The Space of Literature* (trans. A Smock), Lincoln and London, University of Nebraska Press, 1982, pp. 254–63.

34 Blanchot's account of the 'ordinary interpretation' of the image approaches Lacan's analysis of the 'soothing' function of the picture: 'The gratifying aspect of the image is that it constitutes a limit at the edge of the indefinite. . . . In this way the image fulfils one of its functions which is to quiet, to humanize the formless nothingness pressed upon us by the indelible residue of being.' Blanchot, *Space of Literature*, pp. 254 and 255.

35 Blanchot, *Space of Literature*, p. 262.

36 Blanchot, *Space of Literature*, pp. 262–3.

37 Blanchot, *Space of Literature*, p. 263.

forcibly denied, rejected or repressed by the dominant cultural and political formations of the West. If this repression reached a zenith with the forms of nineteenth-century positivism which framed the camera's birth, its effects still linger. Subordinated to the Platonic order of reference, the image is regularly confined to a one-way street: it can reflect or distort the real, but only as its follow-up, the afterthought tailing the origin. Such a standpoint is far too limited and limiting for evaluating the impact of 'media culture'.

Sontag's statement concerning the secular revival of a 'primitive' relation to the image alerts us to another crucial aspect of this debate. While the camera formed the pinnacle of the objective and objectifying eye desired by nineteenth-century positivism, its uncanny fusion of object and image forced a confrontation with much that has otherwise been deliberately submerged in modernity. As fast as the camera has been annexed to the eye of the self, it has opened the eye of the other; its look cannot grant certainty without tracing new wounds of uncertainty. To name this ambiguous relation 'primitive' signals the immense political investments concentrated here. The duplicity by which 'primitivism' has been appropriated by modern art and culture, while so-called 'primitives' have been violently excluded by the political and economic rationality of modernity, is more than an unfortunate accident. The stakes bound up in the distinction between 'modern' and 'primitive' are immense. It seeks to define the movement from the sacred to the secular and the transition from 'superstition' to 'science' as the historical progress proper to 'the West'. In acknowledging the photographic image as the truth of representation, positivist reason sought to exploit the camera's evidentiary power, while conserving the operational distinction between image and reality on which positivist rationality itself depends. But, in the long term, this investment has defaulted – or perhaps its dividends have been too great – exacting a toll upon the absolute priority accorded the real. The looming equivalence of 'direct' and 'indirect' perceptions in the age of television marks a potentially terminal threshold in this trajectory.

It is on this conflictual historical scale that the consequences of the dramatic rise of the image-culture of the twentieth century need to be calculated. If the era of representation predicated on the 'Platonic interpretation' of mimesis is perhaps drawing to a close, this promises a realignment of the fundamental conceptual allegiances which have so decisively shaped the 'history of the West'. It is difficult to address the possibilities and risks of this shift in terms of traditional political affiliations. This is not to posit it as somehow beyond politics – on the contrary – but to suggest that the mutation of spatial and temporal parameters currently entrained by telematics must be analysed as a crucial frame for any future politics.[38] Nor is it to suggest that this threshold is purely emancipatory, according to the dubious idealization of 'relativism' which often substitutes pluralist choice for a more rigorous analysis of hierarchies of power. (This amounts to little more than the consumer's choice of different channels on

38 See my discussion in 'Interzones' and 'Unstable architectures' below.

'Reality TV', according to Coca-Cola's slogan: 'Everyone's got a *right* to reality.') Nevertheless, the 'crisis' in the relation between image and reality which situates the threshold of postmodernism in the West has also contributed to a process of cross-cultural questioning in which new sorts of questions have emerged. The extent to which otherness will be acknow-ledged, refused, incorporated – or will in fact interrupt and redefine the space of the self – has become a critical political issue.

The difficulty in addressing these long-term shifts stems directly from the fact that contemporary media culture is so tightly bound to the functioning of capitalism that looking for other possibilities inevitably risks being seen as Utopian or naive. Yet refusing to look beyond present circumstances risks sacrificing strategic points of intervention. One of Benjamin's most import-ant insights was his insistence that the mass culture of capitalism was not only the source of phantasmagoria and false consciousness, but also of the collective energy to overcome it. If the revolutionary role that he gave to the new media seems less assured today, this is not simply because he overestimated the media's potential to catalyse social change, but also because that potential is still systematically directed elsewhere.

While the vision machine feeds the instrumental rationality underpinning the techno-scientific appropriation of the world, facilitating the commodifi-cation of the other as spectacle, and enabling the policing of identity in an ever-tightening mesh of bureaucratic and self-surveillance, it also points towards an equivocal realm 'where "I" does not recognize itself'.[39] In this zone, one necessarily departs from the certitudes of originary subjectivities and fixed identities, and begins to approach the radical questioning of the natural order that Kracauer long ago posited as the revolutionary effect of the camera. Insofar as thinking identity as a process of invention, negotiation and contestation demands a different understanding of the space and time of representation, this may yet prove to be the camera's most important stimulus to contemporary thought.

39 Blanchot, *Space of Literature*, p. 262.

PART 2
PHOTOMNEMONICS

Perhaps we have an invincible resistance to believing in the past, in History, except in the form of a myth. The Photograph, for the first time, puts an end to this resistance: henceforth the past is as certain as the present, what we see on paper is as certain as what we touch. It is the advent of the Photograph – and not, as has been said, of the cinema – which divides the history of the world.

Roland Barthes

1

The Eye of the Camera Faces Backwards

Speed is at the bottom of it all; the hundredth of a second caught so precisely that the motion is continued from the picture indefinitely: the moment made eternal.

Hart Crane

Photographic images often appear to defy time or, at least, partially to escape its implacable sequence. The ability to withdraw the appearance of the moment and preserve it from time's deliquescence looms large in the history of our fascination with the camera. Barthes suggests: 'looking at a photograph I inevitably include in my scrutiny the thought of that instant, however brief, in which a real thing happened to be motionless in front of the eye.'[1] It seems to matter little that this 'decisive moment', which Henri Cartier-Bresson fashioned into a complete photo-ontology, is mythical; a techno-magical revelation performed by the guillotine action of the camera's shutter, which can suspend a running man over a pool of water forever awaiting the imprint of his foot on its mirror. Yet, as photographer Harry Callahan once noted: 'A photograph is able to capture a moment people can't always see with their eyes.'[2]

In this ambivalent space between recording and revelation one finds the unique possibilities that the camera has brought to the representation of history. Born as a machine offering a novel grip on time, fixing it, freezing it, immobilizing its ineluctable flux, the camera expanded its claims by reconstituting time's 'living flow' in the celluloid ribbons of film which entranced viewers at the gateway to the twentieth century. Around half a century later, as broadcast television inaugurated its uncanny domain of an extended present in which an audience dispersed right across the world is invited to 'watch history take place', the seduction of time seemed complete. Like Borges's fantastic map which merged with the terrain it originally sought to represent, 24-hour television forms a radically different cartography: a temporal map without edges, origins or ends, pulsing incessantly throughout the real.

What is it to remember? What will remain? What materials will construct history? What precepts will structure historical understanding? Questions such as these pose themselves with renewed force and urgency in the late twentieth century as both personal and collective memory are relocated in the virtual landscapes of new media technologies. History – which has

1 Barthes, *Camera Lucida*, p. 78.
2 Quoted in *The Camera*, New York, Time-Life International, 1970–1, p. 42.

always been dominated by recorded history – will inevitably be transformed by changes in the mode of record. According to Illich and Sanders:

> History only becomes possible when the Word turns into words. . . . The historian's home is on the island of writing. He furnishes its inhabitants with subject matter about the past. The past that can be seized is related to writing.[3]

To the extent that this proposition was ever true, it is today no longer sustainable (unless one follows Derrida in radically rethinking the traditional concept of 'writing').[4] Contemporary 'memory-supports', which transcribe not only words but sounds and visual appearances, have surpassed even the imaginings of previous eras. As images created by cameras have increasingly constituted much of the 'evidence' from which we gain knowledge and draw inferences about the nature of reality, they have necessarily assumed greater importance in the production and legitimation of history. From the personalized visual history of the photo-album to public collections in museums and libraries to commercial stockpiles in television stations and film studios, the result has been the unprecedented expansion of all that might constitute an archive.

Despite these manifest changes, academic history has largely remained written history in the traditional sense. While historical scholarship is increasingly supplemented by images, or informed by film or video footage as 'raw materials', there has been all too little consideration of the deeper implications of this transformation of the historical archive.[5] But the impact of the camera cannot be limited to filling in gaps in historical content. On the contrary, the profound technological mutation of the archive necessitates questioning the very concept of history, and exposing the collusion between representation and time it has long presupposed.

*

In his final book, Roland Barthes argued that the fusion of reality with the past constituted the uniqueness of photography: '. . . in Photography I can never deny that *the thing has been there*. There is a superimposition here: of reality and of the past. And since this constraint exists only for Photography, we must consider it, by reduction, as the very essence, the *noeme* of

3 I. Illich and B. Sanders, *The Alphabetization of the Popular Mind*, San Francisco, North Point Press, 1988, p. ix.

4 Derrida notes: '. . . history is itself tied to the possibility of writing; to the possibility of writing in general, beyond those particular forms of writing in the name of which we have long spoken of peoples without writing and without history.' Derrida, *Of Grammatology*, p. 27.

5 There are notable exceptions to this rule, particularly the work of Walter Benjamin and Siegfried Kracauer, whose writings on history were deeply informed by the camera. Both treat the camera as a central aspect of modern experience, while exploring its possibilities as a metaphor for historical representation. Their increasing influence in philosophy of history can be read, at least partly, in terms of this convergence.

Photography.'[6] For Barthes, photography's primal force lies in its unsurpassed power of authentification: 'Photography never lies: or rather, it can lie as to the meaning of the thing, being by nature *tendentious*, never as to its existence.'[7] The relation of the camera to figuring a past, a history, a memory, is thus an ontological relation: 'this has been' is the assertion made by every photographic image before it says anything else. Barthes concludes that nothing else can confer the same sense of certainty.

Yet, even prior to the digital threshold, this certainty proved difficult to maintain. As always, the disturbance posed by the camera is intrinsically linked to the scandalous cohabitation of its images with the real. For this reason, Barthes called photography mutant: 'neither image nor reality, a new being really: a reality one can no longer touch'.[8] To the extent that the photograph radiates a guarantee of presence beyond the jurisdiction of all previous media, it inevitably blurs the sharpness of the line thought to divide past from present, then from now. From the sight of Niepce's dinner table (photographed circa 1823) to electronic images of other worlds relayed across inconceivable distances by the Voyager spacecraft, the camera has formed a unique conduit enabling absence to touch present observers, like delayed rays of light arriving from stars already long vanished. This enigmatic experience, in which the immediacy of the absent invades the security of the present, is central to the camera's ambivalent relation to figuring the past.

While the camera has always excited ambitious claims with respect to memory and history, it also triggered new doubts. Baudelaire's dictum concerning photography – 'Some democratic writer ought to have seen here a method for disseminating a loathing for history . . . among the people' – has returned again and again as the verso side of the positivist dream of encyclopaedic memory.[9] The paradox confronting contemporary societies dominated by audio-visual media and the computerization of traditional writing is the widely countenanced emergence of *amnesic cultures*: societies entranced by spectacle and immediacy but lacking any sense of history.

*

John Berger once asked: 'What served in the place of the photograph before the camera's invention?', replying: 'The expected answer is the engraving,

---

6 Barthes, *Camera Lucida*, pp. 76–7. Like many other critics, Barthes's photographic essence is an essence of 'realist' photographs, excluding montage, collage, superimposition and other 'trick' effects (Barthes, *Camera Lucida*, pp. 33 and 87). But he distinguishes his realism from those predicated solely on the conventions of geometric perspective: 'To ask whether a photograph is analogical or coded is not a good means of analysis. The important thing is that the photograph possesses an evidential force, and that its testimony bears not on the object but on time', Barthes, *Camera Lucida*, p. 89.

7 Barthes, *Camera Lucida*, p. 87.

8 Barthes, *Camera Lucida*, p. 87.

9 Baudelaire quoted in V. Burgin (ed.), *Thinking Photography*, London, Macmillan, 1982, p. 96.

the painting, the drawing. The more revealing answer might be: memory.'[10] In taking this 'more revealing answer' as my starting point, I want to examine the camera's relation to the transformation of memory and history in the last century and a half. But, rather than adopting the conventional perspective which begins from the camera's unique abilities in the domain of time, it seems more illuminating to ask: what are the social relations of time which have enabled the camera to assume such decisive sovereignty over its dimensions? The camera's capacity to furnish evidence, its facility for documenting and preserving, even the unrivalled 'realism' and 'fidelity' of its records, all involve a temporal component. Or rather, these terms are themselves already temporalized. The concept of the 'instant' to which a photograph might correspond itself depends upon a prior assumption about the nature of time: that time is a continuous but infinitely divisible line, supporting partition into smaller and smaller units, in which the order of the microsecond can be paralleled by the multiple exposure of sequential frames. But thinking of time as a continuous line of points/instants leaves us close to Zeno's paradox and the aporia of the now which, in a certain fashion, has governed the dominant Western concept of time over a long period.[11] Under the eye of the camera, it may be that this understanding of time is increasingly forced to confront its own limits.

The status given to photographs as a material form of memory, and the deference to photography, film and videotape over other forms of record and recall, signals an important threshold of modernity. If, as Milan Kundera has suggested, the key political struggle of the twentieth century is the struggle of memory over forgetting, the camera has been a crucial force in this contest. Kundera himself situated something of the complexity of the photo-effect by relating the story of a certain comrade Clementis who was photographed standing next to the Czech communist leader Klement Gottwald as he addressed a crowd in Prague in February 1948.[12] It was snowing and the solicitous Clementis had placed his fur cap on Gottwald's bare head. The image was used by the Party to symbolize the birth of a new era of Czech communism. Hundreds of thousands of copies were distributed across the country. Every Czech citizen was familiar with it from books, posters and museums. Four years later Clementis was found guilty of treason and executed. He was exorcized from Czech history and airbrushed from the photograph as well. All that remains of him is the fur cap on Gottwald's head.

The significance of this story lies not in its uniqueness but in its ubiquity. If photographic images can become memory, they can equally be used to block memory. Kundera's tale registers the need to scrutinize images in order to discern traces of the repressed; lines of other histories which are

10 Berger, *About Looking*, p. 50.

11 See 'Telepresence and the government of time' below.

12 M. Kundera, *The Book of Laughter and Forgetting* (trans. M.H. Heim), Harmondsworth, Penguin, 1983, p. 3.

excluded, rubbed out or defaced. Who knows, in the 1990s Clementis may return; a little retouching and history would be restored. Or would it? Perhaps it is precisely in a new awareness of historical mutability – revealed in the unstable oscillations between 'fact' and 'interpretation' which affect the dominant currency of both history *and* photography – that the most profound consequences of photomnemonics can be discerned. It is in this space that a politics of historical representation begins to be defined as an integral part of contemporary political struggles. As Foucault recognized: 'if one controls people's memory one controls their dynamism.'[13] Attempts to recover 'lost histories' and to forge new practices of remembering have become critical to the political strategies of marginalized peoples: the displaced and diasporic whose pasts have been transplanted into foreign presents; dispossessed indigenous peoples written out of the narrative of progress; women contesting the univocity of history told as the tale of great men. Paralleling the intense questioning of the transparency of the photographic image, the dominant image of historical knowledge as a cumulative process of gathering and collecting has found itself under increasing pressure.

The struggle of memory over the rule of death has always been anxious. But the contradiction between the massive technological apparatus of cameras and computers developed in the name of remembering, and the uncertainty and anxiety currently surrounding history and memory, has never seemed more acute. What photographs often 'preserve' today is only the nostalgia arising from a pervasive and intractable sense of loss. To better understand this condition – which is one of the currents of 'postmodernity' – we need to examine the passion for photomnemonics geared up in the nineteenth century; a passion born in intense struggles over history, knowledge and the social relations of time itself.

13 'Michel Foucault: interview', *Edinburgh '77 Magazine*, 2 (1977), p. 22.

2

The Law of Progress

The concept of the historical progress of mankind cannot be sundered from the concept of its progression through a homogeneous, empty time.

Walter Benjamin

Within a decade of the public unveiling of the camera in 1839, Marx and Engels published their famous *Communist Manifesto*, in which they asserted:

> The bourgeoisie cannot exist without constantly revolutionizing the instruments of production, and thereby the relations of production, and with them the whole relations of society. Conservation of the old modes of production in unaltered form, was, on the contrary, the first condition of existence for all earlier industrial classes. Constant revolutionizing of production, uninterrupted disturbance of all social conditions, everlasting uncertainty and agitation distinguish the bourgeois epoch from all earlier ones. All fixed, fast-frozen relations, with their train of ancient and venerable prejudices and opinions, are swept away, all new formed ones become antiquated before they can ossify. All that is solid melts into air . . .[1]

The passage offers both an analysis of – and a clarion call for – the modern condition. At the crux of the new bourgeois order was a revolution in the social relations of time, the ignition of a logical/ideological motor whose dynamic force would reshape every aspect of human existence. Faith in the guiding star of progress inherited from the Enlightenment intersected with the Industrial Revolution to alter fundamentally the equilibrium of history: for the first time change rather than stasis became the normal expectation.

The political consolidation of capitalism has depended enormously on this re-evaluation of the value of change. Innovation – the newest, the latest, the most modern – has metamorphosed from carrying the stigma of the unproven to be accorded an absolute worth in itself. Such a transformation breaks with tradition on every front, not only reshaping the apparatus of production, but the logic of consumption, including the dominant forms of culture and knowledge. As Walter Benjamin wryly commented, modern commodities circulate according to the dictates of fashion in 'the eternal return of the new', a cycle paralleled by the paradigm of avant-gardism in art and the dominance of news in the sphere of information.[2]

1 K. Marx and F. Engels, *Manifesto of the Communist Party* (1848) (trans. S. Moore), Moscow, Progress Publishers, 1977, pp. 45–6.

2 Benjamin quoted in B. Thomas, 'The new historicism and other old-fashioned topics', in H.A. Veeser (ed.), *The New Historicism*, New York and London, Routledge, 1989, p. 187.

Progress has replaced tradition as the ideological grout of modernity, forming a common matrix of legitimation for nation states otherwise considered culturally and politically diverse. As traditional continuities such as kinship networks have been increasingly fragmented by the accelerated processes of modern life, even the basic co-ordinates of human identity have been transformed. The claims of collective identity have receded in favour of accounts of eruptive autogenesis. Foucault pointed to Baudelaire as a pivot of modern sensibility: 'Modern man, for Baudelaire, is not the man who goes off to discover himself, his secrets and his hidden truth; he is the man who tries to invent himself.'[3] While Nietzsche's description of the desire 'to pull oneself into existence out of the swamp of nothingness by one's own hair' satirized modern faith in the possibilities of individual self-creation, the 'New Man' became a primary point of reference across numerous discourses in the first decades of this century.[4]

Revolutionaries, scientists, entrepreneurs and artists all enthusiastically embraced the notion of modernity as a decisive watershed in human consciousness. From Marinetti's Futurist Manifesto of 1909 to the scandalous mechano-morphic images of Picabia and Duchamp to the mesmerizing robot in Fritz Lang's *Metropolis* (1926), the modern world was gripped by powerful fantasies of technological birth which promised absolute liberation from the past. The desire to overreach history, disavowing all legacies and overthrowing all traditions, formed the heart of a modern sensibility proud of its ability to part the curtains of habit and cast off the blinkers of convention. To be without memory enables one to invent the future, to pluck a new beginning from the wings of time itself.[5]

Part of the complexity of representing such a shift is that what might be called the 'age of progress' both depends on, and yet at the same time produces, dramatic changes in the experience and understanding of time. While the comprehension of time as a destroyer is very ancient (the myth of Chronos being one example), the forms and rhythms of destruction have altered significantly in the modern period. Where the most common medieval figure for representing time was the circle (whether referring to the agrarian cycle of planting and harvest, or the movement of the planets around the heavenly spheres), industrial culture replaced this image with that of the line; most strikingly, the endless parallel lines of steel railway tracks puncturing the visible horizon. From this moment, it proved increasingly difficult to conceive of time as a cycle in which birth and death are

3 'What is Enlightenment?', in P. Rabinow (ed.), *Foucault Reader*, New York, Pantheon Books, 1984, p. 42.

4 F. Nietzsche, *Beyond Good and Evil* (trans. R.J. Hollingdale), Harmondsworth, Penguin, 1973, p. 32.

5 Paul de Man argues: 'Modernity exists in the form of a desire to wipe out whatever came earlier, in the hope of reaching at last a point that could be called a true present, a point of origin that marks a new departure. This combined interplay of deliberate forgetting with an action that is also a new origin reaches the full power of the idea of modernity . . .' P. de Man, *Blindness and Insight*, Minneapolis, University of Minnesota Press, 1983, p. 142.

complementary terms rather than opposites. Instead, time has become unidirectional, a juggernaut which threatens to consume everything. Divorcing destruction from renewal produces a quite different relation to 'the past'. John Berger argues that, since the French Revolution, history 'no longer speaks of the changeless, but of the laws of change which spare nothing'.[6]

The model of the line and the teleology of linearization saturate the modern concept of progress, conditioning belief in the endless growth of productive capacities and intellectual capabilities, the march of history as cumulative, the order of time as successive and irreversible.[7] The consolidation of progress as a socio-political law (paralleled in biology by Darwin's principle of natural selection and preceded in physics by Newton's concept of absolute and irreversible time) corresponds to a period of vastly accelerated social change. Technological developments which regulate social velocity to an unprecedented degree have themselves become subject to shorter and shorter lifespans: wheeled transport existed in more or less the same form for 2,000 years before steam; Watt's steam engine was working for 102 years after it was built; contemporary cars are designed with a projected life of under a decade; the computer and software (purchased last year) with which I am writing this text are already deemed obsolete. The emergence of speed as a primary social value, coupled to notions of productivity, efficiency and profit, has allowed the instrumental reorganization of time to form an apparently self-regulating system: while technology increases social velocity, people find themselves demanding new technologies in order to 'keep up'.

*

The key site in the historical transformation of time – the lever for bringing *time* into *line* – was the industrial workplace. The shift from the country to the city, which has been the dominant demographic tendency of the last two centuries, made time a social and political issue in new ways.[8] First, work was measured less according to the time of specific tasks (cultivating a field, mending a wheel, etc.) and more in terms of how many hours one worked, the rate of pay per hour, the length of the working day, and so on. (Hence the rise of trade unionism around these issues.) Secondly, labour was less susceptible to direct climatic variations, but was instead rendered increasingly subject to the abstract seasons of the market and the vagaries of its

6 Berger, *And Our Faces*, p. 12.

7 Derrida suggests that the linearization of time enshrined in the concept of progress also consolidates a certain model of representation: 'This linearist concept of time is therefore one of the deepest adherences of the modern concept of the sign to its own history.' Derrida, *Of Grammatology*, p. 72.

8 The growth of industrial cities in the nineteenth century was phenomenal; for instance, Glasgow's population increased five-fold from 1801 to 1861. By the 1850s, more people in Britain lived in the city than in the country, the first time such a threshold had been crossed. By the year 2000, it is estimated that more than 50 per cent of the *world's* population will live in cities.

'invisible hand'. Thirdly, and most significantly, the reconstruction of work practices by machine production meant that workers lost control over their own working pace. The new machinery demanded clockwork responses: constant work rhythms, unvarying work rates.[9]

Taylorist principles of 'scientific management' and the Fordist production line were both 'logical' extensions of the demand to co-ordinate the human body with the order of machine time.[10] With its idiosyncrasies and irregularities, the body often found itself lodged as a bottleneck in the industrial process, defined as redundant – unless nothing cheaper could be found to perform the task at hand.[11] In the enforcement of work values such as punctuality, exactitude, efficiency and repetition, industrial culture imposed a new discipline of time central to the modern exercise of power. Foucault highlighted the way that Taylorist changes in work practices altered classical forms of authority by refining attention to detail, regulating the rhythm of actions, and correlating the relation between body, gesture, and object.

> The act is broken down into its elements; the position of the body, limbs, articulations is defined; to each movement are assigned a direction, an aptitude, a duration; their order of succession is prescribed. Time penetrates the body and with it all the meticulous controls of power.[12]

The new discipline of time affected not only the industrial workforce, but touched the entire population. As Marx's analyses consistently stress, the buying and selling of time is at the heart of the capitalist social order. Labour time is all the worker has to sell, while profit depends upon appropriation of the surplus time of others (whether directly through the employment of wage labour or indirectly by utilizing the stored time of technology). Underlying these distinctive socio-economic relations is the abstraction of time into a general system of exchange whose key equation is undoubtedly 'time = money'. Construing time as an abstract measure involves the suppression of specific temporal differences in favour of the general equivalence of all periods of time: a flattening of time which Heidegger characterized as the

9 It is not surprising to learn that many of the early machines in the cotton and wool manufacturing industries were built by clock and watchmakers. The mechanism of the movie camera would come from similar quarters.

10 Taylor's 'time and motion' studies were predicated on analysis, planning and homogenization of working practices as the pathway to efficiency: 'Scientific management requires first, a careful investigation of each of the many modifications of the same implement, developed under rule of thumb; and second, after time and motion study has been made of the speed attainable with each of these implements, that the good points of several of them shall be unified in a single standard implementation, which will enable the workman to work faster and with greater ease than he could before. This one implement, then, is adopted as standard in place of the many different kinds before in use and it remains standard for all workmen to use until superseded by an implement which has been shown, through motion and time study, to be still better.' F. Taylor, *Scientific Management* (1911), New York, Harper and Row, 1964, p. 119.

11 This logic is continued in the current global division of labour in which labour intensive forms of production which have largely disappeared in 'developed' countries resurface in the low wage 'off-shore' production sites favoured by multinational capital.

12 Foucault, *Discipline and Punish*, p. 152.

quintessential modern experience of temporality.[13] In his influential analysis, Guy Debord argued:

> The time of production, commodity time, is an infinite accumulation of equivalent intervals. It is the abstraction of irreversible time, all of whose segments must prove on the chronometer their merely qualitative equality.[14]

Under pressure of commodity production, the lived time of everyday life slid inexorably towards that 'Absolute, True and Mathematical Time' that Newton declared to be the measure of the universe. Newton's concept of time profoundly influenced the course of the Industrial Revolution by grounding the transformation of physics, and thereby enabling the development of new productive machines dependent upon precise calculations of mechanics, new techniques for harnessing energy, controlling force, and manipulating the mass of inert objects. What proved equally decisive to the groundswell of modernity was the manner in which Newtonian physics legitimated the extension of mathematical time into virtually every sphere of existence. John Berger offers a graphic image of this epochal shift: 'The factory which works all night is a sign of the victory of a ceaseless, uniform and remorseless time. The factory continues even in the time of dreams.'[15] The political battles of modernity are continually fought at the border between this new order of industrial time and other, older temporal rhythms.[16]

The emergence of uniform social time, mirroring the theoretical time of Newtonian physics, was critically linked to struggles over new modes of transportation, especially the railway. Rail companies in England pioneered the introduction of uniform national time in the 1840s to facilitate their growing networks, thereby displacing the taxonomic table of the classical era with the timetable of the industrial era.[17] By 1855, most English clocks kept time based on the great clocks of the Greenwich Observatory (themselves established in the seventeenth century as an aid to sea navigation

13 Positing a direct relation between capitalist social relations of time and Heidegger's analysis is problematic. Like Derrida, Heidegger argues that a particular 'interpretation' of time has in fact dominated the entire history of Western thought. Any evaluation of this position is fraught with difficultly, inasmuch as it can never be one question among others: time is immediately involved with the determination of 'history', 'the West', as well as 'thought' itself. Here it is necessary to no more than sketch out the proposition that the linearization of time integral to industrial capitalism in many respects conforms to a longer historical trajectory, but does not simply continue this trajectory. In fact, the new vehicles and communication technologies on which capitalism depends help to bring the model of continuous, linear time into crisis.

14 G. Debord, *Society of the Spectacle*, Detroit, Black and Red, 1977, paragraph 147.

15 Berger and Mohr, *Another Way of Telling*, p. 106.

16 It is from this perspective that recurrent narratives bemoaning the 'laziness' of the domestic working classes, or colonial accounts of the 'unreliability' of the 'natives' need to be heard: as symptoms of the struggles over the social relations of time.

17 Foucault has emphasized the importance of this transition to the emergence of modern disciplinary power, arguing that the timetable is a vital organizational tool for establishing the rhythms and regulating the repetitive cycles of industrial production. See Foucault, *Discipline and Punish*, p. 149.

underpinning the emergence of Britain as a colonial power). When Greenwich time became law in England in 1880, the victory of the town hall clock over the tolling church bell was almost complete. In 1884 the Prime Meridian Conference in Washington formally adopted Greenwich Mean Time (GMT) as Universal Time for the entire world.[18] The same conference also decided the exact length of the day, divided the world into 24 time zones one hour apart and installed Greenwich as zero meridian of longitude. In these determinations was consecrated the new spatio-temporal order of capitalism as a global economy predicated upon incessant movement and ever-increasing speed.[19]

*

This new world order of accelerated social processes and 'everlasting uncertainty and agitation' (Marx) demanded a radically different relation to the past. In the rush towards the industrial future, much was destroyed, declared redundant, or simply left behind. History became indispensable, not only as a measure of progress, but as a safety net; a means of assuaging fears that what Benjamin called the storm of progress might represent time out of control.

The concept of progress has always been linked to what might be termed the *militarization* of time. Not only is modern military hardware dependent on the hyper-accurate measurement of time, but military-led technological developments have effectively shaped modern industrial production. (This includes both production *for* military consumption – war as accelerated technological development – and production according to the logistics of military organization and strategic planning. It is no accident that Lenin recognized military training as a base from which to build an industrial work force in the Soviet Union.) In this respect, the militarization of time is the key aspect of modern political economy: to reverse von Clausewitz, it pertains to a society which has taken on the form of a perpetual war machine.

As a consequence, the social importance of quantifying time has dramatically increased. Technical means for measuring time have become more and more accurate, first to the hour, then the minute, then the second, the millisecond and so on. In the process, they have generated other machines dependent on the possibility of precise temporal co-ordination. Today, sophisticated time-based machines not only saturate contemporary modes of production – including the production of signs, images and information – but condition the entire social framework. However, this critical nexus between

18 Uniform time was adopted in the United States on 18 November 1883, the so-called 'day of two noons'. See Kern, *Culture of Time and Space*, p. 12.

19 In 1912, the International Conference on Time in Paris devised a method for maintaining accurate time signals and transmitting them around the world. France resisted the imposition of GMT and continued to refer to it as 'Paris Mean Time retarded by 9 minutes 21 seconds' until 1978. The French eventually gained revenge for the 'indignity' of GMT: currently, Universal Time is based on the mean of 24 atomic clocks co-ordinated from Paris.

technology and social practice harbours an instability which threatens to overwhelm its domain from within.

The militarization of time which orchestrated the long march of progress has entered a period of crisis. There may be a logical continuity between John Harrison's prize-winning clock of 1765, with its accuracy to within one second a day, and contemporary atomic clocks such as the caesium NBS-6, considered accurate to one second in 300,000 years. But one should not ignore the transgressions of logic this progress also brings. Where Harrison's clock enabled a great leap forward in sea navigation in the eighteenth century, hyper-accurate atomic timing mechanisms allow the delivery of nuclear missiles across continents in the twentieth. Atomic physicists operating in terms of picoseconds (trillionths of a second) and femtoseconds (thousandths of a picosecond) actively undermine the temporal order on which they draw for their authority. Consider (if you can!) that there are more femtoseconds in one second than there were seconds in the past 31 million years and you begin to grasp the inflation of the sign system, the absolute vertigo of the inflationary spiral which grips contemporary physics.

Such inflation has broad repercussions. The much-countenanced legitimation crisis precipitated by the perceived failure of the 'grand narratives' is not only a crisis of reference – where to find the real? – but also of dimension: the continual haemorrhaging of orders of magnitude, the blurring of micro and macro, the telescoping of near and far. If the linear time of progress has always produced a certain problem of memory, the current acceleration and atomization of time has today emptied progress of much of its previous authority. In a world where strategies of production and opportunities for consumption are mounted on a stage of potential ecological collapse, overlayed by the obscenity of mass malnourishment while a privileged minority suffer eating disorders of a different kind, the promise of the future has been rendered hollow. History is indispensable as a measure of progress. But, in the crumbling of faith in the future, remembering can also become terrifying and catastrophic.

3

The Crisis of Memory

People robbed of their past seem to make the most fervent picture takers, at home and abroad.

Susan Sontag

While nineteenth-century Europe is often represented in terms of great self-confidence – confidence in the future forming the fundamental pillar supporting the ideology of progress – the scope and rapidity of change in this period also produced an immense disjunction in social and cultural reproduction. If, as John Berger suggests, the French Revolution marked the point at which the past seemed to crack wide open, negating the claims of tradition with the promise of radical change, subsequent political and economic developments only accentuated this rift. The sense of the eternal which had previously bounded the course of earthly life was deeply questioned by the immense cultural transformations, from revolutionary struggles to projects of colonial expansion, which swept the world in the nineteenth century. Both the hopes and the uncertainty of this period reflect a new consciousness of time: the desire to leave the past behind in order to create the present competed with the sensation that time was running too fast, or was in some way out of synch with itself.[1]

The sense of disjunction was heightened by the fact that the new political order was still in the process of inventing itself. The search for myths of origin to consolidate the hegemony of manufacturers and industrialists over the proletariat moved in concert with the first appearances of what Adorno and Horkheimer would later call 'the culture industry'. Mass newspapers, new experiences of sport, novel forms of entertainment and shopping (the first department stores), and new rituals of national celebration reshaped the social and political terrain. Much of what we now take to be the essence of tradition (such as the pomp of the English monarchy) was born at this time,

---

1 Marx's contention that 'the social revolution of the nineteenth century cannot draw its poetry from the past, but only from the future', and Nietzsche's advocacy of the 'strength' to 'bring the past to the bar of judgement, interrogate it remorselessly, and finally condemn it', both stand as indexes of the emergence of a distinctive modern temporality. Increasing awareness of the limits of these revolutionary demands to break absolutely with the past, which were taken up so forcefully by the political and artistic avant-garde in the first decades of this century, marks an important fault line between modernism and postmodernism. See K. Marx, *The Eighteenth Brumaire of Louis Bonaparte* (1852), New York, International Publishers, 1963, p. 18; F. Nietzsche, 'The use and abuse of history' (1874), in O. Levy (ed.), *The Complete Works of Friedrich Nietzsche* (trans. A. Collins) New York, Gordon Press, 1974, vol. 5, part II, p. 28.

either as the renovation of shabby old ceremonies, or the wholesale creation of new ones. What Hobsbawm aptly termed 'invented traditions' began to assume decisive importance in securing individual lives to the demands of the state.[2]

Heightened awareness of public time provided new opportunities for the integration of individual subjects into the nascent capitalist order. E.P. Thompson has described the popularity of 'watch clubs', which enabled workers to purchase their own pocket watches with a series of subscriptions.[3] Here one can discern the extension of Cartesian mechanism, which imaged the entire universe as a great clock, into the crevices of daily life. But, more than this specific symptom, the new consciousness of time was reflected in a profound change in the way the past was remembered. Collective memories depend largely on the daily practices and micro-practices that people live. Throughout the nineteenth century, the displacement of the cyclical time of the country with the accelerated social rhythms of the city corroded traditional mechanisms of social reproduction, as the nexus between practices of memory and their webs of significance was systematically severed on a scale and at a speed never before experienced.

The most crucial change was the declining importance of the oral tradition. The oral transmission of history depended upon an intricate network of working and living spaces to bring together what Benjamin called 'the community of listeners' – those who heard the story and themselves became the text of history as they retold it in the future.[4] Factories which were too noisy to talk in, and working days and work cycles which were so long that they severely diminished common leisure time, interrupted the chain of storytelling. Increasingly, the story's function as a memory-text was transferred to the newspaper, the novel and the film.

Benjamin discussed the decline of the story and the rise of the novel in terms of a new subjectivity: 'The birthplace of the novel is the solitary individual . . . To write a novel is to carry the incommensurable to extremes in the representation of human life.'[5] But rather than bemoan this shift as 'a modern symptom of decay', he argued that it was 'only a concomitant symptom of the secular productive forces of history, a concomitant that has quite gradually removed narrative from the realm of living speech and at the same time is making it possible to see a new beauty in what is vanishing'.[6] In the process of 'removing narrative from the realm of living speech', the

---

2 See E. Hobsbawm and T. Ranger (eds.), *The Invention of Tradition*, Cambridge, Cambridge University Press, 1983.

3 See E.P. Thompson, 'Time, work discipline and industrial capitalism', *Past and Present*, 38 (1967), pp. 56–97.

4 Benjamin, 'The storyteller', in *Illuminations*, p. 87

5 Benjamin, 'The storyteller', p. 87.

6 Benjamin, 'The storyteller', p. 87. Benjamin was perhaps more ambivalent towards this loss than this statement indicates. But his concern for history was far removed from the nostalgic logic of 'preservation' which is the correlate of progress.

past came to signify a new sense of remoteness, in which tradition was less the repository of the familiar than the out of date.

The oral tradition did not completely disappear. But it could no longer carry the burden of cultural reproduction in a context in which every element of the social habitus, from work practices to modes of transport to property rights to the calendar of festivals, holidays and celebrations – all of which had housed distinct forms of memory and identity – were themselves fundamentally shifting. In this wholesale displacement of traditional sites and techniques of remembering was inaugurated the problem which remains endemic to modernity: the constant threat to memory carried by a social form predicated on the continual revolution of its social relations of production. The triumph of capitalism produces a crisis of memory which could only be alleviated by placing relations to the past on an entirely different footing.

What might be called 'modern history' is born with this new sense of the anachronism of the past. As Terdiman points out, once time became disjointed, knowledge had to be redeployed.[7] In the nineteenth century, the past began to be conceived in terms of its inexorable dislocation from the present, and the present began to be defined through the prism of a discipline capable of focusing the past. This is not to suggest that previous cultures had simply ignored history. But, as Lyotard has noted, a community characterized by an oral narrative tradition does not remember in the same way.

> It finds the raw material for its social bond not only in the meaning of the narratives it recounts, but also in the act of reciting them. The narrative's reference may seem to belong to the past, but in reality it is always contemporaneous with the act of recitation.[8]

In contrast to oral tradition, the industrial culture of the nineteenth century generated memory machines of a different order: theories which investigated history and disinterred it as a mortician might slice open a cadaver. A profusion of academic disciplines and official institutions which brooded on the past were geared up at this time. Exemplary was the work of Leopold von Ranke, who sought to constitute history as a distinct field of knowledge by removing it from its previous abode in between literature and philosophy. Ranke's formalization of the protocols for constructing a more 'scientific' history, particularly his emphasis on the distinction between 'primary' and 'secondary' sources and his preference for the former over the latter, situate the inception of modern history in terms of a new desire: 'It wants only to

---

7 Terdiman writes: 'As the transparency characterizing areas of social existence not previously experienced as problematical is lost, the effort to master such areas in their transformed state attempts . . . to reproduce a dying innocence through the concerted mobilization of knowledge.' *Discourse/Counter-Discourse: The Theory and Practice of Symbolic Resistance in Nineteenth Century France*, Ithaca, NY, Cornell University Press, 1985, p. 97.

8 J.-F. Lyotard, *The Postmodern Condition* (trans. G. Bennington and B. Massumi), Manchester, Manchester University Press, 1984, p. 22.

show what actually happened.'[9] This shift towards the constitution of history as an 'objective science' was not monolithic – major nineteenth-century historians such as McCauley and Carlyle resisted this model – but the principle came to dominate the field of historical understanding.

If this new historical consciousness corresponded to a burgeoning interest in the document and the archive, it was part of a broader shift. Foucault suggests:

> . . . at the beginning of the nineteenth century, in the great upheaval that occurred in the Western *episteme*: it was discovered that there existed a historicity proper to nature . . . moreover, it became possible to show that activities as peculiarly human as labour or language contained within themselves a historicity that could not be placed within the great narrative common to things and men: production had its modes of development, capital its modes of accumulation, prices their laws of fluctuation and change . . .[10]

The 'discovery' of history and the positing of ceaseless change as the natural law of existence marked the point at which knowledge was translated into the temporal economy of industrial culture. This modification was not so much a progress in thought as the thought of progress extending itself in all directions to measure diverse phenomena against the line of time. Toulmin and Goodfield have suggested: 'Whether we consider geology, zoology, political philosophy, or the study of ancient civilizations, the nineteenth century was in every sense the Century of History – a period marked by the growth of a new, dynamic world-picture.'[11]

*

Significantly, this period also witnessed the rise of the great public museums.[12] As an institution designed to collect, catalogue and exhibit the past in order to render it exhaustively visible, the museum plays a key role in the ideology of progress. In the final analysis, the legitimacy of progress rests on the belief that the present constitutes the pinnacle of history. The satisfaction of the present with itself depends partly on the constant creation of the new in the form of intellectual and technological 'advances'. But, as well as coming first, the present must also be figured as last. Faith in progress demands that the present be capable of gathering the past to itself, according to the model of endless accumulation developed in Hegel's

---

9 L. Ranke, from the preface to *Histories of the Latin and Germanic Nations 1494–1514*, reprinted in F. Stern (ed.), *The Varieties of History: From Voltaire to the Present*, New York, Vintage Books, 1973, p. 57.

10 Foucault, *Order of Things*, pp. 367–8.

11 S. Toulmin and J. Goodfield, *The Discovery of Time*, Harmondsworth, Penguin, 1967, p. 232.

12 While private collections belonging to Royalty and the wealthy nobility had existed for centuries, the nineteenth century saw the formalization of the museum as a public institution. Led by France and Britain, all major European cities opened public museums in this period. Many other countries followed these models, which is not surprising as the museums were often established by colonial powers (for example, in Cairo).

influential philosophy of history. Hegelian Spirit finds its self-realization in world history: 'Nothing in the past is lost for it, for the idea is ever present; Spirit is immortal, with it there is no past, no future, but an essential *now*.'[13] The ramifications of Hegelian thought as a conceptual matrix are still being unwound.[14] As Derrida has pointed out, the Hegelian dialectic, in which everything is 'conserved' by being transformed to a higher state, constitutes '*the* concept of history and teleology': the past is maintained precisely by being surpassed.[15] (Lyotard has suggested another affiliation to this double movement of negation and preservation: 'This description of the dialectic of spirit by Hegel is also that of the capitalist's getting richer and richer by Adam Smith.')[16]

The Hegelian prohibition against historical loss saturates the logic of the museum. The possibility of loss – whether loss of knowledge, of species, of culture, of the past in general – remains anathema to the ideology of progress. It raises the spectre that things are not getting 'better and better', but are changing in a less predictable and more complex fashion. Here it is unnecessary to decide whether or not history is 'really' a process without a destiny – no religious or technological Utopia, no single path to certain enlightenment, no Party, no unified end or final meaning – it is enough to observe that this is what has always been strenuously denied and systematically disavowed *in the name of progress*.

While the museum undoubtedly functions to 'preserve' history, it does so in a particular way. The great public museums of the West were born in an era of rapid colonial expansion, and have been indelibly shaped by the political and ideological affiliations of colonialism. Jean Fisher argues: 'Museums cannot present what is illegible to dominant culture; they can only appropriate cultural difference to the imaginary sign of white history and exoticism.'[17] Metropolitan museums filled with cultural 'artefacts' formalized the modern sensibility which values objects not so much for their beauty (the criteria of the art gallery), but simply because they have survived. Awe in the face of survival, coupled to a fetishization of 'authenticity', governs the museum's disposition in this age of disappearances. Objects in the museum often seem to have fallen out of time, even if they are in fact recent or contemporary. Discussing the expropriation of Native American culture, Fisher adds:

13 G.W.F. Hegel, *The Philosophy of History* (trans. J. Sibree), New York, Dover, 1956, p. 79.

14 Fukuyama's recent controversial success, which merely shifted the realization of Hegel's Liberal state from 1808 to 1989, is the latest instalment in a long line. See *The End of History and the Last Man*, New York, Free Press, Toronto, Maxwell Macmillan Canada and New York, Maxwell Macmillan International, 1992.

15 See Derrida, *Of Grammatology*, p. 25.

16 J.-F. Lyotard, 'Adrift', *Driftworks* (trans. R. McKeon), New York, Semiotext(e), 1984, p. 12.

17 J. Fisher, 'The health of the people is the highest law', *Third Text*, 2 (Winter 1987/88), p. 73.

The museum or privately-owned Indian artefact bears witness to history, it is true, but it is not the history of the Indian. It testifies to the history of white conquest: to the disempowerment of native peoples, to the discrediting of their values as 'primitive', and to the theft of their cultural heritage. Above all, official emphasis on historical arts throws a veil over Native Americans as *contemporary* peoples . . .[18]

Despite the best (or worst) intentions, investment in the 'historical fragment' excavated and relocated in the museum's belly has always tended to guillotine the past, producing a disjunctive temporality in which 'primitive' peoples are excised from the present.[19] 'Museifying' indigenous cultures provides an effective means of symbolically and politically relocating them from the realm of the living to that of the dead: denied contemporaneity, they are converted into a totem feast whose consumption has engendered a sense of power vital to the identity of the modern West.[20] The great museums incubate the dream of swallowing whole those 'archaic' cultures which are unable to keep up with the present, and of preserving them for eternity in the metropolitan heartlands: London, Paris, Berlin, New York.

*

It is no accident that photography develops first and fastest in precisely these centres. The camera is dependent on industrial culture, not only to produce its technical apparatus, but also, and perhaps more importantly, to produce its social conditions of existence. The camera corresponded perfectly to the demands of a society which found itself in the flux of rapid industrial transformation. It offered a talisman for memory in an era in which the past was under threat and time itself seemed to be accelerating.

It is in the context of a looming memory crisis that the immediate enthusiasm which surrounded the camera can be understood. Photography was seized, often quite consciously, as a technology capable of filling an emerging void. With its speed, relative low cost, infinite reproducibility, and aura of neutrality, the photograph seemed to answer the problem the past was threatening to become. In his inaugural Presidential address to the Photographic Society of London in 1855, Sir Frederick Pollock eulogized the camera as history's saviour:

The varied objects to which Photography can address itself, its power of rendering permanent that which appears to be as fleeting as the shadows that go across the

18 Fisher, 'Health of the people', p. 73. Such a standpoint situates the political ambivalence of Western nostalgia for 'authentic' oral traditions located in countries and cultures outside the West.

19 Museums are often patronized by the very corporations ('Esso Presents Civilization' was a major exhibition at the State Museum of Victoria in 1990) which continue to marginalize indigenous peoples in the present.

20 In this respect, the shift of Australian Aboriginal cultural production from artefact to art and from museum basement to art gallery in the 1980s was significant. While it didn't resolve all the problems of exhibition and appropriation, it did challenge the polarity between 'modern' and 'traditional' in Western thought.

dial, the power that it possesses of giving fixedness to instantaneous objects, are for purposes of history . . . a matter of the deepest importance. It is not too much to say that no individual – not merely individual man, but no individual substance, no individual matter, nothing that is extraordinary in art, that is celebrated in architecture, that is calculated to excite the admiration of those who behold it, need now perish, but may be rendered immortal by the assistance of Photography.[21]

As early as 1874, prosperous Londoners could subscribe to a Society for Photographing the Relics of Old London. In 1897, Sir Benjamin Stone, a rich British industrialist and Conservative MP, founded the National Photographic Record Association with the aim of documenting dying rural ceremonies and traditional festivals in England. Stone contended: 'Every village has a history which might be preserved by the means of the camera.'[22] Similar projects were undertaken almost everywhere that the growth of capitalism collided with local traditions and regional ways of life. As colonization expanded rapidly towards the end of the nineteenth century, extending a pseudo-Darwinian banner of racial hierarchy to new frontiers, the 'primitive' world and its inhabitants were declared to be dying out. At one level, this chilling prophecy, which became a recurrent theme of anthropology, reflected the catastrophic impact of disease, slaughter and dispossession. But it also served to mask cultural genocide as historical destiny. The camera assumed a prominent role in the funeral ritual, exemplified by Woolley's famous images of Truganini, which were misleadingly labelled, 'The Last of Her Race'.[23] The photographing of Native American Indians by the army of travellers who streamed West following the opening of the railroad in 1869 was only a foretaste of other photographic invasions to come.[24] All over the world anthropologists, ethnographers and tourists set out to 'document' the 'primitive' past before it disappeared.

What the camera established for the first time was a means of producing an archive on a scale and rhythm in accord with the demands of capitalism. Capitalism needed the camera as a means of negotiating the social disjunction produced by its convulsive expansion. Foucault's comments on the role of continuous history are suggestive in this regard:

Continuous history is the indispensable correlative of the founding function of the subject: the guarantee that everything that has eluded him may be restored to him; the certainty that time will disperse nothing without restoring it in a reconstituted unity; the promise that one day the subject – in the form of historical conscious-

---

21 Quoted in Hawarth-Booth, *Golden Age of British Photography*, p. 9.

22 Quoted in Sontag, *On Photography*, p. 56. A two-volume set, *Sir Benjamin Stone's Pictures: Records of National Life and History*, was published in 1905.

23 This labelling assumes keen political overtones, not least in the present struggle for Aboriginal land rights in Australia. Positioning Truganini as 'the last of her race' obviates the necessity to recognize land rights in the state of Tasmania.

24 Such images played an important propagandistic role. Dipple suggests these photographers 'recorded a picturesque yesterday, serving as memorabilia of the once noble, vanishing Indian; and they recorded a hopeful, if less colourful present, serving as propagandists for assimilation'. 'Representing the other: the Native American Indian', in Edwards, *Anthropology and Photography*, p. 136.

ness – will once again be able to appropriate, to bring back under his sway, all those things that are kept at a distance by difference, and find them in what might be called his abode.[25]

In the camera, the sovereign subject found an umbrella apparently capable of sheltering the philosophy of consciousness in a time zone increasingly alien to it. In sympathy with the museum and its investment in the historical object, the camera offered symbolic objects, signs which rendered 'the past' freely available for possession and circulation; simultaneously monuments to the triumph of progress and placebos for anxiety felt in face of the loss that progress inevitably brings. In offering the image of a stable and unchanging record in an era of increasing instability and rapid social change, Bann argues that: 'photography and subsequently cinematography . . . might be seen as the Utopia to which nineteenth century historical representation is valiantly striving.'[26]

Modern identity is tethered to time in a distinct way. The Western differentiation of other cultures through a network of temporal hierarchies ('backward', 'primitive', 'archaic') has been paralleled by the re-evaluation of its own past as a sign of difference: the difference over time of modern culture from itself. In the memory banks generated by the proliferation of cameras and the stockpiling of images, the era of progress finds one of its principal measures. But as much as the camera has mapped the transformation of the social and physical environment, it has helped to transform our conceptions of history and memory. Can we imagine a mode of record more exact than that provided by the camera? Perhaps not. But what if, as Kafka once suggested, we photograph not in order to remember, but in order to forget?

25 M. Foucault, *The Archaeology of Knowledge* (trans. A.M. Sheridan Smith), London, Tavistock, 1972, p. 12.

26 S. Bann, 'The sense of the past: image, text and object in the formation of historical consciousness in nineteenth century Britain', in Veeser, *New Historicism*, p. 111.

4

Amnesic Cultures

People once remembered more readily: an assumption, a half-truth at best.

Christa Wolf

In one of his lectures, Borges recalled the poet John Milton whose sight was destroyed writing pamphlets supporting the execution of King Charles I. Milton composed most of his poetry, including the monumental *Paradise Lost*, following the onset of his blindness, conjugating up to 40 or 50 hendecasyllables of verse in his head, which he would later dictate to whoever came to visit.[1] Such a prodigious feat of memory seems startling, perhaps even more so in an age in which hypomnemonics – photography, phonography, film, video and audio recordings, as well as the computerization of traditional writing – seem to have obviated the need for such proficiency.

Yet, despite the profusion of technologies which have vastly expanded the capacity to record events and to construct archives, both personal and collective memory have entered a period of extreme uncertainty in the present. Since the 1960s, debates concerning history and memory have been increasingly linked to the role of visual and audio-visual media in figuring a usable past as an integral part of a dominant ideological matrix. If the Left has contributed most to this discourse, it is noticeable that its concern about the 'falsification' of history has increasingly been shared by the Right. Orwell's *Nineteen Eighty-Four* has become a tutor text for diverse political tendencies, suggesting that the current transformation of the social terrain of memory cannot be easily contained within the traditional divisions of the political spectrum.

What has increasingly made itself felt is the discrepancy between the immense growth in devices and institutions designed to collect and preserve the past and what seems to be a shrinking of historical consciousness in the present. Interviewed in the 1970s, Foucault suggested:

There's a real fight going on. Over what? Over what we can roughly describe as *popular memory*. It's an actual fact that people – I'm talking about those who are barred from writing, from producing their books themselves, from drawing up their own historical accounts – that these people nevertheless do have a way of recording history, or remembering it, of keeping it fresh and of using it . . . Now, a whole number of apparatuses have been set up ('popular literature', cheap books and the stuff that's taught in school as well) to obstruct the flow of this popular

---

1 J.-L. Borges, *Seven Nights* (trans. E. Weinberger), New York, New Directions, 1984, pp. 116–17.

memory . . . Today, cheap books aren't enough. There are much more effective means like television and the cinema. And I believe this was one way of *re-programming* popular memory, which existed but had no way of expressing itself. So people are shown not what they were, but what they must remember having been.[2]

These sentiments have been widely shared. In *On Photography*, Sontag grants the camera a pivotal role in the contemporary rewriting of history. By removing a discrete moment from the temporal continuum and 'conferring on the event a kind of immortality it would never otherwise have enjoyed', Sontag suggests that photographs constitute, at best, an unreliable or false support for memory.[3] At worst, she finds photography is not a memory aid at all, but a mechanism of a different and more threatening order: 'not so much an instrument of memory as an invention of it or a replacement'.[4] Roland Barthes was another who agreed that the photograph is not only *never* a memory 'but it actually blocks memory, quickly becomes a counter-memory'.[5] He arrives at this point of view under pressure of a photographic excess which he suggests remains alien to the process of remembering: 'The photograph is violent: not because it shows violent things, but because on each occasion it fills the sight by force, and because nothing in it can be refused . . .'[6] Barthes provides numerous examples of photographic compulsion, but none more striking than the following:

> One day I received from the photographer a picture of myself which I could not remember being taken, for all my efforts; I inspected the tie, the sweater, to discover in what circumstances I had worn them; to no avail. And yet, *because it was a photograph*, I could not deny that I had been *there* (even if I did not know *where*).[7]

For Barthes, like Sontag, part of the problem is that, by conferring exemplary authority on the recorded moment, the camera enables this instant to dominate all others. The fragment aggrandizes itself; the part swallows the whole. But Barthes also shifts his analysis to another level:

> [B]y making the (mortal) photograph into the general and somehow natural witness of 'what has been', modern society has renounced the Monument. A paradox: the same century invented History and Photography. But History is a memory fabricated according to positive formulas, a pure intellectual discourse

---

2 'Michel Foucault: interview', *Edinburgh '77 Magazine*, 2 (1977), p. 22. Foucault's appeal to authentic experience – the difference between what people 'were' and what 'they must remember having been' – runs against the grain of much of his other writing. In the context of debates over the representation of French resistance to Nazism, he frames the issue primarily as one of *control* over the apparatus. One suspects he would never have tolerated this idealization of *content* with regard to language.

3 Sontag, *On Photography*, p. 11.

4 Sontag, *On Photography*, p. 165. This position resembles her ambivalence to photorealism, restating the same unacknowledged paradox in which, on the one hand, photography *fails* to represent truly, while, on the other, it succeeds too well and so threatens to replace what it should only re-present.

5 Barthes, *Camera Lucida*, p. 91.

6 Barthes, *Camera Lucida*, p. 91.

7 Barthes, *Camera Lucida*, p. 85

which abolishes mythic Time; and the Photograph is a certain but fugitive testimony; so that everything, today, prepares our race for this impotence: to be no longer able to conceive duration, affectively or symbolically.[8]

Here Barthes touches another pressing concern: fear that the culture of the camera is antagonistic to the rhythm of History. While the photograph is often criticized because of its excessive fixity, images – particularly on television – can also move too fast. A 1985 editorial in the *New Yorker* concluded:

The new communications media may be giving rise to a new ignorance . . . You cannot look back up the page of a television broadcast to check what you have just seen, or down the page to see how it might relate to what follows. The pictures flicker on the screen and are gone for ever.[9]

In a similar vein, Fredric Jameson has suggested:

One is tempted to say that the very function of the news media is to relegate . . . recent historical experiences as rapidly as possible into the past. The informational function of the media would thus be able to help us forget, to serve as the very agents and mechanisms for our historical amnesia.[10]

Elsewhere, Jameson expands this judgement to assert that 'memory seems to play no role in television, commercial or otherwise (or, I am tempted to say, postmodernism generally).'[11] These perspectives could be multiplied almost at will. From Guy Debord, who declared the spectacle to be 'the paralysis of history and memory' and the imposition of a 'false consciousness of time', to Baudrillard's vision of technological apocalypse ('TV, the veritable final solution to the historicity of every event'), history seems destined to become what Virilio terms 'the lost dimension'.[12]

The photographic image which offers to show how things were has today been overtaken by television images which unite programming from the Olympic Games to the Gulf War with the slogan *watch history being made*. Instead of referring to a determinate past, television locates viewers in a mythic present in which history constantly 'happens' right before their eyes. Virilio suggests: 'Chronological and historical time, which passes, is thus succeeded by a time that instantaneously exposes itself.'[13] In television's perceptual logistics, the time for judgement seems to vanish. Does this imply the failure of the historical project? Not only the dispersion of its unities, the

8 Barthes, *Camera Lucida*, p. 93.

9 *New Yorker*, 15 April 1985. Of course, this ignores the impact of video recorders and the growth of video libraries which facilitate such 'checking'. However, it is the automatic recourse to the book as the proper standard of historical representation which interests me here.

10 F. Jameson, 'Postmodernism and consumer society', in Foster, *Postmodern Culture*, p. 125.

11 F. Jameson, 'Reading without interpretation: postmodernism and the video text', in N. Fabb et al. (eds), *The Linguistics of Writing: Arguments Between Language and Literature*, New York, Methuen, 1987, p. 202.

12 Debord, *Society of the Spectacle*, para. 58; Baudrillard, *Evil Demon of Images*, p. 22; Virilio, *Lost Dimension*, pp. 101–19.

13 P. Virilio, 'The over-exposed city' (trans. A. Hustvedt), *Zone*, 1/2 (1986), p. 19.

dissolution of its regularities, the fragmentation of causes and effects, but an even more radical failure? Less the overwhelming of one culture by another (with all the forms of resistance, adaptation and hybridity that this involves), but the *overwhelming of time itself*?[14] Oscillating between excessive hypo-statization of the past and relentless erosion of the stability on which the very possibility of historical knowledge is thought to depend, camera technologies stand charged with ushering in a shadowy age in which collective memory gives way to generalized amnesia. This prospect is so far removed from the general enthusiasm which first greeted the camera that the passage from *then* to *now* is of profound interest.

But, before examining the relation between the camera and the archive in more detail, it is worth recalling another facet of the history of memory: what Derrida has called the 'implacable law that always opposes good (living) memory to bad memory (mechanical, technical, on the side of death) . . .'.[15] The spectre of the artificial support or technical prosthesis consuming and replacing the very faculty it was originally designed to supplement has long haunted the discourse around memory, at least since Plato's judgement on the invention of writing:

> The fact is that this invention will produce forgetfulness in the souls of those who have learned it because they will not need to exercise their memories, being able to rely on what is written, using the stimulus of external marks which are alien to themselves rather than, from within, their own unaided powers to call things to mind. So it's not a remedy for memory, but for reminding you have discovered.[16]

Derrida's reading of this Platonic warning is instructive. While contemporary perceptions of an emergent cultural amnesia should not be dismissed lightly, critical evaluation of this threat cannot proceed from a merely reactive base. It also needs to take into account the long history of splitting 'living' memory from a so-called artificial or technological memory. This seems even more important when the forms of 'artificial' memory such as the camera and the computer, and the modes of archivation they sustain, have so little in common with those of the past. Derrida argues that the enormity of the current technological transformation affects not only 'the quantitative economy of so-called artificial memory, but also its qualitative structure – and in doing so obliges us to rethink what relates this artificial memory to man's so-called psychical and interior memory, to truth, to the simulacrum and simulation of truth, etc.'[17] Refusing to rethink the status of 'Man' as the ground capable of regulating the network of relations between thought and technology, nature and artifice, interior and exterior, living and dead, risks conforming to an agenda of a different kind. Lamentations concerning the 'disappearance of history' so easily mask the mourning for

14 This will be taken up further in 'Telepresence and the government of time' below.

15 J. Derrida, *Memoires: For Paul De Man* (trans. C. Lindsay et al.), New York, Columbia University Press, 1986, p. 70.

16 Quoted in Derrida, *Dissemination*, p. 102.

17 Derrida, *Memoires*, pp. 107–8.

the disappearance of a particular kind of history: the dream of continuous history which comforted the Western subject with an image of its own sovereignty.

Displacing this ideal image involves less the complete abandonment of history than the interrogation of historical presumptions. A strategic point of departure is the manner in which the camera first lent itself to the totalizing model of history established under the sway of nineteenth-century positivism, while at the same time exceeding its limits and destabilizing its laws in provocative and unpredictable ways. All the precepts sedimented around the concept of objectivity – the concern for stable origins and ends, the demand for transparency in representation, the desire for a fixed centre enabling the totalization of knowledge – have been made newly contentious in the process. Neither pessimism based on nostalgia for the book, nor optimism based on unlimited faith in technological progress seem adequate to understanding the complexities of this transformation.

5

Eternity's Hostage: The Camera and the Archive

Shakespeare, Rembrandt, Beethoven will make films . . . all legends, all mythologies and all myths, all founders of religions and the very religions . . . await their exposed resurrection . . .

Abel Gance

There is no such thing as *documentary* – whether the term designates a category of material, a genre, an approach, or a set of techniques.

Trinh T. Minh-Ha

You put him on the six, ten *and* the twelve o'clock news, then he be real.

Medium Cool

Like the museum, the camera has often inspired delirious dreams of containing the history of the world in its entirety. A phantasm of the total archive stalks photographic history joining official public collections and commercial stockpiles to the more subterranean realms of private collections and personal albums. Allan Sekula has argued:

> Within bourgeois culture, the photographic project has itself from the very beginning been identified not only with the dream of a universal language but also with the establishment of global archives and repositories according to models offered by libraries, encyclopaedias, zoological and botanical gardens, museums, police files and banks.[1]

As images produced by the camera have become significant historical sources and resources, they have also transformed history's image, affecting the way in which historical evidence can be produced, mobilized and legitimated. Here I want to examine these modifications under three headings: the status of the eye-witness; the relation between the particular and the general in historical discourse; and the threshold of photographic simulation.

*

Hayden White once suggested:

> Historical events, whatever else they may be, are events which really happened or are believed to have really happened, but which are no longer directly accessible

1 Sekula, 'Reading an archive', in Wallis, *Blasted Allegories*, p. 118.

to perception. As such, in order to be constituted as objects for reflection, they must be described in some kind of natural or technical language. The analysis or explanation, whether nomological or narrativistic, that is subsequently provided of the events is always an analysis or explanation of the events as previously *described*.[2]

It is precisely by blurring all previous protocols for demarcating 'description' from 'direct perception' that the camera has most dramatically transformed the frame within which history is now constructed. To the extent that eye-witness accounts have been privileged in the writing of history, the multiplication and dispersion of eyes – photo-eyes, cine-eyes, video-eyes, as well as what Vertov termed the 'radio-ear' – has introduced a series of new variables into the equation. Barthes's assertion that 'photography's inimitable feature (its *noeme*) is that someone has seen the referent . . . *in flesh and blood* or again *in person*' succinctly locates the camera's intervention: it functions as a space–time machine capable of instantiating a potentially infinite chain of eye-witnesses.[3] By positioning each observer as eye-witness to events long gone, the camera seems to offer not mere re-presentations, but resurrections, not memories 'but reality in a past state: at once the past and real'.[4]

Yet, it is no accident that the question of context – perhaps *the* question of history – has become so contentious in the present: the relation between image, context, and meaning is the question incessantly posed by the industrialization of the camera.[5] While the accumulation of images into a visible archive carries the powerful, culturally embedded, assertion that 'this has been', simply establishing the existence of what is shown has never satisfied questions as to its significance. Sekula argues that archives constitute a '*territory of images*', adding, 'Not only are the pictures in archives often literally for sale, but their meanings are up for grabs.'[6] This situation creates both possibilities and risks. John Berger suggests: 'All photographs are possible contributions to history, and any photograph, under certain circumstances, can be used to break the monopoly which history today has over time.'[7] Photographs can interrupt dominant narratives by providing other views of historical experience. Or existing photographic archives may themselves be changed by being opened to new historical frames of reference.[8]

But equally photographs can function to naturalize dominant interpretations of history. Sekula argues: 'Clearly archives are not neutral; they embody the power inherent in accumulation, collection, and hoarding as

---

2 H. White, 'New historicism: a comment', in Veeser, *New Historicism*, p. 297.

3 Barthes, *Camera Lucida*, p. 79.

4 Barthes, *Camera Lucida*, p. 82.

5 See 'Promiscuous meanings' above.

6 'Reading an archive', in Wallis, *Blasted Allegories*, p. 116.

7 Berger and Mohr, *Another Way of Telling*, p. 109.

8 An excellent example is Malek Alloula's symptomatic reading of colonial postcards from Algeria, with the stated aim of returning them to their senders. See his *The Colonial Harem* (trans. M. and W. Godzich), Minneapolis, University of Minnesota Press, 1986.

well as that power inherent in the command of the lexicon and rules of a language.'[9] If the camera's evidence has never been self-evident, it can often be made to seem so, by the use of a caption, a text, a voice-over, or merely as a function of the design and layout, which selects from a penumbra of potential meanings to produce an authoritative interpretation. Naive faith in photo-realism provides what film maker Alexander Kluge termed 'a unique opportunity to concoct fables'.[10]

All simple assertions of the realism of the image betray the desire to naturalize the camera's function as eye-witness to history. But the dominant form of this naturalization has itself passed through several phases. The enthusiasm displayed by Arago and his colleagues in the nineteenth century for the total detachment and absolute transparency of the mechanical eye has been revealed as just that: enthusiasm. Taine's positivist dictum ('I want to reproduce the objects as they are, or as they would be even if I did not exist') has ceded ground to a growing awareness of the observer's irreducible implication in the scene observed.[11] Heisenberg's recognition that 'science does not simply describe and explain nature; it is part of the interplay between nature and ourselves: it describes nature as exposed to our method of questioning' stands as an influential point of reference for this shift.[12]

Yet the claims of objectivity have never been entirely negated, nor its attractions wholly surrendered. In the 1930s, John Grierson's famous definition of documentary film as the 'creative treatment of actuality' differentiated the raw image from the cooked text in order to elevate documentary over reporting and newsreel. In this way, Grierson relocated realism from the apparatus to the editor, from the isolated image to the textual system.[13] In the 1960s, influential *cinéma vérité* proponent Jean Rouch validated the camera's role as eye-witness as a kind of subjective objectivity:

> [Y]ou ask the audience to have confidence in the evidence, to say to the audience, 'This is what I saw. I didn't fake it, this is what happened . . . I look at what happened with my subjective eye and this is what I believe took place. . .' It's a question of honesty.[14]

These positions represent less the overturning of objectivity than an internal adjustment of its workings: faith in the machine is supplemented by trust in the integrity of its human masters (the camera operator who frames

---

9 Sekula, 'Reading an archive', in Wallis, *Blasted Allegories*, p. 118.

10 *Alexander Kluge: A Retrospective*, New York, Goethe Institutes of North America, 1988, p. 4.

11 Taine quoted in S. Kracauer, *Theory of Film: The Redemption of Physical Reality*, Oxford, Oxford University Press, 1960, p. 5.

12 See W. Heisenberg, *Physics and Philosophy*, London, Allen and Unwin, 1959, p. 75.

13 Grierson argued: 'Here we pass from the plain (or fancy) descriptions of natural material to arrangement, rearrangements and creative shapings of it.' Grierson, *Grierson on Documentary*, p. 36. Dziga Vertov's first 'Life caught unaware' films were similarly suspended between a positivist valorization of the image and a constructivist ethic of editing.

14 Quoted in G.R. Levin, *Documentary Explorations: Fifteen Interviews with Film-Makers*, New York, Doubleday, 1971, p. 135.

the image, the director or editor who selects and reassembles it, the organization such as the 'news team' which produces and narrates it). Shifting from 'this is what happened' to 'this is what *I* believe happened' is not insignificant – it paves the way for the rise of personality-based news services, for example – but it still leaves the old matrix of 'seeing is believing' largely in place. It acknowledges the partiality of the camera only to limit any disturbance this might cause to existing regimes of truth by offering to position the viewer as a *perfectly organized eye-witness*.[15]

Disputes over realism have consistently led to a series of dualistic positions concerning the treatment and presentation of the camera's evidence. One might point to Cartier-Bresson's well-known prohibition against cropping or retouching the photographic negative as the obverse of Grierson's faith in editorial organization. Yet, Cartier-Bresson's influential thesis of the 'decisive moment' ('I prowled the streets all day, feeling very strung up and ready to pounce, determined to "trap" life – to preserve life in the act of living. Above all, I craved to seize the whole essence, in the confines of one single photograph, of some situation that was in the process of unrolling itself before my eyes')[16] does not deny the camera's intervention. Instead, he aims to make the chosen moment 'representative' of the whole.

In contemporary documentary film circles, one finds many similar expressions of the desire to record with 'minimal impact'. But while current orthodoxy tends to reverse Grierson's more interventionist practice, it retains his aim of reaching 'actuality'. Mamber argues that *cinéma vérité* is at its best when '[t]he camera just watches, scarcely commenting upon what it sees', adding: 'The respect for the long take and the attempt to keep cutting at a minimum in most cinema verite films stems from combined desires to approximate the feeling of being an actual witness to the event and not to enforce a specific interpretation through editing upon the filmed material.'[17]

This desire 'to approximate the feeling of being an actual witness' raises a number of questions. It is not a matter of arguing that the techniques that Mamber describes are in themselves wrong. Rather that, once habitualized and hierarchized, stylistic preferences all too easily become alibis for avoiding other questions concerning the politics of representation and the production of realism. Why is 'real' time now thought to be more truthful than Grierson's 'narrative' time? Why are the untreated image, the long take and the wide angle privileged as signs of immediacy, as if treatment, montage and framing have not already taken place in conception and filming? What concept of truth and direct vision is being mobilized here? How is the unity of image and sound, face and voice, linked to notions of

---

15 This is the level at which most news organizations legitimate themselves in the present: not by claiming they are absolutely comprehensive, but that they show everything *worth* showing.

16 Quoted in Sontag, *On Photography*, p. 185.

17 Mamber, *Cinema Verite*, pp. 174 and 188.

'authenticity' and 'presence' in order to promote the self-evidence of the image? In whose interests do such alignments operate?

Trinh T. Minh-Ha argues that much contemporary documentary practice, drawing on 'progressive' anthropological conventions originally developed to contest an homogenizing ethnocentrism which rendered all others the same, has itself resulted in disciplinarian guidelines of 'cultural authenticity'. She contrasts the faith in representing so-called 'primitives' with 'straight' images which claim to 'let people speak for themselves' with the very different techniques often employed in representing metropolitan experience, and asks: are these different standards a sign of respect for the other, or are they a continuation of the master's discourse which defines the other as different, and cloaks the exercise of power in the name of respect?[18] The whole notion of 'giving voice', which informs so much documentary practice, is highly problematic in its appeal to the universal subjectivity of an anonymous eye-witness. Who gives? What is the gift? And who is given in this scene?

These questions of style relate to some of the great controversies of film history. Kuleshov's demand for a simple image without ambiguity, which could be placed in a montage sequence and 'read' like a Chinese character, is diametrically opposed to Bazin's advocacy of deep-focus and long takes as the means of allowing ambiguity to enter the field of representation.[19] However, this long-running argument must now be taken elsewhere. Bazin's demand that camera reality be established without 'trickery' – that objects or events juxtaposed in close-ups must be shown together in a single shot or else be rendered less believable – was partly levelled against Kuleshov's concept of 'creative geography'.[20] Doubtless, as viewers became more cinematically literate, Kuleshov's early experiments (such as cutting scenes of Moscow buildings together with shots of the White House in Washington DC) would have seemed less than convincing. But digital imaging has rendered Bazin's equation of realism with spatial unity as naive as he once thought Kuleshov's theory of montage. Films such as *Forrest Gump* (1994), or *Jurassic Park* (1993), in which *we see what we know doesn't exist*, indicate not only the extreme malleability of camera reality, but the vital need to reconsider the status of the eye-witness in the present. In 1985, film historian John O'Connor warned that future computer systems '. . . will allow a still picture (of some world leader, for example) to be manipulated and animated (with a computer synthesized voice) in such a way that he

18 See Trinh T. Minh-Ha, *Framer Framed*, New York and London, 1992, p. 124.

19 See *Kuleshov on Film*, pp. 62–3; Bazin, *What is Cinema?*, p. 36.

20 Discussing the film *Where No Vultures Fly*, Bazin writes: 'Up to this point everything has been shown in parallel montage and the somewhat naive attempt at suspense has seemed quite conventional. Then suddenly, to our horror, the director abandons his montage of separate shots that has kept the protagonists apart, and gives us instead parents, child and lioness all in the same full shot. This single frame in which trickery is out of the question gives immediate and retroactive authenticity to the very banal montage which has preceded it.' Bazin, *What is Cinema?*, p. 49. On 'creative geography', see 'Flickering in eclipses' above.

appears to make whatever public statement the technicians may put in his mouth'.[21] That future has now arrived.

*

Counterpointing these shifts in the status of the eye-witness are the effects of technological selection on the formation of the audio-visual archive. Because dreams of complete recording have always dogged the photographic imagination, it is constantly necessary to emphasize the practical finitude of the camera's reach. For instance, limitations of early cine-cameras meant that the first 'actuality' films were largely confined to the recording of pre-announced daytime events such as official ceremonies, sporting contests and military parades, for which the camera could remain static.[22] When researching this period – the phrase 'looking back on history' comes so readily to one's lips – it is likely that the visibility of these events will overshadow others that were unrecorded. In the case of still photography, it wasn't until the 1920s that new lenses and film stocks enabled the 'snapshot' photo-journalism with which we are so familiar today.[23] This not only brought a new range of events within reach of the camera, but changed the entire approach to photographic recording. Where early news pictures, such as Roger Fenton's Crimean War photographs, recorded the aftermath of events, the emblematic modernist desire was to photograph 'people involved in the process of everyday living' (as Paul Strand put it).[24] Dziga Vertov summed up the modern reportage ethic:

> I cannot, like some correspondents, write an article on events, on spectacles, on carnivals, several days after they have taken place. I do not demand that a cameraman be at a fire two hours before it breaks out. But I cannot permit that he goes to film a fire a week after the fire has gone out.[25]

Another threshold in this regard occurred around 1960, when lightweight cine-cameras and changes in sound-recording equipment gave the flexibility of filming in 'real' situations that we now take for granted. Richard Leacock, a camera operator on the landmark film *Primary* (1960) recalled: 'For the first time we were able to walk in and out of buildings, up and down stairs,

21 'Not the past as it really happened: an interview with John O'Connor', in T. O'Regan and B. Shoesmith (eds), *History on/and/in Film*, Perth, History and Film Association of Australia, 1987, p. 167.

22 P. Sorlin, *The Film in History: Restaging the Past*, Oxford, Basil Blackwell, 1980, p. 11.

23 The invention of the compact Ermanox and Leica cameras in 1924 and 1925 paved the way for pioneering photojournalism of those such as Erich Salomon, and Robert Capa and Henri Cartier-Bresson (who later helped to found the influential Magnum agency).

24 Quoted in C. Tompkins, 'Look to the things around you: profile of Paul Strand', *New Yorker*, 16 September 1974, p. 51.

25 'The writings of Dziga Vertov', *Film Culture*, 25 (Summer 1962), p. 58.

film in and out of taxi cabs, all over the place, and get synchronous sound.'[26]

The point is that these technical transformations are inseparable from transformations in the archive. Sorlin comments:

> Of Hitler's accession to power, the cinema shows us only the official version –
> Hitler in the Reichstag, the screaming crowd in the streets, the enthusiasm of the
> victors . . . after the *coup d'état* in Chile . . . [w]e know not only the official truth
> – elections, parliamentary debates, speeches, processions – but we also have
> filmed records of dozens of incidents unknown to the press – the occupation of
> land, the shopkeeper's strike, confrontations between workers and lorry drivers
> and arrests made by the army in September and October. . . . The history of
> the American involvement in the Vietnam War, the *coup d'état* in Chile, or the
> Portuguese revolution will be known through audio-visual records as much as
> written ones . . .[27]

One could easily multiply Sorlin's examples, particularly in light of the growing availability of domestic video equipment and highly portable, high-definition video cameras. If low-cost access to the means of production enables different groups to construct their own records at a local level, this may well assist the formation of less centralized archives. But 'democratization' of the means of representation is less a convincing answer to the problem of history than a reorientation of the historical problematic.

Pluralism of sources always seems an attractive solution to liberal demands to respect 'cultural diversity' – until one runs up against the hard edge of existing practices and their implication in established hierarchies of power and privilege. It can be readily acknowledged that wider availability of photography and video may help to 'fill in' gaps in the historical archive (along the lines in which amateur video, such as the footage of the Rodney King beating, is incorporated into network news where no professional footage is available). But universalizing discourses are deeply entrenched in Western epistemology. If seeing with 'different eyes' merely confirms television's role as the ubiquitous eye-witness reporting on a global culture to an anonymous audience, struggles over history will remain confined to struggles over equal screen time, as if television is a 'universal language' itself capable of transcending all political and cultural differences. Of course, systematic forgetting of the ideological and technological filters which operate to screen events, determining whether and in what form they enter memory, has always been integral to the camera's identity as eye-witness.

This is not to deny the pressing need to 'relativize' historical knowledge

26 *Primary* was a Time-Life-sponsored film dealing with the Kennedy–Humphrey contest
in the Wisconsin Democratic Primary election of 1960. Leacock quoted in Mamber, *Cinema
Verite*, p. 30.
27 Sorlin, *Film in History*, pp. 6–7. The recent release of additional material, including Eva
Braun's 'home movies' and Hans Feierabend's 1939 colour films of Hitler in Munich,
undermines Sorlin's specific example, but not the general trajectory he indicates.

(which Kracauer saw as 'the key problem of modern philosophy'),[28] but to question the language in which such an exchange might take place. Can a single discourse or medium in fact hope to encompass global multiplicity, and to unite these differences in and as 'history'? Lyotard discusses the problem of 'universal history' in terms of a 'litigation over the names of times, places, and persons, over the senses and referents attached to those names. . . . This litigation, though, has no tribunal before which it can be presented, argued, and decided. For this tribunal would already have to be "universal". . .'[29] *Decolonizing* history demands more than supplementing the record and filling in the empty spaces according to the existing structures of knowledge: as Jay Ruby puts it, 'the social and human sciences must themselves be decolonized.'[30] For this to be achieved, the subject of historical knowledge – which today includes the ready-made subjectivity of the viewer as eye-witness – must itself be put at risk.

*

In addition to radically disembodying the eye of the eye-witness, the invention of the camera took historical narrative across the threshold of what Barthes termed *infra-knowledge*: '. . . how long were nails worn in a particular period'? Photography can tell me this much better than painting.'[31] Photography renders visible much that had previously existed below the reach of historical documentation. From the mid-nineteenth century, the past – its fashions, its faces, its architecture, its day to day minutiae and detritus – crystallizes in our imagination in a manner simply not possible for pre-photographic eras. This shift is both qualitative and quantitative: the camera not only offers a new level of detail and a new form of precision, but mechanical reproduction vastly multiplies the number of historical documents which can be produced. Sontag notes:

> For example, now all adults can know exactly how they and their parents and grandparents looked as children – a knowledge not available to anyone before the invention of cameras, not even to that tiny minority among whom it was customary to commission paintings of their children. Most of these portraits were less informative than any snapshot. And even the very wealthy usually owned just

28 For Kracauer, the philosophical problem of relativity is itself an effect of a new mode of apprehending history: 'Nineteenth century historicism is very much responsible for the firm establishment of the consciousness of man's historicity, the belief in the formative powers of time as well as place. Dilthey was perhaps the first to fully realize the consequences of this belief. According to it, there are no 'eternal truths'; rather all our thinking is a function of time. Consciousness of man as a historical being necessarily contains a conviction of the relativity of human knowledge.' *History, the Last Things Before the Last*, New York, Oxford University Press, 1969, pp. 195–6.

29 *The Differend: Phases in Dispute* (trans. G. Van Den Abbeele), Minneapolis, University of Minnesota Press, 1988, p. 157.

30 J. Ruby, 'Exposing yourself: reflexivity, anthropology and film', *Semiotica*, 30 (1980), p. 16, quoted in Trinh T. Minh-Ha, 'Documentary is/not a name', *October*, 52 (Spring 1990), p. 93.

31 Barthes, *Camera Lucida*, p. 30.

one portrait of themselves or their forebears as children, that is, an image of one moment of childhood, whereas it is common to have many photographs of oneself . . .[32]

Yet, the multiplicity of images has never simply completed life's picture in all its variety. Despite the camera's complicity with the encyclopaedic dream of universal history, it has also been instrumental in exposing certain flaws in this logic. In the wake of the great photographic projects culminating in the universal aspirations of Steichen's *Family of Man* (1955), it has become more and more difficult to believe that the camera could ever have hoped to contain life. Increasing scepticism to this prospect is not simply a matter of asserting the empirical infinity of possible subjects; rather, there is something about photographic evidence which is itself antagonistic to the project of historical totalization.

Historical discourse has traditionally placed great emphasis on the incorporation of particular cases within the embrace of general principles or wider laws. If, as Adorno and Horkheimer argued, this conforms to the general thrust of Western knowledge at least since the Enlightenment, it is an orientation which gained momentum in the nineteenth century when new institutional and intellectual frames of history were geared up at the height of positivism. Within this matrix, local events tend to be subordinated to the demands of more inclusive explanatory structures, culminating in the teleology of progress which functions to unify the most heterogeneous phenomena. Nevertheless, this 'unity' is always selective: as Foucault argued, historical 'events' tend to become visible only to the extent that they conform to established discursive patterns, while those which resist or transgress the existing order often remain below the threshold of 'knowledge'.

On the other hand, the nineteenth century was also marked by the desire to separate history from philosophy, theology and literature, manifested in the rise of what Kracauer termed 'technical' histories: specialized studies which claimed to eschew the pretensions of overarching, unified systems of explanation. Ranke's voluminous work, which modestly abandoned the 'high office' of judging the past for the instruction of future generations (while replacing it with the rather immodest ambition of showing 'what actually happened'), frequently returns to the relation between particular and general (or universal) history. While the historian 'must feel a participation and pleasure in the particular for itself', this is not sufficient: a good historian must also 'keep his eye on the universal aspect of things'.[33] Clearly, 'balance' is required. Kracauer's distinction between 'macro' and 'micro' (or general and technical) histories situates the problem succinctly. On the one hand, above a certain level of generality, history risks becoming 'philosophy' abstracted from empirical evidence, while, on the other hand, the more one descends into detail, the more history risks losing its powers of

---

32 Sontag, *On Photography*, p. 165.
33 L. Ranke, 'A fragment from the 1830s', reprinted in Stern, *Varieties of History*, p. 59.

explanation. Modern history is inscribed in this field of tension, suspended between its powerful belief in the teleology of human progress and an increasing awareness of the fragmentation and dispersion of knowledge.[34]

How does the camera intervene in this situation? If the most prominent heading has undoubtedly been the alignment of photographic images with historical 'facts', another tendency exerts a growing influence in the present. This concerns the manner in which the audio-visual archive has altered the balance between the particular and the general in the representation of history. In contrast to language, which promises to separate the abstract from the concrete (and in fact gives rise to this distinction, as well as its distinct limitations), the photograph or film acquiesces in this division only to a degree. Beyond a certain point, the irreducible specificity of each image asserts itself, stubbornly refusing to surrender to the demands of the 'example'. Even the most rigorously 'scientific' photographs, such as Muybridge's studies with their gridded backgrounds which were designed to assist the formulation of general laws of locomotion, display this resistance. Despite his own aims, Muybridge cannot avoid what Benjamin termed the photograph's 'spark of contingency', what Barthes termed the photographic *punctum*. The laughter and surprise provoked by one female model dousing another with a bucket of water forms an inseparable part of the precise record of their sequence of movements.[35]

Unlike words built from a finite alphabet, each photographic sign is unique: a one-off in a lexicon that can only be radically open-ended. It is the difficulty of dominating the image, of systematizing its proliferous effects, which led Barthes to inquire of the photograph: 'why mightn't there be, somehow, a new science for each object? A *mathesis singularis* (and no longer *universalis*).'[36] What would such a science be? Would it enable us to think of difference outside the law of identity? Or would it promote the disintegration of discourse into an unmanageable heterogeneity of iso-morphic elements? Such questions recall Borges's Funes the Memorious for whom the world was recreated anew in each instant and from every perspective:

> Not only was it difficult for him to comprehend that the generic symbol dog embraces so many unlike individuals of diverse size and form; it bothered him

34 Kracauer's solution to the incommensurability of particular and general histories is ingenious: he offers Griffith's 'admirable non-solution' of montage, in which the close-up shot is both integrated as part of the narrative and yet remains apart. See Kracauer, *History, the Last Things*, pp. 108–38. Walter Benjamin pursued a similar line in his unfinished 'Paris Arcades' project whose conceptual armature, developed with the aim of dispelling the myth of progress, was 'most tightly linked to that of montage'. Benjamin quoted in S. Buck-Morss, *The Dialectics of Seeing: Walter Benjamin and the Arcades Project*, Cambridge, MA and London, MIT Press, 1991, p. 422.

35 Muybridge's 11-volume *Animal Locomotion* (first published in 1887) is a complex study in itself, especially with regard to the gendering of its scene. While some actions, such as walking and carrying, are performed by both sexes, those of men wrestling and women undressing are not.

36 Barthes, *Camera Lucida*, p. 8.

that the dog at three-fourteen (seen from the side) should have the same name as the dog at three-fifteen (seen from the front).[37]

But, while the camera might indeed raise such possibilities, it has never fulfilled them, neither in promise nor threat. There is always movement from the particular to the general. Photographs are constantly drawn into networks of significance and generate much of their meaning from general classifications such as subject matter, genre, photographer, or period. Even the most specific photographic images are never bereft of symbolic qualities and frequently come to exemplify abstract values, ideas or emotions, even to the point – Hitler among the cheering crowds at Zeppelinfield, Neil Armstrong stepping down to the surface of the moon – of symbolizing an entire era.

Yet the force of my earlier point remains. Because its images are so deeply indebted to a particular weave of space and time, the camera finds it difficult to generalize with the ease of other forms of representation. This peculiar quality, which is the camera's undoubted strength, has particular consequences for the formation of history. Perhaps the Zapruder film of the Kennedy assassination can serve to highlight this point (but in fact any widely screened film of a significant historical event would do). In the traditional writing of history, the act of the shooting and its significance can be demarcated (or so it seems). Description of the sequence of events and analysis of their import obey different dictates. But on film these two planes merge irresistibly. The symbolic weight of the killing fuses with the violent arc of the President's body at the moment of impact, the bloody tissue spattered across his wife, the erratic swerving of the limousine with a security agent hanging on grimly to its rear, the glimpses of the infamous grassy knoll in the background. The fascination of this sequence of film – *and this is the fascination of film generally* – is precisely the manner in which it promotes this fusion of the particular and the general.[38]

Even if it had not been filmed, there is no doubt that Kennedy's assassination would be a modern landmark. But the fact (somewhere between accident and inevitability) that it was filmed has conferred a particular quality on its remembrance. The compulsive repetition of the sequence in countless documentaries, re-enactments and dramatizations ensures that the scene remains at the forefront of the Kennedy legacy. If death inevitably finalizes our understanding of a life and its historical significance, rarely has the process of interpretation been arrested so visibly and instantaneously for so many people, focusing cultural attention onto a single sequence of film which, by its very nature, invites repetition. The exhaustive frame by frame scrutiny to which investigators and viewers everywhere have subjected the footage (has a piece of film ever been more

37 *Labyrinths* (trans. D.A. Yates et al.), Harmondsworth, Penguin, 1970, pp. 93–4.
38 Another example is the video recording of the Rodney King beating. In the retrial each blow was analysed in slow motion, each action was subjected to the most minute scrutiny. Judgement was eventually pared down to the very second, and the force was deemed to be 'illegal' after 63 seconds. Has such a precise relationship to a past event which is in contention as 'history' ever before been possible? Would it have ever made sense before?

closely watched?) testifies not only to a deeply embedded faith in the camera's power to reveal hidden secrets, but to its role in the formation of a wound which no amount of repetition can heal. The theme of Antonioni's *Blow-Up* (1966) is not far away: under pressure of excessive attention, certainty of meaning recedes; interpretations drift and multiply. By visibly repeating the impact of the bullets as historical impact, the Zapruder film accentuates a problem of mourning whose effects are by no means limited to this particular example. It forces a confrontation with Kennedy's death as a unique event. Despite the apparatus of culture which inevitably pulls the unique happening towards a common ground of meaning, a residue of singularity remains. Repeated viewing of the film precludes distance from the event: hence its fecundity as a narrative machine, a prolific generator of controversy, speculation and rumour, a fertilizer of conspiracy and counter-conspiracy theories.

This example indexes the new problems that history faces in the development of audio-visual archives. The stubborn singularity of the audio-visual signifier – the fact that, beyond a certain point, the detail refuses to lie down, refuses to be accommodated within a broader structure, refuses to be integrated in a linear temporality – conditions the new uncertainty surrounding protocols for representing history. If, as Kracauer suggested, good history demands a 'balance' between the particular and the general, the camera has upset something in this equilibrium. Under pressure of photographic scrutiny, the past remains all too visible, open for reassessment and reinterpretation. When historical 'evidence' multiplies exponentially, the line of time no longer coheres. Both the concept of the archive and the model of historical understanding with which it has been associated threaten to decompose.

This decomposition affects the movement from the particular to the general which has long regulated the translation of experimental data into scientific theory, of evidential 'fact' into historical record, of 'event' into narrated context. The crisis of holistic theories which dominates the postmodern moment stems from a perceived inability to contain the particular, to domesticate the thought of the exception which every generalization provokes. As Derrida has pointed out, the value of universality has always been intrinsically linked to the possibility of exemplarity, and all that allows the example to divest itself of the birthmarks of culture, language, accent, idiom, singularity – to divorce itself from the materiality of time and place in general. Yet no example can ever be completely isolated or it would remain entirely beyond the reach of 'culture'.[39] There is a paradox here: discourse cannot do without examples, and yet particular examples can never remain entirely singular nor yet be wholly justified. Should one respond to this paradox by seeking to reconcile the claims of the particular and the general, or instead place the accent upon their irreducible disjunction? This is not a

39 See J. Derrida, *The Other Heading: Reflections on Today's Europe* (trans. P.A. Brault and M.B. Naas), Bloomington, Indiana University Press, 1992, pp. 72–3.

dilemma I am aiming to resolve here: my point is rather that it is precisely this problem that the camera exposes, by interrupting the established forms of circulation between theory and example, and destabilizing their habitual terms of exchange. From this perspective, as much as it has conformed to the positivist demand for a technique of objective recording – a technique capable of precisely locating objects and events in time and space – the camera has finally disrupted positivism's capacity to generalize.

Obsession with the Zapruder film reflects a cultural preoccupation with the 'decisive moment', as if tracing events to a putative source could somehow purify their meaning, and thereby alleviate the problems of interpretation which bedevil all claims to historical truth. What remains striking is the extent to which such an understanding of time, extending to the hypothesis that life itself might be comprised of a series of singular moments, seems peculiarly photographic in conception.

*

The third broad shift entrained by the camera with regard to historical representation relates to the threshold of simulation. It might be thought that disappointment with the fantasy of the perfect memory machine belongs to a new awareness of the disarming ease with which the truth of photo-realism can be faked.[40] But consciousness of the malleability of photographic truth has a history as long as photography. The earliest exhibitions of retouched negatives at the Paris World Fair in 1855 caused a sensation with their revelation that the camera could 'lie'. (Interestingly, this also served to increase the popularity of photography, especially for portraiture.) Likewise in cinema, historical reconstructions have often achieved great success, and not only in so-called 'fiction' films. Films made by the Edison company depicting the Anglo-Boer war were feted, although shot entirely in the Orange Mountains of New Jersey. Barnouw has noted: 'Memorable genuine footage came back from the 1906 San Francisco earthquake but other footage contrived in table top miniature was equally applauded.'[41] The dazzling special effects of *King Kong* were still 25 years away. Newsreels such as *The March of Time* (begun in 1935) specialized in combining 'actuality' footage with free-wheeling dramatizations.

In fact, throughout this century it is noticeable that 'actuality' films and photographs which claim to document the past have always been supplemented by those which aim for its wholesale reconstruction. Crucial to this enterprise has been the realization that, on screen, the 'presence' of every

40 Beyond the digital threshold, photographic manipulation is virtually undetectable. As one expert in the legal authentication of photographs points out: 'You will never be able to tell which is the original even under a microscope. The resolution of the digital work is higher than the resolution of the photograph. I could not stand up in a court of law to tell you which is which.' Professor Robin Williams (Head of Photography at RMIT University, Melbourne), quoted in L. Simpson, 'The Lying Eye', *The Age Magazine* (Melbourne), 31 July 1993, pp. 21–2.

41 Barnouw, *Documentary*, p. 25.

image is equal, the 'fake' can be presented as convincingly as the real. In fact, with the increasing sophistication of cinematic narrative, the fake has often seemed better than the real. Griffith's declaration that he was 'very disappointed with the reality of the battlefield' after visiting the front towards the end of the First World War is symptomatic of the new dilemma.[42] After centuries in which representation disappoints the real, modernity is defined by a reversal in which it is the real which begins to disappoint its spectators.[43] Vertov, who was one of the first to recognize the uncertainty that the camera engenders, saw it as a problem to overcome:

> If a fake apple and a real apple are filmed so that one cannot be distinguished from the other on the screen, this is not ability, but incompetence – inability to photograph. The real apple has to be filmed in such a way that no counterfeit is possible . . .[44]

But can one in fact exclude the possibility of the counterfeit? Even putting aside this most enigmatic and essential question, it must be acknowledged that it has been exactly the reverse tendency – filming 'fakes' so as to confer the experience of filmed 'reality' – which has dominated cinematic practice. As film making became more expensive, the use of studio sets or carefully controlled locations became imperative. What else has studio production been but a war against chance, an attempt to exert absolute control over events in order to force appearances into a diabolical conformity with the dictates of a pre-scripted narrative? White's suggestion that *the* historical fantasy is that '*real* events are properly represented when they can be shown to display the formal coherence of a story' situates the stakes in this move which affected both 'documentary' and 'fiction'.[45]

The Birth of a Nation (1915) played a critical role here, redefining the manner in which it was thought possible to depict the past in narrative cinema. Griffith placed great emphasis on historical research and the accuracy of period detail, arguing that, as a viewer 'you will actually see what happened. There will be no opinions expressed. You will merely be present at the making of history.'[46] If such a boast, which directly restates Ranke's principles, were made today, it would be received cautiously, perhaps even provoking a knowing smile in the belief that the myth of cinematic transparency has been debunked. But has it? As Deleuze points out, the frequent dismissal of 'Hollywood history' as necessarily corrupted

42 Quoted in Virilio, *War and Cinema*, p. 15.

43 Barthes wrote: 'Looking around at the customers in a cafe, someone remarked to me (rightly): "Look how gloomy they are! Nowadays the images are livelier than the people." One of the marks of our world is perhaps this reversal: we live according to a generalized image-repertoire.' Barthes, *Camera Lucida*, p. 118.

44 'The writings of Dziga Vertov', *Film Culture*, 25 (Summer 1962), p. 55.

45 H. White, 'The value of narrativity in the representation of reality', in W.T.J. Mitchell (ed.), *On Narrative*, Chicago, Chicago University Press, 1981, p. 4.

46 Quoted in Sorlin, *Film in History*, p. ix. Sorlin notes that many contemporary reviewers shared this line. One wrote: 'History repeats itself on screen with a realism that is maddening.' *Film in History*, p. ix.

history still appeals to a bottom line: *that there be a bottom line.*[47] This is not to idealize the representation of history in Hollywood cinema, but to suggest that judging it with reference to 'what really happened' is as problematic as simply accepting it on its own terms.

Contemporary responses to the reality of an image tend to be determined not so much by the image itself, but by assumptions concerning the origin of the image. These assumptions often seem to derive from the image itself, but are usually determined more by the context of viewing.[48] To put it simply, if we are watching the news, we tend to assume that the image refers to reality; if we are watching a feature film, we usually don't.

In the first case, the image seeks less to 're-present' real events than to forge an identification with reality itself. 'Actuality' footage, which mobil- izes the complex heritage of photo-realism, seeks to position the real world – 'pure, concrete, fixed, visible, all-too-visible' – as its single unshakeable referent.[49] 'Eye-witness' reports remain the bastions of news, current affairs and documentary programmes, proclaiming (along with Griffith) that what we see on screen is history making itself. In the second category, one might point to texts which explicitly recreate 'real' historical events, but present them as 'fiction'. So-called 'period' films tend not to be judged simply as 'fakes', but in terms of their faithfulness to an Ideal History (Ranke's 'what actually happened') – insofar as they are judged against history at all.

These divisions seem self-evident. They respect the boundary commonly posited between 'documentary' and 'fiction'. But – and this is where the problem begins again and again – no matter how carefully we draw the line, counter-examples which contravene its sovereignty jostle for attention. Cross-fertilization of genres has been of enormous importance to film and television production: contemporary news, for example, shares a similar narrative organization to much contemporary television fiction, while fiction can (and often does) mobilize the conventions, and even the footage, of news. A landmark in this regard was Haskell Wexler's *Medium Cool* (1969), which cut footage of the demonstrations surrounding the 1968 Democratic convention in Chicago together with footage depicting a (fictional) tele- vision reporter covering the same events. The film's impact derives from its exploitation of this fusion: towards the end an off-camera shout, 'Watch out, Haskell, it's real!', marks the uncertainty of this conjunction as violence erupts with a police charge. (Subsequent revelations by protesters that

47 Deleuze writes: 'It is easy to make fun of Hollywood's historical conceptions. It seems to us, on the contrary, that they bring together the most serious aspects of history as seen by the nineteenth century.' Deleuze, *Cinema 1*, p. 142.

48 There are many photographs of objects such as UFOs, or the Loch Ness monster. Some people believe in these images and others don't: my point is that it is not the image itself but the cultural network inflecting its referent which is decisive.

49 As Trinh T. Minh-Ha puts it: 'The real world: so real that the Real becomes the one basic referent – pure, concrete, fixed, visible, all-too-visible.' 'Documentary is/not a name', *October*, 52 (Spring 1990), p. 80.

network camera crews asked them to stage the real demonstrations provide another twist in this scene.)

In fact, the present is increasingly characterized by hybrid texts which mix the language of fictional narrative with 'actuality' footage. 'Recreated' sequences appear in even the most prestigious current affairs programmes, extending the trajectory of *Medium Cool* (or perhaps simply refiguring the earlier tradition of *The March of Time*), while archival footage regularly crosses over into feature films, video clips, advertisements, and the like.[50] The point here is that awareness of the uncertain relation of the audio-visual 'fact' to invented or imagined pasts is being sharpened in the present. Shifting attitudes to Robert Flaherty, who single-handedly defined documentary style in the 1920s, are revealing. Flaherty was perhaps the first documentary film maker to appreciate the importance of a lengthy shooting time to do justice to his subject matter. His emphasis on filming and then 'discovering' his story in the process of editing proved enormously influential. However, subsequent revelations concerning his vision of 'authentic primitivism' belied what many disciples had seen as a strategy for achieving 'objectivity'. The fact that the harpooning sequence in *Nanook* (1922), the tattooing ceremony in *Moana* (1926), and the fishing expedition in *Man of Aran* (1934) were all redesigned by Flaherty to efface the intrusions of modern culture and technology has inspired numerous critiques of his work.

But the lessons here should point more than one way. If Flaherty's invasive anthropology is out of step with contemporary practice, this shouldn't negate the worth of his films in the name of a supposedly non-invasive practice. Every film maker shapes reality in the act of filming. The problem should not be one of finding an absolutely authoritative means of demarcating fiction from fact, but of maintaining a reflexive attitude to the specific relations of representation mobilized in any historical representation.

This touches another significant issue. While turning a 'real' story into fiction is usually called 'licence', claiming that an 'invented' story is 'real' is likely to be called 'deception'. Even as the collusion between reality and representation has become more widely acknowledged, the assumption remains that, at some point, the two domains are finally separable, and that, for this reason – in the very name of reason – taking liberties with the real is a more serious matter than anything that passes under the name of fiction. This belief situates the threshold of a mutant form of history unique to the twentieth century: the unprecedented register of false history which appears under the pejorative sign of propaganda.

The difficulties of distinguishing 'propaganda' from Grierson's definition of documentary as the 'creative treatment of actuality' are notorious. Of

---

50 For example, Oliver Stone's ambitious film history of the recent US past is notable for blending of archival and dramatic footage, particularly in *The Doors* (1991), *JFK* (1991) and *Nixon* (1995).

course, for Grierson, like many of his contemporaries, the term 'propaganda' didn't carry the overwhelmingly negative connotations it would later assume.[51] However, the experience of fascism and the cold war ensured that, while 'truth' was annexed to the self, propaganda became the discourse assigned to the other. This separation remains fraught with difficulty. To take a prominent example: Leni Riefenstahl's *Triumph of the Will* (1935), which is undoubtedly the most commonly cited example of film propaganda, is also the film most widely chosen to show the 'real' nature of Nazi Germany (the Führer cult, the hysteria of nation, the deification of the athletic body, etc.) Barnouw's assertion that this is possible because 'Riefenstahl's cameras did not lie . . .' demonstrates a recurrent obeisance before the camera's authority.[52] Even as the possibility of 'distortion' is recognized and criticized, desire for the undistorted image, or, more specifically, for that image in which historical truth can be read despite all human veiling, returns time and again. Celebration of the camera as a mechanism of objective record slides into a celebration of the camera as a mechanism capable of doing more than simply record. Today, *Triumph of the Will* has become a major source of 'actuality' footage for new documentaries on Nazi life, histories which consider themselves far removed from the taint of 'propaganda', but often fail to acknowledge the circumstances in which the images they appropriate were first created.[53] As Sekula has pointed out, to use the archive in this fashion is, at best, naive.[54]

The crux of the matter is that the question should not be whether or not Riefenstahl's cameras 'lied', but how they might both 'lie' and 'tell the truth' at the same time. This demands a rigorous engagement with the itinerary of desire that invested the camera with the potential to reproduce absolute truth in the first place. Clearly, this investment has returned unexpected dividends in the present. One might follow Metz in arguing that 'every film is a fiction film.'[55] Such an aphorism is useful in contesting positivist readings of the camera image, by emphasizing that the image is always partial, selective, discriminatory, constructed around a perspective which determines a blind field, and so on. But this is only one half of the photographic bind, which closes with the realization that *every film is also a document*. Even the most fantastic studio-made film is built from fragments of 'actuality'. This marks a point of return to my earlier description of

51 Grierson's rather paternalistic theory of democracy led him to assert: 'There are some of us who believe that propaganda is the part of democratic education that the educators forgot . . . If you recall the origin of the word propaganda, you will remember it was first associated with the defence of a faith and the concept of civilization.' Grierson, *Grierson on Documentary*, p. 109.

52 Barnouw, *Documentary*, p. 105.

53 Avisar notes that 'there is no film whose footage has been used so extensively in other cinematic works, or has directly inspired other cinematic versions on subjects directly related to Hitler's era.' I. Avisar, *Screening the Holocaust*, Bloomington, Indiana University Press, 1988, p. 23.

54 Sekula, 'Reading an archive', in Wallis, *Blasted Allegories*, p. 122.

55 Metz, *Psychoanalysis and Cinema*, p. 44.

Medium Cool as a fiction which uses 'actuality' footage: isn't there a sense in which every film does this? Isn't this precisely the point on which the camera's ambivalent relation to history turns: the constant slippage between the fiction of its images and the reality of its fictions, the incessant movement from 'textuality' to 'reality' as the privileged point of reference?

This threshold is of particular pertinence to *Triumph of the Will*. It has been widely acknowledged that the film documents not an event but a cinematic event. Post-war versions of the film released by the Allies were prefaced with warnings that the rallies were 'staged' like a 'film-set'. Sontag cites a book contemporary with the making of the film in which Riefenstahl related supervising the construction of elaborate bridges, towers and camera tracks: 'A photograph on p. 31 shows Hitler and Riefenstahl bending over some plans, with the caption: "The preparations for the Party Congress were made hand in hand with the preparations for the camera work." '[56] Recognizing that the rally was conceived as a film production in which the camera eye was given right of way over all others, that spoilt footage of loyalty pledges to Hitler was re-shot weeks later on a studio set designed by Albert Speer, serves to contradict Riefenstahl's later assertion that: 'Not a single scene is staged. Everything is genuine. And there is no tendentious commentary for the simple reason that there is no commentary at all. It is *history – pure history.*'[57] But engaging with the deeper issues raised by *Triumph of the Will* demands further analysis.

One reason that *Triumph of the Will* remains so contentious is that its techniques remain so contemporary. If it was in Nazi Germany that the possibility for establishing a national polity integrated by new media technologies was first systematically explored, this political space has clearly spread in the present. The staging of mass events for the camera and the orchestration of the 'public sphere' via television has become integral to the legitimation of most contemporary nation states.[58] But this context is rarely acknowledged: like many other excavations of the Nazi past, responses to *Triumph of the Will* tend to be coloured by a desire to seal that history off from the present.

*

56 'Fascinating fascism', in *Under the Sign of Saturn*, New York, Farrar Strauss and Giroux, 1980, p. 79. The internal quote comes from *Hinter den Kulissen des Reichparteitag-Films*, Munich, 1935.

57 Interviewed in September 1965, quoted in Sontag, 'Fascinating fascism', p. 82. In the same interview, Riefenstahl claimed she hadn't written a word of the 1935 book on the film's production which had appeared in her name.

58 See 'Unstable architectures' below. This leads on to another point. One feature which always troubled me about *Triumph of the Will* was that it was *so good*: not only did it invent a new genre (the 'cine-event'), but it remains arguably its most perfectly realized example. In fact, Riefenstahl shot a film (*Sieg Des Glaubens/Victory of Faith*) of the Party convention at Nuremberg in 1933. Surviving fragments of this film (included in Müller's *The Wonderful, Horrible Life of Leni Riefenstahl* (1993) to Riefenstahl's obvious displeasure), demonstrate that she, as much as Hitler, used the earlier occasion as a dress rehearsal.

Is there still a place for 'documentary' when television turns the world into spectacle and reality endlessly retreats under its stare? Despite the fact that the disappearance of 'documentary' – like 'objectivity', and even reality itself – has been proclaimed for decades, and is proclaimed anew with each new wave of film makers who reinvent the conventions of cinematic language, it seems unlikely that these categories will simply vanish. When faced with such recalcitrant terms, it is less a matter of departing them absolutely than of analysing them patiently and redeploying them critically. The problem of representing history in the age of the camera will not be resolved by escaping from fiction into fact, or vice versa. Critical history is generated, not when the lines of authority which divide 'the truth and nothing but' from the 'it's just a story' are stabilized, but when they are crossed. Trinh T. Minh-Ha argues:

> A documentary aware of its own artifice is one that remains sensitive to the flow between fact and fiction. It does not work to conceal or exclude what is normalized as 'non-factual', for it understands the mutual dependence of realism and 'artificiality' in the process of film making.[59]

Contemporary enthusiasm for simulating history in cinema and on television testifies not only to the political importance of remembering the past, but also to the political imperative of modernizing the forms of memory. One of the first tasks undertaken by every emergent national cinema this century has been its own 'birth of a nation' saga, translating myths of national identity and narratives of national formation into an audio-visual archive.[60] As Walter Benjamin once pointed out, if this is an effective way of 'preserving' the past, it is also a most efficient way of liquidating traditional forms of memory.[61]

This is perhaps another history lesson from *Triumph of the Will*: in committing himself so decisively to the new media, it seems Hitler has ensured his survival in the twentieth century and beyond. In Syberberg's epic, *Hitler: A Film from Germany*, the character of Goebbels proclaims: 'I'll make sure that in a hundred years, every word that any of us speaks will reappear in films. It's up to you to decide which part you want to play. I'll make you a legend, a myth if you like, through your deaths.'[62] The monumental architecture which Hitler thought would be his permanent epitaph has all but gone, but the ephemera of those ghostly flickering images remain.

---

59 'Documentary is/not a name', p. 89. This flow can be discerned in a number of recent films, including Trinh's *Surname Viet Given Name Nam* (1989), Errol Morris's *The Thin Blue Line* (1988), Reece Auguiste's *Twilight City* (1989) and John Akomfrah's *Who Needs a Heart* (1991), which operate in a 'factual' terrain no longer regulated by the goal of 'objectivity'. The significance of this shift (reminiscent of certain avant-garde documentaries of the 1920s) is the manner in which it displaces what were previously limit terms.

60 See 'The myth of the centre' below.

61 See Benjamin, *Illuminations*, p. 224.

62 H.J. Syberberg, *Hitler: A Film from Germany* (trans. J. Neugroschel), New York, Farrar Strauss and Giroux, 1982, p. 66.

6

Intolerable Memories

> But this slaughter pretends to be without memory, without trace, and through this testifies again to what it slaughters: that there is the unthinkable, time lost yet always there . . .
>
> Jean-François Lyotard

Certain horrific images – a Vietnamese child drenched with napalm running down a road screaming in pain and fear – have perhaps been indelibly etched into contemporary memory. But how does such a memory function? Can an image of atrocity assist in preventing its recurrence? Or does it short-circuit political engagement in favour of sensationalism, facilitating political detachment through the soft murder of voyeurism?[1]

Some memories are perhaps intolerable. All that is named by 'the Holocaust' forms an extreme case, one which tests the limits of representation and challenges the very notion of historical responsibility, imposing an obligation to confront the fact that, here, what was previously unimaginable actually occurred: 'unreality' became 'real'. Can representation ever hope to preserve the lacerations of such a history? What might 'preservation' involve here? Is it better to remember the intolerable as intolerable, to preserve the trauma in all its intensity? Or would this only freeze time, leaving the present immobilized in the face of the past? Should we instead let time 'heal our wounds', even if this prepares us to 'forget' what disturbs us? Does memory succeed in bringing experience close – and making it available as acquired knowledge – only at the cost of transforming its original object? How, then, might we remain true to the past and repay our obligations to its debts? And what of historical responsibility? To whom should history respond?

From the outset, it must be said that my concern here is not to attempt to represent 'the Holocaust'. This is a task for which I am ill-equipped; moreover, if others apparently better equipped to perform it have 'failed',

---

1 This is how I read John Berger's comments on war photography: 'It is generally assumed that its purpose is to awaken concern. The most extreme examples . . . show moments of agony in order to extort maximum concern. Such moments, whether photographed or not, are discontinuous with all other moments. They exist by themselves. But the reader who has been arrested by the photograph may tend to feel this discontinuity as his own personal moral inadequacy. *And as soon as this happens his sense of shock is dispersed*: his own moral inadequacy may shock him as much as the crimes committed in the war. Either he shrugs off this sense of inadequacy as being only too familiar, or else he thinks of performing a kind of penance – of which the purest example would be to make a contribution to OXFAM or UNICEF.' Berger, *About Looking*, pp. 39–40.

this is perhaps for essential reasons (as Blanchot gives us to think).[2] 'The Holocaust' names a cataclysmic event whose scale and severity exceeds comprehension; it is the disaster for which (as Primo Levi put it) even the survivors 'are not the true witnesses'; the catastrophe to which it is impossible to respond.[3] And yet, in the name of the silencing of the dead, it imposes an irreducible obligation to speak, to remember and to bear witness.[4] Memory faces a double injunction: the imperative of preserving, bringing close, and making familiar what must nevertheless remain unfamiliar, alien, discontinuous.

My concern here is what 'the Holocaust' can teach us about the functioning of the camera archive in the present. For it was the camera which made the world at large witnesses to this horror, and which has since been given a heavy responsibility in maintaining this memory. When 'the facts' so greatly exceeded comprehension, the camera became indispensable as a means of providing criminal evidence and producing cultural conviction. In the final stages of the war, material concerning the death camps was gathered by special units of Allied troops. They included teams of camera operators, who filmed the mountains of human hair, teeth, eye glasses and other remains that testified to the magnitude of the killing. These images were instrumental, both in the Nuremberg trials which made unprecedented use of photographic and cinematic evidence in prosecuting war criminals, and in convincing often sceptical publics about the extent of the 'final solution'.[5]

2 Blanchot provides the most searching examination of the relation between representing the catastrophic 'event without response', and the shattering and infinite dispersal of language, identity, and time. See M. Blanchot, *The Writing of the Disaster* (trans. A. Smock), Lincoln and London, University of Nebraska Press, 1986.

3 Primo Levi writes: 'We, the survivors, are not the true witnesses. . . . We are those who by their prevarications or abilities or good luck did not touch bottom. Those who did so . . . have not returned to tell about it or have returned mute. . . . They are the rule, we are the exception.' *The Drowned and the Saved* (trans. R. Rosenthal), New York, Vintage Books, 1989, pp. 83–4.

4 This double bind – the impossibility of writing and representing conjoined by the impossibility of *not* writing and representing – has been a consistent theme of Holocaust literature traumatized by the guilt of survival, the inadequacy of testimony, and the failure of language in face of excessive experience. Adorno charged this failure not to the intrinsic qualities of language, but to an 'audience' (a community, a society) incapable of responding to what the Holocaust revealed about its own culture: 'Auschwitz demonstrated irrefutably that culture has failed. That this could happen in the midst of the traditions of philosophy, of art, and of the enlightening sciences says more than that these traditions and their spirit lacked the power to take hold of men and work a change in them. There is untruth in those fields themselves.' *Negative Dialectics* (trans. E.B. Ashton), New York, Seabury Press, 1973, p. 366.

5 The entire war crimes trials were themselves filmed and became the basis for two feature documentaries, the Soviet-produced *Judgement of the Nations* (1946) and the US-produced *Nuremberg* (1948). The latter was screened in occupied West Germany as part of 'denazification' programmes after the war, but was never released in the USA, apparently in deference to pleas from West German Chancellor Konrad Adenauer. It was withdrawn from all circulation by the US Department of Defence in 1950. See Barnouw, *Documentary*, pp. 173–5.

What effect has the widespread dissemination of such images had? Susan Sontag described her own experience as a rite of passage:

> One's first encounter with the photographic inventory of ultimate horror is a kind of revelation, the prototypically modern revelation: a negative epiphany. For me it was photographs of Bergen-Belsen and Dachau which I came across by chance in a bookstore in Santa Monica in July, 1945. Nothing I have seen – in photographs or in real life – ever cut me as sharply, deeply, instantaneously . . . When I looked at those photographs, something broke. Some limit had been reached, and not only that of horror; I felt irrevocably grieved, wounded, but a part of my feelings started to tighten; something went dead; something is still crying.[6]

Nevertheless, she argues that representing the horrific does not necessarily preserve the sense of horror, nor work to prevent its recurrence. It may also serve to domesticate it, normalize it, and, in time, absolve it. Sontag added:

> At the time of the first Nazi camps there was nothing banal about these images. After thirty years, a saturation point may have been reached. In these last decades, 'concerned' photography has done at least as much to deaden conscience as to arouse it.[7]

It is perhaps tempting to attribute Sontag's general pessimism about 'concerned' photography to her perception that not even these images – despite their immense impact on her as a twelve-year-old – have been able to secure the past as a lesson learned once and for all, immutable, unchangeable, unforgettable. But such a convenient (psycho)analysis remains superficial, and not only because she makes Holocaust imagery a partial exception to the trajectory she indicates. What Sontag points to is the fact that any attempt to remember atrocity through 'actuality' images faces a new dilemma in the present. It is no longer a question of authenticity – apart from an extremist minority, few doubt the veracity of such events – but of banality.[8] Resistance to believing has been overrun by the perception that such evil is 'human, all too human' – itself another, more intractable form of resistance.

*

And yet one cannot abandon the responsibility to remember. One film which consciously attempts to counter the threat of historical banality is Alan Resnais's *Night and Fog* (1955).[9] It is easy to recall other documentaries which deploy the same images of shapeless bodies being bulldozed into mass graves, or of the living dead staring with uncomprehending eyes

6 Sontag, *On Photography*, p. 20.

7 Sontag, *On Photography*, p. 20.

8 Elsewhere, Sontag extends this perspective to 'recreations': 'To simulate atrocity convincingly is to risk making the audience passive, reinforcing witless stereotypes, confirming distance and creating fascination', adding 'Like its simulation as fiction, the display of atrocity in the form of photographic evidence risks being tacitly pornographic.' Sontag, *Sign of Saturn*, p. 139.

9 The film takes its title from the notorious 'Night and Fog' decree of 7 December 1941, issued to make those 'endangering German security' simply vanish without record.

unable to believe that the horror is over; the multiplicity of examples is part of the effect to which Sontag is pointing.[10] But *Night and Fog* remains quite distinct, even (perhaps especially) after four decades. This is not only because its script was written by former camp inmate Jean Cayrol. The authority of the narrative voice is necessarily 'compromised' here in the manner common to all eye-witnesses in this field; he did not experience everything he must nevertheless address. The film's strength is not its claim to authenticity, but the manner in which it negotiates memory's double injunction, bringing the past close and yet keeping distant.

On the one hand, *Night and Fog* refuses to isolate the 'concentration camp universe' from the host of mundane activities which were required to sustain its daily life. It points out that the building of the camps involved contractors, tenders, competitive bids, *profit*; the running of this other world mimed the institutions of the world outside, with hospitals (the site of grotesque medical 'experiments'), social hierarchy (Jews and 'politicals' at the bottom ruled over by common criminals, Kapos, the SS, and finally the Commandant), brothels (the narrator reminds us that these women were 'prisoners still, like the others doomed to death'), and an emphasis on productivity. This logic even informed the apparatus of death. Following details of the initial attempts to orchestrate mass extermination (the machine gunning of an estimated two million victims), the narrator bluntly states: 'Killing by hand takes time. Cylinders of Zyklon gas are ordered.' The 'final solution' mimed the drive for efficiency and speed which is the hallmark of industrial production. It is all a matter of 'appropriate technology' in a process in which the human body had itself become raw material. These are the everyday facts that Cayrol recuperates from forgetful silence.[11]

But one cannot say or show everything.[12] What enables *Night and Fog* to redeem these images of atrocity not only from the forgetfulness of historical absence, but also from the forgetfulness of banality, is its refusal to efface its own limits in representing the past. Despite the 'factual' tone of the narration, and the constant recourse to archival images, its circuit of positive evidence is consistently interrupted by recognition of the inevitable failure

10 One might contrast *Night and Fog* with the sensationalized presentation of similar images in *Judgement of Nations*, which operates very much in the memorial mode of revenge.

11 Here *Night and Fog* approaches the criteria Godard laid down for a film about the concentration camps: 'The only real film to be made about them – which has never been made because it would be intolerable – would be if a camp were filmed from the point of view of the torturers and their daily routine. How to get a human body measuring two metres into a coffin measuring fifty centimetres? How to load ten tons of arms and legs on to a three-ton lorry? How to burn a hundred women with petrol enough for ten? One would also have secretaries making lists of everything on their typewriters. The really horrible thing about such scenes would not be their horror but their very ordinary everydayness.' Godard, *Godard on Godard*, p. 198.

12 In this regard, *Night and Fog*'s lack of specific reference to Germans as perpetrators or Jews as principal victims has disturbed and angered a number of critics. See Avisar, *Screening the Holocaust*, pp. 15–16.

of words and images when confronting 'the Holocaust'. Discussing the use of human bodies to make soap, the narrator breaks off, acknowledging: 'But there's nothing left to say . . .' A shot of a scarred ceiling in a concrete bunker is accompanied by the narrator's voice: 'The only sign – but you have to know it – is this ceiling dug into by finger nails.' The bunker was a gas chamber. Even the photographic image cannot impart this knowledge by itself. One gradually realizes that the peaceful green fields surveyed by the camera are fertilized by the blood and bones of countless victims whose presence cannot be shown directly, merely revealed symptomatically.

This awareness of the limits of documentation is vital. It informs the network of strategies by which *Night and Fog* forces us to bring the concentration camp close – too close for the comfort of objectivity – and yet this nearness does not promote the sort of comprehension that would only be another form of comforting distance. The film constantly weaves between 'past' and 'present', mixing archival and contemporary images as its formal structure, in a pattern which displaces the resolution of chronology by suspending the viewer over an abyss of time.[13] By disrupting linear time, *Night and Fog* preserves memory *and* the disjunction of memory; it respects history's demand to show 'what really happened' while acknowledging the impossibility of ever really showing what happened.

Perhaps the principal achievement of *Night and Fog* is that it treats the Holocaust as a problem of memory; not in the conventional sense that it offers recovery and mastery of a lost past, but by its recognition that the extermination was itself a monstrous attempt to forget absolutely. The question the film continually poses, and continues to pose, amongst the silence and desolation, the abandoned railway lines, deserted buildings and weed-covered assembly yards, is just how 'the Holocaust' could ever be forgotten, and why this forgetting (of a people, a culture, a something Lyotard has called 'the jews')[14] can itself still be forgotten, lost not only once, but over and over again.

> The crematorium is no longer in use. The devices of the Nazis are out of date. Nine million dead haunt this landscape. Who is on the lookout from this strange tower to warn us of the coming of new executioners? Are their faces really different from our own? Somewhere among us, there are lucky Kapos, reinstated officers, and unknown informers. There are those who refused to believe this, or

13 This mixing of past and present is a strategy that Resnais would pursue in many of his feature films, particularly *Hiroshima, Mon Amour* (1959), *Last Year at Marienbad* (1961), *Muriel* (1963) and *Je t'aime, Je t'aime* (1968).

14 For Lyotard, this forgotten 'something', which he polemically terms 'the jews', is an anxiety or terror in face of radical heterogeneity. He argues that the socio-political conditions which enabled and eventually 'authorized' the Holocaust are linked to the refusal of Occidental thought to take account of this forgotten 'something' in every representation; a forgotten 'which persists not so much at the limits but rather at the heart of representation; this unnameable in the secret of names, a forgotten that is not the result of a forgetting of a reality – nothing having been stored in memory – and which one can only remember as forgotten "before" memory and forgetting, and by repeating it'. *Heidegger and 'the jews'* (trans. A. Michel and M.S. Roberts), Minneapolis, University of Minnesota Press, 1990, p. 5.

believed it only from time to time. And there are those of us who sincerely look upon the ruins today, as if the old concentration camp monster were dead and buried beneath them. Those who pretend to take hope again as the image fades, who pretend to believe that this all happened only once, at a certain time and in a certain place, and those who refuse to see, who do not heed the cry to the end of time.[15]

Some memories are more intolerable than others. *Night and Fog* was originally withdrawn from the 1956 Cannes Film Festival, ostensibly because the French government did not want to offend another participating country (Germany). This rationale does not explain the demand to delete an image in the film which showed a French gendarme in the control tower of the Pithiviers assembly camp. Eventually the screening went ahead with the uniform obscured.[16] Remembering French collaboration in the final solution was clearly felt to be more unpalatable than viewing other images arising from such a policy.[17]

*

If *Night and Fog* forms a benchmark for documentary approaches to the Holocaust, what might be said of those texts which eschew the archive and instead take on the burden of recreating that history? A landmark in this regard was the NBC mini-series *Holocaust* (1979), which broke new ground when it attracted massive audiences world-wide for its re-enactment of the wartime experiences of a family of German Jews. Even more remarkable was its impact in Germany. It came at a time when a number of young German film makers were reopening the question of the Nazi past, often figuring this history as an Oedipal conflict ironically expressed in the discomfort occasioned by the traditional child's question: 'What did *you* do in the war, daddy?' (As Elsaesser wrote of those who formed the core of the 'New German Cinema': 'They found history in the home and fascism in the family unit.')[18] But it was also a time when Nazism enjoyed something

15 This is the concluding statement from *Night and Fog*.

16 See J. Monaco, *Alan Resnais*, New York, Oxford University Press, 1979, p. 22.

17 Resistance to acknowledging French complicity in the 'final solution' was underlined by the controversy surrounding Ophul's *The Sorrow and the Pity* in 1969. It wasn't until 1992 that President Mitterrand made the first 'official' high-level acknowledgment of French participation in the deportation of French Jews.

18 Elsaesser, *New German Cinema*, p. 239. Elsaesser points out that early post-war West German films dealing with fascism, made under Allied control, tended to treat the subject as a crime thriller, with Nazism figured as a Mabuse-like conspiracy perpetrated by an isolated clique of fanatics, criminals and lunatics. Any question of widespread complicity and participation was thus peremptorily excluded. (See *New German Cinema*, p. 249.) Apart from a few exceptions such as Straub's *Not Reconciled* (1965), it wasn't until Syberberg's *Our Hitler* (1976), Fassbinder's *The Marriage of Maria Braun* (1977), Sanders-Brahm's *Germany Pale Mother* (1979) and Kluge's *The Patriot* (1979) that Nazism became a subject for cinematic investigation in Germany. International arthouse films dealing with the issue included *The Sorrow and the Pity* (1969), Visconti's *The Damned* (1969), Caviani's *The Night Porter* (1973), Malle's *Lacombe Lucien* (1974), Wertmuller's *Seven Beauties* (1975), Losey's *Mr. Klein* (1976), Bergman's *The Serpent's Egg* (1977) and Truffaut's *The Last Metro* (1981).

of a resurgence, variously manifested in a growing interest in wartime 'souvenirs', the so-called 'Hitler wave' in cinema, and the widespread eroticization of Nazi iconography.[19]

The ambivalence of these currents of interrogation, avoidance and fascination was reflected in the public response *Holocaust* generated. It immediately inspired thousands of phone calls, and sparked extensive public debate. According to film maker Edgar Reitz: 'More than any other documentary or personal account, this fiction film, although of mediocre quality, provoked a truly emotional outburst.'[20] Peter Marthesheimer (Fassbinder's scriptwriter on *The Marriage of Maria Braun*), who acquired *Holocaust* for German television, likened it to 'the psychodrama of a therapeutic experiment'.[21] Marthesheimer saw the televising of *Holocaust* as a means to free viewers 'from the horrible paralysing anxiety which has remained repressed for decades, that we in truth were in league with the murderers', adding that, through watching, 'we are able to experience every phase of the horror we are supposed to have committed against the other in ourselves . . . to feel it and to suffer it . . . deal with it as our own trauma.'[22] He thus situates Holocaust squarely as a response to Germany's 'unresolved' past and what the Misterlichs described as the German people's 'inability to mourn'.[23]

Could *Holocaust*, which takes the story of an ordinary German family who just 'happen' to be Jewish, remedy this memory problem? In the tradition of novelistic cinema, *Holocaust* 'works' by polarizing the audience between identification with the victims – 'this could be you' – and rejection of the brutality of the Nazi perpetrators. While this is undoubtedly a powerful technique (as the emotional response showed), representing 'the Holocaust' within the traditions of melodrama raises certain problems. No matter how 'realistic' one tries to be, within this narrative matrix the events inexorably assume the classical dimensions of tragedy. Germany becomes a closed historical universe with the death camps as inescapable destiny and final narrative destination. The politics of history gives way to the certainty of historical outcome, leaving viewers nostalgic for their lost innocence, but safely distant from 'the Nazi past'.

19 Foucault linked the association of Nazism with sex to attempts to re-eroticize power: 'The monarchy and its rituals were created to stimulate this sort of erotic relationship towards power. The massive Stalinist apparatus, and even that of Hitler, were constructed for the same purpose. But it's all collapsed in ruins . . .' 'Michel Foucault: interview', *Edinburgh '77 Magazine*, 2 (1977), p. 23.
20 Quoted in Elsaesser, *New German Cinema*, p. 271.
21 Elsaesser, *New German Cinema*, p. 272.
22 Elsaesser, *New German Cinema*, p. 272.
23 The Misterlichs argued that, because post-war Germany lacked the political space to acknowledge that the Nazi state had represented an object of love for many Germans, the pain of loss created by its defeat also went unacknowledged. As a result, instead of confronting their history, Germans buried it in the frenzy of post-war reconstruction. See A. and M. Misterlich, *The Inability to Mourn*, London, Tavistock, 1975.

Despite the catharsis it inspired, *Holocaust*'s easy division between the 'goodies' and 'baddies' of history outraged many critics. Edgar Reitz was particularly scathing of the response in Germany:

> Along comes the Uncle from America, pulls Holocaust out of his pocket, millions watch the box, thousands phone in, ten thousand break into tears . . .[24]

For Reitz, the tears were crocodile tears, and the outpouring of emotion showed that German audiences in fact had no inclination to accept responsibility for the past: 'Their longing for a block-buster is like the petit-bourgeois yearning for a *Führer* – even today.'[25] Reitz argued that *Holocaust* did not exhume the past so much as entomb it under the guise of exhumation.[26] By providing an abstract alibi of 'collective guilt', considerations of personal responsibility could be avoided by appealing to the limits of a private sphere ('I didn't see those things'), or to the passing of time ('that was all long ago').[27] Far from providing historical therapy by increasing historical consciousness, Reitz charged *Holocaust* with promoting cultural amnesia, enabling fascism to be perceived as a self-contained 12-year exception to the rule of civilization. Anything which threatened this belief – whether it be the return to power of former Nazi officials, or the disturbing proximity of this 'exception' to the 'normal' functioning of the state apparatus – could be guillotined by the sharp edge of linear chronology and historical teleology.[28]

Largely as a result of *Holocaust* and what he saw as Hollywood's expropriation of German history, Reitz was spurred to make *Heimat* (1984), a 16-hour serial film chronicling the experience of an extended family in Germany from 1919 to 1982. *Heimat* was pitched in similar narrative terrain to *Holocaust*, but aimed to perform 'memory-work' in a way that Reitz believed was impossible for both *Holocaust* and the repetition of archival images of 'the Holocaust'. In his film, Reitz claimed to restore not so much the historical record as historical reflexes. He argued:

24 Quoted in T. Elsaesser, 'Memory, home and Hollywood', *Monthly Film Bulletin*, 52, 13 (February 1985), p. 64.

25 Quoted in Elsaesser, 'Memory, home and Hollywood', p. 64.

26 Baudrillard made a similar analysis, although he placed greater emphasis on the role of television in the process of forgetting. *Holocaust* 'replays the extermination – but too late for it to profoundly unsettle anything, and above all it does so via a medium which is itself cold, radiating oblivion, dissuasion and extermination in an even more systematic manner, if this is possible, than the camps themselves. TV, the veritable final solution to the historicity of every event.' Baudrillard, *Evil Demon of Images*, p. 22.

27 Barta argues that the extreme polarization of Left and Right, reflected in the cold war partition of Germany, created the conditions for a wholesale denial of the past via retreat into a hermetic private sphere. See '*Heimat* and the ideology of innocence', in O'Regan and Shoesmith, *History on/and/in Film*, pp. 131–40.

28 Foucault has observed: 'One of the numerous reasons why they [fascism and Stalinism] are, for us, so puzzling, is that in spite of their historical uniqueness they are not quite original. They used and extended mechanisms present in most other societies. More than that: in spite of their own internal madness, they used to a large extent the ideas and devices of our political rationality.' 'The subject and power', *Critical Inquiry*, 8 (Summer 1982), p. 779.

Even now forty years after the war we are still troubled by the weight of moral judgements, we are still afraid that our little personal stories could recall our Nazi past and remind us of our mass participation in the Third Reich. That is the problem. We have so many stories that make up our past that can't be told, can't be true, that are stifling us, perhaps because they are so normal and for that reason so blind to history.[29]

To this end, Reitz called for a 'cinema of experience' utilizing cinema's unique capacity to saturate viewers with material detail. *Heimat* represented the past not by replicating the large-scale drama of major political events, but by redirecting attention from the monumental to the commonplace. Such a 'strategy from below' builds history as a mosaic of small decisions and temporary accommodations, sins of omission as much as commission, silences and compromises as much as political rhetoric and heroic stands. Through these means, Reitz hoped to cathect the common experiences which are differently inflected through each individual life, thereby bringing the most private memories to judgement at the table of politics. For Reitz:

> The difference between a scene that rings true and a scene written by commercial scriptwriters, as in *Holocaust*, is similar to that between 'experience' and 'opinion'. Opinions about events can be circulated separately, manipulated, pushed across desks, bought and sold. Experiences, on the other hand, are tied to human beings and their faculty of memory, they become false or falsified when living details are replaced in an effort to eliminate subjectivity and uniqueness.[30]

Such 'truths' are inevitably contentious. While *Holocaust* and *Heimat* take different approaches to representing the past, it is noticeable that Reitz's belief that film can create the conditions for 'memory-work' mirrors Marthesheimer's rationale for screening *Holocaust*. Anton Kaes has argued that *Heimat* suffers many of the problems common to melodrama, including a nostalgic tendency to conflate 'mother' and 'home': 'the film's secret message is that where she is there is Heimat.'[31] However, it is significant that Reitz's emphasis on using a 'cinema of experience' to represent history included the experience of cinema as a determinant of that history. *Heimat* consistently framed its character relations through the impact of communication technologies such as photography and radio, as well as the inclusion of extracts of a 1938 film also called *Heimat*. These references to the mediatization of politics and identity offer a crucial strategy for negotiating the excesses of that historical sensibility all too ready to accept the camera's transparency. Elsaesser comments:

> In spite of his diatribe against Hollywood, Reitz is clearly aware that in our century, to talk about memory is to talk about audio-visual representations of events. . . . One might even go so far as to say that Reitz's film is not so much a review of German history as a review of German *film* history . . .[32]

29 Quoted in Barta, 'Ideology of innocence', p. 131.
30 Reitz quoted in Elsaesser, *New German Cinema*, p. 272.
31 A. Kaes, *From Hitler to Heimat*, Cambridge, MA, Harvard University Press, 1989, p. 168.
32 Elsaesser, 'Memory, home and Hollywood', p. 64.

   The importance of this standpoint lies in the fact that National Socialism was an intensely narcissistic cultural formation, predicated on mass spectacle and the inculcation of a mode of subjectivity which itself resembled the experience of cinema. Simply employing conventional mechanisms of cinematic identification to 'work through' the experience of a past significantly *constituted* by those mechanisms is inherently problematic.[33] However, if Nazi Germany remains an extreme case (the total mobilization of technologies of representation prefigured total war), the trajectory it indicates has not been unique to Germany so much as an integral part of modern experience.

*

While Reitz sought to displace the 'opinion' of *Holocaust* with the 'irritatingly detailed experiences' of *Heimat*, an even more uncompromising critique of the limits of representation in this domain was undertaken by Claude Lanzmann in his epic *Shoah* (1985). Uniquely, *Shoah* not only eschewed archival imagery, but also refused to dramatize the past. Instead, the film records the testimony of survivors – perpetrators, victims and bystanders – by filming these different protagonists at the sites of their torn histories. Locating the conductor from one of the trains used to transport Jews to Treblinka, Lanzmann put him on the train and filmed his arrival at the now derelict camp.

> We arrived at the station and he made this incredible gesture staring back toward an imaginary chain of boxcars. He made as if he was going to cut his own throat. To me that was an image of truth which made the archival photos which we had seen completely irrelevant.[34]

How might we understand this 'irrelevance'? Is it simply, as Lanzmann has suggested, that the particular archival images he needed were missing? 'As far as the process of extermination goes, nothing – and there was a rather simple reason for this – the Nazis formally prohibited any filming of the extermination in order to keep it a secret.'[35] Or is it rather that resistance

---

33 This situates the need felt by film makers such as Fassbinder, Kluge and Syberberg to represent the Nazi past by foregrounding the *mediatization* of history. Fassbinder often utilized melodrama to narrate history; but while a film like *Lili Marleen* (1980) is full of period detail, it also quotes cinematic manifestations of period to reflect upon cinema's role in historical memory. In *The Patriot* (1979), Kluge eschewed the terrain of the historical blockbuster, with its 'realism' of swastikas, marching masses and book burnings, and instead approached the past by patching together bits of newsreel footage with snapshots and 'fictional' segments, focusing on the seams and disjunctions of these intersections to explore the collusion between spectatorial pleasures and historical truths. Syberberg's *Hitler: A Film from Germany* (1979) is the most extreme example of this tendency, entirely shaped by the thesis that critiques of Nazi Germany cannot afford simply to repeat the spectacle of that history, but must explore the politics of spectatorship to activate critical impulses.

34 Interview in *Cahiers du Cinéma*, 374 (July–August 1985), pp. 19–20, quoted in R. Burnett, 'Lumière's revenge', in O'Regan and Shoesmith, *History on/and/in Film*, p. 141. In *Schindler's List*, a child performs a similar gesture.

35 Quoted in Burnett, 'Lumière's Revenge', p. 141.

to the images that do exist, not of actual killings but of their aftermath, was judged to be too great? The risk of recycling atrocity as spectacle is particularly acute in this domain. Lanzmann has stated: 'If I had stumbled on a real SS film – a secret film because filming was strictly forbidden – that showed how 3 000 Jewish men, women and children were gassed in Auschwitz's crematorium 2, not only would I not have shown it but I would have destroyed it.'[36] In the same essay, his comments on Spielberg's critical and commercial success with *Schindler's List* (1994) reveal the gulf between their approaches. For Lanzmann:

> [T]here are some things which cannot and should not be represented. When I saw *Schindler's List* I remembered how I felt on watching the TV serial *Holocaust* . . . I suddenly realized that everything I refrained from showing is shown by Spielberg . . . For him, the Holocaust is a backdrop. The blindingly dark sun of the Holocaust is not confronted.[37]

Yet none of these concerns about the limits of representation address the immensely disquieting effect that *Shoah* often produces in its spectators. The nine-and-a-half-hour running time is vital in this regard. This length is not a sign of comprehensive treatment, even in a naive empirical sense. *Shoah* was cut from some 350 hours of footage, and its selectiveness is accentuated by its deliberately narrow focus on the East European death camps. What the length does create is an experience of duration. Viewers are made to witness the eye-witnesses as they tell their own stories, replete with evasions, admissions, accusations, prevarications and confessions; stories which unfold anguished experiences over an anguished time of telling; stories whose process of narration works a change in the demeanour of their narrators. What begins with confidence and control often ends with silence, tears, or defiance. The extraordinary scene in which a group of villagers in Chelmno, Poland, initially welcome the return of a Jewish survivor whom many remember as a boy singing in their church, and then gradually become defensive and almost aggressive in his mute presence, upbraiding him with accusations that the Jews did not resist extermination because *they them-selves accepted guilt* for the death of Christ, exemplifies this traumatic transposition of 'past' to 'present'.

For Lanzmann: 'The worst crime, from both a moral and an artistic standpoint, in making a film devoted to the Holocaust, is to regard the Holocaust as something in the past.'[38] *Shoah* seeks to demonstrate that 'the Holocaust' does not belong to a past which once existed but is now over and done with. Instead it aims to reveal another order of time. Lanzmann suggests:

> Legends are never laid to rest by pitching them against memories. They must, if possible, be confronted in the inconceivable present from which they draw their

36 'Why Spielberg has distorted the truth', *Guardian Weekly*, 3 April 1994, p. 14.
37 'Why Spielberg has distorted the truth', p. 14.
38 Lanzmann quoted in *36th Melbourne Film Festival Programme* (1987), p. 13.

being. The only way to achieve this is precisely by resuscitating the past and making it present, by resuscitating it in a timeless present.[39]

Like Resnais in *Night and Fog*, Lanzmann inserts numerous shots of railway lines, stations, trains and trucks throughout *Shoah*, material remnants of the mass deportations. Repetition here signals the strangeness still transfiguring these all-too-ordinary items which once belonged to the world of the camps. Like the dream objects André Breton wanted to fabricate in order to prove the reality of journeys into the unconscious, these images are evidence from the other side, 'concrete reality' wrapped in a malignant residue of historical incomprehension. A similar incomprehension grips the contemporary viewer asked to bear witness to stories from that other world; alien stories emanating from living bodies, traced in habits, gestures and faces; stories which split the present with what resists being told or shown but nevertheless makes its presence felt.[40] *Shoah* produces an immensely disquieting 'present' in which history finds no rest. But this infinite sleeplessness is not without hope: as Trinh T. Minh-Ha has observed: 'hope is alive as long as there is a witness – or . . . as long as the witnesses themselves do not die without witnesses.'[41]

*

What can be learned from these different strategies for representing 'the Holocaust'? Most evidently that there can be no single way of encapsulating such an 'event', which in its enormity and complexity challenges the very concept of history conceived as a narrative series of motivating causes and effects. But, perhaps more importantly, what is also registered in struggles to respond meaningfully to 'the Holocaust' is a disjunction within contemporary historiography. There is a gap between those who believe that memory can best be kept by marshalling facts and assembling evidence in order to establish (or at least try to establish) a complete picture, and those who believe that memory is best kept – *here especially* – by rigorously questioning the precepts which authorize or impose any such totalizing perspective, even as history's ideal. In question is precisely the politics of totalization,

39 Lanzmann quoted in *36th Melbourne Film Festival Programme* (1987), p. 13.
40 Lyotard writes: 'Representing "Auschwitz" in images and words is a way of making us forget this [the "unpresentable" in every representation]. I am not thinking here only of bad movies and widely distributed TV series, of bad novels or "eyewitness" accounts. I am thinking of those very cases that, by their exactitude, their severity, are, or should be, best qualified not to let us forget. But even they represent what, in order not to be forgotten as that which is the forgotten itself, must remain unrepresentable. Claude Lanzmann's film *Shoah* is an exception, maybe the only one. Not only because it rejects representation in images and music but because it scarcely offers a testimony where the unpresentable of the Holocaust is not indicated, be it but for a moment, by the alteration in the tone of a voice, a knotted throat, sobbing, tears, a witness fleeing off-camera, a disturbance in the tone of the narrative, an uncontrolled gesture.' Lyotard, *Heidegger and 'the jews'*, p. 26.
41 Trinh T. Minh-Ha, *Framer Framed*, p. 209.

and the negotiation of historical responsibility, including our responsibility to that which resists representation.[42]

Today, perhaps under pressure of subsequent events (other genocides, the nuclear threshold), but also a certain use made of 'the Holocaust' as the means of evading history and avoiding discussion of 'the Palestinian question', the historical significance of the event it names has been dispersed. This is not necessarily a bad thing. Any identification of 'the Holocaust' as an absolute evil which seeks to place its memory beyond question has always served to relegate it to a zone of abstract morality. In the face of such forgetting, one must ponder the extent to which horror of 'the Holocaust' belongs not only to its inhuman scale and techniques, but also to the fact that it occurred at the heart of Europe – the self-styled centre of civilization – rather than in Europe's colonies and satellites where racial policies tantamount to genocide were frequently institutionalized.

Most disturbingly, the lesson some now draw from 'the Holocaust' is not that we should remember in order that it will never happen again, but that we should remember so that it will never happen again to Jews. Instead of redefining 'the nation' in terms of an injunction to remember the heterogeneity of its people, the memory of 'the Holocaust' has returned as the byword for national security. The pain of history becomes a justification for any and all measures of aggressive self-defence against 'enemies' who threaten the existence of the state of Israel.

Some memories are intolerable. But if the immense technological archive cannot guarantee remembrance of 'the Holocaust', nor prevent the political structures and ideological formations which orchestrated its final solution from resurfacing, even and especially in contemporary Israel, there is an urgent need to rethink the model of history predicated on the preservation of history's singular truth. The demands of such a task can work strange inversions.

---

42 In his response to the 'de Man affair', Derrida posed the need to examine carefully the relation between theoretical axioms and political practices. He asks: 'Is there a systematic site of utterances, axioms, evaluations, hierarchies which, forming a closed and identifiable coherence of what we call totalitarianism, fascism, nazism, racism, antisemitism, never appear outside these formations and especially never on the opposite side? . . . To say that I do not believe that there is, not absolutely, means at least two things. (1) Such a formalizing, saturating totalization seems to me to be precisely the central character of this logic, whose project, at least, and ethico-political consequence can be terrifying. One of my rules is never to accept this project and consequence, whatever they may cost. (2) For this very reason, one must analyze as far as possible this process of formalization and its program so as to uncover the statements, the philosophical, ideological or political behaviours that derive from it and wherever they may be found. The task seems to me both urgent and interminable.' J. Derrida, 'Like the sound of the sea deep within a shell: Paul de Man's war' (trans. P. Kamuf), *Critical Inquiry*, 14 (Spring 1988), pp. 645–6.

7

Biodegradable Histories

> We cannot say anymore that the immutable is truth, and the mobile,
> transitory is appearance. The mutual indifference of temporality and
> eternal ideas is no longer tenable . . .
>
> T.W. Adorno

In every remembering something is always forgotten. But perhaps what is most actively forgotten is precisely the irreducibility of forgetting. And yet, forgetting is essential to remembrance: as Borges once remarked, 'If something were unforgettable, we could never think of anything else.'[1] However, most discourses around memory resist speaking this condition, resist knowing their own conditionality. What seems so difficult to remember, or at least so easy to forget, is that everything – even the unforgettable itself – is liable to be forgotten.

This is certainly a function of time. But perhaps not in the common sense that time passing necessarily removes us from the past. Distance from the past is less a simple measure of chronology than a complex effect of culture. The permanence or impermanence of any memory always depends on others, on the extent to which the living are prepared to assume responsibility for the lives of the dead. It is this constant need to reanimate the past which explains the urgency with which Holocaust survivors such as Primo Levi took on the mission to which they felt life had appointed them: to *testify*, to labour to keep memory near, to bear witness in order to ensure that 'never again' remained the watchword of the present.

If we admit that all remembrance is predicated on an intractable and irreducible forgetting, what might be a 'good' memory? Not all forms of forgetting should be presumed equal. Memory necessarily implies selection, ordering, narration, perspective; historical significance is fragile and events are liable to become unmoored in time; official 'history' is formed by the power to ignore and exclude as much as the power to name and include. What is recorded and preserved by a culture inevitably transmits the values and world-views of its dominant groupings. Benjamin's warning that '[i]n every era the attempt must be made to wrest tradition away from a conformism that is about to overpower it', which prefaces his famous injunction 'to brush history against the grain', remains indispensable.[2]

How might this necessity be related to what Lyotard terms the 'unpresentable', referring not to that which is merely left out, as if it might have been

1 Quoted in Virilio, *Lost Dimension*, p. 101.
2 W. Benjamin, 'Theses on the philosophy of history', *Illuminations*, pp. 257 and 259.

included, but that which resists representation? An amnesia deeper than the silence of negligent forgetfulness, belonging to a forgetting which plumbs the depths of cultural oblivion. While the first mode of forgetting is more susceptible to political intervention – the articulation of a programme of recovery, the formulation of a project of education – the second resists direct engagement. One of the most important lessons of deconstruction has been to insist on the necessity of political strategies which are (at least) double, which allow the 'unpresentable' to make itself felt at the limit of all directly political programmes. This seems crucial in negotiating the disjunctions of history and memory produced by new technologies in the present.

In light of the problematic that Derrida has called *writing* – of which the camera is something less than a cause but more than a symptom – what has become increasingly evident is a realignment of subjectivity, knowledge and representation which brings the time of history into contention. What interests me here is the manner in which previously fundamental oppositions – the poles of subjective and objective history, the psychic interiority of living memory and the exteriority of artificial or technological memory – have begun to break down and mutate in the present. The camera offers a strategic point of entry to this zone, not only because it has generated new practices of memory, but because it has so often been used as a metaphor capable of representing a certain historical ideal. This double identity situates its critical ambivalence: even as the camera has conformed to the objectifying and monumentalizing model of memory which stood at the heart of nineteenth-century historicism, it has pushed that paradigm towards ends which remain uncertain.

*

Like other forms of knowledge inherited from the nineteenth century, memory has consistently been split between the poles of objectivity and subjectivity. Objective memory demanded the reproduction of the past as it was, without mediation or alteration. According to this determination, remembering consists of preserving or restoring an original presence – an actual event, experience or encounter of some kind – which constitutes a stable point of origin. The belief that meaning is fully present at this point situates the importance granted a 'neutral' mode of representation in this economy. Objective memory demands a sign or medium which can re-present the origin without deviation. Within the same conceptual space, 'defective' memory designates re-presentations which depart from their point of origin or original identity, distorting it in some way, even to the point of falsifying its truth. It is difficult to overstate the extent to which our investment in the camera as a memory-machine has been shaped by this matrix, even today.

This understanding of the dictates of 'good' and 'bad' memory clearly has a long history, at least since Plato dreamed of a memory uncontaminated by signs. But if the Platonic goal of perfect repetition has remained ostensibly the same, the means to this end have undergone profound transformation. Classical mnemonics emphasized the 'placement' of expressive images in the mind according to a familiar topography such as the buildings in a street, or the rooms of a house. As one imagined moving through the space, the memories stored at different sites could be collected along the way.[3] However, as science became the matrix of modern knowledge, personalization was rigorously excluded, and good memory was instead reformulated in terms of the exteriority of objective reproduction. Following Bacon and Newton, scientific truth came to centre around the possibility of repeating experimental results under controlled conditions. This epistemological shift helped to create a new terrain for history and memory predicated on exact repetition. By the nineteenth century, the scientific claim to penetrate the reality of what is was replicated by history's claim to show only what was.

What becomes increasingly evident from this time are the twin paths – or rather the mutually supporting sides of a single path – along which the social relations of memory have been canalized in modernity. The governing face has been the rising demand for memory to be 'supported' in order that its testimony be granted authority. Like 'hard' science, historical truth demanded 'hard' evidence and repeatable proofs. This instrumental rationality conditions a cultural frame in which all that is *not* recorded is implicitly devalued, placed under the sign of unsubstantiated experience or 'mere hearsay' and thereby prevented from entering the highest realms of knowledge.[4] Moreover, in the quest for a supported past, not just any 'supports' would do. The dictates of objectivity which made it imperative for history to demarcate itself from 'speculative' discourses such as philosophy, theology and literature, also orchestrated the preference for photography over painting, and, indeed, over any other means of record. In the quest for objectivity, the camera-eye has consistently bested the human eye. So susceptible is reality to definition by the camera, that all that is not filmed, photographed or televised in the present begins to assume an ethereal quality; as if it only barely exists, unproven, unsubstantiated, illegitimate.

The other side of this dominant trajectory has been a tendency to appraise so-called 'living memory' reactively as an organic skill which functions completely outside any technical support. The problem here is not that 'scientific' history could not learn from other models – on the contrary – but that eulogizing the 'natural' over the 'artificial' only serves to homogenize a diversity of practices on both sides of this divide. Challenging the political hierarchy authorized in the name of 'objective history' is not simply a matter

3 See F. Yates, *The Art of Memory*, London, Routledge, 1966, pp. 6–7.

4 The automatic disqualification of virtually the entire oral tradition has been a decisive weapon in the imposition of structures of colonial power, especially with regard to land tenure. In Australia, for example, the inadmissibility of oral testimony regarding land ownership by indigenous peoples, coupled to their 'lack' of written records, underpinned the infamous doctrine of *terra nullius*. This notorious fiction was partially overturned in 1992 by the *Mabo* case, in which oral testimony in the Meriam language was granted new legal status.

of reversing the routine domination of the 'supported' over the 'un-supported', but of displacing the structure of opposition. If 'objectivity' was never as disinterested as it believed itself to be, neither was 'subjectivity' as prone to error nor as foreign to *technics* as was often asserted.

Clearly, the seductive potential of the camera to the scientific imagination lay in its capacity to objectify vision. A mechanical device capable of registering the most transitory appearances and repeating them to infinity carried unprecedented promise for preserving history without mediation, memory without text. Insofar as the discourse of history in the nineteenth century was marked by a strong desire to shift its domain from the speculative to the factual ('what actually happened'), its allegiance to the camera as both a source of evidence and a powerful conceptual model was the embodiment of logic itself. The camera seemed to offer that neutral mode of recording essential to the new age of historical certainty, parrying the crisis that the past was threatening to become in a period of rapid social change.

But as well as serving history, the camera transformed its terrain. In generalizing the function of the eye-witness, the camera blurred the distinction between expert and lay observer on which historical authority had been wagered. In industrializing the image and destabilizing the balance between detail and context, the camera began to dethrone the totalizing frameworks on which positivist historiography depended. And, by exposing the partiality and mutability of its own supposedly impartial and immutable representations, the camera finally made the entire line of objectivity – that line which co-ordinated the fantasy of the disinterested memory machine – far more problematic to sustain.

These contradictory movements situate the contemporary ambivalence to the camera as a memory device. In coming so close to that pure transcription of fact for which positivist knowledge hungered, and yet still finding itself distant – held at a distance, in its own terms, by an inability to secure meaning – the camera has exposed fatal flaws within this entire orientation. As much as it has formed a pinnacle of history's scientific leanings, the camera has also been instrumental in corrupting the very notions of objectivity, incontrovertible evidence and historical certainty for which it was once a shining light.

What photo-technologies have revealed this century is not only a new range of facts and new horizons of knowledge, but also the fragility of every fact, and the mutability of every image's truth. Where the camera once extended belief in the possibility of constructing a purely factual discourse about the past, it now promotes resistance towards this possibility: resistance crystallized in the understanding that, like a photograph, a 'fact' must be seen from somewhere, that it has a duration, a context, a configuration in time and space.

*

If the camera both opens and breaks open the dream of a perfect memory machine, this ruinous perfection invites us to rethink all that links identity to memory and time. Identity has historically been governed by the principle of non-contradiction: the self is self-identical by virtue of repeating (remembering) itself without alteration, without the intrusion of alterity. But what if 'good memory' is something other than recall without fail? In *The Ravishing of Lol Stein*, Marguerite Duras explored the burden of a memory which refuses to forget. Lol is prostrated by her past and lives without time for the present. Identity can atrophy not only by forgetting, but by remembering too much. One can be imprisoned in time.

Freud also warned of the dangers of obsessive memory. In one of his earliest texts, he declared that '*hysterics suffer mainly from reminiscences*', an opinion he would periodically re-cite.[5] The transformation of memory into a burden perhaps lies in an excessive fear of forgetting, a paralysing fear of loss, obliteration, oblivion, or death. But between the 'healthy' desire to remember and an 'unhealthy' anxiety at forgetting there is only a slender margin resembling the enigmatic movement/moment which divides past from present and future. The good memory posited as essential to 'healthy' identity so easily slides towards a memory which is too good and therefore 'unhealthy': fixated, brooding, obsessive. Once again, memory finds itself subject to a double injunction: the need for a stable memory to prevent a radical loss of identity must be 'balanced' against the risk of memory becoming wedded to an unchanging past, a memory condemned to repeat the fiction of unified identity, whether the referent is personal or collective ('self', 'nation', 'people'). How can one respect this double demand, to remember, and to remember the limits of remembering? What would be the fulcrum to balance that which should perhaps remain unbalanced?

To be without memory is to risk being without identity. In *Total Recall* (1990), when the mystic mutant Kwato asks Schwarzenegger's character: 'What do you want, Quaid?', he replies, 'Same as you. To remember. To know who I am.' The stranger is often a figure without a past, or with an interrupted or broken past: spatial displacement is overlaid by temporal disjunction as memory becomes the sole abode of the former home. Memory is frequently used to distinguish the properly 'human' from both the animal and the machine. Somewhere between the blind force of instinct and the

---

5 See S. Freud and J. Breuer, 'Studies in hysteria' (1893–5), *Standard Edition*, vol. 2, p. 7. Freud repeats this observation in 'Beyond the pleasure principle', *On Metapsychology: The Theory of Psychoanalysis*, Harmondsworth, Penguin, 1984, p. 282. And yet, it is worth noting that Freud's entire 'system' is predicated on the impossibility of *absolute forgetting*. The forgotten, even that active forgetting which constitutes the unconscious through the dynamics of repression, always returns to influence the present. Or rather, it is constantly present yet *elsewhere*; present without constituting something which could be re-presented. As we will see, even while Freud remains close to the Hegelian understanding of history as a dialectic without loss, his text begins to proceed in a quite different direction. Hence Derrida's desire to 'radicalize' the Freudian concept of the trace and to extract it from a metaphysics of presence by thinking the trace as 'constituted by the threat or anguish of its irremediable disappearance, of the disappearance of its disappearance'. See Derrida, *Writing and Difference*, p. 230.

mechanical repetition which drives the robot, human memory is inevitably linked to consciousness. In *Bladerunner* (1982), when android replicants are 'humanized' to increase their productivity, part of the process involves giving them a personalized memory complete with family photographs. As a result they become all too human with disastrous consequences: they no longer want to die. But positing 'healthy' memory as a function of properly human consciousness is less a resolution of the relation between memory and identity than a concentration of its essential ambiguity.

Do you select your past, or does it select 'you'? As Proust knew, involuntary remembrance can easily assume a life of its own. Freud also argued that memory, like forgetting, could never be simply 'voluntary': it is in the interval in between the voluntary and the involuntary that the whole question of the unconscious is posed. In his 1925 text, 'A note upon the "mystic writing-pad" ', Freud begins by observing that neurotics are remarkable for the extent to which they distrust their memories and then immediately reassures the rest of his readers by adding 'but normal people have every reason to do so as well'.[6] However, his real break in this field lies less in identifying this uncertainty than in locating it in the stratification of consciousness: 'Such memory traces . . . have nothing to do with the fact of becoming conscious. Indeed, they are often most powerful and enduring when the process which left them behind was one which *never entered consciousness.*'[7]

Tracing the effect of memories which 'never entered consciousness' is a major concern of the Freudian project. How might it relate to thinking the historical presence of what Lyotard has termed the 'unpresentable'? What protocols might respect the double demand to remember and to remember the limits of remembering? Most evidently, the Freudian text necessitates departing from spatial models in which remembering is conceived as the process of recovering a stable past located 'within' the mind as if in a wall safe or filing cabinet. (Here one might recall Sherlock Holmes, the doyen of nineteenth-century intellectuals whose persona tested the bounds of fiction; Conan Doyle described Holmes's mind as an attic which was not to be cluttered with extraneous bits of information, but only used to store the most useful and precious items.) By contrast, Freud describes less the stable architecture of a lumber room than a chamber without an entrance, whose only mode of access is not the daylight of consciousness but the twilight of dreams, jokes, hesitations and slips. This other place obeys an other time in which recollection can no longer conform to the mechanical retrieval of an original experience because the origin is no longer the indisputable self-presence of consciousness. The implications of this economy of deferral, detour and delay – which Derrida argues are the 'concepts which govern the whole of Freud's thought and determine all his other concepts' – are

6 S. Freud, 'A note upon the "mystic writing-pad" ', in *On Metapsychology: The Theory of Psychoanalysis* (Pelican Freud Library vol. 11), Harmondsworth, Penguin, 1984, p. 429.

7 Freud, Beyond the pleasure principle, p. 296 (my italics).

immense.[8] If memory and identity threaten to come unmoored, what also emerges is the possibility of a different protocol for relating to the past.

Freud's analytic cure is itself fundamentally concerned with memory-work: the analysand 'must be brought to recollect certain experiences and the affective impulses called up by them which he has forgotten'.[9] But the aim cannot be simply to render the unconscious available to consciousness:

> The patient cannot remember the whole of what is repressed in him, and what he cannot remember may be precisely the essential part of it. . . . He is obliged to *repeat* the repressed material as a *contemporary* experience instead of, as the physician would prefer to see, remembering it as something belonging to the past.[10]

There is a disjunction here: 'the past' is not remembered as past, but is repeated as present. Or, as Lacan will later put it (adopting a scriptural metaphor which demands further reflection), what is at stake for the subject 'is less remembering than rewriting the history'.[11]

How can we read the mutability of a memory which can never simply belong to the past, but is always refracted by the index of the present? Does it simply confirm modernity's emphasis on 'objective' or 'supported' memory and reinforce the technological apparatus as the site of reliability and certainty? Or does it repeat, on the terrain of the psyche, the logic of what Kracauer termed 'present-interest' theories of history, summarized by Croce's dictum: *all history is contemporary history*. Kracauer, who also placed Carr, Collingwood, Dewey and Dilthey in this school, remained critical of its orientation, not so much because of its focus on the present but because of its overemphasis on historical continuity. He argued that if the present is thought to 'encapsulate' the past, the tendency towards a Hegelian teleology of history proves irresistible.[12]

It would misleading to posit too neat a convergence between Freud and 'present-interest' theories of history. Clearly, Freud was disturbed by the present repetition of the repressed past: what the subject experiences is the anguish of trauma without the knowledge that it 'belongs' to the past. What is useful to take from Freud is the insistence that the past must always be interpreted in the present. Yet such an insistence must itself be coupled to a knowledge – a memory – that this experience has always already happened before. What comes into question is the adequacy of the model of origin on which historical knowledge has often been based.

The rupture in time opened by the Freudian text is useful in this regard, if

8 Derrida, *Writing and Difference*, p. 203.

9 'Constructions in analysis', *Standard Edition*, vol. 23, pp. 257–8.

10 Freud, 'Beyond the pleasure principle', p. 288 (second emphasis added).

11 Quoted in S. Heath, 'Contexts', *Edinburgh '77 Magazine*, 2, 1977, p. 38.

12 On the other hand, while Kracauer stressed the heterogeneity of historical phenomena and the significance of rupture, he was also critical of Benjamin's 'Theses' which he saw as moving too far towards the *discontinuist* side of the dialectic. See Kracauer, *History, the Last Things*, pp. 62–79 and pp. 191–214.

taken beyond conventional 'Freudianisms'. Throughout his life, Freud deployed various schemas to represent the relation between perception and memory. The problem which continued to fascinate him was the psyche's simultaneous facility for both 'an unlimited receptive capacity and a retention of permanent traces'.[13] How did the same system enable new data to be constantly registered while also storing a body of previous experience against which the incoming information could be weighed and judged? What model could represent this infinitely differentiated and yet permanently virginal apparatus? Derrida traces three principal metaphoric clusters that Freud deploys to this end: (1) the *energetics* of the *Project* (1895), where the psyche is conceived as a relation of forces, stratified by the differential excitation of mental particles; (2) the *topographics* of *The Interpretation of Dreams* (1900) in which the psyche is represented as an optical mechanism 'resembling a compound microscope, or a photographic apparatus, or something of the kind';[14] (3) the *textual* machine of the 'mystic writing-pad' in the 'Note' (1925). What is perhaps most noticeable in these figures – which inevitably include the camera – is not so much their adequacy or inadequacy as 'metaphors' for the psyche, but the manner in which every attempt to think memory disrupts the unity of the space of consciousness. For Freud, this interruption signals less the failure of identity than the very space–time of its production. Derrida argues that what finally defines the psychic system in the Freudian text is a metaphor of writing which does not displace the earlier schemas so much as unite them with unpredictable consequences.[15]

At first glance, recourse to the metaphor of writing is far from unusual. As Derrida points out, from the time of Plato and Aristotle, the relationship between perception and memory has regularly been illustrated by the image of writing (as notation, registration, inscription, recording, etc.). However, these relations have always been anchored by the prior determination of writing as secondary, the sign of a sign, a deferred presence which is therefore merely a strategy for mastering absence.[16] What emerges in the Freudian text – unevenly, often written with one hand and effaced with the other – is the necessity of appealing to 'a script which is never subject to, never exterior and posterior to the spoken word'.[17] This 'psychical' script is nevertheless not purely 'internal' because it is precisely the relation between inside and outside – the translation of sensory impressions into mental signs – which is in question.

13 Freud, 'A note upon the "mystic writing-pad" ', p. 430. Freud offered almost identical formulations in *A Project for a Scientific Psychology* (1895) in *The Standard Edition*, vol. 1, London, Hogarth Press, 1966, pp. 295–397, and *The Interpretation of Dreams* (1900).
14 Freud, *Interpretation of Dreams*, vol. 5, *Standard Edition*, p. 536.
15 See J. Derrida, 'Freud and the scene of writing', *Writing and Difference*, pp. 196–231.
16 See my earlier discussion in 'Writing with light'.
17 Derrida, *Writing and Difference*, p. 199. Barthes also entertains this other possibility: 'However, another notion of writing is possible: neither decorative nor instrumental, i.e. in sum secondary, but primal, antecedent to man, whom it traverses, founder of its acts like so many inscriptions.' *Sade Fourier Loyola* (trans. R. Miller), New York, Hill and Wang, 1976, p. 40.

What Derrida develops, following Freud's attempts to describe the logico-temporal relations of the unconscious, is the threshold of a 'concept' of the sign as writing or trace.[18] This endeavour to rethink the sign profoundly unsettles existing configurations of the space and time of representation. If what Freud calls 'the unconscious' interrupts consciousness, not as a buried experience (a present which is now past), but as the repository of an experience which has never been present, 'bringing to consciousness' could never amount to the repetition of a pre-existent text or body of signs. Instead, it is the very idea of a simple origin, of a 'first time' which could be subsequently repeated, which is made enigmatic. Since a sign only becomes a sign by virtue of its potential to be repeated, this possibility necessarily intrudes upon the purity of the 'living present' by always already dividing the point of departure of the 'first time'. For Blanchot: 'all this alludes to the initial error which might be expressed as follows: what is first is not beginning, but beginning over, and being is precisely the *impossibility* of being for the first time.'[19]

Awareness of this 'initial error' suggests that 'remembering' something involves less the repetition of a stable past than the reinscription of the putative origin. The Freudian logic of the 'deferred effect' suggests that each repetition must be its own origin, but, instead of happening just once, the origin is itself a weave of differences which incessantly point elsewhere. From this perspective, memory would name the enigmatic event of originary repetition: a repetition which – if only by dint of repeating – differs from that which it repeats. Such an understanding confounds the plenitude of the origin on which dominant structures of meaning, subjectivity, knowledge and memory have long been determined. Above all, it throws into disarray the prevailing sense that time is essentially linear and irreversible.

But if Freud continually announces the heterogeneity of time – and allows it, through the problematics of detour, deferral and delay, to shape his entire text – he also shies away from its most radical implications. Non-linear time necessarily undermines the metaphysics of truth to which psychoanalysis, in its desire to become a science, always remained committed. This bind was insoluble for Freud: while psychoanalysis posits itself as a certain truth of memory, it also reveals the disquieting possibility that the time in which this truth might be re-presented is itself inherently problematic. Derrida concludes:

> That the present in general is not primal but, rather, reconstituted, that it is not the absolute, wholly living form which constitutes experience, that there is no purity

18 As I have argued earlier in 'Promiscuous meanings', Freud oscillates between espousing systems of interpretation where the reading of dream symbols resembles traditional acts of oneirocriticism and decoding, and a radical awareness of the decisive importance and irreducible open-endedness of *context* which would prevent any simple closure of meaning. It is this second current that Derrida has consistently explored.

19 Blanchot, *Space of Literature*, p. 243.

of the living present – such is the theme, formidable for metaphysics which Freud, in a conceptual scheme unequal to the thing itself, would have us pursue.[20]

Pursuing the implications of this other time – time no longer governed by the value of presence – returns us to the problem of the camera's relation to history. But differently.

*

Memory has always troubled the serenity dreamt of by philosophies of consciousness and ontologies of substance. Repetition which lacks the symmetry of sameness threatens the presumption of homogeneous time in which the self-presence of identity finds a proper home. In the twentieth century, as the concept of linear and irreversible time, and its correlate of a unified subject capable of synthesizing temporal difference with relation to itself, have come into increasing dispute, the problem of memory has intensified. Without the guiding line of irreversible time, memory could not be determined as the repetition of an original thought or experience, or of any simple origin determinable as such. Yet, for much of its history, analysis of the photographic archive has been regulated by the problematic of 'restoration' with regard to 'original' meaning and context. As I have argued earlier, this model has always proved unsatisfactory, even on its own terms.[21] The fact that images can – and constantly do – appear in contexts unimagined by those who produced them cannot be regarded simply as the corruption of 'proper' meaning. Rather, this promiscuity demands new protocols for framing the archive. If photographs, films, or video tapes do preserve a past, it is the trace of a past which was never simply present, but was always already heterogeneous, discontinuous and forking: a time which reserved (deferred) some portion of its 'being-present' for unspecified futures.

From this perspective, the permanence of the past and the closure of history, promised as the 'scientific' gathering and summation of historical knowledge, appears as chimeric as the 'myths' that science sought to overtake. It is evident that the ideal memory posited by nineteenth-century history – so easily named photographic memory – obeys only one side of memory's double injunction. In valorizing repetition without alteration, this ideal memory remembers to remember, but forgets the irreducibility of forgetting, and so risks becoming a fixation, a blockage, a form of cultural constipation; an ethnocentrism which abandons the memory of the other traced in the heart of the self. *Lapsus*, absence, transformation and loss have their own claims on memory. With regard to the camera's role in perpetuating traditional festivals, one writer has commented:

> Obviously, the act of memory – which verse comes next, which way do we turn?
> – is very important to this continuity. But lapses of memory are also very much

20 Derrida, *Writing and Difference*, p. 212. Derrida's neologism of *différance* is one attempt to pursue this theme.
21 See 'Promiscuous meanings' above.

part of the developing process of a custom . . . It's the agglomeration of mistakes and additions through lapses in memory which give life and vitality to the event for the local community . . . Now, the act of recording or filming might prevent these changes happening by fixing the event. So the custom might become stagnant.[22]

Under the hammer of progress, solutions to the problem of history have most often taken the form of a quest for certitude. The desire to pull something back from the ruin of time, to secure an unchanging image which endures beyond the ceaseless mutability of life's flux, is deeply rooted within the modern psyche. And for good reason. A monumentalizing memory often seems to be all that can protect us from the time in which we are destined to lose everything, even ourselves. But, in the process of arming ourselves to the teeth with protection against life's transience, we find ourselves embedded in contradictions which open 'the past' to the most sentimental investments. The more we seek to seize the moment as a Kodak 'golden memory', the faster time seems to rush by.

Today, each act of recording has acquired a new poignancy. Photographic rituals of remembrance no longer hold back the tide of historical oblivion (as nineteenth-century photo-archivists such as Sir Benjamin Stone once hoped), but instead seem to presage it, to rehearse it, to bring it ever closer. We no longer fear that everything not recorded might soon be lost, but that many things, even if they are recorded, are somehow already lost. Everywhere today a camera stands ready to record phenomena, from historic buildings to biological species or ways of life, threatened with 'disappearance'.[23] The contemporary stockpiling of images to ward off loss – of species, of habitat, of culture, of the past in general – registers the acute anxiety affecting memory in the present.[24] Where the nineteenth century invented history, late twentieth-century imagination is gripped by melancholy. Nostalgic visions of the past as a time of lost innocence have proliferated in the cold light of social dysfunctions and environmental destruction which diminish the allure of progress. Often what photographs, films or video recordings preserve today is merely this sense of irredeemable loss.

Conditioned by the rapid disappearance of the past, modernity has developed technologies of memory such as the museum, the camera and the computer, which are charged with the task of securing a permanent record. But overinvestment in exact appearances, or in the authenticity of specific objects, transforms their significance. Recent controversy over the 'desecration' of a '5,000-year-old' cave painting in Western Australia highlights the

22 Quoted by B. Bushaway, 'Cameras and festivals', in C. Rawlence (ed.), *About Time*, London, Jonathan Cape, 1985, p. 93.

23 Symptomatic are photo-essays such as James Balog's *Survivors: A New Vision of Endangered Wildlife*, H.N. Abrams, New York, 1990. In forming a photographic *zoo*, these images reproduce an environment in which, as Berger once noted, the animals already 'constitute the living monument to their own disappearance'. Berger, *About Looking*, p. 24.

24 To the photo-archive and the museum, one could add current attempts to establish 'gene banks' of endangered species. One project involves preserving the genetic materials of all Australian marsupials: the story of Noah's Ark reappears in and as technology.

disjunction between chronological history in which the goal is the recovery and restoration of an original presence, and history conceived in terms of a non-linear interweaving of 'past' and 'present'.[25] The case concerned some Aboriginal rock paintings in remote north-western Australia, which, according to media reports, had been 'ruined' by some young Aboriginal men employed to restore them. What provoked the outcry was the modification of the existing designs, and the use of non-traditional materials (acrylic paints rather than ochres). Putting aside the question of whether the criticisms were justified, it is notable that they conform to the logic which ascribes the poor copy or defective imitation, like a bad memory or false history, to deformation of the original.

But what was the 'original'? Despite the headlines, a '5,000-year-old painting' is not necessarily one with 5,000-year-old paint. While the media stressed the importance of fidelity to an existing image (stemming, in part, from a tenant farmer who had an interest in promoting the site for tourism and later suggested that 'the safeguarding of these relics is too important to be left to Aborigines'), David Mowjarlai, the Aboriginal elder who administered the project, emphasized the pedagogical function of cyclical repaintings.[26] In contrast to the tourist economy with its concern for 'authentic' objects, Mowjarlai understood that 'memory' was part of a learning process. Questioned on *Sixty Minutes* as to why the young men doing the repainting didn't 'try out' on some other rocks, he replied: 'Aborigines don't practise'. Such a reply, which is both direct and supremely ironic in the circumstances, should not be read as advocating an 'anything goes' approach to tradition, but as questioning the fetishization of a limited concept of exactitude as the sole measure of 'good' memory. Preserving objects and appearances is not the same as periodically renewing cultural practices through which history and memory are kept 'alive'.[27]

What this controversy highlights is a cultural disjunction of great political significance. Irreversible, linear time has always sought to legislate the

25 Eric Michaels discussed this episode in his article 'Bad Aboriginal art', *Art & Text*, 28 (March–May 1988), pp. 59–73. Michaels's concern was primarily the potential for collective traditions of Aboriginal cultural production to interrupt the discourses of individual creativity and aesthetic innovation which dominated the market in which Aboriginal art began to circulate in the 1980s. My point is that these different practices also embody different conceptions of history and memory.

26 This situation is hugely complicated by the legacy of colonial dispossession. David Mowjarlai, who organized and administered the grant, seems to have acted outside traditional lines of authority, and it is uncertain whether the elders actually responsible for the caves were on site or elsewhere during the 'restoration'. My interest here is the defence Mowjarlai mounted.

27 Similarly, Nigerian writer Chinua Achebe describes the deliberate neglect of traditional *mbari* houses with their collection of art objects. The house is valued not as a physical site or precious object but because of the collective experience generated by its building and decoration. Veneration of the object and desire to preserve it is thought to diminish the creative urge of the new generation. See J. Clifford, 'Histories of the tribal and the modern', in R. Ferguson et al. (eds), *Discourses: Conversations in Postmodern Art and Culture*, New York, New Museum of Contemporary Art and Cambridge, MA, MIT Press, 1990, p. 418.

chronology of 'history' as something distinct from 'myth' and has functioned to differentiate other cultures temporally, stigmatizing them as
'backward', 'archaic', and 'primitive' often on the basis of their different
time sense. Linear, irreversible time has thus been both a fundamental
marker of cultural difference and an essential attribute of the dominant
language and logic within which such differences have been articulated.[28]
Defining an Aboriginal painting as a '5,000-year-old relic' is a powerful way
of denying Aboriginal Australians a stake in contemporary politics. The
example also highlights why the survival of indigenous peoples in the late
twentieth century is so awkward for Western cultures: it not only challenges
the pyramids of racial hierarchy and the models of cultural domination
which have figured history as the history of Western progress, but it disrupts
the means of defining 'the West' within that narrative by problematizing its
reliance on an other whose time has supposedly passed.

*

It is no accident that the expansion of telematics and the increasing
dominance of the camera in the historical archive corresponds to a new crisis
in history. 'History', which has long been written history, has been disturbed
by contemporary questions concerning its own textuality: the legitimacy of
its master narratives, the systematization of its modes of inquiry and the
formation of its distinct temporality. The natural order of the past has been
disrupted by the dispersion of sources and the excess of information
characteristic of the televisual era, and this diaspora has contributed to an
emerging awareness that there is in fact *no* natural way of ordering the past.
But this realization does not resolve the problem of history so much as
realign its tensions.

What is called history is never homogeneous, made up only of positivities
and positives, all that is solid, enduring, visible, memorialized and saved, but
also, and as importantly, is formed by processes of selective amnesia,
strategic illegibility, repression, avoidance, neglect, and loss. Recognizing
that history is biodegradable, that it belongs as much to the decay of origins
and archives as to their preservation and 'museification', demands new
protocols from those which have operated in the name of absolute origins,
authentic relics and photographic truths.[29]

Biodegradable history presages the end of the encyclopaedic model of
totalization. As Derrida has pointed out, the dream of totalization which
underwrote the nineteenth-century concept of historical truth can be judged
to be impossible in (at least) two ways. One is drawn from the classical
standpoint, presuming an infinite richness and variety which the empirical

28 This resembles what Fabian calls *allocentric* discourse: others positioned in another
time; *Time and the Other: How Anthropology Makes its Object*, New York, Columbia
University Press, 1983.
29 See J. Derrida, 'Biodegradables: seven diary fragments' (trans. P. Kamuf), *Critical
Inquiry*, 15 (Summer 1989), p. 845.

subject can never master: there is always more to see, to read, to learn, to say, to photograph. However, this model does not disturb the project of totalization, which may continue to orient knowledge as its ideal. The photographic project of the infinite archive follows this logic. By contrast, the other hypothesis is no longer that of an infinite field which resists saturation by a finite glance or discourse. Rather, it supposes 'a field of infinite substitutions only because it is finite, that is to say, because instead of being an inexhaustible field, as in the classical hypothesis, instead of being too large, there is something missing from it: a centre which arrests and grounds the play of substitutions'.[30]

What is this missing centre if not the Eurocentric myth of universal Man, and its temporal correlate of the homogeneous time of historical progress? To the extent that the camera has contributed to the undermining of the model of universal history as a continuous process of collecting and gathering whose proper end is unity – by multiplying potential historical sources, destabilizing the balance between particular events and general theories, and interrupting the established lines of historical authority – its effects can be placed in accord with the currents analysed by contemporary feminism, postcolonialism and postmodernism. But this is a necessarily complex accord, circumscribed by Western dominance in media products and infrastructure, and bound up with the political ambivalence of 'relativism'. For those long denied representation within the official texts of dominant history, there is reason to be suspicious of the forces seeking to dissolve the stable grounds of historical truth at the moment it seemed possible to set foot within their domain. Recognizing the ambivalence of historical knowledge is productive, not when it leads to the paralysis of judgement, but when it delimits absolutism.

It has often been noted that Walter Benjamin's 'Theses on the philosophy of history' broke radically with tradition; firstly in finding historical significance in 'the rags, the trash' of commodity culture, but above all in the emphasis that he placed on the transitory and shifting meanings of historical phenomena.[31] For Benjamin:

> The true picture of the past flits by. The past can be seized as an image that flashes up at the instant when it can be recognized and is never seen again. . . . For every image of the past that is not recognized by the present as one of its own concerns threatens to disappear irretrievably.[32]

This threat of irretrievable loss distinguishes historical time from the empty, homogeneous time of progress (which Benjamin saw as merely the modern face of 'eternal recurrence', except that what was repeated was the 'monotony of the new').[33]

---

30 Derrida, 'Structure, sign and play in the discourse of the human sciences', *Writing and Difference*, p. 289.

31 Benjamin quoted in S. Buck-Morss, *The Dialectics of Seeing: Walter Benjamin and the Arcades Project*, Cambridge, MA and London, MIT Press, 1991, p. 218.

32 Benjamin, 'Theses on the philosophy of history', *Illuminations*, p. 257.

33 Benjamin quoted in Buck-Morss, *Dialectics of Seeing*, p. 104.

Belief in progress, in endless perfectibility . . . and the conception of eternal recurrence are complementary. They are ineluctable antinomies, in the face of which the dialectical concept of historical time needs to be developed.[34]

The 'dialectical concept of historical time' aimed not to preserve the past, but to activate it. Benjamin's theory of 'dialectical images' which flash up at a moment of danger was explicitly conceived as a historical pedagogy – a means of transmitting the past while drawing attention to the particular way in which that past is seen in the present. Benjamin stressed the need to 'blast open' the historical continuum (hence the importance of film as 'the dynamite of the tenth of a second') in order to detach historical objects from their linear developmental histories. Through a montage of dialectical images, Benjamin sought to promote political awakening by highlighting the way the original Utopian promise of industrial culture had been betrayed under capitalism.

Bomber planes make us remember what Leonardo Da Vinci expected of the flight of man; he was to have raised himself into the air 'In order to look for snow on the mountain summits, and then return and scatter over city streets shimmering with the heat of summer'.[35]

Is such a project still viable today? While there are many reasons to doubt it, perhaps it is better to reverse the question and ask: is history possible in the present without undertaking such a project in relation to the images which circulate in the mass media? For these images inevitably contain historical traces, but transmitted in such a way – with the aim of humanizing commodities and charging them with existential significance – that their histories remain mute. Rather than surrender the 'mass media' as a zone without history, what becomes critical is our ability to detach these images from the atomized and empty 'now-time' of the televised present and to reconstruct them in an historically charged 'now-time' (what Benjamin called *Jetzzeit*).

If relinquishing visions of a permanent and stable past seems inherently risky, technological change has undoubtedly exacerbated our sense of this risk. One of the problems faced by the Waste Isolation Pilot Plant (WIPP) project, the world's first 'permanent' dump for nuclear waste in New Mexico, is to construct a monument capable of marking the site for 10,000 years.[36] This so-called 'Sign of Ages', due to be erected by 2030, must outlast all human monuments ever built – more than twice the current span of the pyramids. It must also preserve its meaning for a period vastly exceeding that of 'recorded' human history. The US Energy Department has

34 Benjamin quoted in Buck-Morss, *Dialectics of Seeing*, p. 108. Benjamin described the aim of his 'Paris Arcades' project as 'to demonstrate a historical materialism within which the idea of progress has been annihilated . . .' Quoted in Buck-Morss, *Dialectics of Seeing*, p. 78.

35 Quoted in Buck-Morss, *Dialectics of Seeing*, p. 245.

36 This is the period decreed by the US government, despite the fact that some of the waste will be toxic for at least 24,000 years. WIPP has been under construction for 15 years and is due to open in 1998. It consists of five kilometres of caverns some 300 metres below ground in which an estimated 300,000 drums of nuclear waste will be stored.

assembled a panel of experts – architects, anthropologists, semioticians, linguists, geomorphologists – to face this challenge.

What makes the WIPP project so fantastic is the disjunction it reveals in our sense of time. WIPP's manager is a geophysicist who assisted with nuclear tests in the 1950s. He notes that while radiation effects were then measured in milliseconds, today they are calculated in millennia. This future seems unimaginable – and unreachable – not only because of the dubious record of the nuclear industry in waste disposal, but because *memory takes time*, while time is the dimension most occulted by the culture of speed. While demanding monuments, museums and archives at every turn, the present seems unable to find the time in which they could be read.

PART 3
THE NEW PLASTICITY OF SPACE AND TIME

A few centuries ago our ancestors had the luck
to make the voyages of great discovery
We, the grandchildren of Columbus,
are creating the epoch of the most glorious inventions
They have made our globe very small
but have expanded our space
and intensified our time
My life is accompanied by unprecedented sensations
Barely five years old I had the rubber leads
of Edison's phonograph stuck in my ears.

El Lissitzky

1

Pure Speed: From Transport to Teleport

We must try to find a form to express the new absolute – *speed* – which any true modern spirit cannot ignore.

Umberto Boccioni

Video isn't I see, it's I fly.

Nam June Paik

In 1825, on a gentle 20-mile descent between Shildon and Stockton Quay, George Stephenson's *Locomotion* became the first steam train to haul passengers along a public railway. Wild scenes ensued as an excited band of riders accompanied it to its journey's end before a crowd of 40,000. The 21-one gun salute celebrating the achievement announced the emergence of a new era in which mechanically powered vehicles would finally sever traditional links between force and motion. Subsequent history has been so decisively shaped by this revolution that different incarnations of the engine – steam, combustion, jet, rocket – have been used to mark successive thresholds of a modern era which is itself characterized by perpetual movement. The train, the automobile and the aeroplane have completely modified all human relations to distance and speed, approaching a terminal point with rocketry in which the earth itself becomes merely a launching pad for potentially infinite journeys into endless space.

If velocity has been at the heart of each of these revolutions, it is not only the increased speed each new wave of vehicles has achieved, but also the ascending rate at which they have transformed social and political relations. Over a century ago Marx noted the critical importance of rapid movement to the development of a global capitalist economy:

> [W]hile capital on one side must strive to tear down every spatial barrier to intercourse, i.e. to exchange, and conquer the whole earth for its market, it strives on the other side to annihilate this space with time, i.e. to reduce to a minimum the time spent in motion from one place to another. The more developed the capital, therefore, the more extensive the market over which it circulates, which forms the spatial orbit of its circulation, the more does it strive simultaneously for an even greater extension of the market and for greater annihilation of space with time.[1]

This trajectory underpins the emergence of speed as the prime quotient of modern social relations. When Marinetti proclaimed in his Futurist Manifesto of 1909 that 'Time and Space died yesterday. We already live in

1 K. Marx, *Grundrisse: Foundations of the Critique of Political Economy* (trans. M. Nicolaus), London, Allen Lane/NLR, 1973, p. 539.

the absolute, because we have created eternal, omnipresent speed', he was voicing a desire which became a destiny for the new century.[2] Modernization has become synonymous with acceleration across all areas of social life. Speed has been the mechanical soul of modernity; not only for the avant-gardes whose aspirations to burn the libraries and wreck the museums transformed art, but for entrepreneurs, inventors, adventurers and all the other apostles of progress who were captivated by the impulse to go faster and travel further, to dynamize life and propel it into the future – by force if necessary.

In the excitement generated by the opening of transcontinental railways and intercontinental sea-routes, and especially the unbounded public adulation of early aviators such as Bleriot and Lindbergh, we can read parables of the emergent culture of speed.[3] Pleasure in the novelty of dynamic vehicles and pride in the 'conquest of the skies' converged with the immense possibilities for economic growth and colonial expansion that they created. Imperialism was the political corollary of modern dynamism: as Robinson, Gallagher and Denny observed: 'Expansion in all its modes not only seemed natural and necessary, but inevitable: it was preordained and irreproachably right. It was the spontaneous expression of an inherently dynamic society.'[4] The rapid extension of 'the West' as a political and economic force in the nineteenth century, which laid the foundation for the systematization of world trade and the global division of labour in the twentieth, has been paralleled on the domestic front by the development of the distinct modern culture of *auto-mobility*: the Brownian motion of mass urban populations for whom the 'freedom to drive' has become a fundamental article of political faith.[5]

Under pressure of these new forms of circulation which mobilized people and products on regional, national and transnational circuits, the centres of lived existence have mutated in a process whose ends are still not clearly defined. Suspended between house and car dwells an antagonism internal to modern culture. A fault line stretches between the desire for home as a stable site, a secure space of shelter and enclosure, and the constant drift towards the frontier as a liminal space of perpetual transformation and potential conquest. Modern identity belongs neither in the home nor on the road, but

---

2 F.T. Marinetti, 'The founding and manifesto of Futurism 1909', reprinted in Apollonio, *Futurist Manifestos*, p. 22. Marinetti also considered 'Dynamism' as the name for the movement.

3 Louis Blériot was the first pilot to fly the English Channel in 1909, an act whose full strategic implications were scarcely appreciated until 1940. Charles Lindbergh made his thirty-three-and-a-half-hour trans-Atlantic flight in 1927, a feat acclaimed in a manner unrivalled until the Apollo moon landings.

4 R. Robinson, J. Gallagher and A. Denny, *Africa and the Victorians: The Official Mind of Imperialism*, London, Macmillan, 1972, p. 3.

5 Although the 'freedom to drive' has never been codified, it clearly resembles the successive doctrines concerning the freedom of the seas, freedom of the skies and freedom of space which have been integral to the geopolitical order of capitalism.

is perpetually split by the psychic and social contradictions of its attachments to both these poles.

*

Despite constant acceleration throughout this century, and the technological attainment of speeds beyond human endurance, locomotive machines have themselves been overtaken by what Paul Virilio aptly termed 'the last vehicle': the audio-visual one.[6] Following Marinetti's tracks, Marshall McLuhan remains perhaps the most famed post-war prophet of the manner in which transport would be displaced by communication:

> During the mechanical ages we had extended our bodies in space. Today, after more than a century of electric technology, we have extended our central nervous system itself in a global embrace, abolishing space and time as far as our planet is concerned . . . As electrically contracted, the globe is no more than a village.[7]

If McLuhan's 'global village' was forever embedded in what could be called – perhaps for the first time – 'global consciousness' with the Apollo moon landing telecast of 20 July 1969, the trajectory he indicated had been evident for some time.[8] The advent of the telegraph in 1794 inaugurated the ability for messages to outpace messengers. By the nineteenth century, the expansion of telegraph services and the successive invention of the camera (1839), the telephone (1876), the phonograph (1877), the wireless radio (1894), and the cinematograph (1895) completely redefined the practice of 'communication' and the notion of 'proximity'. The dichotomy between being present in one place and therefore necessarily absent elsewhere began to waver, as physically separated sites of action were bridged and juxtaposed in new ways. Stephen Kern points to the spectacular blaze of publicity the wireless received in 1910 when it enabled the arrest of Dr Hawley Crippen (a US physician accused of murdering his wife) while he was on board the ocean liner *Montrose*. But the new possibilities of 'action-at-a-distance' went beyond merely extending traditional forms of social interaction and political authority; rather, they fundamentally changed the socio-political field itself.

The instantaneous 'live' connection offered by the telephone (and then radio) provided the model that other media sought to emulate. When Charles Lindbergh set off on his epoch-making trans-Atlantic flight in 1927, Fox–Movietone rush-released a four-minute sound newsreel of his take-off to a packed cinema audience in New York's Roxy Theatre that same night.[9] It

6 P. Virilio, 'The last vehicle', in D. Kamper and C. Wulf (eds), *Looking Back on the End of the World* (trans. D Antal), New York, Semiotext(e), 1989, pp. 106–19.

7 McLuhan, *Understanding Media*, pp. 11 and 12–13.

8 Arthur C. Clarke discussed the possibilities of geostationary orbit and the communications potential of satellites (now known as 'the Clarke belt') in his 1946 paper 'Extra-terrestrial relays'. Television link-ups to all five continents via satellite occurred in 1964, the year that McLuhan's *Understanding Media* was published.

9 See D. Gomery, 'Towards an economic history of cinema: the coming of sound to Hollywood', in Heath and De Lauretis, *Cinematic Apparatus*, p. 44.

received a standing ovation, a response worth recalling when the surpassing of such feats has become a part of daily life. Equally notable is the fact that similar examples are spread across what are usually posited as the great political divides of this period. The Soviet *ciné-train* project led by Alexander Medvedkin in the 1930s (adapted from the civil war agit-trains) also strove to exhibit films the same day they were shot.[10] In Nazi Germany, propaganda Minister Goebbels ordered the airlifting of footage from the battle front so that it could be included in the latest newsreels, while the finished products were then flown around the entire country so they could be released on the same day.[11] All these examples may be read as attempts to establish film services which approach the speed of television. The desire for simultaneity, which coursed through modern sensibility at the beginning of the century, has transformed the social and political terrain, creating radical new 'communities' dispersed in space but joined in time. What Paul Virilio has termed the displacement of geo-politics by chrono-politics situates the manner in which television has been able to present itself as the destiny and destination of modernity.[12]

Television hybridized the camera with radio to fuse vision and speed in a new way. *Rapid seeing* – spanning distance without losing time – has become the hallmark of modern perception, defined by the ubiquity of live broadcasts which enable vast audiences distributed across continents to see events happening outside the horizon of their own 'presence'. The fact that the appearance of broadcast television redefined the roles of all other media, including print, radio, photography and cinema, only underlined the extent to which modernity is a speed-driven culture, in which the relative velocity of different media vehicles determines their social utility. With television, photographic and cinematic images lose their edge and prove unable to keep up with demands for a rapid information flow. Finally, it is television and not the newspaper or newsreel which works around the clock.[13]

Where it once took military organization to deliver images and information at a speed which ensured that events did not outstrip communications,

10 The cine-train was equipped as a mobile film studio, processing plant and cinema. It made six expeditions into the Ukraine and Caucasus between 1932 and 1933, producing some 70 short films. The aim was to use the experience of seeing one's own community represented on film to generate feelings of collective goodwill and national fervour. See S. Crofts and M. Enzensberger, 'Medvedkin: investigation of a citizen above suspicion', *Screen* 19, 1 (Spring 1978), pp. 71–89. See also the films *The Train Rolls On* (SLON Collective, 1971) and Chris Marker's *The Last Bolshevik* (1993).

11 See S. Kracauer, *From Caligari to Hitler*, Princeton, Princeton University Press, 1974, pp. 276–7.

12 See Virilio, *Lost Dimension*, p. 124.

13 Although there had been experimental broadcasts since the 1920s, television did not gain sizeable audiences until after the Second World War. The direct relation between the rise of television and the decline of cinematic newsreel and news-related programmes can be seen in the demise of the major US productions: *The March of Time* and *This is America* ceased in 1951, *Pathé News* in 1956, *Paramount News* in 1957, *Fox–Movietone News* in 1963, *MGM News of the Day* and *Universal News* in 1967.

today it is the media who are on permanent war alert and events which cannot move fast enough. If the Gulf War was notable for the extent to which television cameras stalked each action and searched restlessly for the decisive event, an even more striking threshold (but destined, one suspects, to become banality itself) was the landing of US troops in Somalia in December 1992: by the time the marines arrived, the camera crews already had a beachhead, and were beaming the action live to domestic audiences over breakfast. The much-prophesied creation of a single terrestrial zone of total visibility suddenly seemed very close: the world as global TV studio. Decades earlier, Heidegger had evoked the darker side of McLuhan's 'global village' by casting television as the force of a new tyranny:

> All distances in time and space are shrinking . . . The peak of this abolition of every possibility of remoteness is reached by television, which will soon pervade and dominate the whole machinery of communication . . . Yet this frantic abolition of all distances brings no nearness; for nearness does not consist of shortness of distance . . . despite all conquest of distances the nearness of things remains absent.[14]

'Nearness' is undoubtedly a complex and elusive quality. For Heidegger, it belonged to the essential distance which opens the dimensionality of 'true time'.[15] For Benjamin (who was certainly no disciple of Heidegger), 'distance' was an essential attribute of aura, and, as is well known, it is precisely the decay of aura that he posits as the revolutionary effect of the camera. By allowing viewers to approach the previously unapproachable, Benjamin argued that the camera contributed to the displacement of 'cult value' in every sphere, bringing the secular disenchantment of the world to a new pitch.[16] Yet, under the eye of Hollywood and global television, the political effects of this revolution have diverged from those Benjamin once envisaged.[17]

From one man's first steps on the moon to a football match with an audience a billion strong, the entirety of the world and its beyond has been structured as the set of an ongoing spectacle. In his seminal analysis, Guy Debord argued that this seizure of the world as spectacle exceeds traditional

---

14 M. Heidegger, 'The thing', *Poetry, Language, Thought*, p. 165.

15 See M. Heidegger, *On Time and Being* (trans. J. Stambaugh), New York, Harper and Row, 1972, p. 15.

16 For Benjamin, cult value belonged to the myth-laden sacred world: 'The definition of aura as a "unique phenomenon of a distance however close it may be" represents nothing but the formulation of the cult value of the work of art in categories of space and time perception. . . . The essentially distant object is the unapproachable one. Unapproachability is indeed a major quality of the cult image.' Benjamin, *Illuminations*, pp. 245 and 224–8. In contrast, he argues that the camera is characterized by the dominance of exhibition value: its images exist to be seen, and this fact instils them with new political possibilities.

17 This point is complicated, insofar as Benjamin did not subscribe to the thesis, most commonly attributed to Max Weber, equating post-Enlightenment modernization with the process of 'disenchantment'. Rather, Benjamin understood the rise of commodity culture in the nineteenth century as the imposition of a new mode of enchantment. He posited the historic role of the camera as its ability to 'awaken' the masses from their commodity-induced slumber.

questions of vision and representation, and points instead to the historic moment in which technologies of vision effectively penetrate the interstices of all social relations.[18] For Debord, the primary characteristic of the spectacle is the pervasive commodification of time and space, manifested in the homogenization of territory and the domination of temporality by 'pseudo-cyclical rhythms' of consumption.[19] Yet, the prospect of a completely unified and totally homogenized world has also produced counter-tendencies of conflict and contestation. Today, the imposition of global media empires is marked by the resurgence of cultural difference, and the reassertion of claims of locality and regionalism, even the much discussed 'collapse' of universalizing theories.

For this reason, it is important to recognize that, inasmuch as television provides an exemplary image of the capacity of communications technology to produce a 'global culture', it also offers a powerful metaphor for the disjunctive spatial and temporal experiences of the present. The confusion of near and far accentuated by television's drive for a global horizon engineers a new psychogeography in which locality and universality are no longer opposed but in series. Television often seems to upset something in our thinking: the fact that it so regularly slides to an extremity of thought (recalling Heidegger: 'the *peak* of the abolition of every possibility of remoteness') may yet constitute one of its most strategic attributes.

*

From the first successful photographs of the moon taken in the 1840s to space-age images of the earth seen as a solitary luminous orb suspended in a vast black universe – perhaps the most long-awaited 'reverse shot' in history – the camera has been instrumental in opening new vistas to the human eye.[20] Images of the terrestrial surface seen from aeroplanes, or of whole continents seen from satellites, or of entire galaxies imaged via radio-photography are counterpointed by photomicrographs which penetrate the bounds of the discrete atom. The opacity of solid surfaces has dissolved before X-rays, while the shades of darkness are everywhere lifted by infra-red images and thermography. Even the integrity of the living body has been penetrated, as if from within, by endoscopy. Movement of all kinds has been decomposed beyond the threshold of the human eye, and the most transient phenomena, such as sub-atomic particles whose longevity lies at the edge of nothingness, can now be 'seen' by human observers. Contemporary techniques of 'ideography', using positron cameras to register the movement of

18 For Debord: 'The spectacle is not a collection of images, but a social relation among people, mediated by images.' *Society of the Spectacle*, paragraph 6.

19 See *Society of the Spectacle*, especially chapters 6–7. It is worth comparing Debord's text with Heidegger's analysis of the 'ground plan' of science. See 'The geometric universe' above.

20 The first full disc colour photographs of the earth taken from Apollo 17 in December 1972 represented a new threshold of the Copernican revolution – a previously unattainable perspective became visible to all eyes.

air around the brain, once again raise the age-old dream of submitting the psychic to the physical by rendering visible the 'event' of thought itself.[21] In short, the bounds of the perceptible universe have been completely redefined.

Yet to focus solely on this series of spectacular limit cases would be misleading. The camera's most profound effects on contemporary experiences of time and space are perhaps to be found in those perceptual shifts which have today become so prosaic that they pass almost unnoticed: the snapshot, the close-up, the moving-image, montage, the time-lapse sequence, the live broadcast, the instant replay. In what follows, I am most interested in the profound modulation of social rhythms, the reconstruction of living and working spaces, the emergence of new social relationships and the deployment of new forms of power in a world in which every site and situation is subject to potential incursion. The institutional forms different camera technologies have taken – postcards, illustrated magazines and newspapers, domestic photography, cinema, broadcast television, and so on – have been instrumental in the production of a network of functional spaces, new scenes of watching which are both sites of consumption and cells for surveillance. In the uncertainty generated by the camera's disjunctive effects on the authority of embodied perception, qualities of time and space long thought to be 'fundamental' are themselves shifting. In one sense, 'modernity' can be defined by this shift which affects both physical boundaries and psychic formations: the destabilization of architectural and geographical borders (the room, the nation) as much as the disruption of discursive traditions (the unity of the book, the universality of reason) are part of the crisis of referents and dimensions currently testing the limits of thought and experience.

It is important to treat the emergent space–time of what is commonly called 'media culture' as more than a distorted manifestation of some earlier, more 'genuine' social form. Ever since the invention of the telegraph, developments in transport and communication technologies – from the railway and cinema to television and the space age – have been hailed or condemned for engineering the 'disappearance' of space and time. Since so many pronouncements of 'the end' have proved premature, it seems prudent to be less hasty in equating transformation with annihilation. Contemporary challenges to the authority of values such as linearity, continuity and homogeneity from discourses emphasizing relativity, rupture and discontinuity have fundamentally affected the legitimation of the political field. In the process, the profound and often neglected links between politics and time and space have been thrown into relief. Situating the camera in this scene is critical insofar as camera technologies have themselves generated new spatio-temporal experiences crucial to the political force lines of

---

21 One scientist involved in this research, Jean-Pierre Changeaux, argues: 'It is not utopian one day to think we will be able to see the image of a mental object appearing on a computer screen.' Quoted in Virilio, *Lost Dimension*, p. 114.

modernity and postmodernity. Today, our task is to reckon with a novel horizon in which 'direct' and 'indirect' perceptions gravitate towards a radical interchangeability in everyday life. This condition undermines the presumption of spatio-temporal continuity which founded the Cartesian–Newtonian universe, and orchestrates a new distribution of bodies, gazes and identities as the frame of contemporary subjectivity. If the front line of every war zone has the potential to cross every living room as a present event, it is the terms of this 'new world order' that we need to understand.

2

Reconstructing 'the World'

The 'world' was never more than an image, a regulative idea, a normative concept for planning and implementing a global society.

Dietmar Kamper and Christoph Wulf

The European conception of the world which came into being during the sixteenth century was vastly different from that which preceded it. In the wake of Columbus, the globe had been circumnavigated and maps began to assume the territorial outlines and distribution of land masses with which we remain familiar today. But, more significantly, the world was becoming integrated in a new sense, conceived as a geophysical continuity without edges or ends. If its place in the Copernican universe was no longer centre stage, the belief that the earth possessed a continuous spherical surface meant that all terrestrial journeys could potentially interconnect if extended far enough. There was no underneath, no other side, no place which remained absolutely discontinuous or completely apart.[1]

Clearly, it is only in retrospect that this threshold can be discerned at such a distance. Despite epoch-shaping events such as the conquest of the Americas and the colonization of India and Australia, in practical terms the unity of the world remained amorphous until well into the nineteenth century. In this period, the development of transcontinental railways linking the intercontinental sea routes and the expansion of telegraph and telephone networks began to stitch the world's surface together in qualitatively new ways. It became possible not only to think of the world as a single entity, but to traverse and administer it as one.[2] With further reductions in the time of circumnavigation, the isolated European 'voyager' was displaced by the ascendancy of the trader, the missionary, the soldier, the colonial functionary, and eventually the ubiquity of the tourist, as the growth of organized travel to 'foreign' places emerged as a distinctive part of modern experience.

1 A fact dramatically demonstrated by Howard Hughes in his 1938 solo flight circumnavigating the globe when, upon landing, he taxied his plane to the exact point from which he had departed four days earlier.

2 Jules Verne's *Around the World in Eighty Days* (1873), which symbolized the shrinking of the world into a traversable surface, was itself inspired by a travel timetable published in 1870 following the completion of the Suez Canal, the American Transcontinental Railroad and the Trans-Indian Peninsular Railroad. The first international phone line was established between Paris and Brussels in 1887, and the first overseas phone line between France and England in 1891. See Kern, *Culture of Time and Space*, pp. 211–15.

This invasion of every periphery presaged deeper cultural mutations, as changes in transport and communication fed transformations in political economy. The global trajectory of capitalism which spurred the dramatic expansion of colonialism in the period up to the First World War made it feasible to represent the world as a single unit organized by the relation between various metropolitan centres and their diverse satellites.[3] If this unprecedented expansion of 'the West' gave birth to new political hierarchies founded on a racial basis, it also demanded new strategies for managing cultural and racial difference. From its inception, the camera proved pivotal to this scene.

Like the new vehicles which transported people and products across the globe, the camera transported vistas and sights, mapping the earth's surface and joining the foreign to the familiar in new ways. It fused pleasure in seeing the previously unseen to power in the form of a knowledge with normalizing aspirations. The camera was instrumental in the advance of imperialism, linking the 'hard' gaze of military–bureaucratic surveillance with the 'soft' panoptic pleasures of the voyager–voyeur, overlaying territorial dominion with a veneer of cultural and psychological domination. Photography, and later cinematography, not only facilitated the direct exercise of military force and colonial rule, but enabled the colonizers to believe they had taken possession of unfamiliar territories. For the traveller abroad, the camera often functioned literally as a screen for the eye, serving to domesticate foreignness by imposing a standard frame on any encounter with cultural and racial difference. For the viewer at home, images of 'others' became prized objects of consumption, and played a vital role in securing the perimeters of Western self-identity in a time of increased exposure to racial diversity and cultural heterogeneity.

*

As soon as the first photographic images began to circulate, views from distant lands and far-off places achieved an immediate currency in European and North American metropolitan centres. Alongside the portrait, it was unusual and exotic scenes, especially Byronic images depicting the ancient splendours of Egypt, Greece and Rome, which initially fired the public imagination. The success of the first tentative photographic ventures abroad led to a photographic diaspora, as cameras rapidly appeared in all parts of the world. The 1850s saw a host of European photographers descend on the Mediterranean and the Middle East.[4] Along another axis, photographs of foreign events, such as Roger Fenton's images from the Crimean War (1855), began to circulate as part of an information economy with global aspirations.

3 Between 1815 and 1914, direct European colonial dominion expanded from 35 per cent to 85 per cent of the earth's surface.

4 Most renowned was Francis Frith, whose journeys up the Nile and through the Middle East from 1856 to 1859 generated sizeable profits, which Frith used to found what became the world's largest publisher of picture postcards.

The ability of the camera to bring the world back home astonished, excited and enthralled. The photographic stamp of authenticity ensured favourable comparisons to all previous media, exposing the often fertile imaginations of painters to the critical eye of an age eager for objective knowledge. Photography quickly surpassed the contemporary popularity of the Panorama and the Diorama and rivalled the new public museums with their treasure hoards and plaster models in laying out foreign lands for domestic consumption. The blank spaces and mysterious absences surrounding legendary sites and mythical places gave way to an increasingly detailed photo-topography. The unprecedented extension of horizons seemed palpable: one photographic enthusiast was moved to proclaim: 'Every day now lessens the distance between the travelled and the untravelled man.'[5]

But this increased exposure of the outlands did not so much erase their antipodality as confirm its essential truth. While photography undoubtedly expanded the range of knowledge available to people about countries and cultures outside their own experience, this knowledge was indelibly shaped by its historical setting. The fact that the camera was invented and popularized just after the young Victoria's ascension to the throne of England can scarcely be overstated. Increased access to the colonies – the gift of the new vehicles – created new demands for comprehensibility. In his seminal work, Edward Said noted the 'modernization' of orientalist discourse in the nineteenth century.[6] Photography became a lynchpin in the trade in foreignness and fuelled the new discourses of the other – from anthropology and ethnography to popular accounts of travel and colonial life – which blossomed in the second half of the nineteenth century. As the most versatile tool for 'worlding' the world (as Spivak puts it),[7] the camera was instrumental in orchestrating a colonial vision, making visible the previously unseen and unknown, shaping its apparent shapelessness and instilling form where it was felt to be lacking.

By dint of their magnetic realism, photographs offered unique properties of symbolic possession which translated into an ideal means of collecting and cataloguing the new world. The camera's utility here can be measured by its ubiquity, as photography spanned an immense array of audiences and disciplines. As the amateur traveller of the 1850s gave way to the professionals who streamed forth following the industrialization of photography in the 1880s, scholarly reports to learned societies, but also travel books for the general public, were increasingly distinguished by their reliance on photographic illustration. Even images produced with specific viewers in

---

5 Review by 'Theta' in *Journal of the Royal Photographic Society*, 1857, p. 215, quoted in Haworth-Booth, *Golden Age of British Photography*, p. 82.

6 E. Said, *Orientalism*, New York, Pantheon, 1978, p. 22. However, Said ignores the camera's place in this scene.

7 Spivak borrows the term from Heidegger, but sharpens the sense in which one 'worlding' always excludes others, sometimes to a pathological extent. See her 'Three women's texts and a critique of imperialism', *Critical Inquiry*, 12 (Autumn 1985), pp. 243–4.

mind often crossed over between audiences. Scientific and popular curiosity converged in ethnographic exhibitions which attracted large crowds, and picture postcards of ethnographic 'specimens' – including various indigenous peoples who had been kidnapped for public display – found wide audiences. A similar terrain was sought by the circuit of world fairs and international expositions which became landmark events in the second half of the nineteenth century, joining education – especially inculcation of the value of progress – to entertainment, in the form of new objects, spectacles and experiences.[8]

One of the most significant of these new objects was the postcard: a cheap, disposable, collectible sign of the global horizons of modernity. The circulation of postcards rose exponentially at the end of the nineteenth century: by the First World War over one billion postcards were delivered annually in England and Wales alone.[9] The picture postcard became a key discursive space in the construction of national identity, joining the concerns of the anthropologist and the demands of the administrator to the pleasures of the traveller and the curiosity of those at home. With its repertoire of stereotypical images – where the myth of the noble savage was counterpointed by images of 'native' degeneracy, and the foreign city metamorphosed into a set of ornamental facades and monumental sites – the postcard epitomized the West's desire to render the colonies totally visible and completely legible.[10] In his evocative study of colonial postcards, Malek Alloula writes:

> The postcard is everywhere, covering all colonial space, immediately available to the tourist, the soldier, the colonist. It is at once their poetry and their glory captured for the ages; it is also their pseudo-knowledge of the colony. It produces

8 Many writers have pointed to the nineteenth-century exhibition circuit as an important site for the construction of imperial identity. Schneider argues: 'ethnographic exhibitions developed as a new medium of popular culture that played a powerful role in shaping European popular attitudes to non-westerners.' W. Schneider, 'Race and empire: the rise of popular ethnography in the nineteenth century', *Journal of Popular Culture*, 11, 1 (1977), pp. 78–109. Street cites the display of the Batwa pygmies at the London Hippodrome in 1905, and adds that 'Eskimos, so-called "Aztecs", members of Bantu races, Australian aboriginals and Sioux Indians . . . were all variously brought to Europe to be exhibited to the general public . . .', B. Street, 'British popular anthropology: exhibitions and photographing the other', in E. Edwards (ed.), *Anthropology and Photography*, p. 122. See also C. Fusco, 'The other history of intercultural performance', *English is Broken Here*, New York, New Press, 1995, pp. 42–3.

9 See J. Walvin, *Victorian Values*, London, Cardinal, 1988, p. 82.

10 It is worth adding that it was not only the 'periphery' which was reorganized for visual consumption. Naomi Schor links the Paris World's Fair of 1900 to the dissemination of Paris by postcard, an undertaking which became a major industry employing some 30,000 people in France alone. The 'age of the exposition' clearly inspired panoptic obsession: the principal series on Paris included some 10,000 views to which Schor suggests 'we must add many smaller more specialized series'. See '*Cartes Postales*: representing Paris 1900', *Critical Inquiry*, 18 (Winter 1992), p. 217.

stereotypes in the manner of great seabirds producing guano. It is the fertilizer of colonial vision.[11]

The postcard exemplified the manner in which the camera concretized nineteenth-century discourses on race, enabling the bodies of others to be divided into visual categories and inserted into evolutionary and developmental hierarchies.[12] A recurrent theme of ethnography in this period was the establishment of a photographic catalogue of all the world's races, a project which is repeated endlessly in the postcard's search for signs of 'local colour' which nevertheless belong to a universal schema: that of the representative type.[13] The imperial posture of the photographic gaze directed abroad deftly reflected the profusion of domestic projects for scrutinizing the poor, the insane, the sick and the deviant at home.[14]

The social relations of photography themselves enacted a microcosm of the political relation between metropolis and periphery. As much as the camera served to create images of the new world, it was the image of the photographer which became emblematic of modern cross-cultural encounters. Overwhelmingly, representatives of the West *took* photographs, while other cultures became photographs. This is not to posit the practice of photography as homogeneous or fixed, nor to deny different forms of resistance and different levels of local control which were exerted over photographic practices. (These ranged from refusal to be photographed, to registering displeasure by scowling and grimacing on camera, to inciting photography by displaying oneself or demanding payment, even to integrating photography into traditional practices such as mourning rituals, or employing photographs in new political struggles.) But there are remarkably few recorded examples of 'native' photographers in this period.[15] This fact alerts us to the extent to which photographic practice was embedded in the

11 Alloula, *Colonial Harem*, p. 4. Alloula emphasizes the intolerance that colonial culture displayed to *invisibility*. Confronted with the veil, and the closed space of the harem, French colonizers invented the phantasm of semi-nude, unveiled Algerian women whose images circulated on pornographic postcards (pp. 7–16).

12 The period also saw the first publication of new journals joining geography to perceptions of cultural and racial difference: *National Geographic* (1889), *Annales de Géographie* (1891) and *Geographische Zeitschrift* (1895).

13 As I have argued in 'Promiscuous meanings', this project was internally flawed: the mastering of the world as photographic genre has been counterpointed by the collapse of traditional generic boundaries. The industrialization of image production, which ensures that images connect less to unique referents than to an image world of generalized substitutions, has confirmed, not the scientific and systematic aspirations of anthropology and ethnography, but the fragile 'truth' of the postcard.

14 Like their anthropological counterparts, the urban photographer was often depicted as a heroic explorer descending into dangerous and unknown lands. Henry Mayhew's monumental *London Labour and London Poor* (1851) was the precursor of a long line of work, often with an explicitly reformist bent, which sought to reveal the social underbelly 'at home'. See also 'The mechanical eye of reason' above.

15 One account of a nineteenth-century 'native' photographer is given in I. Jacknis, 'George Hunt, Kwakiutl photographer', in Edwards, *Photography and Anthropology*, pp. 143–151.

racial theories on which colonialism stood. By dividing the colonial observer from the 'natives' who were observed, the act of photographing fitted perfectly into the lines of technological progress, scientific objectivity and reasoned detachment with which the West sought to clothe its power, while photographic images seemed to confirm racial difference as a visible sign of cultural hierarchy.

Like the booty that flowed into metropolitan museums and art galleries across Europe and North America at this time, photographs depicting the past splendours of ancient ruins intermingled with images of contemporary colonial life to fuel the colonial imagination. Significantly, the 'periphery' was not only represented by ruins, it was often figured *as* a ruin, distanced in time even as it was made closer in space. This translation of cultural difference into temporal disjunction by virtue of the law of progress has been pivotal to the construction of the modern global polity. The designation of non-European races as relics, archaic survivors whose creative moment belonged to an irretrievable past, has been intrinsic to the West's sense of its modern destiny. Even when the 'primitives' were seen as childlike, they were children who could never grow up: cast out of the present, their only possible future was deemed to be assimilation.[16]

The camera played a key role in securing popular consent to this unhappy destiny. Unprecedented ability to see the distant frontiers, the places of legend and the people of interest offered the newly constituted 'mass public' a stake in the imperial enterprise. Like the mercenaries in Jean-Luc Godard's *Les Carabiniers* (1963), who return from bloody conquest with a treasure of postcards, metropolitan populations were seduced by photographic title pages to the imperial project. The capacity to incorporate selectively and exhibit other cultures via the camera helped to orchestrate a seemingly unshakeable faith in Imperial identity.[17] In the photographic 'Grand Tour', the military, economic and technological weight of Europe was focused into a cultural, moral and racial superiority, a pathology which helped to establish unprecedented European hegemony across virtually the entire globe.

*

While photography in all its guises did much to put the world into circulation in new ways, it was the moving image which intensified the hallucinatory effect of travelling without leaving home, indelibly tattooing it onto the perceptual experience of this century. The successful public debut of the *cinématographe* in 1895 consolidated the growing sense that 'the

16 As I have noted earlier, the driving force behind so many photographic projects from the 1880s onwards was the belief that indigenous peoples were 'dying races' whose lifestyles needed to be recorded before they vanished for ever. See 'The crisis of memory' above.

17 The persistent refusal to limit photographic licence (for example in photographing the religious practices and sacred sites of non-European cultures) belongs to a culture which has already consumed the space in which its own sacred images once existed.

world' formed a single entity, interconnected not only by transcontinental flows of trade, products and people, but by an international trade in spectacle. There was immediate demand in Europe and North America for films from abroad, especially before transformations in the film industry made it cheaper, easier and safer to simulate the 'foreign'.[18]

Within six months of its Paris opening, the *cinématographe* had been launched by the Lumière organization across Europe, Russia and the United States and soon thereafter in Algeria, Tunisia, Egypt, Turkey, India, Australia, Indochina, Japan and Mexico. Within two years, Lumière operators had been on every continent except Antarctica. The fact that each licensed representative was both camera operator and projectionist enabled the collection of new film material to proceed in tandem with the penetration of new markets. Cinematograph operators generally opened in each new city with a range of pre-made films, before introducing the novelty of 'local' events into a second programme. For domestic audiences, these short location films (such as *Melbourne Races*, 1896) were the ultimate proof of the authenticity of the new medium. For audiences elsewhere, they became part of the rich international assortment the Lumière catalogue soon boasted as a major selling point.[19]

While the Lumières gained a head start over their competitors, by the time they withdrew from film production and exhibition to concentrate on manufacture of raw stock in 1897, numerous rival companies were vying to occupy the same market. In the United States, there was the Edison Vitascope, Biograph, Vitagraph and others; in France, Méliès, Pathé, Gaumont; in England, Urban, Hepworth, Williamson; in Germany, Messter; in Denmark, Nordisk; in India, Madan, and so on. However, it is noticeable that the leading film producing countries (France, Britain and the United States) all possessed extensive colonial empires or international interests. It was these other places which provided 'raw material', not only for trade in commodities, but for commerce in national identity. The travel genre proved immensely popular, and was a staple of early film production.[20] Against a

18 Up to 1906, 'actuality' films outnumbered 'fictions'. The shift to a predominantly narrative cinema around 1914 altered the manner in which other cultures would be represented in films. As the industry demanded more complex plots and spectacles, and films became more expensive to produce, location shooting was more risky. The arrival of sound further enshrined the rule of the studio for several decades, especially in Hollywood. The fact that a film like *Casablanca* (1941) – one of the most popular and enduring pastiches of cultural difference – was shot entirely in Los Angeles merely confirms Hollywood, with its simulated geographies and famed studio backlots, as the modern rival of Calvino's infinitely variable Venice.

19 A Lumière programme screened in New York in March 1897 included films taken in France, Germany, Italy, Austria and England. By the end of 1897 the Lumière catalogue offered over 750 short films. See Barnouw, *Documentary*, p. 13.

20 Charles Musser notes that in 1902, 61 out of 62 films copyrighted by Edison concerned foreign countries (the West Indies, Europe, the Near East), while half the feature items in Vitagraph's 1903 catalogue were travel subjects. See his 'The travel genre in 1903–1904: moving towards fictional narrative', in Elsaesser, *Early Cinema: Space, Frame, Narrative*, p. 123.

projected backdrop of otherness, myths of progress, the colonial mission and the racial superiority of Western civilization were narrated over and again.[21] These productions assumed an important role in neutralizing potential dissonance within the metropolitan centres, displacing class tensions by elevating the industrial working class above 'native' underclasses, and legitimating the imperialist scramble for land which dominated the early twentieth century.

Cinematic coverage of 'foreign events', such as the Spanish–American War of 1898 and the Boer war of 1899–1901, were early sensations which helped to secure public acceptance of the notion that the geographical boundaries of the West were rightfully extended in a global embrace.[22] If this represented a 'logical' political extension of the universalizing tendencies of post-Enlightenment notions of progress, it also reflected the practical demand levied by new transport and communication technologies for an international framework of co-ordination. The Prime Meridian Conference, held in Washington in 1884, had fixed Greenwich as the zero degree marker of longitude, determined the exact length of the day, and divided the world into 24 time zones, each one hour apart.[23] Not only was the measurement of time and space calibrated on a global scale, but over 200 international organizations were established between 1900 and 1914 to oversee science and communication.[24] This steady march towards a global administration was exemplified by the collapse of 'local' times in the face of world standard time calculated with reference to a single centre. On 1 July 1913, the Eiffel Tower transmitted the first time signal relayed around the entire world. The German philosopher Oswald Spengler eulogized:

> ... the expansion of the Copernican world picture into that aspect of stellar space that we possess today; the development of Columbus' discovery into a world wide command of the earth's surface by the West.[25]

21 Barnouw notes: 'Coverage of "natives" generally showed them to be charming, quaint, sometimes mysterious; generally loyal, grateful for the protection and guidance of Europeans. Europeans were benevolently interested in colourful native rituals, costumes, dances, processions. The native was encouraged to exhibit these quaint matters for the camera.' Barnouw, *Documentary*, p. 23.

22 Footage of the Spanish–American War has been credited with giving cinema a renewed prominence following the waning of its initial novelty value, while the 1902 Catalogue of the Warwick Trading Company (one of the major British film companies) listed 111 films pertaining to the 'Transvaal War'. See E.G. Strebel, 'Imperialist iconography of Anglo-Boer war footage' in J. Fell (ed.), *Film Before Griffith*, pp. 264–71.

23 See E. Zerubavel, 'The standardisation of time: a sociohistorical perspective', *American Journal of Sociology*, 88, 1 (1988), pp. 1–23.

24 The 1912 International Conference on Time held in Paris determined a method for maintaining accurate time signals and disseminating them globally. Other important international agreements consolidating the global framework were the convention on Telegraphy (St Petersberg, 1875), and the determination of standard scientific measurements such as the ohm, volt, coulomb, farad and ampere (Paris, 1881). See Kern, *Culture of Time and Space*, pp. 12–15 and 230–1.

25 *The Decline of the West* (trans. C.F. Atkinson), London, Allen and Unwin, 1926, vol. 1, p. 337. Spengler's manuscript was first completed on the eve of the Great War, but not published until after.

But even this expanded theatre of operations rapidly proved too small. Following the official closing of the American frontier (1890), the conquest of the North and South poles and the annexation of all 'available' territory in Asia and Africa, the scene was set for the first military conflict which would no longer be named by regional or national combatants, but by its global extension.

3

The Myth of the Centre

There *is* no 'There' – There.

Gertrude Stein

The Great War constituted a watershed for the camera along at least two axes. The first was the unprecedented use of photography and cinematography as techniques of military observation. While Nadar's famous aerial photographs of Paris taken from a balloon in 1858 had long foreshadowed this application, Virilio argues that it was Joffre's success at the Marne in 1917 which marked the practical acceptance of photographic reconnaissance, inaugurating the general decoupling of military strategy from human observation which dominates the present.[1] Speed was critical in this displacement of the eye by sophisticated 'sight machines': the immense destructive force of saturation bombardment with high explosive artillery had rendered the front line a fleeting and contingent signifier. As landmarks vanished, traditional maps lost their utility: 'Only serial photography was capable of registering changing troop positions or the impact of long range artillery, and hence the capacity of new weapons for serial destruction.'[2] Photographic reconstruction of the battlefield acknowledged this quintessentially modern landscape as a heterogeneous milieu not fully visible to any single observer. Such an enterprise can be aligned with the earlier projects of Muybridge and Marey, but instead of decomposing a single body into discrete moments or movements, the aim was to reconstitute fragments into a new perceptual whole.

The second major threshold defined by the war was the definitive emergence of Hollywood as the undisputed centre of global film production, and it is the implications of this heading that I want to explore here. By 1919, approximately 80 per cent of films produced in the world were being made in southern California.[3] This shift, paralleling the general ebb of political and economic power across the Atlantic from Europe to the United States (the USA changed from a net debtor to a net creditor during the war), has itself redefined international relations and the manner in which political

1 See Virilio, *War and Cinema*, p. 17. Virilio argues that the history of battle can itself be understood as a history of changing fields of perception. He stresses the importance of image production and processing techniques, such as high-definition and high-speed cameras, infrared film, light enhancing lenses, tele-detection and computer-augmented 'real time' simulations, to contemporary military strategy.
2 Virilio, *War and Cinema*, p. 70.
3 Brownlow, *Parade's Gone By . . .* , p. 36.

power is projected. A number of factors contributed to the rapid rise of Hollywood, but most prominent was easy access to finance at a time of rapid expansion in the US economy. The peculiar status of cinema as an 'industrial art' is only partly a matter of its mechanical apparatus: equally important is the need for capital, and, in the United States, money was readily available as banks eager to garner the enormous profits won by Griffith's *The Birth of a Nation* (1915) gave their support to the notorious studio system. This enabled the swift vertical integration of the US film industry, linking production, distribution and exhibition arms in single corporate enterprises. The monopoly control established by the major studios over chains of domestic and foreign cinemas, which allowed them to enforce preferential block-booking of their own productions, became a fulcrum of the Hollywood system which persisted for several decades.[4]

As Hollywood expanded, film production elsewhere shrank. Shortages of celluloid during the War (film had to compete with demand for high explosive) severely curtailed European production. By 1925, American films had captured some 95 per cent of the feature film market in the United Kingdom and 77 per cent in France.[5] Other early rivals, such as Canada and Australia, were absorbed as they proved unable to compete with the production standards and currency of spectacle that Hollywood, with its economies of scale, could supply much more cheaply than local producers. Others, such as Germany and the Soviet Union, found themselves overtaken by political turmoil.[6]

The culmination of this trajectory was the enormous popularity of synchronized sound from 1927, which massively increased the cost of both producing and screening films.[7] Sound was not merely a technical improvement which brought film closer to its mimetic goal: it redefined cinema as a cultural and political entity. The new language barriers imposed by sound films split the international market into a number of unequal national markets, enabling Hollywood, which operated in the largest domestic

4 It wasn't until 1946 that the US Supreme Court made a ruling under antitrust laws that required Paramount – and by implication the other studios – to divest themselves of their theatre chains. Paramount appealed but complied in 1951, while MGM and Loews Theaters resisted until 1959, arguably the close of Hollywood's 'classical' era.

5 See T. Guback, 'Hollywood's international market', in T. Balio (ed.), *The American Film Industry*, Madison, University of Wisconsin Press, 1985, p. 466.

6 Germany, which was a major film producer in the silent era, found itself caught between the coming of sound and the Nazi takeover of 1933, both of which restricted its film market. With major directors such as Lubitsch, Murnau and Lang already in Hollywood, of the 1150 films made between 1933 and 1945, only a handful were seen internationally. See J. Petley, *Capital and Culture: German Cinema 1933–45*, London, British Film Institute, 1979. Although the Soviet film industry was internationally renowned in the 1920s, it never had the resources to back up Lenin's oft-cited remark that 'cinema is for us the most important art.' However, Stalin's dominance by the late 1920s spelt its death knell, and production shrank to almost zero as charges of 'formalism' intensified in the 1930s. See D.J. Youngblood, *Soviet Cinema in the Silent Era 1918–1935*, Michigan, UMI Research Press, 1980.

7 See P. Wollen, 'Cinema and technology', in Heath and De Lauretis, *Cinematic Apparatus*, p. 17.

market, to consolidate its dominance of the international scene. If the introduction of synchronized sound also heightened pressures to standardize the 'American' voice (increasing demand for theatre-trained actors, especially from the UK), the effect on non-English speakers was far more dramatic. Berg writes: 'If a regional twang could kill a career, a foreign accent was sure to toll disaster.'[8] By the 1930s, 'movies' had become virtually synonymous with Hollywood.

It was in this context that new questions of cultural imperialism emerged, not least in colonial powers such as Britain and France which had themselves long orchestrated cultural exchanges from a position of dominance with regard to other regions. Quotas on US films and attempts to imitate Hollywood were, at best, only moderately successful, while attempts to infiltrate the US market proved spectacularly unsuccessful.[9] What was born in this period was a fascination with 'America' – its cities, its cars, its speech, its fashions, its way of life – which has proved an extraordinarily durable yardstick against which diverse cultures have sought to measure themselves this century, whether in approbation or opposition. Perhaps most significant is the manner in which 'America' came to represent what Virilio aptly termed a 'perceptual luxury'.[10] It is precisely as an *image*, whose quintessential expression is cinema and the iridescent myth of Hollywood itself – immortalized in 'insider' films such as *Singin' in the Rain* (1952) – that 'America' has disseminated itself. A ubiquitous screen familiarity with 'America' haunts this century, exerting a gravitational pull on the rest of the world, affecting our sense of locality as much as our parameters of normality.

*

The importance of cinema as a site for the social construction of difference has constituted a primary theme of recent film theory, especially in its rereadings of classical Hollywood cinema.[11] Hollywood's notorious lack of interest in other countries and cultures as anything more than background

8 A.S. Berg, *Goldwyn*, London, Hamish Hamilton, 1989, p. 176. Against this must be weighed the fact that many of those working in Hollywood – including major writers, directors and studio executives – were themselves immigrants from non-English speaking backgrounds. It should also be noted that this question of linguistic domination has never gone away. See 'Interzones' below.

9 While the United States exported 235 million feet of film in 1925, it imported only 7 million, a situation which remains virtually unchanged in the present. See T. Guback, 'Hollywood's international markets', in Balio, *American Film Industry*, p. 465.

10 Virilio, *War and Cinema*, p. 9. The phrase is borrowed from Bergson.

11 Here I will only mention three examples out of a vast raft of material which may stand as indices of shifting (although not necessarily mutually exclusive) theoretical currents in film analysis, from Marxism to feminism to postcolonialism: 'John Ford's *Young Mr. Lincoln*' by the editors of *Cahiers du Cinéma*, issue no. 123, 1970, reprinted in *Screen*, 13, 3 (Autumn 1972), pp. 5–44; Laura Mulvey's 'Visual pleasure and narrative cinema', *Screen*, 16, 3 (Autumn 1975) pp. 6–18; Homi Bhabha's 'The other question', *Screen*, 24, 6 (November–December 1983), pp. 18–36.

locations for established stars and storylines was matched only by its intolerance toward 'non-American' accents, and its indifference or outright hostility to indigenous peoples, blacks, working-class and migrant cultures. Coupled with the predominance of rigid gender stereotyping and the conservative sexual morality enforced by the Hayes Office, Hollywood cinema became a powerful normalizing force in modern culture. If its representation of an 'America' dominated by white, heterosexual, middle-class men reflected existing relations of power, it also played a critical role in legitimating this hierarchy. The obsessive repetition of standard narrative patterns, and the political repercussions which arose from their transgression in the occasional 'ground-breaking' film testifies to an intimate collusion between textual margins and social and political boundaries.

Of course, such domination is never seamless. The irreducible dependence of the white master's self-identity on all those others who were confined to bit parts – the Indian side-kick, the black servant, the uneducated working-class villain, the colourful migrant, the female 'love interest', the *femme fatale* – inevitably compromised his security. Tracing the strategies by which classical Hollywood cinema excluded or stigmatized images and themes felt to lack conformity with prevailing cultural orthodoxies and political hierarchies, has proved singularly revealing of the deep anxieties and febrile insecurities which fissure a supposedly monolithic national identity.[12]

While re-reading Hollywood's legacy is still an important project for understanding contemporary culture, it is equally important that such read-ings not remain closed to other questions. In this regard, it is worth noting the gap which often separates analysis of film as a textual entity from the analysis of cinema as a global phenomenon. Where the first approach treats specific films in terms of narrative, ideology and subjectivity, the second tends to focus on cinema as a national institution which is merely sympto-matic of broader political and economic relations. This segregation, while always suspect, seems particularly problematic when considering Holly-wood. The predominance of classical narrative textual forms went hand in hand with the emergence of the Hollywood star system and production apparatus in the 1920s, and it is from within this paradoxical centre – the self-styled 'glamour capital of the world' – that the first formations of global culture emerged. From Chaplin to Bogart to Monroe to Schwarzenegger and beyond, Hollywood has colonized the subconscious (to borrow Wim

---

12 Recent theoretical re-evaluations of classical Hollywood cinema have clearly been informed by the cinematic deconstruction of Hollywood's precepts since the Second World War. Within Hollywood, Orson Welles and Alfred Hitchcock are perhaps the most important transitional figures. While their films are integral parts of the classical narrative tradition, they already mobilize the tensions and contradictions of this scene against itself. Other influences could be multiplied almost at will: Italian neo-realism in the 1940s, the French 'new wave' and the 'discovery' of Japanese cinema in the 1950s, New German Cinema in the 1960s, and so on.

Wenders's phrase) of the most diverse audiences, cutting a freeway through the modern imagination.

Understanding this quintessentially modern form of colonization necessitates juggling frames of analysis. Focusing on textual inscriptions of identity and difference while ignoring the geopolitics of film consumption has often led to the assumption that Western audiences (however stratified and differentiated) are the only viewers. Yet Hollywood has always relied heavily on overseas sales for a large part of its profits.[13] On the other hand, eschewing questions of subjectivity for a macro-politics of competition between nation states has often promoted theoretical presumptions of a simple dictatorship of the centre, erecting Hollywood into a monolithic system and reducing the response of the 'periphery' (as producers and consumers) to the margins of creativity and authenticity. Conventional analyses of the rise of Hollywood can themselves be seen as symptomatic of the political culture which favoured centre–periphery models as the primary analytical matrix. Changing this field is not simply a matter of championing the periphery over the centre (for example, by finding unacknowledged 'masterpieces'), but of displacing the presumption that 'centre' and 'periphery' are unified entities.

This is undoubtedly a complex task. A strategic point of departure is to juxtapose Hollywood's role in the formation of global culture against cinema's role as a site for the representation of national identity in modernity. The modern nation state, situated at the intersections of global economics, colonial expansions and mass migrations, has faced unique problems of political legitimation. As Homi Bhabha has argued, the putative unity of the modern nation is irrevocably split by the complexity of affiliations and identifications which function in its name.[14] Securing its identity in face of the increasing heterogeneity of 'the people' has demanded new strategies to manage cultural, racial and ethnic differences. A crucial element of this process has been the capacity to invent histories which project a recognizable national origin, particularly through the restaging of myths of national formation and the narrativization of the significant events of national history. Bhabha contends:

> [T]he political unity of the nation consists in a continual displacement of its irredeemably plural modern space, bounded by different, even hostile nations, into a signifying space that is archaic and mythical, paradoxically representing the nation's modern territoriality, in the patriotic, atavistic temporality of Tradition.[15]

13 Guback argues: 'Probably no other American business is so heavily dependent upon export trade as the film industry.' In Balio, *American Film Industry*, p. 481.

14 Bhabha argues that, while the nation 'fills the void left by the uprooting of communities and kin', it does so uneasily. Nationalist resistance to 'the heterogeneous histories of contending peoples, antagonistic authorities, and tense cultural locations' render the nation 'the measure of the liminality of modern culture'. See his 'DissemiNation' in H. Bhabha (ed.), *Nation and Narration*, London, Routledge, 1990, pp. 300 and 291–2.

15 Bhabha, 'DissemiNation', p. 300.

The nation demands a history in which 'the difference of space returns as the Sameness of time, turning Territory into Tradition, turning the People into One'.[16] Responsibility for performing this role has increasingly fallen to cinema (and television).[17] One of the primary tasks undertaken by all modern nation states has been the creation of a national cinema to symbolize an atavistic self-identity. Yet – and this contradiction exemplifies the modern condition – each national cinema remains virtually unthinkable without reference to Hollywood. This tension highlights the critical importance of Griffith's *The Birth of a Nation* (1915): it is made and remade, not only in Hollywood, but in every emergent national cinema which, even today, cannot avoid its reckoning with the Hollywood legacy.

This inheritance is by no means confined to the particular inscriptions of cultural marginality through which Hollywood has manufactured its own imaginary worlds. While *The Birth of a Nation* is notorious in some circles for the inspiration it gave to the Ku Klux Klan, it is more famous in film history for its role in structural transformation of cinematic language. How might these two headings – too often kept apart– be articulated together? In his study of the emergence of the modern nation state, Benedict Anderson stressed the importance of the temporal structure of the nineteenth-century realist novel as a means of unifying the vastness and diversity of the modern nation into an 'imagined community'. Anderson contends that the displacement of an earlier 'prophetic simultaneity-along-time' by the novel's hinged temporality of 'meanwhile' permitted the linking together of dispersed sites of action to form a national stage dominated by a 'transverse, cross-time marked not by prefiguring and fulfilment but by temporal coincidence and measured by clock and calendar'.[18] He further argues: 'So deep lying is this new idea that one could argue that every essential modern conception is based on a conception of the "meanwhile".'[19] Transposing this analysis from literature to cinema pinpoints the value of Griffith's epic for modern nationalist discourse. *The Birth of a Nation* provided the first effective translation of the narrative structure of the nineteenth-century realist novel into the dynamic language of the feature film. Historically, it defines the threshold beyond which cinema's dependence on what Heath has termed the 'novelistic' genre of narrative was institutionalized.[20]

Griffith's system of parallel montage displaced the narrative consecution of so-called 'primitive' cinema by interweaving actions occurring in differ-

16 Bhabha, 'DissemiNation', p. 300.
17 See 'Interzones' below.
18 Anderson, *Imagined Communities*, pp. 30–1.
19 Anderson, *Imagined Communities*, p. 31.

20 Heath describes the novelistic as 'the ideological category of the narrative elaborated in film', arguing that it plays a critical role in tailoring cinema to the desires of the individual subject. Heath, *Questions of Cinema*, p. 125. *The Birth of a Nation* was less the origin of new cinematic techniques than the sum of the experiments conducted by Griffith and others over the previous decade. However, its extraordinary critical and commercial success redefined cinema and determined its orientation for decades to come.

ent places at the same time. This invention of simultaneity provided the
basic template enabling cinema to claim it could encompass the scope and
diversity of the modern nation as a visual narrative. The bifurcating
movement of parallel montage (the cinematic equivalent of Anderson's
'meanwhile') allowed differences of race, class, gender, ethnicity and
sexuality to be mapped onto a seemingly homogeneous national space; the
uniform space of the screen which alone seemed capable of gathering and
reintegrating all the dispersed and heterogeneous fractions of modern
existence. By instituting textual borders which enforced the boundaries of
dominant cultural and political discourse, counterpointing the alterity of the
foreign and unfamiliar with stereotypical images of self-identity, cinema
assumed a key role at the modern intersection of nation and narration. Film's
unique capacity to join the representation of space to the experience of time,
matching landscape as a nationalist metaphor with the re-enactment of
landmark historical events, has made cinema a primary site for establishing
the modern nation as a textual unity and imagined community.[21]

*

At this point, I want to return to Virilio's analysis of the relation between
modern warfare and 'perceptual arsenals'. Virilio goes beyond conventional
considerations of ideology and propaganda to propose a radical continuity
between military–political strategy and aesthetic pleasure in modernity.
Paralleling the permanent war economy against which Eisenhower warned
as he left Presidential office, Virilio locates a permanent war of perception:
the war of stars, production values and delivery systems (synchronized
sound, colour, wide screen, surround sound) that Hollywood has long been
winning. Hollywood's domination over the currency of spectacle from
Griffith to Spielberg has indelibly marked the aestheticization of politics and
the mediatization of culture which conditions what Henry Luce famously
dubbed the 'American century'.[22] While the Vietnam war showed that the
USA could be defeated militarily, no nation has yet devised a strategy to
defeat the USA cinematically. The victory of capitalism and 'democracy'
across Eastern Europe and the former Soviet Union in 1989–90 was very

21 Again, it is important to stress a dynamic image of this process. Bhabha argues that
Anderson overstates the possibility of nationalist *resolution*, and suggests that the 'meanwhile'
(like the process of signification itself) is comprised of incommensurable temporalities which
threaten its coherence: 'From that place of the "meanwhile", where cultural homogeneity and
democratic anonymity make their claims on the national community, there emerges a more
instantaneous and subaltern voice of the people, a minority discourse that speaks betwixt and
between times and places.' Bhabha, *Nation and Narration*, p. 309.
22 Schiller argues that Luce (head of the *Time–Life* group) was one of the first to
understand that 'the fusion of economic strength and information control, image making and
public opinion formation was the new quintessence of power.' H. Schiller, *Mass Communications and American Empire*, New York, Beacon Press, 1971, p. 1. Virilio stressed the
importance that both Hitler and Goebbels placed on German films matching Hollywood in
terms of production values and spectacle. See Virilio, *War and Cinema*, pp. 8–9.

much a victory for this specular 'America'; its image, its consumption as spectacle and image.

Yet, in the very process of representing the modern nation state, cinematic discourse increasingly threatens to unmoor its putative referent. The telescoping of spatial and temporal dimensions crucial to cinematic narration disturbs the traditional nexus between geography and nation. Virilio suggests:

> When the offer of a trip 'Around the World in Eighty Minutes' shone outside cinemas in the '30s, it was already clear that cinema was imposing itself on a geostrategy which for a century or more had inexorably been leading to the direct substitution, and thus sooner or later, the disintegration of things and places.[23]

This decomposition of material referents functions less as an absence of the real than as a multiplication of its indices and a rearrangement of its signs in conformity with a world picture in which 'embodied' and 'disembodied' perceptions have become radically interchangeable. If Hollywood no longer exists in its classical form, this should not be read as evidence of its disappearance from contemporary culture, but in terms of its saturation of contemporary life: Disneyland, theme parks and shopping malls, not to mention television, all proliferate in its luminous wake. Perhaps there is a certain irony in the fact that the 'real' United States seems to be fast disappearing under the weightlessness of its own images. (For Baudrillard: 'It is not the least of America's charms that even outside the movie theatres the whole country is cinematic.')[24] But, even today, Hollywood remains the primary metaphor for the detonation of the real in modernity: not the destruction of reality, but the destabilization of its previous frames of reference and the decomposition of its centres of existence.

23 Virilio, *War and Cinema*, p. 47.
24 J. Baudrillard, *America* (trans. C. Turner), London, Verso, 1988, p. 56.

4

In the Neon Forest

> What is especially fascinating to me is the so-called 'invisible city': the
> urban structure which is lodged in our nerves, feelings, knowledges.
>
> Alexander Kluge

If the city is modernity's home, modernity is the time of the home's
reinvention. To recognize this is not to attempt to isolate the modern city
from its surrounds but to acknowledge its new dominion over them. The
industrial metropolis increasingly subjugates 'the country' around it, drain-
ing it of food, water, raw materials and people in a parasitical relationship
which now extends transnationally according to the international division of
labour. Within these circuits, the modern city has not only been the physical
destination for countless waves of rural migrants; it has also been a psychic
destination, a locus of symbolic capital, and a lynchpin in the projection of
imperial power. It is the image of a future city – from the first great modern
icon of the Eiffel Tower (1889) to the Manhattan skyline which inspired
Fritz Lang's *Metropolis* (1927) – which reigns over the dreams of this
century.[1]

But, as much as the modern city has been the set for a new image,
modernity names the time in which the city metamorphosed into a profoundly different lived environment. From the 1880s, the city concentrated a
multitude of technological innovations within its domain; innovations which
were themselves dependent on radical breakthroughs in the harnessing and
exploitation of energy (especially the electromagnetic spectrum so important
to the new physics). Electrical power and electric lights, steel construction
and glass-curtained skyscrapers, automobiles and aeroplanes, radios and
telephones, synthetic materials and X-rays, air conditioning and chemical
industries, subways and escalators, assembly lines and cinema, were just
some of the inventions which transformed the urban–industrial life-world
beyond recognition in barely one generation. The city became a vast
perceptual laboratory, a living experiment in 'special effects' whose impact
on the human sensorium has shifted the parameters of human identity. New
spatial and temporal experiences levied new demands upon representation.

---

1 Barthes wrote of the Eiffel Tower: 'The Tower is also present to the entire world. First of
all as a universal symbol of Paris, it is everywhere on the globe where Paris is to be stated as
an image; from the Midwest to Australia, there is no journey to France which isn't made,
somehow, in the Tower's name . . . the symbol of Paris, of modernity, of communication, of
science or of the nineteenth century . . . it is the inevitable sign.' Barthes, 'The Eiffel Tower',
Barthes: Selected Writings, p. 237. The Manhattan skyline of Stieglitz's famous photograph
City of Ambition (1910) became the paradigmatic 'establishing shot' of countless movies.

Increasingly, the urban environment sought to encompass the memory of 'the country', in the form of botanical gardens, zoos, public parks and even backyards. But perhaps its most versatile and successful enclosure was cinema, which captivated audiences by capturing every Outside.

*

The architectural revolution arising from the use of steel, glass and re-inforced concrete as key building materials shifted the primary axis of urban development from the horizontal to the vertical.[2] The 'skyscraper' not only symbolized a radical break with the structures of the past, but transformed the perceptual habits of the present. Gazing down from great heights, the ascendant eye encountered a new topography: the urban landscape laid out as its own map.[3] From the ground, the extreme verticality of high-rise buildings challenged the act of seeing. Seen at a distance, they dominated the horizon, and yet from immediately below they defied the eye's capacity to grasp them whole. Robert Delaunnay's series of Eiffel Tower paintings display the tension between representing the Tower from a distance or from below, a problem he solved by juxtaposing fractured images in a dissonant pictorial space. But it was photographers such as Alvin Langdon Coburn, László Moholy-Nagy and Alexander Rodchenko who most enthusiastically embraced the need to reconstruct perception and representation. Coburn's exhibition 'New York from its Pinnacles' (1912) was a landmark for the Photo-Secession group gathered around Stieglitz. Moholy-Nagy strongly advocated adopting 'unusual views, transverse, top and bottom views, distortions, shadow effects, tonal contrasts . . .', while Rodchenko, who was greatly influenced by Vertov's 'cinema-eye' theories, argued: 'We must remove from our eyes the habit of looking "from the navel".'[4]

Along the horizontal axis, urban landscape was transformed by new generations of vehicles: train, bicycle, electric tram, subway, motor bus and private car. By permitting a new elasticity in the distance between home and work, motorized vehicles enabled the dispersion of the city into suburban dormitories. As well as providing the infrastructure for new social and economic relationships, the new vehicles revolutionized perception. The commuting eye increasingly found itself on a collision course with the urban environment, projected into a series of fleeting encounters which trans-formed the nature of landscape in the abruptness of arrival and the

2 The first skyscrapers were built in Chicago in the 1880s following the great fire of 1871. The spread of high-rise building was facilitated by the invention of the hydraulic elevator, the new vehicle needed for the occupation of vertically stratified space.

3 Robert Hughes notes: 'when the [Eiffel] Tower opened to the public in 1889, nearly a million people rode its lifts to the top platform; and there they saw what modern travellers take for granted every time they fly – the earth on which we live seen flat, as pattern, from above.' *The Shock of the New*, New York, Alfred A. Knopf, 1981, p. 14.

4 L. Moholy-Nagy, 'Photography is creation with light' (1928), in Passuth, *Moholy-Nagy*, p. 303. Rodchenko quoted in Khan-Magomedov, *Rodchenko*, p. 225.

suddenness of departure.[5] Painter and film maker Fernand Léger observed in 1914:

> When one crosses a landscape by automobile or express train, it becomes fragmented; it loses in descriptive value but gains in synthetic value; the railway carriage door or the car windscreen along with speed imparted to them, have altered the habitual look of things.[6]

The city was also galvanized by electrification, which architectural historian Rayner Banham has described as 'the greatest environmental revolution in human history since the domestication of fire'.[7] Electricity not only powered the new machines of production and transportation which fed the acceleration of urban life; it fundamentally altered the city's visual appearance. The incandescent light bulb converted night-time streets into arteries of light and shop windows into commodity fairy lands, charging the urban habitat with spectacular and immaterial qualities previously reserved for specialized show places such as the theatre, diorama and amusement park.[8] Divisions between inside and outside became subject to new forces. Not only night and day, but seasonal patterns and climatic variations, began to decline in importance with developments in lighting, refrigeration and environmentally controlled living spaces. The reign of a non-solar day moved the distinction between the time of work and the time of sleep from the 'natural' order onto the political agenda.

On another plane, it was in the city – or as arterial links between cities – that new communication technologies found their initial purchase. Telephone, radio, picture postcards, daily newspapers, illustrated magazines, the phonograph, and cinema all contributed to the rapid redistribution of the borders of everyday experience. The separation of private zones from public domains began to blur as the interior of the home became directly susceptible to the invisible forces theorized in the field theory of the new physics.[9] An editorial in the *New York Times* observed in 1912: 'All through the roar of the big city there are constantly speeding messages between people separated by vast distances and . . . over housetops and even through the walls and buildings are words written by electricity.'[10] A new fluid con-

---

5 Proust compared rail travel to metaphor, inasmuch as it 'united two distant individualities of the world, took us from one name to another name.' Quoted in Kern, *Culture of Time and Space*, p. 216.

6 F. Léger, quoted in A. d' Harnoncourt (ed.), *Futurism and the International Avant-Garde*, Philadelphia, Philadelphia Museum of Art, 1980, p. 118.

7 R. Banham, *The Architecture of the Well-Tempered Environment*, London, Architectural Press, 1969, p. 64.

8 Edison invented his incandescent lamp in 1879. The first public grid for electric light opened in New York in 1882.

9 Einstein wrote: 'With the invention of the electro-magnetic field, a daring imagination was needed to comprehend that it was not the conduct of bodies, but rather the conduct of *something that existed in between them* i.e. the field, that could be the essential for ordering and interpreting all events.' Quoted in P. Virilio, *Lost Dimension*, p. 97 (my italics).

10 Quoted in Kern, *Culture of Time and Space*, p. 64. By 1914, there were some 600,000 telephones in Great Britain, 1.3 million in Germany and nearly 10 million in the United States.

sistency began to inhere to lived space as the mutual interpenetration of objects and surfaces pronounced by the Futurists achieved the status of social fact.[11] Events were no longer so easily contained by models of thought presuming a simple distinction between presence and absence. What 'took place' at one site could also produce instantaneous effects elsewhere, or across a multiplicity of elsewheres. The elimination of the gap between sending and receiving (radio, telephone) expanded the circumference of the present moment, linking nations and continents in a novel experience of synchronicity which seemed to pass right through the human body.

Visions of technological reconstruction proliferated. Futurist sculptor Boccioni declared: 'Let's split open our figures and place the environment inside them.'[12] The poet Apollinaire proclaimed: 'I am everywhere or rather I start to be everywhere', adding: 'Already I hear the shrill sound of the friend's voice to come/ Who walks with you in Europe/ Whilst never leaving America . . .'[13] Einstein's Theory of Relativity achieved immediate popularity: while understood by few, it symbolized epochal change for many. What avant-garde art and science of the time registered was a rupture in experience and perception joining physical transformations to new psychic dispositions. Simultaneity assumed a palpable reality, confirming the existence of multiple subjective times against the back-drop of the new order of global time. As Nowotny observes, the 'discovery' of simultaneity lends 'the connection between power and time a qualitatively new dimension. Whoever governs simultaneity controls the temporal dependences derivable from it'.[14]

This capacity to draw a heterogeneity of discontinuous sites into the dream of a single information network infused the modern city with its principal signifier: speed. As the power of each metropolis became increasingly dependent on the rapid movement of images and information, as much as products and people, the past suddenly seemed slow in comparison. Spengler asserted: 'In Classical existence years, in Indian centuries scarcely counted; but here the hour, the minute, even the second is of importance.'[15] Punctuality, efficiency, and the co-ordination of complex schedules by 'scientific' time and motion studies became the watchwords, not only of business dealings but human relations; as Benjamin noted: 'Taylor who

11 In their 'Technical Manifesto' of 1910 the Futurist painters proclaimed: 'Space no longer exists: the street pavement, soaked by rain beneath the glare of electric lamps, becomes immensely deep and gapes to the very centre of the earth. . . . Our bodies penetrate the sofa upon which we sit, and the sofas penetrate our bodies. The motor bus rushes into the houses which it passes, and in their turn the houses throw themselves upon the motor bus and are blended with it.' Apollonio, *Futurist Manifestos*, p. 28.

12 'Technical Manifesto of Futurist Sculpture' (1912) in Apollonio, *Futurist Manifestos*, p. 63.

13 Quoted in J. Berger, *The Sense of Sight*, New York, Pantheon, 1985, pp. 165 and 166.

14 H. Nowotny, *Time: The Modern and Postmodern Experience* (trans. N. Plaice), London, Polity Press, 1996, p. 80.

15 O. Spengler, *Decline of the West*, vol. 1, p. 133. It is not so much the truth of Spengler's grand generalizations, but their indication of epochal change which I find significant.

popularized the watchword "Down with Dawdling" carried the day.'[16] The restless dynamism of crowds, industry and traffic conditioned a mode of *rapid seeing* which has now become the invisible frame of modern perception.[17]

*

Merleau-Ponty has noted the manner in which familiarity allows thought to impose habit upon perception. But in the absence of familiarity there can be no such perceptual habitus. In the first decades of this century, the city mutated into an environment which profoundly challenged the senses. Sergei Eisenstein's first impressions of New York register its exhilarating and vertiginous impact:

> All sense of perspective and of realistic depth is washed away by a nocturnal sea of electric advertising. Far and near, small (in the *foreground*) and large (in the *background*), soaring aloft and dying away, racing and circling, bursting and vanishing – these lights tend to abolish all sense of real space, finally melting into a single plane of coloured light points and neon lines moving over a surface of black velvet sky. It was thus that people used to picture stars – as glittering nails hammered into the sky. Headlights on speeding cars, highlights on receding rails, shimmering reflections on wet pavements – all mirrored in puddles which destroy our sense of direction (which is top? which is bottom?), supplementing the mirage above with the mirage beneath us, and rushing between these two worlds of electric signs, we see them no longer on a single plane, but as a system of theatre wings, suspended in the air, through which the night flood of traffic lights is streaming.[18]

The modern city-machine, in which all parts had become mobile and all surfaces seemed to permeate and interpenetrate each other, where darkness or opacity was susceptible to the flick of a switch or the activation of a circuit, where the horizon was continually sliced open by the screen of a billboard seen from the window of a speeding train, was a milieu which deeply disoriented its inhabitants. Or rather, it provided so many orientations that it overwhelmed with its abundance, suspending the eye in perpetual fascination. This environment of visual and sensory excess no longer provided a stable reference grid against which time and space could be measured in traditional terms. The historic function played by the city as a socio-political map and a repository of collective memory gave way to an urban and suburban geography in which the co-ordinates of home, self and community had to be plotted in new ways.

16 Benjamin, *Illuminations*, p. 199.

17 Benjamin speculated: 'The daily sight of a lively crowd may once have constituted a spectacle to which one's eyes had to adapt first. On the basis of this supposition, one may assume that once the eyes had mastered this task they welcomed opportunities to test their newly acquired faculties. This would mean that the technique of Impressionist painting, whereby the picture is garnered in a riot of dabs of colour, would be a reflection of experiences with which the eyes of the big city dweller have become familiar.' W. Benjamin, *Charles Baudelaire: A Lyric Poet in an Era of High Capitalism* (trans. H. Zohn), London, New Left Books, 1973, p. 130.

18 Eisenstein, *Film Sense*, p. 83.

As modernity has outpaced the past, it has often threatened to outstrip itself. The first decades of this century are crossed by an urgent desire for representation to catch up with life: photography became faster, with the development of new lenses and new film stocks; the 'snapshot' was invented to seize life on the run. But it was undoubtedly moving pictures which best moved in step with the new rhythms of the city; the traffic, the crowds, the kaleidoscopic displays of lights, objects and forces in motion. If the city has been one of cinema's primary narrative frames – a line which can be traced from Sennett's silent comedies of urban dysfunctions through the new urban rhythms revealed by Cavalcanti and Ruttman to the mutant, animistic streets and shadowy moral territories of Expressionism and *film noir* – this intersection also reveals the extent to which the modern city is itself cinematic.

Hollis Frampton has suggested: 'Painting "assumes" architecture: walls, floors, ceilings. The illusionist painting itself may be seen as a window or doorway.'[19] Cinema's dynamic perception – 'perception in the form of shocks' as Benjamin put it[20] – 'assumes' not the stable site of a solid building but the variable vector described by a moving vehicle. Experiences of rapid transit through the electrified day–night of the industrial city and of the rapid transmission of images by motor driven projectors converge in the infinitely mobile eye of the modern voyager–voyeur. The unity of travel and tracking shot concentrates the essential ambiguity conditioning modern perception: the endless journeys, the fluctuation of borders and contexts, the displacement of the body as authoritative centre.

It has often been observed that the industrial metropolis depersonalized social relations to an unprecedented degree. Anonymity was the city's gift, offering the prospect of self-invention, but carrying the price tag of alienation. The transition to the machine environment wrought immense physical destruction: the rising body count of railway accidents and factory injuries led to the beginnings of health insurance, that 'calculus of suffering' in which death itself becomes anonymous. (As Adorno and Horkheimer point out: 'Whoever dies is unimportant: it is a question of ratio between accidents and the company's liabilities.')[21] Individual life seemed increasingly susceptible to chance as older patterns of behaviour and explanation were overtaken by new conditions of existence. Kracauer never tired of stressing cinema's natural affinity for urban spaces such as the railway

19 Frampton, *Circles of Confusion*, p. 189.

20 Benjamin, *Charles Baudelaire*, p. 132. Whenever Benjamin compares film to painting, *movement* is the term of differentiation: 'The painting invites the spectator to contemplation; before it the spectator can abandon himself to his associations. Before the movie frame he cannot do so. No sooner has his eye grasped a scene than it is already changed.' Benjamin, *Illuminations*, p. 240.

21 *Dialectic of Enlightenment* (trans. J. Cumming), London, Allen Lane, 1973, p. 84. The phrase 'a calculus of suffering' comes from Pernick's book of the same name, discussed in S. Buck-Morss, 'Aesthetics and anaesthetics: Walter Benjamin's artwork essay reconsidered', *October*, 62 (Fall 1992), pp. 3–41.

station, department store or street; the arenas of transitory and haphazard encounters which impressed themselves on modern consciousness. Cinema not only offered a powerful means for representing these marginal public spaces in which perception was cut open by contingency; it was itself a primary site for experiencing the surreal attractions of the unexpected and the incommensurable.

In positing 'shock' as integral to cinematic form, Benjamin argued that cinema enjoyed an edge in responding to historic shifts in human existence:

> The film is the art form that is in keeping with the increased threat to his life which modern man has to face. Man's need to expose himself to shock effects is his adjustment to the dangers threatening him. The film corresponds to profound changes in the apperceptive apparatus – changes that are experienced by the man in the street in big-city traffic, on a historical scale by every present-day citizen.[22]

Benjamin believed that industrial capitalism had established a new sensibility predicated on technological innovations which had one thing in common: 'one abrupt movement of the hand triggers many steps.'[23]

> Of the countless movements of switching, inserting, pressing and the like, the 'snapping' of the photographer has had the greatest consequences. A touch of the finger now sufficed to fix an event for an unlimited period of time. The camera gave the moment a posthumous shock, as it were. Haptic experiences of this kind were joined by optic ones, such as are supplied by the advertising pages of a newspaper or the traffic of a big city. Moving through this traffic involves the individual in a series of shocks and collisions. At dangerous intersections, nervous impulses flow through him, like the energy from a battery.[24]

Drawing on Freud's work on the relation between shock and defence mechanisms, Benjamin argued that the 'battlefield' of modernity split perception from memory. Overstimulation resulted in numbness. Because survival in the city had come to depend on immediate response, unreflexive submission to the instant led to a deterioration of experience, compartmentalizing time and space, and rigidifying the body's mimetic faculties. The fixed smile on the face of the anonymous individual buffeted by a relentless crowd functioned as a deflective barrier rather than an avenue of communication.[25] Breaking through these barriers became the primary task of political struggle. But the revolutionary role that Benjamin gave cinema in this struggle has remained contentious: hence the political import of debates over whether cinema merely continues to 'drill' the spectator according to the industrial training system of conveyor belt and reified

22 Benjamin, *Illuminations*, p. 252.
23 Benjamin, *Charles Baudelaire*, pp. 131 and 132.
24 Benjamin, *Illuminations*, pp. 176–7.
25 What would he have made of the 'smile-training' offered to the residents of Lillehammer before the 1994 Winter Olympics? Drawing on Simmel's opinion that the city privileges the eye over the ear, Benjamin adds: 'That the eye of the city dweller is overburdened with protective functions is obvious', and laments, 'There is no daydreaming surrender to far away things in the protective eye.' (Benjamin, *Charles Baudelaire*, pp. 151 and 193.)

perception, playing on the spectator as the sinister Caligari directed the somnambulist Cesare, or whether it exposes the alienated conditions of modern existence and so 'redeems' the modern life-world.[26]

*

This ambivalence is reflected in the place cinema came to occupy in the architecture of the modern city. A series of different scenes of watching cut across film's first decades, beginning with the penny arcade, peep-show format of Edison's Kinetoscope. After a brief, but resounding, success, the private viewer of the Kinetoscope was dethroned by the public audience of projected films, often shown as part of travelling vaudeville shows in which the audience joined in sing-alongs and other forms of collective interaction. However, in less than a decade, this theatrical audience was itself re-privatized, as films sought to absorb the individual spectator within the text's movement according to the novelistic model of narrative continuity, shot-matching and suture. While the audience remained collective in form, the viewing experience became more solitary, echoing the mutual anonymity enjoyed by individuals in the crowds of any big city. Within a few years, as films began to attract middle-class patrons, cinemas capable of holding thousands began to appear in every major city staking its claim to being modern.[27]

This journey, from amusement arcade to itinerant travelling exhibit to shop-front Nickelodeon to its 'coming of age' in the great picture palaces of the 1910s and 1920s, symbolizes cinema's growing status, not only in economic terms, but as a cultural force crucial to the political settlement of modern urban–industrial societies. Writing in 1926, Kracauer described the lavishly decorated 'optical fairylands' which dominated the era:

> Elegant surface splendour is the hallmark of these mass theatres. Like hotel lobbies, they are shrines to the cultivation of pleasure, their glamour aiming at

26 I have already discussed the ambivalence of cinematic subjectivity in 'Flickering in eclipses'. Here I will merely add that, in contrast to Benjamin and Kracauer (who never abandons a major role for cinema in answering modernity's need for radical critique – hence his post-war emphasis on film as 'the *redemption* of physical reality'), Adorno seriously doubted 'the viability of a procedure based on the principle of shock'. (See Adorno and Horkheimer, *Dialectic of Enlightenment*, pp. 126–7 where he equates lack of time for contemplation with spectatorial automatism.) Adorno later argued that Benjamin's theory was conceived 'with the explicit purpose of outdoing the provocative Brecht and thereby – this may have been its secret purpose – gaining freedom from him'. While Adorno called Kracauer's the 'most plausible theory of film technique', he criticized its 'sociological abstention'. See 'Transparencies on film', *New German Critique*, 24–5 (1981–2), p. 202.

27 The darkness we now take to be protective of cinematic fantasy was initially perceived as a threat to cinematic popularity. The dingy Nickelodeon had a 'bad' (lower-class) reputation, which the lavish new theatres were designed to overcome. Miriam Hansen has pointed to the deliberate 'de-ethnicization' of the cinematic audience, as nationally slanted programmes and sing-alongs of 'foreign' songs were discouraged by professional organizations of producers and exhibitors. See her 'Early cinema: whose public sphere?', in Elsaesser, *Early Cinema: Space, Frame, Narrative*, pp. 228–43.

edification. . . . This total artwork of effects assaults every one of the senses using every possible means. Spotlights shower their beams into the auditorium, sprinkling across festive drapes or rippling through colourful growth-like glass fixtures. The orchestra asserts itself as an independent power, its acoustic expression buttressed by the responsory of the lighting. Every emotion is accorded its own acoustic expression, its colour value in the spectrum . . . Alongside the legitimate reviews, such shows are the leading attraction in Berlin today. They raise distraction to the level of culture; they are aimed at the *masses*.[28]

As well as granting aesthetic legitimacy, the architecture of the picture palace was instrumental in supporting the new cinematic imaginary. Cinema was the place in which an avowedly rational and secular society prepared itself to encounter the scene of the other – the foreign, the fantastic, the erotic, even that most duplicitous double, 'life itself'. The ritual of entry, the descent of darkness, the comfortable immobilization of the body, the cessation of motor activity, the vastly magnified and intensely luminous images, the soothing or dramatic music, all contributed to the cinematic effect. Cinema demanded separation from the outside world, which nevertheless could never be simply absent, but had to be brought inside, offered for consumption in the enigmatic form of an image created from light alone. Like the camera obscura, cinema offered an inverted interior, but with an endlessly elastic and infinitely mobile field of vision, an enclosed space able to expand its own horizons from within. The spectator's perceptual limits were no longer determined by architectural space, but by fluctuations in filmic space. This effect, in which the inside begins to include the outside – even all possible outsides – marks a crucial moment in the emergence of a distinctively modern sense of place. Immersed in cinema's ludic shell, place seemed to abandon dependence on solidity and materiality.

It is perhaps not surprising that responses to this renovation of the traditional ground of Being (defined as substance, permanence, presence) has often assumed spiritual, if not apocalyptic, overtones. As Paul Virilio has pointed out, the grandeur and opulence of the picture palaces (like the railway stations a generation earlier) resembled nothing so much as the great Gothic cathedrals of past ages:

> Nineteenth century Europeans were forever on the move to *see* new commodities; now, with the coming of cinema, pure visions were for sale. The cinema became a major site for a *trade in dematerialization*, a new industrial market which no longer produced matter but light, as the luminosity of those vast stained glass windows of old was suddenly concentrated into the screen.[29]

The cinematic trade in visual commodities – in vision as a commodity – must be related to other urban spaces, such as the Paris Arcades which fascinated Benjamin, or the world exhibitions which he described in neo-

---

28 S. Kracauer, 'Cult of distraction: on Berlin's picture palaces' (1926), reprinted in S. Kracauer, *New German Critique*, 40 (Winter 1987), pp. 91–2. Kracauer's reference to the 'total artwork' situates cinematic spectacle in relation to grand opera (particularly Wagner, for whom Adorno adopted the phrase).

29 Virilio, *War and Cinema*, p. 32.

religious terms 'as places of pilgrimage to view the fetish Commodity'.[30] Yet, despite evident affinities between the close-up and the icon, cinema does not simply reinhabit the terrain of religion. What the proximity between the picture palace and the cathedral suggests is the importance of a *placeless* place for the cinematic effect to work. For the worshipper, the bricks and mortar of the Church perform a general function unrelated to the building's particular location or physical attributes. It forms a space of seclusion and solitude which mediates the presence of God. What else has cinema been this century but a vast cathedral of fictions, a hole in the real in which time, space and self can be held in suspension, at least for the performance of a film or the span of its prayer?

Today the great movie shrines are virtually extinct, replaced by the multiplex cinemas of suburban shopping malls catering for the more specialized audiences of the post-video/cable-television era. Yet, if the neo-Gothic architecture is gone, contemporary cinema maintains key elements of the earlier tradition. Personal voyeurism in a public forum continues as the dominant mode of film consumption. And contemporary cinemas resemble nothing more than wide-bodied aeroplanes, the ubiquitous vehicles for the end of this century of migrations.

30 Benjamin, *Charles Baudelaire*, p. 165.

5

Interzones

> The very concepts of homogeneous national cultures, the consensual or
> contiguous transmission of historical traditions or 'organic' ethnic com-
> munities – *as the grounds of cultural comparativism* – are in a profound
> process of redefinition.
>
> Homi Bhabha

Cinema's strategic role in the manufacture of information, entertainment and
propaganda during the Second World War enmeshed it in cultural and
political life to an unprecedented degree. But immediately upon the war's
conclusion, the film industry found itself outflanked by a new cultural
dynamic. If the exponential rise of broadcast television has become a
primary symbol of the post-war era, it has also profoundly transformed the
characteristic spaces, linkages and rhythms of post-war life.[1] By exploiting
the possibilities first suggested by radio, but raising experiences of action-at-
a-distance to a new power, television created distinct social relationships
which have come to generate their own momentum. The simultaneous relay
of pictures and sounds to a radically dispersed audience occupying a
multiplicity of viewing sites, and the instantaneous co-ordination of 'live
events' between different locations, has emerged as one of the most
distinctive features of the second half of this century. As this experience has
become integral to everyday life, sending ripples of ambiguity through the
sinews of immediacy, it has confirmed the fundamental shift in the balance
between 'direct' and 'indirect' perceptions initiated by the camera one and a
half centuries ago. This reconstruction of the value of presence goes to the
heart of contemporary crises in epistemology as much as politics.

Originally envisaged as a scientific prosthesis capable of transporting the
researcher's eye into situations beyond the body's reach (Zworykin, who

---

1 The earliest experiments with television date from the early 1920s, when Vladimir
Zworykin patented the iconoscope (1923). In Britain, Douglas Logie Baird introduced wireless
television around 1926. Experimental broadcasts were conducted by General Electric in the
USA and the BBC in the UK from 1928. Limited regular broadcasts occurred in Germany for
the 1936 Berlin Olympics. But the war effectively held up television's advance until around
1948. This can be indexed above all by the post-war transformation of Hollywood. In 1946,
the worldwide cinema audience was estimated at 235 million *per week*, 90 million in the USA
(its peak). By 1948, the US audience was 60 million (the lowest since 1933) as the sale of
television sets doubled. In 1955 (despite the advent of widescreen technologies such as
CinemaScope in 1952), the US cinema audience had shrunk to 45.8 million per week and by
1970 it was 15 million. More recent cinematic revivals have only confirmed the end of the
classical period by instituting different modes of production, marketing, distribution and
consumption.

took his patents to the RCA laboratories in 1927, proposed placing a television camera in the nose cone of a vertically ascending rocket), it soon became apparent that television's potential extended beyond science. Society itself would be the realm of televisual experimentation. If, as McLuhan argued, television has engendered a vastly expanded sense of 'locality' and 'community', the corollary of this shift is the manufacture of modes of relating to place and to social group which find no measure in the past. Under the sway of broadcast television, the demarcation between public and private realms has become increasingly volatile; the perimeter of the home, the orchestration of the public sphere, even the borders of the nation state, have been subjected to new pressures and uncertainties. These movements carry far-reaching implications for the formation of contemporary identity, whether at the level of the self or in terms of the collective referent of 'the people'. If these transformations have now been in motion for at least half a century, it is only recently that they have been recognized as more than intermittent interruptions to the undisputed sovereignty of the nation state and the proper individuality of its citizens.

Foucault's observation that the modern hallmark of power is its capacity to operate simultaneously along the axes of universalization and individualization situates television's paradigmatic utility as a contemporary political technology.[2] Television's expansion has always proceeded on two fronts at once: the globalization of telecommunication flows is counterpointed by the reorganization of domestic life down to the micro-politics of the family and the physical and psychic space of the home. In fact, the most significant change is precisely that where these fronts or frontiers (domestic, local, regional, national, transnational) were once distinct – or were believed to be – they now seem irreducibly imbricated in one another.

The ambivalence of television's place in the political formation of the nation state is symptomatic of the tensions between nationalism and transnationalism which suffuse capitalism. On the one hand, the development of national broadcasting networks has given television unrivalled potential to represent national consciousness and synthesize national consensus on a scale and speed previously unimagined. On the other hand, national broadcasting systems everywhere currently find themselves being integrated within or displaced by transnational networks which have only fragile allegiance to the nation state.[3] Both processes have fundamentally altered the experience of 'nation' and the parameters of nationalist discourse.

2 Foucault suggested that the transition from 'pastoral' to 'disciplinary' power has 'focused the development of the knowledge of man around two roles: one globalizing and quantitative, concerning the population; the other analytical, concerning the individual.' Foucault, 'Subject and power', p. 784.

3 This process really took off in the 1980s, with the emergence of 'global' channels such as CNN and MTV, the increased private ownership of telecommunications (notably in Western Europe), and the growing integration of electronic media with other information technologies such as computer and telephone services.

Benedict Anderson's contention that national communities should not be judged in terms of whether they are authentic or inauthentic, 'but by the *style* in which they are imagined' sets a relevant point of departure.[4] If the nation is as much a textual as a territorial entity, in the post-war era the space and time of the national text has become increasingly televisual. The fact that an entire populace can share the simultaneous unfolding of events has given new shape and form to national archetypes, allowing them to coagulate into the imaginary flesh of a national body. The capacity to channel individual sites of watching and personal mechanisms of recognition onto a collective plane grants television unrivalled prominence in contemporary projections of national identity. Colin McCabe has suggested:

> Just as national literature in the vernacular tongue was an essential component in the constitution of the ruling classes of post-Renaissance Europe, so a national broadcasting system is a crucial element in the current political settlement of the capitalist West.[5]

This analogy is revealing, as much for its limits as for the broad continuities it seeks to authorize. Distinguishing 'the capitalist West' from other regions is always problematic, but doubly so here. The spread of television is symptomatic of the growing disjunction between territorial control and cultural domination: one no longer needs the former to achieve the latter.[6]

*

The instrumental link McCabe posits between national television and contemporary nationalism is exemplified by 'flagship' programmes, such as the four-hour telecast *Australia Live: The Celebration of a Nation*, broadcast on 1 January 1988.[7] In many respects, *Australia Live* drew on familiar nationalist terrain, eulogizing 'the land', and deploying the common colonial narrative describing a pioneering struggle in a harsh environment.[8] Where it departed from earlier nationalist discourses – especially the popular literary culture it otherwise reproduced – was the manner in which these themes

4 Anderson, *Imagined Communities*, p. 15.

5 C. McCabe, *High Theory/Low Culture*, Manchester University Press, Manchester, p. 8.

6 While it is increasingly difficult to contain 'the West' as a geographical entity, it is still important to distinguish television's role in regions such as Australia, where some 98 per cent of the population own television sets, from those such as Indonesia, where television remains beyond the reach of many, except in communal viewing situations. However, if 'developed' nations still dominate total television audiences, this situation is rapidly changing, and the spread of television in 'underdeveloped' nations is itself frequently seized upon as a marker of 'development'.

7 This date, marking two hundred years of colonization of the State of New South Wales, was chosen to commemorate the Australian BiCentennial. *Australia Live* was broadcast simultaneously by three national networks (two public and one commercial), assisted by government telephone and satellite authorities. With over 1000 technicians and celebrity presenters, it remains the largest live telecast undertaken in Australia.

8 On the tensions of such narratives in the Australian context, see R. Gibson, *South of the West: Postcolonialism and the Narrative Construction of Australia*, Bloomington, Indiana University Press, 1992.

were embodied as scenes. Instead of simply describing nation or national unity, *Australia Live* was able to enact it, using the camera's capacity to generalize the role of the eye-witness to cathect nationalist investment in geography as epistemology. The programme was structured as a series of *tableaux vivants*, literally mapping the Australian continent into a textual structure by criss-crossing 'live' between the central studio and some 70 locations. Each new location, from capital cities to tourist icons such as Uluru and Bondi Beach, to the physical extremities of the continent (most northerly point, highest mountain, etc.), was introduced by a celebrity presenter, often accompanied by a group of revellers. In this way, *Australia Live* embodied the 'Celebration of a Nation' theme by figuring 'Australia' as a series of familial and local gatherings which could be seen in living rooms all over the country.

The sheer visibility of such a broadcast – undoubtedly television's most significant technical threshold translated into cultural impact – granted substance to the claim made by one of the presenters that *Australia Live* was 'a great achievement in television technology which will tonight unite an entire nation'. But what is the unity offered by the tele-event? No longer centred around locality, neighbourhood or any mode of physical proximity, it also exhibits a tendency to supplant traditional axes of group identification, such as class, religion, ethnicity, race and gender. (These differences are far from irrelevant – if only as the demographics through which advertisers purchase audiences – but the *mass* media was named precisely for its unprecedented ability to aggregate otherwise diverse social fractions.) Baudrillard once postulated that television has taken us across the hallucinatory threshold beyond which 'events no longer have any meaning: not because they are insignificant in themselves but because they have been preceded by models with which their own processes can only coincide.'[9] But, in highlighting the deformation of 'the real' according to the precession of simulacra, he perhaps underestimates the extent to which the meaning of events now resides precisely in the experience of watching.

What is unique to the national unity proposed by television is that its 'collectivity' belongs to an audience which defines itself in the act of watching. While this may seem self-evident, the full implications of this novel form of collectivity resist easy assessment. Firstly, this shift should not be too hastily aligned with models of audience passivity which figure TV as merely a soporific or narcotic.[10] But nor should such models be countered by the 1980s fashion for celebrating the semiotic heroism of 'active' spectators who 'make their own meanings'. Critical analysis of television cannot be confined to adjudicating between the agency of the individual viewer and the rule of centralized structures of power, but needs to recognize

9 Baudrillard, *Evil Demon*, p. 21.
10 A classic text here would be M. Winn, *The Plug-in Drug*, New York, Viking Press, 1977.

the mutual imbrication of these poles in a scene whose terms of reference no longer obey traditional dichotomies.

This reconfiguration stems directly from the immense uncertainty that live broadcasts generate with regard to distinctions between presentation and representation. Henri Bergson's desire to resolve the equivocality of 'representation' (which he argued 'ought never, according to its etymology, . . . designate an intellectual object presented to the mind for the first time'), finds its Waterloo in live television.[11] Television has taken the modern desire for simultaneity and elevated it onto a new plane. Synchronous viewing and the shared experience of the rhythmic unfolding of events on screen, aware that *others are watching simultaneously but elsewhere*, now constitutes a primary ritual of national identification. Heightened social awareness of synchronicity has given rise to new ways of marking the rings of time.[12] The proliferation of questions of the 'What were you doing when JFK was shot?' type situate the extraordinary reach a single 'moment' can assume when tele-distributed. Television's successful colonization of intersubjective experience also draws on the mobilization of techniques of direct address and the adoption of self-reflexive narrative structures. *Australia Live* was firmly in the mould that Eco has dubbed 'Neo-TV', with one of the hosts proudly announcing 'a show that's prepared to go to any lengths to unite our nation and Australians around the world. . . . You're all in this. If you're in the audience, you're in the show'.[13]

Being 'in' the show assumes novel dimensions when one tries to situate its event. Unlike *Triumph of the Will* (1935), which crossed a certain cinematic threshold in the relation between 'event' and 'representation', *Australia Live* lacked an event which could be located in traditional terms. There was no single gathering, no mass assembly, performance or procession – even one designed to be filmed and subsequently reassembled according to the plastic logic of montage. What *Triumph of the Will* and *Australia Live* share is their desire to reconstruct the experience of community and communal presence for a dispersed national audience.[14] But while *Triumph of the Will* still belonged to an orchestration of 'mass spectacle' based on the populating of space – something exemplified by Hitler's plans for a series of mass assembly halls and stadiums, from the Berlin Dome for 130,000 to Zeppelinfield planned for 400,000 – television has redirected this desire for community and communality along the axis of time.

11 Bergson quoted in J. Derrida, 'Sending: on representation' (trans. P. and M.A. Caws), *Social Research*, 49, 2 (Summer 1982), p. 295. See also 'The ends of representation' above.

12 While synchronicity has undoubtedly been part of human experience for millennia, it is noteworthy that television seized this 'metaphysical' terrain in a context in which intersubjectivity had been radically denied.

13 See U. Eco, 'A guide to the neo-television of the '80s', *Framework*, 25 (1984), p. 19.

14 One might compare the scenes in *Triumph of the Will* in which massed SA members proclaim their place of birth (enacting the unity of Greater Germany) with the narrative format of *Australia Live*.

The 'event' which *Australia Live* 're-presented' never existed. Or rather, it existed in multiple parts and places. What we (symptomatically) call the 'television-event' is radically homeless, which is to say it is fissured at inception. Of course, events have always been capable of being transported beyond the secure co-ordinates of a single occurrence – as Derrida points out, the possibility of repetition inhabits the structure of every present event – but television immeasurably sharpens our awareness of this uncertain destiny. By dis-locating the stable space and time in which events are thought to 'occur' or 'take place', live television suspends representation over the abyssal moment of enunciation.[15] In *Australia Live*, 'Australia' became a performance, the sequencing of a live montage whose reconstructive logic has so saturated contemporary consciousness that it enables our entire relation to the world to be conceived in terms of set and *mise-en-scène*.[16]

The tele-event, with its fundamental de-realization of immediate space in favour of an intermittent, discontinuous and inherently ambiguous topology, openly conflicts with older forms of social organization predicated on the security of borders and the control of territory. The notion of the boundary (whether separating sites of action or categories of thought) has been subjected to a new uncertainty principle, whose impact on social theory may eventually rival quantum theory's redefinition of traditional mechanics. The transient and mobile centres of modern existence have found themselves increasingly volatilized by practices of telemobility which erode the sanctity of origins, the stability of contexts and the finality of ends. Virilio comments:

> We can now see more clearly the theoretical and practical importance of the notion of interface, that drastically new surface that annuls the classical separation of position, instant or object, as well as the traditional partitioning of space into physical dimensions, in favour of an almost instantaneous configuration in which the observer and the observed are roughly linked, confused and chained by an encoded language from which emerges the ambiguity of interpretation, an ambiguity that returns to that of the audio-visual media, especially that of live television . . .[17]

Yet, despite being caught in this rather Derridean cleft – which undoubtedly tugs at the strings of presence as the compass of metaphysics –

15 Homi Bhabha has stressed the disjunctive effect of enunciation as a limit to the metaphysics of presence and the philosophy of consciousness. See Bhabha, *Location of Culture*, p. 34. The effect may also be compared to the problematic of the 'performative' which Derrida analyses as one of the tributaries of *différance*. See Derrida, *Margins of Philosophy*, pp. 307–30.

16 There are numerous examples of such 'performances', such as the *Live Aid* concert of 1989 or the staging of *Tosca* in Rome in July 1992, using 'real' locations as the sets for each act, linked to a national and international audience via satellite and screen.

17 Virilio, *Lost Dimension*, p. 52.

television clings to the very tradition it undermines. The 'you are there' imaginary which dominates broadcast television validates itself wholly by appealing to the traditional value of presence, promising the viewer greater access and faster reports in a frantic quest to circumscribe the real by mastering absence, injecting reality where it is felt to be lacking. The ambiguity of this pursuit and the contradictions in which it is enmeshed are felt again and again in the vacillation of reference that televised images inevitably produce: where does one locate the real? How does one demarcate reality from its images? Attempting to master absence through the live interface of the electronic screen carries the ambition of mastery into uncertain terrain. If classical cinema still belonged to an urban architecture of the city centre, television today engenders an urbanization without centres, and a nationalism without grounding in the soil of the nation state.

*

This focuses another important limit to McCabe's analogy between the role of national literature in post-Renaissance Europe, and the contemporary functioning of broadcast television. Where print media played an active role in forging the cultural and linguistic basis of emergent nation states (especially in the eighteenth and nineteenth centuries), television's historical alignment has most often been with established national formations (including many post-colonial nation states such as India, Indonesia or Nigeria).[18] Of greater significance is the fact that television technology has always exceeded the harmony between geography and politics sought by the nation state. Like the aeroplane, the televisual vehicle eludes traditional forms of border control. Paralleling the manner in which electronic media have reduced the significance of architectural features such as doors and windows in determining 'access' to buildings, television has diminished the strategic importance of geographical features such as rivers, oceans and mountain ranges in demarcating national boundaries. Even before the Berlin wall fell, the closed society of East Germany was infiltrated nightly by Western television. Israel reluctantly approved its own national television broadcaster in 1967 largely because (as Lisa Cohen put it): 'Jordan's plan to begin broadcasting news in Hebrew convinced the Israeli government that failing to establish its own television industry would create a national security

18 McLuhan memorably described the printed word as the 'architect of nationalism'. See McLuhan, *Understanding Media*, p. 184. Benedict Anderson similarly stresses the importance of print as the joint vehicle of national economy and national consciousness, through its creation of unified zones of communication and exchange. Anderson, *Imagined Communities*, pp. 41–55.

risk.'[19] When Ronald Reagan wanted to 'intervene' in Poland in 1982, his chosen vehicle was televisual rather than military.[20]

If these examples (which could be multiplied at will) still seem to belong to a political terrain defined by competition between distinct nation states, it must be added that this map has itself been confused by television. In question is not only the external reach of 'foreign' broadcasters, according to patterns of terrestrial links and satellite footprints, but the ability of soft missiles such as *Dallas* to cross national borders and redefine cultural frontiers from within. In 1982, when French Minister for Culture Jack Lang branded *Dallas* a weapon of 'cultural imperialism', and President François Mitterrand warned that 'the distribution of information developed and controlled by a few dominant countries could mean for others the loss of their history, or even their sovereignty', it had to be acknowledged that, beyond strains of cultural elitism and Gallic pique, a more fundamental shift was involved.[21] According to a report prepared by the French Inter-Ministerial Commission on Transborder Data Flows:

> The current development of transborder flows establishes and amplifies the dominance that multinational systems are achieving over individual countries. Certainly the nation state remains vigorous. But it runs the risk of being steadily drained of its strength.[22]

Such a highly charged image of transnational media as a parasite corrupting the health of the national body is problematic in assuming the political desirability of the nation state. However, it does serve to situate the *radical* challenge that new media and information technologies pose to the philosophical tradition and political heritage from which the nation state

19 L. Cohen, 'Conflict and consensus: television in Israel', in C. Schneider and B. Wallis (eds), *Global Television*, New York, Wedge Press and Cambridge, MA, MIT Press, 1988, p. 50.

20 The concept of using broadcast media to bypass foreign governments in order to influence 'the people' directly has been part of US foreign policy for decades. The Reagan-inspired television spectacular *Let Poland Be Poland* was created by Charles Wicks (director of the *Voice of America* network), and was broadcast across the USA and around the world by satellite in a 'weekend of solidarity' with Poland. It featured a plethora of old movie stars such as Bob Hope, Frank Sinatra and Charlton Heston, as well as numerous political leaders and heads of state expressing support for the Polish people and opposition to their Soviet-backed government. However, it failed where it most wanted to succeed – in the ratings market.

21 Mitterrand (speaking at the Versailles Summit in June, 1982) quoted in Mattelart et al., 'International image markets', in Schneider and Wallis, *Global Television*, p. 19. The issue resurfaced with a vengeance in the 1993 debate over GATT, and France's demand for 'cultural exception' to agreements on trade in goods and services. In a speech to the biennial Francophone summit (a body representing 46 French speaking states), President Mitterrand asked: 'who can be blind to the threat of a world gradually invaded by an identical culture, Anglo-Saxon culture, under the cover of economic liberalism?', and questioned whether 'the laws of money and technology are about to achieve what totalitarianism failed to do'. Quoted in C. Bremner, 'US "imperialism" galls Gallic pride', *Australian Higher Education Supplement*, 27 October 1993.

22 Quoted in Mattelart et al., 'International image markets', in Schneider and Wallis, *Global Television*, pp. 18–19.

emerged.[23] Moreover, if the prospect of cultural domination appears daunting to Europe (leading the European Commission to propose that 'the creation of a common market for television production is thus one essential step if the dominance of the big American media corporations is to be counterbalanced'), this situation is manifested far more starkly elsewhere.[24] At the time *Television Without Frontiers* was written, US programming constituted about half of total European television imports and occupied about 10 per cent of total air time. This might be contrasted to the case of Papua New Guinea, where the sole television licence is held by an Australian consortium who programme it identically to their national Australian network (US, UK and Australian product), leavened only by local news and a weekly sports programme.

Television has clearly made national sovereignty a political issue in a new way, which is doubtless one reason for the frequent 'moral panics' which dot its history.[25] Television crosses all those lines, from the threshold of the private home to the perimeter of the nation state, which previously helped to secure individual and collective identity. By exposing the fragility of territorial boundaries, it has accentuated the intense questioning of the cultural and linguistic borders of the nation state which grips the late twentieth century. It also means that debates on restricting the circulation of knowledge, which were once primarily concerned with the regulation of illicit flows of information (political or moral censorship of state secrets or cultural taboos), are today equally concerned with explicit information flows.[26] If this allows us to see the nation state as an historical entity rather than the apex of 'civilization', it also raises new questions. Lipschutz argues: 'At the end of the twentieth century we are seeing the leaking away of sovereignty from the state both upwards, to supra-national institutions, and downwards, to subnational ones.'[27]

*

23 In his meditation on 'Europe', Derrida pointed out that current ruptures mean that no radical politics can afford to define itself simply *in opposition* to the state: 'in certain cases the old state structures help us to fight against private and transnational empires.' Derrida, *Other Heading*, p. 37.

24 Commission of the European Communities, *Television Without Frontiers*, Brussels, 1984, p. 47.

25 This was how a number of critics read the *Dallas* episode, suggesting that *Dallas* became an easy target for a political Right nostalgic for its own cultural centrality, and a political Left concerned at the seduction and 'feminization' of the working class. See I. Ang, *Watching Dallas*, London, Methuen, 1985.

26 This was made clear in September 1993, when Chinese Radio, Film and Television Vice Minister Wang Feng described uncensored foreign television broadcasts as an issue of national sovereignty and proclaimed a ban on satellite dishes (largely in response to Rupert Murdoch's STAR TV and Murdoch's much-publicized proclamation that satellite television would be 'an unambiguous threat to totalitarian regimes everywhere'). Murdoch responded by dropping the offending BBC World Service News from STAR's line-up.

27 Lipschutz quoted in D. Morley and K. Robins, *Spaces of Identity: Global Media, Electronic Landscapes and Cultural Boundaries*, London and New York, Routledge, 1995, p. 183.

The 1991 Gulf War will undoubtedly be remembered as the moment in which global television fully entered public consciousness. Boosted by the publicity its war reporting received, CNN expanded into 135 countries by 1992. This success was partly a function of the extent to which CNN's coverage seemed to abolish traditional information hierarchies.[28] All over the world, political leaders watched CNN and discussed 'the war' from what they saw there, what 'we' all saw together. Politicians became spectators, and spectators became experts. The much noted construction of war-as-video-game and spectator-sport went hand in hand with this democracy-effect, which has been one of television's most persistent ideologemes in legitimating its trajectory towards universal access and global coverage.

To better situate this threshold, some historical reference points are helpful. The 1990s' cyberpunk slogan, 'Information wants to be free', is scarcely new. Following the Second World War, US State and commercial interests converged in pervasive demands for a 'free flow of information' and 'worldwide access to news', especially in previously occupied Europe.[29] US influence was largely responsible for inscribing this objective into the Unesco charter constituted in London in 1945.[30] The extent to which this amounted to a direct attempt to break the grip of European news cartels was widely recognized at the time, but won support in the cold war climate as a means of embarrassing the Soviet Union.[31] On a similar ideological terrain, Hollywood films were again saturating the world market, even in previously protected areas.[32]

What was orchestrated in a period in which the USA enjoyed un-precedented political and economic dominance was a framework in which the dissemination of information, as much as entertainment, would be

28 This extended to the controversial presence of CNN correspondent Peter Barnett 'behind enemy lines' in Baghdad. If both sides understood the strategic importance of the battle of representations, Washington enjoyed a vast superiority here too. Learning from its experience in Vietnam, the US military maintained tight rein over all war reporting; a vital element of a 'controlled' conflict is media control.

29 In a 1946 speech, William Benton, then US Assistant Secretary of State, proclaimed: 'The State Department plans to do everything within its power along political or diplomatic lines to help break down the artificial barriers to the expansion of private American news agencies, magazines, motion pictures, and other media of communication throughout the world. . . . Freedom of the press – and freedom of exchange of information generally – is an integral part of our foreign policy. . .' Quoted in H. Schiller, *Communication and Cultural Domination*, New York, International Arts and Sciences Press, 1976, p. 29.

30 Section 2 of Article 1 of the Unesco Charter recommends 'such international agreements as may be necessary to promote the free flow of ideas by word and image'.

31 See F. Wete, 'The new world information order and the US press', in Schneider and Wallis, *Global Television*, p. 139.

32 Following the war, restrictions on US films were eased or removed in countries including the UK, Australia, Italy, France, and West Germany. Jill Forbes notes that the 1946 agreement by the French government to impose no quotas on US films reversed the pre-war stance 'out of gratitude' to the Americans. See her 'The internationalization of French television', in Schneider and Wallis, *Global Television*, p. 62.

dominated by Western interests under US leadership. Currently, as Wete points out:

> [T]he overwhelming majority of news flows from the developed to the developing countries and is generated by four large transnational agencies – AP, UPI, AFP and Reuters. . . . Moreover, the West dominates the use of satellites, the electromagnetic spectrum controlling the use of airwaves, tele-communications, micro-electronics, remote sensing capabilities, direct satellite broadcasting and computer related transmission.[33]

The extent to which 'America' would act as the arbiter of the emerging global culture was underlined by its leadership in post-war television production, building on its established dominance in film production. While US television producers rapidly became the largest programme exporters in the world, the US market has remained virtually closed; not by the 'artificial barriers' of quotas, but through the more efficient prophylactic of a dominant culture with little interest in foreign programming.[34]

It wasn't until the 1960s, when some 70 former colonies gained independence and joined Unesco, that there was any serious questioning of the terms of the US-dominated world information order.[35] Throughout the 1970s, a series of proposals to correct the imbalance gained momentum, but also met increasing opposition from Western press organizations, especially in the USA.[36] Amidst powerful calls to 'no longer authorize discussions and activities which relate to propositions unacceptable to the West', the US eventually moved to withdraw funding from Unesco, a marked reversal of the role it had originally taken in establishing Unesco as a key institution in the global information structure.[37] Lyotard's speculation that 'it is conceivable that the nation-states will one day fight for control of information, just as they battled in the past for the control of territory . . .' seemed eminently

33 Wete, 'New world information order', p. 139.

34 In his 1983 study, Tapio Varis found that the USA imported only 2 per cent of its total programme output (the lowest of any country). Varis concluded: 'One might claim that foreign programmes are not shown at all in the United States.' 'Trends in international television flow', *International Political Science Review*, 7, 3 (July 1986), p. 237. While the decline of network dominance – around 30 per cent of their audience has been ceded to specialist cable 'narrowcasters' exploiting niche markets in the last decade – complicates this situation, the major networks remain 'virtually devoid of foreign programming'. See P. McCarthy, 'The horror grip of Hollywood', *The Age* (Melbourne), 30 December 1993, p. 9.

35 Mehan cites a meeting in Montreal in 1969 as the first UN reference to a change in the 'information order'. See J. Mehan, 'Unesco and the US: action and reaction', *Journal of Communication*, 31, 4 (Autumn 1981), p. 160.

36 US press coverage of the 1980 Unesco General Conference in Belgrade virtually ignored Unesco's basic activities combating illiteracy, and concentrated solely on communication policy. See A.H. Raskin, 'US news coverage of the Unesco Conference', *Journal of Communications*, 31, 4 (Autumn 1981), pp. 164–74.

37 From the Declaration of Talloires issued by Western media organizations at the 1980 Unesco conference. Quoted in Mattelart et al., 'International image markets', in Schneider and Wallis, *Global Television*, p. 18.

plausible.[38] But the question remains as to whether such battles can still belong to the political tradition of the nation state.

*

While theses of 'media imperialism' – like the theories of 'underdevelopment' they emerged alongside – remain prone to oversimplification by foreclosing tensions in favour of a spurious unity accorded both dominant and dominated cultures, the decisive advantage enjoyed by US media products cannot be ignored in considering the lines of force which bind the 'global village'. A primary index is the emergence of English – or Anglo-American – as the *de facto* universal language 'destined to overtake or dub all the idioms of the world' (as Derrida puts it).[39] If this reflects the economic and political hierarchies of this century, it also depends on contemporary audio-visual hierarchies (which can scarcely be divorced from economic or political relations).[40] As the global reach of television grows, the need to remember that its culture does not belong equally to everyone in the world becomes more pressing.

Yet this cannot rest upon simplistic assertions that 'the media are all American', nor on Pavlovian models of 'audience response'. The first assumption has been challenged by the emergence of major non-Western television networks such as Televisa (based in Mexico), and particularly by the increased role of Japanese corporations in the audio-visual industry.[41] The second presumption has been challenged by empirical research into viewing habits, and growing awareness of the variety of readings that the same programming can sustain. The 1980s also saw the emergence of new delivery systems (cable, microwave) which facilitate 'narrowcasting' and the division of national audiences into niche markets. Around the same time, structural limits to globalization became more apparent.[42] While the Gulf War propelled CNN into its pioneering role as the first effective global

38 Lyotard, *Postmodern Condition*, p. 5.

39 Derrida, *Other Heading*, p. 23. This pattern continues with the Internet. The fact that the USA alone requires no country code has a familiar ring. More telling is the statistic that, in 1993, nearly 94 per cent of Internet bytes flowed into just four countries: the USA, Canada, the UK and Australia. India accounted for 0.01 per cent, China for so little it didn't register.

40 After aerospace, the entertainment industry was the USA's largest export earner, taking $4.9 billion in 1986. See C. Hoskins and R. Mirus, 'Reasons for US dominance in international trade in television programs', *Media, Culture and Society*, 10, 4 (1988), pp. 499–515.

41 On Televisa, see J. Sinclair, 'Television in the post-colonial world', *Arena*, 96 (1991), p. 132. The purchase of Columbia by Sony in 1989 and MCA–Universal by Matsushita in 1990 marked a new round of vertical integration in the media industry with significant political implications.

42 Morley and Robins point out that global programming tends to be more successful where it has less dependence on language (*MTV*), or where there is no direct local competition. See Morley and Robins, *Spaces of Identity*, p. 63.

network, its success also inspired a variety of national reactions.[43] Schneider and Wallis have argued that: 'the movement towards global formations often has the opposite effect . . . at the very moment when television distribution is most versatile, local and national producers have become most aggressive.'[44]

However, 'regional' studies often seem as inadequate as the global paradigm they purport to replace. For example, Richard Collins used an analogy to audience response research to argue that 'the same differential found at the microlevel of consumption is found at the macrolevel.'[45] If true, this would challenge the very concept of 'media imperialism'. However, his qualifications (relying on the single example of US–UK trade which, because of linguistic compatibility, he admits is 'exceptional') turn out to be minor: basically that the trade is not completely one way. More alarming is Collins's justification of US domination of foreign markets in terms of cost efficiency: the availability of higher production values at a lower price per viewer hour than domestic production can achieve. Advocating economies of scale as the sole arbiter of cultural production effectively cedes the entire issue of television's role in constructing national identity to the most universalizing discourse of all: that of the global free market.

If it is increasingly inadequate to demand evidence of the nexus between media domination and cultural imperialism in terms of an 'Americanization' of audiences, this should not simply be a function of faith in market democracy. A more promising point of departure is the new instability of the referent 'America': who now speaks in its name? As Homi Bhabha points out, the grounding presumption of nationalism – that the ideal nation state occupies a unified political space mirrored by a homogeneous cultural space – has increasingly been fractured from within. Bhabha argues that: 'The Western metropole must confront its post-colonial history, told by an influx of post-war migrants and refugees, as an indigenous or native narrative *internal to its national identity*.'[46] A visible index of this change is the changing face of US television. Where classical Hollywood cinema sought, consciously and unconsciously, to create a normalized national subject by centring specific figures (prototypically the white, middle-class, English-speaking, educated, heterosexual, male), it also relied heavily on a process of cultural subtraction, regulating signs of difference by confining 'Others' to positions of narrative marginality, or often simply excising them from the

43 CNN has spawned direct rivals, such as BBC World Service Television, Sky News and Reuters, while 'vernacular' CNN subsidiaries are proposed in Germany, Japan, Latin America and elsewhere. Similarly, the phenomenal success of *Dallas* in the 1980s (screened in over 100 countries) sparked a series of national imitations, such as *Chateauvallon* in France, *Vanderburg* in Canada, and *Herrenstraat 10* in the Netherlands.

44 Schneider and Wallis, *Global Television*, p. 8.

45 R. Collins, 'Wall-to-wall *Dallas*: the US–UK trade in television', *Screen*, 27, 3–4 (May–August 1986), p. 67.

46 Bhabha, *Location of Culture*, p. 4.

dominant texts of national representation.[47] By contrast, contemporary US television grants conspicuous visibility to various 'minorities', particularly women and blacks – something symbolized by the status of Oprah Winfrey as the world's highest-paid television performer since 1994. The political import of this shift from a strategy of exclusion to one of inclusion – which echoes the displacement of assimilation by pluralism as the official paradigm for dealing with racial and ethnic difference – remains uncertain. Do new talking heads herald deeper social changes, or merely new strategies for the management of cultural difference without disturbing the consensus of the centre?

These questions highlight the contemporary importance television has assumed in orchestrating a 'public sphere'. This is a point to which I will return in the next section: here I merely want to observe that, as much as television's power arises from the transmission of normalized and normalizing narratives, it is also in the creation of a new matrix of social relations, in which the screen is the ubiquitous centre, that the media's current 'imperialism' is to be found. For Eric Michaels, the most urgent questions that television and video raise for remote Aboriginal communities in Australia are not those of imported programming, but the structural effect of the new media on traditional forms of cultural reproduction. Michaels emphasized the disjunction between traditional culture in which knowledge is restricted according to specific, locally-based kinship networks, and the spatio-temporal extension at the heart of electronic media.[48]

This situates the pressing need to rethink conceptual and analytical frames so as to avoid subjugating national and regional differences to universal teleology, while acknowledging the upsurge of discourses and processes (from advertising to feminism to land rights movements and environmentalism) which cut across the political space of the nation state. It cannot be a matter of aggregating regional analyses to form a comprehensive global pattern, nor of definitively demarcating 'local' concerns. While one tendency of contemporary television leans toward the obliteration of cultural difference according to what Virilio has termed 'a geo-strategic homogenization of the globe', there is also the strategic production of difference.[49] Strategies of 'localism' and 'inclusionism' may well play important roles in the process of globalization. Samuel argues: 'The more cosmopolitan capitalism becomes, the more it seems to wear a homespun look: the more nomadic its

47 In his exhaustive study of Hollywood's representation of African Americans, Cripps notes: 'in dealing with racial issues before the war they often preferred erasing blacks.' *Making Movies Black: The Hollywood Message Movie from World War Two to the Civil Rights Era*, New York and Oxford, Oxford University Press, 1993, p. 251.

48 E. Michaels, *For a Cultural Future: Francis Jupurrurla Makes TV at Yuendumu*, Melbourne, Art & Criticism Monograph Series, 1987, pp. 76–7. It must be added that Michaels did not subscribe to a nostalgic view of 'authentic primitivism', but underlined the importance of Warlpiri attempts to run a television service of their own which could be articulated with their traditional law.

49 P. Virilio, *Speed and Politics* (trans. M. Polizzotti), Semiotext(e), New York, 1986, p. 135.

operations, the more it advertises its local affiliations.'[50] Guattari also argues that development of an homogenizing global culture is not inconsistent with the emergence of defiant and ostentatious parochialisms:

> In fact, the two phenomena are complementary. It is just when there is the most universality that we feel the need as far as possible to return to national and regional distinctness. The more capitalism follows its tendency to 'de-code' and 'de-territorialize', the more does it seek to awaken or to re-awaken artificial territorialities and residual encodings, thus moving to counter-act its own tendency.[51]

Instead of reinscribing the problematic of cultural difference with reference to the heterogeneity of every national identity, globalization can lead to national and regional chauvinisms, and aggressive assertions of ethnicity according to the polemical determination of 'pure' identities. Clearly, television's endeavours to provide a range of role models often travel this path, amounting to little more than selective incorporation of the margins. Targeting different groups with fantasies of social inclusion (*you* are part of the viewing family) assumes heightened strategic importance as local and regional stations are increasingly integrated in national and transnational structures of programming and control. Yet, even if 'localism' and 'inclusionism' often barely exceed tokenism, they also stand as signs of the limits to television's universalizing trajectory, marking the point at which 'global culture' is forced to deal with the anxieties and contradictions of the irreducibly plural nation state.

Television has emerged as a major force in the contemporary redefinition of cultural and political space. Electronic media form the primary matrix of an unhomely space in which the global and the local are no longer in opposition but in tandem; a place for the emergence of cultural hybridity, but also a powerful frame for regulating cultural difference. While the period of national television networks has been instrumental in creating and maintaining a national polity by integrating a geographically dispersed audience into the grid of a national information landscape, the globalization of tele-communications increasingly unmoors this constituency. Transnational media flows produce a new world order of internationalized nationalism, in which national identity can no longer be secured with reference to a self-evident territory, whether geographic, ethnic, linguistic or cultural. On another trajectory, the multiplication of channels and the fragmentation of national audiences raises the spectre of the disintegration of the national public. Under pressure from supra-national economic blocs and political formations on the one hand, and the effects of racial and cultural heterogeneity which is the legacy of colonialism and a century of mass migrations on the other, the autonomous and unified nation state, like the national broadcasting system which once nourished its dreams, is already a nostalgic reference point.

50 Quoted in Morley and Robins, *Spaces of Identity*, p. 59.
51 F. Guattari, *Molecular Revolution* (trans. R. Sheed), Penguin, Harmondsworth, 1984, p. 36.

6

Unstable Architectures

[T]he way one gains access to a city is no longer through a gate, an arc of triumph, but through an electronic audiencing system . . .

Paul Virilio

There will be a road. It will not connect two points. It will connect *all* points. Its speed limit will be the speed of light. It will not go from here to there. There will be no more there. There will only be here.

Network MCI

The vacillating formations of globalism, nationalism and localism which dominate broadcast television have produced significant spatial mutations, most notably the confusion of public and private realms affecting contemporary identity. These pressures can be linked to the manner in which television's permeable boundary redefines the stability of social context, including the domestic space of the home. The scene of watching is instructive: where cinema developed an enclosed viewing space to separate its predominantly voyeuristic narratives from the everyday world, television rapidly found its characteristic place as the electronic hearth of the modern home.

If this divergence has today acquired an air of inevitability, it is worth recalling that in Germany initial experiments with broadcasting were directed towards collective viewing situations. The Nazi state, arguably the first to recognize fully the political importance of simultaneity as a means of generating national unity, favoured public television halls seating between 40 and 400 as an ideal mechanism for relaying important events to a mass audience. This enthusiasm for television was undoubtedly related to their innovative use of radio, such as the famous occasion when over one million Party members gathered around loudspeakers across the country to hear Rudolph Hess take his oath of allegiance to Hitler, and to recite it in unison with him.[1]

The fact that television achieved mass audiences on a scale exceeding even Goebbels's hopes, not by replicating the cinematic prototype, but according to a cellular model of individuated viewing sites, has played a

---

1 See W. Urrichio, 'Rituals of reception, patterns of neglect: Nazi television and its postwar representation', *Wide Angle*, 11, 1 (1989), p. 49. As Adorno and Horkheimer commented: 'The National Socialists knew that the wireless gave shape to their cause just as the printing press did to the Reformation', adding that the charisma of the Führer belonged to the 'gigantic fact that the speech penetrates everywhere'. Adorno and Horkheimer, *Dialectic of Enlightenment*, p. 159.

major role in structuring the contemporary social and political terrain. In direct contrast to the closed texts and darkened rooms of cinema, which promote an intense experience of personal voyeurism in a public place, the serial text of television belongs to an open viewing lattice. Each viewer's awareness of others watching in their own private spaces elsewhere forms an integral part of the viewing experience. If this orientation was dictated partly by technical difficulties (the cost of producing large-screen televisions, problems of projection), it also fitted other currents of post-war society.

The centrifugal dispersion of the city into suburban dormitories in the first half of the century depended upon new generations of public vehicles such as the tram, train and bus. In the second half of the century, it has been the victory of private vehicles – both automotive and audio-visual – which have transformed the urban terrain. The car, aptly described by Virilio as a detachable room of the suburban house, has confirmed the ascendancy of a commuter lifestyle dependent on rapid transit between home and work, while the television screen has redefined the home for an era of vastly expanded consumption.[2] Both vectors have been instrumental to the rapid decomposition of urban–industrial space in the wake of the Second World War, affecting not only the density and distribution of population, but the demarcation of zones of domesticity, production and leisure. Virilio comments:

> Basically, just as the television set posted before the sofa is an object that punctures the walls, the garage must also be considered in the context of its effect on the rooms of the house. Both are thresholds of transformation that provoke anamorphoses of constructed architectural and urban structures.[3]

Where vehicles of public transportation supported the division between public and private space crucial to classical capitalism, the triumph of auto-mobility vastly exceeded the bourgeois logic of city centre and suburban dormitory. Desire for unimpeded movement, expressed in the fantasy of an infinite system of freeways, resulted in the emergence of sprawling, a-centric cities whose prototype was Los Angeles. While the car confronts the old city centre merely as a barrier to circulation, it is one which proves impossible for mechanical vehicles to transcend. The decline of traditional urban reference points (the town hall, the city square, the public monument) entrained by the culture of auto-mobility has laid the grounds for the contemporary victory of the electronic data screen, whose ubiquity situates it as the new *polis* at the crossroads of public and private.

Heidegger once defined the *polis* as 'the historical place, the there *in*

2 Virilio, *Lost Dimension*, p. 80. Television's emergence as the principal marketing route has joined 'life-style' advertising to emphasis on the home as the key site for the consumption of new products such as white goods and electronics. Ironically, most entrepreneurs initially dismissed television as an advertising medium, believing the prohibitive cost of receivers would curtail audience reach. However, intense public desire to own a television placed a significant part of the cost of establishing TV networks on the audience.
3 Virilio, *Lost Dimension*, p. 80.

which, *out* of which, and *for* which history happens.'[4] To suggest that television has now taken this role is firstly to indicate the need for a profound rethinking of our understanding of 'society'. What happens to the social bond when traditional modes of linkage, including the very notions of place, presence and situation, are being completely redefined by instantaneous communications?[5] As 'organic' forms of community based on the primacy of locality and the durability of extended family and kinship networks have been displaced by more highly individuated modes of living, electronic media have assumed critical roles in bridging the gaps, and in bringing people into 'contact' with one another. As social life has become more privatized and fragmented, and individual experience (the experience of self *as* individual) more solitary, the inclusive, integrative fantasies which suffuse broadcast television have assumed heightened importance in locating each person within an imagined communal body, in wiring us to ourselves. Much as family photo-albums remain the last symbolic traces of the unity of the extended family, the family and communal orientations of long-running soap operas such as *Coronation Street* or *Neighbours* represent ghostly forms of community and communality which for many scarcely exist.[6] Virilio comments: 'After the explosion of the ancient extended family that arose from rural living, the present disintegration of the urban nuclear family progressively relieves threatened populations of any prospect for organized resistance.'[7]

*

The threshold of the tele-community (like that of tele-nationalism) depends upon the increased availability of the public sphere to the circuits of household perception. One way to approach this shift is to consider the imbrication of television and sport. Declining attendances at sporting events have everywhere been counterpointed by increasing audiences for televised sport. Even where crowds remain high, the proportion of tele-spectators far outweighs those at any game – crowds now function more as 'extras' in terms of the televised spectacle. As a corollary, professional sport has become an integral part of television programming, according to a tightening circle of spectacle, sponsorship, celebrity and advertising. (In fact, sport is

4 Quoted in P. Lacoue-Labarthes, *Heidegger, Art and Politics* (trans. C. Turner), Oxford, Blackwell, 1990, p. 17.

5 This is the problematic Lyotard identified as that of postmodernity, in which each 'self' becomes a 'nodal point' 'in a fabric of relations that is now more complex and mobile than ever before'. Lyotard, *Postmodern Condition*, p. 15.

6 Between 1960 and 1981, the number of people living alone in the USA doubled to one in four. See J. Meyerowitz, *No Sense of Place: The Impact of Electronic Media on Social Behaviour*, New York and Oxford, Oxford University Press, 1985, p. 148.

7 Virilio, *Lost Dimension*, pp. 126–7. One need not agree with his analysis of the family 'as a basic cell of resistance to oppression' – which leaves the question of patriarchy hanging – to acknowledge the profound changes to social bonding in a culture implored to 'keep in touch' by telephone.

the largest single category of television programming, forming a major nexus between television and nationalism.)

It would be foolish to reduce this shift to another sign of the enforced passivity of the television spectator. More complex psycho-social relationships seem to be involved, particularly when techniques promoting viewer involvement have been instrumental to television's popularity.[8] Learning from Leni Riefenstahl's path-breaking multi-camera coverage of the 1936 Berlin Olympics for her award-winning *Olympiad* (1938) – 'we turned the stadium into a film studio' as one of the camera operators recently put it[9] – contemporary television constructs the sporting field as an arena of total surveillance. The technical arsenal to ensure that nothing passes unseen or unheard (multi-camera coverage of all angles, remote cameras in motor vehicles or the cricket stumps, effects microphones, instant replays, slow motion, close-ups, split-screen inserts) is designed to give the television viewer not only the best seat in the house, but a seat which is better than the best according to the capacity of live montage to extend perception outside bodily limits.[10] What was once cinematic fiction has become everyday experience for a culture in which spectatorial omniscience has been completely normalized.

However, it would be negligent to isolate sport as an example. If the live action beamed from the front line of the 1991 Gulf War, complete with instant replays and an 'us' and 'them' scoreboard of casualties, demonstrated the commercial potential for televising war as sport, it also confirmed a trajectory which had been underway for some time. In a prescient footnote to his 'Artwork' essay, Walter Benjamin observed the manner in which new communication technologies reframed the scene of politics:

> The present crisis of the bourgeois democracies comprises a crisis of the conditions which determine the public presentation of the rulers. Democracies exhibit a member of the government directly and personally before the nation's representatives. Parliament is his public. Since the innovations of camera and recording equipment make it possible for the orator to become audible and visible to an unlimited number of persons, the presentation of the man of politics before camera and recording equipment has become paramount. Parliaments, as much as theatres, are deserted. Radio and film not only affect the function of the professional actor but likewise the function of those who also exhibit themselves before this mechanical equipment, those who govern. Though their tasks may be different, the change affects equally the actor and the ruler. The trend is towards establishing controllable and transferable skills under certain social conditions.

8 Here it is important to disentangle arguments over 'active' and 'passive' viewers from Debord's characterization of the spectacle as a social relation dominated by the principle of non-involvement. One can easily be an active viewer with a high degree of semiotic agency, while remaining withdrawn from social or political involvement.

9 Interviewed in *The Wonderful, Horrible Life of Leni Riefenstahl* (1993).

10 Equally indicative are the camera's direct interventions into sporting practices. From the 'photo-finish' which took the line between winning and losing beyond human perception to the sight of players on the field watching instant replays of their own acts, or the roar of the crowd approving not a spectacular play but its televised replay, we are currently witnessing the wholesale reconstruction of sport by television.

This results in a new selection, a selection before the equipment from which the star and the dictator emerge victorious.[11]

Benjamin's evaluation, made under the shadow of Hitler but prior to the spread of television, identifies a condition which still resists easy analysis. But the problem today is not so much lack of development obscuring a new trajectory as overdevelopment rendering the condition all too visible. However, a good starting point remains Benjamin's analogy between 'dictator' and 'star', which suggests the need to situate the immense political impact of the star system on public life.

Historically, the development of the star system was intimately related to structural developments in the film industry: as the thrill of simply watching motion pictures waned, the need for spectacle and narrative to attract new audiences raised production costs. Increased capital investment was secured by replacing the anonymity of the early 'players' with a cinema marketed by familiar names and faces.[12] However, the cult of cinema stardom bore little relation to any previous manifestations of fame or notoriety. In the exponential swelling of star persona – literally *public image* – cinema exploited the latent energy released by the camera's ability to separate the actor's body from its immaterial image. It constructed a new public ritual, violent in its intensity, in which the line between screen image and 'real person' was deliberately blurred. One reason it doesn't seem all that inaccurate to speak of the 'worship' of film stars is that the demand to embody an ideal image – as face, voice, physique, movement and even lifestyle – amounted to the attempt to incarnate a god. The personal cost exacted on many who attempted to live such disjunctive identities has become all too evident this century.[13]

Of course, the star system has undergone substantial modifications since its peak in Hollywood in the 1930s, when major movie stars received thousands of letters each week, and studio publicity machines maintained military watch over the images of their charges. It is often nostalgically observed that we no longer have *real* stars in the present, because they have become too real, or rather, too close; the protective distance sheltering their aura has been compromised.[14] But this represents less the end of the system or the termination of its contract than the dispersal of its logic and the

11 Benjamin, *Illuminations*, p. 249.

12 The story of the 'Biograph Girl', Florence Lawrence, is offered by some as the origin of the 'movie star', while others point to the fame of Asta Nielsen in Europe around 1910. But it was the emergence of Mary Pickford, Douglas Fairbanks and Charlie Chaplin in Hollywood between 1910 and 1913 that transformed both cinema and the notion of stardom with repercussions which would be felt around the world.

13 It seems no accident that Faustean 'price of fame' stories are a privileged cinematic genre, exemplified by the 'tragic fate' of Marilyn Monroe which continues to fuel an industry in her image beyond the grave.

14 For a time in the 1980s the British Royal family assumed the role previously accorded classical film stars. But, like other stars under the accelerated surveillance of television (which equally affects the press), the façade of a perfect family image found itself increasingly susceptible to rumour, innuendo and, finally, direct attack.

general dissemination of its effects. Stars appear over many horizons today: rock musicians, entrepreneurs, athletes, intellectuals and even 'ordinary people' can all become stars – or rather celebrities – according to Warhol's democratic formula, whose 15-minute duration belongs to the accelerated time of television. If 'celebrity' is only a small 's' version of star, exploiting the intimacy of 'personality' rather than the inaccessibility of archetype, it also testifies to the emergence of a cultural milieu in which the demarcation of media roles and the distinction between 'actors' and 'non-actors' has become increasingly problematic.

Ronald Reagan's metamorphosis from actor–politician (as president of the Screen Actors' Guild he was one of the 'friendly witnesses' for the first McCarthy inquiry into Hollywood) to politician–actor bears out Benjamin's prognosis concerning the profound *continuity of skills* (photogeny, performance, script) now needed to succeed in each domain. The calculation of public appearances on the basis of photo-opportunities and the structuring of public pronouncements to provide succinct 'sound bites' underlines the dominance of *mise-en-scène* in political as much as cinematic productions. Technical effects also converge: Reagan's specially designed lecterns, with auto-cues (borrowed from television) able to flash dialogue complemented by information such as journalists' names, enabled him to give the impression that he was not only on top of his lines, but also on a first name basis with the entire press corps. (Less seamless were his notorious homilies in which he would draw on a fund of 'personal experience' later revealed to be significantly coloured by his previous film roles. As Michael Rogin quipped, President Reagan is a man 'whose most spontaneous moments . . . are not only preserved and projected on film, but also turn out to be lines from old movies'.)[15]

In Reagan's aftermath, it seems that everybody 'knows' that politics is performed for the media, especially television. But focusing on Reagan as if he were an exceptional case is actually a way of resisting the full implications of this knowledge. Reagan was less the origin than another example of a trajectory which can be traced from Roosevelt and Churchill, as much as Hitler and Stalin.[16] One reason that all these political leaders from the 1930s remain 'larger than life' in the present is that politics divides at this point: they were the first to use the audio-visual media to 'personalize' their political images, projecting them into the public sphere in a manner which has since become second nature. Subsequent thresholds, from Nixon's

15 M. Rogin, *'Ronald Reagan' The Movie and Other Episodes in Political Demonology*, Berkeley, University of California Press, 1988.

16 Robert Herzstein discusses Roosevelt's ties to Henry Luce (controller of Time Inc.) and the importance of *The March of Time* newsreel series which 'became a virtual mouthpiece for Roosevelt's interventionist policy'. R. Herzstein, *Roosevelt and Hitler: Prelude to War*, New York, Paragon House, 1989, p. 344. Echoing Syberberg's cinematic analysis of Nazism, Virilio proposes of Hitler and Stalin: 'Perhaps it has not been properly understood that these miracle working dictators no longer ruled, but were themselves directors.' Virilio, *War and Cinema*, p. 53.

Checkers speech to Kennedy's victory in the first televised Presidential debates of 1960 (broadcast to the then largest-ever television audience) to the dominance of prime-time news images and the growing importance of 'non-news' programmes, merely confirm the escalating dependence of official politics on television.[17] When Bob Hawke appeared (playing himself as Australian Prime Minister) on the popular series *A Country Practice* in 1986, he seemed to be only preparing his post-parliamentary transition to occasional roving reporter for *Sixty Minutes*: both of these acknowledged acting roles segued into his earlier performances as a political leader. Rather than isolating individual cases, we need to reposition this shift at the heart of the political field itself.[18]

The reversibility of the actor–politician and the politician–actor, which seems set to rival the unholy alliance of military personnel and arms manufacturing corporations, highlights the present political function of celebrity. Celebrities function in the media as what Lacan termed *points de capiton* – they are the 'anchoring points' which arrest the sliding of discourse in (temporary) configurations of coherence.[19] Celebrities mediate public and private domains by providing nodes of identification – stereo-types – which enable the privatized viewing audience to project a common public sphere. But if celebrities dominate television programming as the star system once ruled cinematic genre, it is important to recognize their construction as provisional and ambivalent. While the celebrity stereotype undoubtedly exerts a normative power by distributing and hierarchizing positive and negative qualities, its dependence on identificatory processes of doubling and splitting also generates an irreducible instability.[20]

The political ethos of modernity, circling an ideal vision of democracy, has been closely tied to the political function of television celebrity. Meyerowitz's claim that television has 'the potential of the closest thing the

---

17 The definitive image of the 1992 US Presidential campaign was arguably Bill Clinton's saxophone solo on the *Arsenio Hall Show*. In 1996, Clinton launched his successful campaign for re-election on a set designed by the set designer of *Jurassic Park*.

18 This is clearly not a matter of simply opposing 'image' politics to political 'substance'. Lacoue-Labarthe's analysis of Nazism remains an essential point of reference here. Firstly, he refers to Syberberg's 'radicalization' of Benjamin's thesis, arguing that 'the political itself is instituted and constituted (and regularly grounds itself) in and as work of art' – a 'representa-tion' whose paradigm would be cinema. But secondly, he speaks of an 'immanentism' in which the entire 'community' produces itself as a collective artwork: 'That is why that process finds its truth in a "fusion of the community" (in festival or war) or in the ecstatic identification with a Leader . . .' Here the paradigm would be television and the tele-event. See Lacoue-Labarthe, *Heidegger, Art and Politics*, pp. 64 and 70.

19 See Lacan, *Écrits*, p. 154.

20 Homi Bhabha stresses the *productive* ambivalence of the stereotype, which makes it both a fulcrum of dominant ideology, but also a site of dis-ease which can be transformed into a language of contestation and resistance. For Bhabha: 'The stereotype is not a simplification because it is a false representation of a given reality. It is a simplification because it is an arrested, fixated form of representation that, in denying the play of difference (which the negation through the Other permits), constitutes a problem for the *representation* of the subject in significations of psychic and social relations'. Bhabha, *Location of Culture*, p. 75.

earth has ever witnessed to participatory democracy on an enormous scale' is characteristic in its exorbitant equation of democracy and tele-visibility.[21] In fact, the trope of transparency which underwrites television's image of political openness leads directly to the overexposure of personal life which produces media celebrity. Yet there is a sense in which Meyerowitz is correct. Where royalty demanded divine birth, celebrity can accrue to anyone: it is simply a matter of being well-known, or rather well-distributed, across a multiplicity of circuits.

*

In the cold war era, when each nation state was dominated by one, or, at most, a handful of national networks, television assumed an unprecedented role in defining a national 'public sphere'. Even without accepting the nexus posited by conservative commentators lamenting a 'loss of standards' in this period, it is clear that the rise of television has been accompanied by a sustained decline in the authority of traditional institutions of social integration: church, school, police, judiciary, parliament. This is demonstrated above all in the current integration of legal, educational, religious and political institutions with the telecommunications media. When Bill Clinton wants to hold public meetings with an 'old-fashioned' flavour, his chosen forum is not the town hall but the television studio which can distribute the feeling of a town hall to an entire nation. The rise of television churches and tele-evangelists, the spread of tele-education, the growth in televised court proceedings, and the increased tele-visibility of parliament and other public forums, all confirm television's status as the key forum of contemporary public life.[22] Today, public proceedings *need* to be televised, not simply to show 'democracy in action', but to shore up their legitimacy; to reassure us that parliament, for example, still has primary importance in a political process dominated by executive government and extra-parliamentary forces. There is a powerful convergence between the ideal image of representative democracy – the accessibility of the representatives, the visibility of decision making, the transparency of the political process – and the desire for transparency in representation which found its home in the camera. This convergence underwrites the extraordinary extent to which the official public sphere has today become internal to television.

Alexander Kluge argues that the current transformation of telecommunications, in which public ownership of the airwaves and state control of broadcasting is becoming subject to new levels of privatization and corpor-

---

21 Meyerowitz, *No Sense of Place*, p. 323.

22 The televising of public affairs is most 'advanced' in the USA, where broadcasts of the HUAC inquiries in the 1950s set a powerful precedent culminating in ratings successes such as the trials of Oliver North and O.J. Simpson. But the general reach of this trajectory was perhaps exemplified by the live broadcasts from the Russian Congress of People's Deputies in 1992: the fiery debates contrasted directly with both the closed doors of the Kremlin, and the tightly controlled footage of the Stalinist show trials of the 1930s, which previously stood as the dominant images of the Soviet political process.

atization, represents a profound transformation of political space: 'when this public sphere threatens to disappear, its loss would be as grave today as the loss of the common land was for the farmer in the Middle Ages'.[23] This is not to deny the deep antagonisms concealed in the bourgeois notion of a 'public sphere' which purported to universal representation while working by strategic exclusion. Kluge argues against surrendering the term, while advocating contesting its 'naturalization': 'What we understand by "naturalized" is evidenced by the ambivalence – in almost every case unrecognized – of the most important concepts associated with the key phrase *public sphere*: public opinion, public authority, freedom of information, the production of publicity, mass media etc.'[24] In the context of the emergent public sphere increasingly appropriated by private enterprise (what Kluge dubs 'the industrialization of consciousness'), he contends that any counter-public sphere must work on and against the contradictions of each of these historic forms. If every claim to inclusivity must be tested from the vantage point of the marginalized and excluded, even the most overdetermined sites of commercial television offer some possibilities for political intervention and cultural contestation.[25]

*

The full implications of the televisual restructuring of the public sphere can be grasped by returning to television's direct implantation in the interior of the home. The privilege of intimacy as television's dominant mode of address – politicians as much as advertisers quickly discovered that formality makes you seem dishonest – stems from the fact that the favoured scene of watching is the space of privacy itself. But the very concept of private space has been significantly transformed by the ambiguous illumination of what Virilio calls the 'third window'.[26] With television, access to the home belongs to the threshold of perception as much as locomotion, while the

23 A. Kluge, 'The public sphere', in Schneider and Wallis, *Global Television*, p. 69. Kluge is writing from a Western European perspective, where broadcasting services were traditionally the function of state-controlled monopolies, and the expansion of commercial television belongs to the convergence of 1980s ideologies of financial deregulation with the development of new delivery systems such as direct satellite broadcasting. But, apart from the USA, where telecommunications was always dominated by corporate interests, increased pressures on public broadcasting are clearly discernible elsewhere.

24 A. Kluge and O. Negt, 'The public sphere and experience' (trans. P. Labanyi), *October*, 46 (1988), p. 63.

25 For Kluge: '[T]he fence erected by corporations, by censorship, by authority does not reach all the way to the base but stops short – because the base is so complex – so that one can crawl under the fence at any time. Even television producers and board members can be examined in light of this calculation of marginal utility.' Kluge and Negt, 'Public sphere', pp. 69–70.

26 Virilio uses the phrase to place television in historical succession to the first window – the entrance door which granted access to dwellings – and the second window, which was concerned with the entry of light. See 'The third window', in Schneider and Wallis, *Global Television*, pp. 187–97.

perceptual horizon, divorced from material constraints, becomes contingent, shifting and radically discontinuous. By compromising the physical integrity of the traditional dwelling, television has profoundly deterritorialized the home. Because of its capacity to enter without knocking, interrupting lines of household security and parental authority, television has often triggered acute social tensions.[27]

The other face of this invasive trajectory is, of course, the overexposure of the private that dominates contemporary television. From talk show confessionals such as *Donahue* and *Oprah* to the growth of 'home video' shows and the recurrent fascination of television-as-life series such as *Sylvania Waters*, television increasingly offers the private sphere for public consumption. How has this affected the gender split which has traditionally assigned public and private spaces to 'male' and 'female' subjects respectively?[28] Meyerowitz argues that the 'flowering' of feminism since the 1960s has been aided by television's merging of male–female information systems: television's 'demystified image of the male world' revealed to women their lack of place in the public sphere.[29] While this analysis gives television a progressive role in 'democratizing' the public sphere, other currents are clearly discernible. Television's focus on domesticity is less the affirmation that 'the personal is political' than the submission of the personal to a new level of scrutiny. The contemporary political crisis arising from the overexposure of politicians' personal lives is counterpointed by the personal crises engendered in the increased commodification of private space and the subjection to normalized and normalizing images this brings. If the problem of finding 'clean' candidates for public office is one index of the first process, the rise of body image-related eating disorders such as anorexia symbolizes the second.

Television's unique capacity to expand the perceptual horizon heralds a new mode of relation to the outside, the scene of the other. It doesn't so much offer to take you there – this is more the promise of cinema with its seductive power to suspend self, body, place and time – as to bring the *there* to you. The psychic ambivalence of this contract, and the contradiction between the viewer's involvement in watching and the same viewer's frequent detachment from what is shown, resonates in the duplicity of the term *screen*. To screen something is to project it as a representation, but it is equally to camouflage or filter what is shown. This double register straddles the tension suffusing televisual spectatorship.

27 The producers of *Julia*, one of the first prime-time US series to give black actors leading roles, reported receiving letters from white viewers irate at the 'invasion' of their homes. See Morley and Robins, *Spaces of Identity*, p. 131.

28 This division has never been neat. While the home is often coded as a female space in opposition to the male public domain, it may still remain subject to the master of the house. Empirical studies of family viewing habits reveal that the person who wields the remote control is still most often the husband/father. See D. Morley, *Family Viewing: Culture, Power and Domestic Leisure*, London, Comedia, 1986.

29 Meyerowitz, *No Sense of Place*, p. 224.

The underlying assumption of liberalism, inherited from the Enlightenment, is that access to information and knowledge will eventually provide the remedy for social injustice. But the cry, 'The whole world is watching' (made famous by protesters pointing out news camera crews to the police at the 1968 Democratic Convention in Chicago), seems increasingly hollow today. Is it simply that the type of knowledge we receive via the screen militates against engagement? Or are there also more structural problems? Dufour and Dufour-Gompers argue that witnessing horror on the screen is more likely to function as personal exorcism:

> I see that these anxieties, hatreds, killings are not me . . . I see that these inhibited, distorted sexual appetites are not me . . . in a word, all this craziness is not me.[30]

Such psychological distancing mechanisms are undoubtedly augmented by the social architecture of the scene of watching. The fact that the television viewer is located inside his or her own domicile colours the entire experience. While enjoying a direct line to the outside, the viewer remains insulated; able to witness the fascinating spectacle of the other but also to withdraw from the threatening spectre of the other. Disavowal plays a critical role in this scene: the alternation of belief and disbelief characteristic of our ambivalent relation to camera-reality means that anxiety generated via the screen can always be alleviated by dismissing what is seen as 'mere representations'.[31]

What must be added to this analysis is a collective focus. It is worth recalling that television images from Vietnam – often credited with ending the war – did not in themselves build a political position. However, in the context of diverse counter-cultural struggles, the reading of such images was transformed so significantly that – for a moment at least – the spectacle began to work against its own principle of non-intervention. Television images became catalysts for social activism. To a certain extent, television is always capable of working like this, which is why its promise is so hard to surrender even as its political effects are increasingly removed from individual and collective empowerment.

*

Television technology has always lagged behind the dream–nightmare of the 'global village'. Recent developments in video cameras and satellite technology have once again put flesh on the bones of the old promise of a sight machine which allows us all to see *anything anywhere anytime*. In this bold

---

30 Quoted in Morley and Robins, *Spaces of Identity*, p. 144. See also my discussion of images of atrocity and their potential to encourage withdrawal into a private sphere in 'Intolerable memories' above.

31 While Baudrillard's polemical characterization of the television image as 'pure simulacrum' without any relation to the real serves a role in contesting the powerful naturalization of the screen image, it does so by sacrificing any possibility of recognizing the responsibility to the other that television images may hold.

guise, contemporary television offers itself as a meta-medium or master-discourse: *the frame which is not itself framed*. This fantasy of total visibility returns us to the panoptic metaphor which has always maintained a close watch over the camera. But in which direction does the mechanism point? As much as each individual viewer resides at the centre of the apparatus, experiencing the heightened sense of power engendered by surveying an apparently infinite horizon, it is the mass audience which fulfils another social contract. This reverse-shot – the captivated or captive audience – is, of course, precisely what advertisers buy.[32]

While the radical open-endedness of television's textual forms cannot be discounted (what would finally *end* the news?), television clearly remains close to the Enlightenment tradition of discourse which seeks control over its limit, and in fact legitimates itself precisely by the continual reincorporation of its own margins.[33] Despite its extraordinary technical possibilities, which are translated into bold promises to show us 'the world' at large, television programming rarely strays beyond a schema for incorporating and domesticating the 'foreign'. Its excursions into the outside resemble nothing so much as another form of – or forum for – global tourism, with the role of tour guides played by programme presenters, and the standardized tourist infrastructure and leisure activities provided by established narrative structures.

And yet, as with tourism, other effects may nevertheless ensue. As telematics has become more influential in economic, political and social life, customary spatial divisions have given way to a proliferation of ambivalent spaces which are neither entirely here or there. Lived experience of space has assumed a fluctuating existence, less adequately described by inherent and stable qualities (area, extension, volume) than by evaluations of its potential states. For Virilio, the disappearance of 'elementary' reference points in the architecture of our cities, but also of our concepts, has increased our dependence on new technologies such as television to provide the means for evaluating space and time. But because telematics, with its permeable, osmotic and interactive boundaries, has so little common ground with mapping and measuring systems of the past, this dependency only further heightens the current crisis of dimensions.

> This crisis of the notion of dimension then appears as a crisis of the whole, a crisis
> of substantive, continuous and homogeneous space inherited from classical

32 In contrast to Baudrillard, who described television as 'the end' of panopticism, Crary uses television to question Foucault's 'dismissal' of spectacle in favour of surveillance as the hallmark of power in a disciplinary society. Crary writes: 'I suspect Foucault did not spend much time watching television or thinking about it, because it would not be difficult to make a case that television is a further perfecting of panoptic technology. In it *surveillance* and *spectacle* are not opposed terms, but collapsed into one another in a more effective disciplinary apparatus.' J. Crary, 'Spectacle, attention, counter-memory', *October*, 50 (1989), p. 105.

33 One might compare televisual mechanisms of textual reflexivity with the traditions of Western philosophy. As Derrida notes, philosophy has never simply been blind to its other, but has always been anxious to think its other *in a certain way*. See Derrida, *Margins of Philosophy*, pp. x–xii.

geometry in favour of an accidental, discontinuous and heterogeneous space, one in which all the parts and the fractions, the points and the various fragments become once more essential, as if they were an instant, a fraction or fragmenting of time.[34]

Such a 'crisis' – which is also the invention of the new – makes itself felt at both the level of 'theory' and 'lived experience', and in fact often manifests itself precisely in terms of a disjunction in the relation between theory and experience. The saturation of everyday life with practices of telemobility has created a pervasive technical deformation of location and locality. Distance – the space which once held things apart and maintained sites, and also concepts, in a hierarchical system of differences – has collapsed in the ubiquity and instantaneity of the screen. The eviction of 'the people' from the older political theatres – agora, forum, street, town hall, parliament – prefigures their reconstitution as a dispersed audience whose commonality is established through the grid of a programming schedule. This reorientation highlights the extent to which the tradition of geopolitics, grounded on divisions between country and city, manifested in distinctions between local, regional, national and international spheres of action, and operationalized in the rule of the metropolitan over the antipodes – in fact the entire tradition of power being defined and exercised primarily in relation to demarcated spatial territories – is currently giving ground to what Virilio terms 'the non-site of contemporary chrono-politics'.[35] It is along the axis of time, in the cleft of immediacy, impelled by the urgent desire for the now, that television orchestrates its present dominion.

34 Virilio, *Lost Dimension*, p. 35.
35 Virilio, *Lost Dimension*, p. 78.

7

Telepresence and the Government of Time

> Time, a matter, presumably *the* matter of thinking, if indeed something like time speaks as presence.
>
> Martin Heidegger

In Jean-Luc Godard's *Alphaville* (1965), the future is controlled by the Alpha-60 computer which is programmed to organize society on a purely rational basis. Predictably the scheme fails: drawn into a contest of wits by secret agent Lemmy Caution, Alpha-60's logical functions disintegrate (as HAL-2000's would in *2001: A Space Odyssey*). Their encounter concludes with the computer soulfully intoning a monologue drawn from Borges. The 'answer' to Caution's riddle ('something that never changes with the night or the day, as long as the past represents the future, towards which it will advance in a straight line, but which, at the end, has closed in on itself into a circle')[1] was, of course, time: that elusive and enigmatic concept which, despite its status as the 'universal' condition of human existence, has always resisted the grasp of the universe of reason.

This disjunction between time's natural existence and reason's perennial difficulty in explaining time's nature finds expression in the recurrent paradoxes evoked by the question, 'What is time?' Spengler once suggested this is the question *no-one* should be allowed to ask. For Augustine: 'If nobody asks me, I know: but if I were desirous to explain it to one who should ask me, plainly I know not.'[2] Of course, the question of time has always been 'answered' in various ways (even by Augustine), but what emerges most consistently is the restatement of an aporia which has itself been critical in defining 'Western thought'.

What concerns me here is the relation between this aporia – which circulates around the duplicity of the now – and the extraordinary proliferation of technologies designed to deliver instantaneity and immediacy as the ever-present condition of modern existence. While modernity defines itself in the force of its acceleration, current developments in telecommunications

---

1 *Alphaville* (trans. P. Whitehead), London, Lorrimer and New York, Simon and Schuster, 1966, p. 70. Alpha-60's final words paraphrase a passage from Borges's essay, 'A new refutation of time': 'Time is the material of which I am made . . . Time is the stream which carries me along . . . but I am Time . . . it is a tiger which tears me apart . . . yet, I, too, am the tiger . . . For our misfortune, the world is a reality . . . and I . . . for my misfortune . . . I am myself – Alpha-60.' *Alphaville*, p. 74. See Borges, *Labyrinths*, p. 269.
2 Augustine, *Confessions* (1631) (trans. W. Watts), London, Heinemann, 1913, p. 239.

mark a fault-line in the culture of speed whose ends remain unclear. How might the desire for presence, which has long stood as the matrix of desire itself, be affected when its traditional parameters such as substance, permanence and proximity are increasingly displaced and outweighed by the immediacy of that which is absent, immaterial, or ephemeral? And what of the regimes of temporality generated by telematics? In the ambiguity of televised instantaneity, does reason find its destiny, or the necessity to subject its history to a critical displacement?

Such questions must be posed in relation to the series of profound changes in the experience and understanding of time which frame modern consciousness. The weakening of religious cosmology by Enlightenment philosophy, the displacement of God as an ultimate principle of causality, the rise of scientific explanation, the growth of machine culture in the wake of the industrial revolution, the global expansion of capitalism, have all helped to dethrone the eternal in favour of a new consciousness of history coupled to a strong belief in human progress. In the nineteenth century, the cosmic time postulated by sciences such as physics, biology and geology redefined the origins and ends of the universe in a manner difficult to reconcile with humanist conceptions. But if Darwin's theory of evolution or Kelvin's analysis of the age of the earth removed 'Man' as time's proper referent, they nevertheless left Newton's idea of 'absolute time' more or less untouched. In contrast, Einstein's space–time fields completely departed Newton's image of universal clock, displacing it with a radical relativity in which each observer is effectively his or her own clock.[3] Today, even as television renders global instantaneity a palpable phenomenon (resembling the Lockean universe in which 'this present moment is common to all things now in being'),[4] time's line wavers in quantum uncertainty. This conjunction of theoretical and experiential ruptures suggests the stakes at play in this scene.

*

3 Einstein's Special Theory of Relativity (1905) drew on the work of Maxwell, Mach, Lorentz and others to propose the final emancipation of field theory from any kind of substratum (ether, etc.). In contrast to Lorentz's earlier explanation for the unexpected outcome of the Michelson–Morley experiment (1888), Einstein argued that the dilation of time they measured was not a 'real' effect located in the object (the measuring apparatus), but rather a 'perspectival' effect generated by the relative motion between the observer and the thing observed. In positing a perspectival effect which is not an optical function of angle or distance but of the *relative velocity* between two frames of reference, Einstein effectively repudiated the possibility of attaching absolute dimensions to time and space. In his General Theory of 1916, he extended this proposal to all accelerated bodies. Since all matter in the universe exerts a gravitational force (which is a form of acceleration), Einstein concluded that 'every reference body has its own time'. A. Einstein, *Relativity: The Special and General Theories* (1916) (trans. R.W. Lawson), New York, Crown, 1961, p. 26.

4 J. Locke, *An Essay Concerning Human Understanding* (1690) (ed. P.H. Nidditch), Oxford, Clarendon Press, 1975, p. 203.

To understand the fascination of television, it is helpful to situate its technology in relation to the aporia of time which haunts Western thought. The essential paradox of time – the paradox of essence itself – relates to the ambiguity of the present moment: time is always now, and yet the now itself cannot really exist. This is the problem formulated by Aristotle and restated down through the centuries.[5] Aristotle's argument may be summarized under three (related) headings:

1   If we consider the nature (*physis*) of time, the only part of time which properly exists (or *is*), is the present. But time is not thought to be made only of the present, but of past, present and future. How can time's essence be composed of that which lacks essence?
2   While time can be divided into parts, the relation between the part and the whole is problematic. If the present is a part of time, it necessarily has duration. But if the present has duration, at no point could it be said to be wholly present. Yet, without duration, how can the present be part of time?
3   Since the present is always 'now', how can time pass? Each now must be 'destroyed' by its successor for time to pass. But the now cannot be destroyed 'in itself' – at the very moment when it *is* – or it would never have existed.[6]

Lurching between the sameness of an eternal present and the vertigo of an instant whose transience confuses the dimension it would measure, time resists simple definition. Aristotle's observation ('Some of it has been and is not, some of it is to be and is not yet') returns like clockwork in Augustine ('The past is now no longer, and that to come is not yet. As for the present, should it always be present and never pass into times past, verily it should not be time but eternity'), and again in Hegel ([Time] 'is that being which, inasmuch as it *is*, is *not*, and inasmuch as it *is not*, *is*').[7] Nor is it entirely foreign to Kant. While Kant reformulated time as 'nothing but the form of inner sense', he remained close to tradition by representing time as 'a line progressing to infinity', with the exception 'that while the parts of this line are simultaneous the parts of time are successive.'[8] (As we will see, transferring the problem of duration onto the space occupied by individual

5 In this discussion, I am drawing largely on the work of Heidegger and Derrida, who (with certain differences) both argue that the Aristotelian determination of time proved decisive for Western thought.

6 Aristotle, *Physics*, Book IV (trans. E. Hussey), Oxford, Clarendon Press, 1983, pp. 41–2.

7 Aristotle, *Physics* (Book IV), p. 41; Augustine, *Confessions*, p. 239; G.W.F. Hegel, *Philosophy of Nature* (trans. A.V. Miller), Oxford, Clarendon Press, 1970, s.258, p. 34.

8 I. Kant, *Critique of Pure Reason* (trans. N.K. Smith), New York, St Martin's Press, 1965, p. 77.

'points' in a line is precisely the move Aristotle made.)[9] Even Bergson, who explicitly criticized philosophy's tendency to spatialize time, perhaps remained closer to Aristotle than he thought.[10]

Clearly these brief selections cannot do justice to the texts to which they refer. What I am interested in here is the repetition of time's aporia, and the manner in which it is negotiated. The paradox of the now is less solved or resolved than displaced *with reference to itself*, according to a course laid out by Aristotle. After bringing us back to the problem he initially formulated ('The now is in a way the same, and in a way not the same'),[11] Aristotle develops a correspondence between 'now' and 'point', time and line, which proves seemingly irresistible. (Hegel, as well as Kant, will follow a similar path.) Of course, the analogy is difficult, because treating the now as a point with a determinate beginning or end means that time would not be a continuous flow, but subject to a series of halts, irregularities and stop-pages.[12] For this reason, Aristotle represents time as a line conceived not as the sum of its individual points, but only in terms of its extremities.[13] Time is a line in which the points ('nows') have ceased to be discrete, with precise limits, absolute origins or determinate ends. (As Hegel will put it, the problem of punctuality and the relation between point, line and plane is dialectically resolved as non-spatial spatiality. Derrida argues that Aristotle is already forced to make this move *in a Hegelian sense*.)[14] The form of a

9 For Heidegger, Kant constitutes a certain breakthrough, insofar as he 'subjected time and the "I think", each taken separately, to a transcendental interpretation, . . . [and thereby] succeeded in bringing them together in their primordial sameness – without, to be sure, having seen this sameness expressly as such'. *Kant and the Problem of Metaphysics* (trans. T.S. Churchill), Bloomington, Indiana University Press, p. 197. In contrast, Derrida argues: 'the Kantian revolution did not displace what Aristotle had set down, but on the contrary settled down there itself, changing its locale and then refurbishing it.' *Margins of Philosophy*, p. 44. These textual affiliations are complex. But, if Heidegger's reading of Kant is perhaps less *approving* than Derrida makes it out to be, Derrida's critique of Heidegger's reliance on a distinction between 'vulgar' and 'primordial' is more far reaching. See Derrida, *Margins of Philosophy*, p. 63.

10 Heidegger argued: 'Bergson's view of time too has obviously arisen from an interpretation of the Aristotelian essay on time.' Heidegger, *Being and Time*, p. 500, note 30. After citing a passage in which Bergson restates time's aporia ('Its essence being to pass, none of its parts is still there when another presents itself . . .'), Derrida concurs partially: 'it appears that Bergson, perhaps in a sense different to the one indicated by Heidegger, is more Aristotelian than he himself believes.' Derrida, *Margins of Philosophy*, p. 57.

11 Aristotle, *Physics* (Book IV), p. 44.

12 This is, in fact, exactly how Paul Virilio proceeds. For Virilio, technological transformation has foregrounded the importance of *interruption* to temporality, producing a generalized *picnolepsy* or paradoxical state of 'rapid waking': 'to the question: who is picnoleptic? we could possibly respond today: who isn't, or hasn't been?' Crucial are the new vehicles of transport and communication: 'the rapid tour, the accelerated transport of people, signs or things, reproduce – by aggravating them – the effects of picnolepsy, since they provoke a perpetually repeated hijacking of the subject from any spatio-temporal context.' Virilio, *Aesthetics of Disappearance*, pp. 14 and 101.

13 See Aristotle, *Physics* (Book IV), p. 45.

14 G.W.F. Hegel, *Philosophy of Nature (Encyclopaedia Part Two)* (trans. A.V. Miller), Oxford, Clarendon Press, 1970, s.256, p. 31; Derrida, *Margins of Philosophy*, p. 54.

line in which the beginning *is* the end is, of course, a circle.[15] For Derrida, recourse to the figure of the circle here means that 'the contradictory terms in the aporia are simply taken up and affirmed together in order to define the *physis* of time': dialectics, whether Aristotelian or Hegelian, only makes time 'the affirmation of the aporetic.'[16]

What are the consequences of taking the 'now' as the proper measure of time? Augustine makes the stakes explicit:

> Nor do we properly say, there be three times, past, present and to come; but perchance it might properly be said, there be three times: a present time of past things; a present time of present things; and a present time of future things.[17]

It is this privilege of the present that Heidegger argued has been critical to the forgetting of time in the question of Being:

> Is not the immediate comprehension of Being developed from a primordial but self-evident *projection of Being relative to time?* . . . The essence [*Wesen*] of time as it was fixed – and, as it turned out, decisively – for the subsequent history of metaphysics by Aristotle does not provide an answer to this question. On the contrary, it would be easy to show that it is precisely Aristotle's conception of time that is inspired by a comprehension of Being which – without being aware of its action interprets Being as permanent and present [*Gegenwart*], and consequently determines the 'Being' of time from the point of view of the *now* [*jetz*], i.e. from the character of time which in itself is always *present* [*anwesend*], and thus properly *is*, in the ancient sense of the term.[18]

While Derrida disputes certain aspects of Heidegger's reading, he does not challenge its general orientation:

> From Parmenides to Husserl, the privilege of the present has never been put into question. It could not have been. It is what is self-evident itself, and no thought seems possible outside its element. Non-presence is always thought in the form of presence . . . or as a modalization of presence. The past and the future are always determined as past presents or as future presents.[19]

For both Heidegger and Derrida the question of time therefore cannot be one question among others, but is rather that which has framed an entire history of questioning – which is also the history of 'the West'. Hence the redundancy of asking, 'What is time?', a question which, in privileging the *is* as the linguistic predicate proper to Being, already inscribes an answer according to a prior determination of time.[20] The relation between time

15 Aristotle makes this clear in *Physics* (Book IV), p. 50.

16 Derrida, *Margins of Philosophy*, p. 54.

17 Augustine, *Confessions*, p. 253. Augustine relates these 'three' times to memory, sight and expectation.

18 Heidegger, *Kant and the Problem of Metaphysics*, pp. 248–50 (translation modified according to Derrida's reading in *Margins of Philosophy*, p. 32). If Heidegger gave Kant an ambiguous filiation to this tradition, he located Hegel firmly within it. Not only does the 'priority which Hegel has given to the "now" which has been levelled off' place him at the centre of the 'vulgar' concept of time, 'it can even be shown that his conception of time has been drawn *directly* from the physics of Aristotle.' *Being and Time*, p. 500.

19 Derrida, *Margins of Philosophy*, p. 34.

20 See M. Heidegger, 'On the grammar and etymology of the word "Being" ', in *An Introduction to Metaphysics* (trans. R. Mannheim), New York, Anchor Books, 1961, p. 42 ff. Also J. Derrida, 'The supplement of copula: philosophy before linguistics', *Margins of Philosophy*, pp. 198–205.

thought on the basis of the now to the determination of essence as stability or permanence, existence as being-present, identity as non-contradiction (or non-simultaneity) – in other words, to the dominant Western narratives of origin, end, cause and effect – can scarcely be overstated.[21] The historical repression of the heterogeneity of time (what Heidegger will counter with his notion of *presencing*, what Derrida will contest with the neologism *différance*) culminates in the modern desire to annihilate distance with speed, to overcome absence with the limitless body of technology, to reside in the enigmatic interval of the absolute instant.

*

This detour through philosophy doesn't offer the writ of truth so much as a register of desire, inscribed in concepts, logic, and also techno-logic. In a sense, television is the enigmatic gift that modernity has always sent itself; it is the radically open horizon through which modernity has fashioned itself as the culture which achieves absolute mastery over time and space. Even the mechanical vehicles which moved bodies and objects from place to place with ever-increasing velocity have lost their primacy, as the strategic importance of territory and position is annulled by the ubiquity of the screen and the instantaneity of tele-transmissions. To switch on the TV is to plug the self into an optical–electronic field of immediacy, a zone of accelerated perceptions generating the aura of instant availability so crucial in defining 'the world' today. With television, the now finds itself in terrestrial extension, linking an audience of global proportions in an overexposure which promises the erasure of antipodality.

Yet this technological transcendence of time and space is perhaps less the fulfilment of the tradition it intersects than the concentration of its essential ambiguities. (For Adorno: 'The cliché which claims that modern technology has fulfilled the fantasies of the fairy tales only ceases to be a cliché if one adds to it the fairy tale wisdom that the fulfilment of wishes rarely benefits those who make them.')[22] All the contradictions entrained by the camera in this regard – the disembodiment of perception, the industrial mobility of perspective, the profound redefinition of 'context', the displacement of permanent and stable representations by transient and immaterial projections – have been immeasurably sharpened by television.

Effectively, television seizes instantaneity as the mark of 'presence', while dislocating the bonds of place which once held this matrix together. But, because tele-presence is a function of pure speed without necessary relation to place, the increasing reliance on television as a means of cultural

---

21 Derrida lists a host of 'subdeterminations which depend upon this general form and which organize within it their system and their historical sequence (presence of the thing to sight as *eidos*, presence as substance/essence/existence (*ousia*), temporal presence as point (*stigme*) of the now or of the moment (*nun*), the self-presence of the cogito, consciousness, subjectivity, the co-presence of the other and of the self, intersubjectivity as the intentional phenomenon of the ego, and so forth)'. Derrida, *Of Grammatology*, p. 12

22 Quoted in Hansen, 'Benjamin, cinema and experience', p. 253.

and political integration rapidly generates new social tensions. This is evident in the instability of the traditional sites of political and social interaction (room, home, street, city), as well as the growing uncertainty of the borders of cultural belonging (national territory, linguistic unity, ethnic homogeneity). This is not to posit this transformation as a cause for despair, but to insist on thinking its epochal implications.

McLuhan once declared television to be an extension not of the eye but 'of the sense of touch'.[23] If his recourse to the metaphor of tactility was drawn, consciously or unconsciously, from an earlier history of optics, it didn't simply restore the body's traditional claims in this scene.[24] Rather, it belongs to the profound redefinition of body and consciousness which suspends the viewer in the equivocal space between 'representation' and 'reality' that live television makes its own. Blanchot alerts us to uncertainties of this domain:

> Seeing presupposes distance, decisiveness which separates, the power to stay out of contact and in contact avoid confusion. . . . But what happens when what you see, although at a distance, seems to touch you with a gripping contact, when the manner of seeing is a kind of touch, when seeing is *contact* at a distance?[25]

Isn't this precisely the dilemma of tele-presence, and the confusion of presence and proximity it brings? How should we understand the force of these perceptions which arrive from outside our own body's time and space, but enter our experience so directly they rupture the perceptual horizon as if from within? Is it simply that television becomes 'raw experience', as the McLuhanesque Professor O'Blivion (from Cronenberg's *Videodrome*, 1982) suggested? Or is such an equivalence better read as an index of desire: what is it that we want television to be? The dream–image of global television belongs to a culture driven by the desire for pure presence, a presence without gaps, without invisibility, illegibility or silence. Such a plenitudinous presence is far removed from the so-called 'eternal present' of cyclical time, but can only be measured by the currency of the *now*. The impossibility of ever fulfilling this desire – at least on this side of death – situates the essential ambivalence of televised instantaneity and the endless and frustrating fascination of its attempts to 'keep up'.[26] In this configuration, one also finds the heightened importance that contemporary television places on staging its own processes of representation: it addresses a perfectly reflexive subject who resides not in the passage between two distinct moments, but

23 McLuhan, *Understanding Media*, p. 358.

24 Crary notes the long history (including Descartes) of grounding vision in the sense of touch; hence the oft-posed 'Molyneux problem': would a blind man recognize objects upon regaining his sight? *Techniques of the Observer*, pp. 59–62. See also Merleau-Ponty's discussion in *The Primacy of Perception*, pp. 169–72.

25 Blanchot, *Space of Literature*, p. 32.

26 Blanchot opens our eyes to the precipitous desire for the absolute instant which fires modernity's soul: 'He who kills himself is the great affirmer of the *present*. I want to kill myself in an "absolute" instant, the only one that will not pass and will not be surpassed. Death, if it arrived at the time we choose, would be an apotheosis of the *instant*.' Blanchot, *Space of Literature*, p. 103.

in a time without duration, a measureless present amidst a whirlpool of perceptions.[27]

Of course, there is still the problem of the body in this scene: the faster the media become, the more static its watchers seem to be. Does TV prepare us for domestic inertia, the ultimate sedentariness, as the contours of consciousness are dissolved and redistributed along the telematic network? The rule of the electronic *polis* threatens to obviate the necessity for motor functions: Virilio argues that 'from now on everything will happen without our even moving, without us even having to set out.'[28]

*

With the ubiquity of the screen, identity loses its once elementary reliance on place: who you are and what you know are less and less a function of where you are. If modernity has always demanded realignments in patterns of cultural belonging and group identification, displacing relations of locality, neighbourhood and proximity with information hierarchies determined by speed, the era of live television has vastly accentuated this leaning. What Kracauer once analysed as the camera's spatialization of history has today been redirected to television's direct implantation in the social relations of time.[29]

This shift suggests another element in the fascination of live television. With cinema, while we might see something unexpected on screen, we always know that it has been chosen out of a number of shots. Even the most contingent phenomena – a fleeting look, an enigmatic gesture, a momentary configuration of shadows – has to be, consciously or unconsciously, pre-selected. Cinematic pleasure is, at bottom, the pleasure of repetition: the ideal observer, the perfect image, the familiar narrative. Television heralds another possibility: it is the first medium to promise a structure of 'representation' equal to the 'event'.[30] All the ambiguous affiliations of television converge here, in the desire for – or fear of – the radically open, the outside, the unknown, the scene of the other. Claiming dominion over the 'event' is

---

27 See also 'The ends of representation' above.

28 Virilio, 'Last vehicle', p. 112. Virilio deploys images including a runner on a running machine and a swimmer in a tidal pool to represent the growing disjunction between the mobility of our perceptions and the immobility of our bodies. See Virilio, 'Last vehicle', pp. 106–9; 'Cataract surgery: cinema in the year 2000', in A. Kuhn (ed.), *Alien Zone*, London and New York, Verso, 1990, p. 170.

29 See my discussion in 'The ends of representation' above.

30 For Derrida, the event 'is a name for the aspect of what happens that we will never manage to either eliminate or to deny (or simply never manage to deny). It is another name for experience, which is always the experience of the other. . . . The happening of the event is what cannot and should not be prevented: it is another name for the future itself. Not that it is good – good in itself – that everything or anything should happen; nor that we should give up trying to prevent certain things from coming to pass. . . . This is why thinking about the event always opens up a kind of messianic space, however abstract, formal, deserted and desolate it may be, and however little it may have to do with religion.' Derrida, 'Deconstruction of actuality', p. 32.

a very marketable quality. As Deese Schonfeld, first President of CNN, put it when explaining the attractions of live broadcasts:

> [W]hat you want to do is have the audience want, not what you have up there now, but what they think you might have up there in the next five seconds and will miss forever if they should just turn off for a minute. You want to lock everyone in the world into the belief that the next minute, the world's greatest catastrophe, the world's greatest joy, may occur, and if they leave CNN they will have lost that one great moment in their lives that people will talk about forever . . .[31]

Clearly, the appearance of any event on television is always mediated, and the mode of narrative framing governs the extent to which the medium will in fact domesticate what it shows. One can never tire of insisting on this point, particularly because it is precisely what television is so often concerned to deny. But this insistence must be tempered by the recognition that live television carries the unique possibility that, for the first time in a 'representation' which we experience as an image, we don't really know what will happen next.

The orchestration of simultaneous experiences has become increasingly important to the constitution of the contemporary public sphere, and this transposition makes itself felt everywhere on television, which is organized according to the logic of 'time share' rather than the parcelling of space. This is obvious at many levels. Viewers congregate in time while remaining aloof from one another in space. Television's socio-economic hierarchy is less one of centre versus periphery than prime-time versus off-peak. Advertisers buy time rather than the column space of a page, raising the commodification of time to a new power: never before has the price of a few seconds, tele-distributed on national and international networks, been so high.[32]

The fact that television is so time-driven can be traced in every facet of production and programming. From the need to compress news stories into one or two minutes, to the desire to accelerate information delivery through faster montage, to the socio-economic importance of each network's sequencing schedule, the most common battle on television is fought against the pressure of time. Where the average news sound bite in the 1960s was around 40 seconds, by the 1980s it was 10 seconds.[33] Where advertisements were initially in 90-, 60- and 45-second blocs, today we are schooled in 30- and 15-second ads with shorter durations mooted. Even 'world leaders' must

31 Interviewed on 'The tycoon', Episode 1 of *Naked News*, Channel Four Television Corporation, 1995.

32 The highest price television advertising – a 30-second spot on the US Superbowl telecast – was US$1.2 million in 1996. Television has also changed the mode of advertising at sports grounds. Rather than dividing the available space (such as perimeter fences) between permanent displays, the tendency is now to use revolving signs so as to sell the entire space to different groups for short periods of time (akin to time share holidays).

33 See D.C. Hallin, 'We keep America on top of the world', in T. Gitlin (ed.), *Watching Television*, New York, Pantheon, 1986, p. 16.

obey this implacable law and submit to the interviewer's ubiquitous closing line: 'I'm sorry but we're out of time.' (And yet, it must be remarked, on television there is nothing but time.)

The contemporary ritual of the viewing day underlines the extent to which television has now assumed responsibility for regulating time in a culture where the exercise of power is dependent on precise temporal control. The emergence of distinct time zones related to different audiences and programming strategies testifies to television's deep integration with contemporary social rhythms, from the daily routines of meal times and leisure times to seasonal patterns of school holidays and religious festivals. In conjunction with the pulsing of peak hour traffic ('rush hour'), television has become a key pacemaker for urban–industrial societies which operate according to the light of a day which has dawned beyond all seasons.

The rule of the supplementary day points to what is arguably television's primary social function in the present: the occupation of time.[34] Under capitalism, the organization of time has become an increasingly important aspect of social life, according to rhythms established by the timetable and the production schedule. These temporal regimes have become important structural co-ordinates of consciousness. But, in the absence of these structures, time doesn't pass easily. The decrease in necessary labour time, which has resulted from reformist political struggles (mainly in 'developed' nations) throughout this century, has been accompanied by significant increases in available leisure time. But the growth of 'free time' has itself been accompanied by the rise of sophisticated leisure and tourism industries. To ensure the reintegration of subjects into its temporal economy, capitalism demands that 'free time' be commodified. It is no accident that television watching has become the most popular leisure activity in all 'developed' countries. And within those societies it is no accident that those defined as having surplus time – the unemployed or retired, children, the sick or incarcerated – are the leading television watchers. Beyond all its other functions, television maintains an essential relation to the time of waiting; that disquieting and uncertain time in-between that Beckett identified as modernity's own.

Yet television never identifies itself under this sign, the time in which expectation is blunted and events don't arrive. Instead, it proclaims its dominion precisely over the plenitudinous time in which events happen. The elision of 'dead time' by means of pre-production, editing and the narrative compression of events, the trimming of 'unnecessary' details, the montage of privileged instants, is so much a part of the rhythm of television that it is

---

34 This seems so obvious that I feel something akin to Barthes's embarrassment at the conclusion of *Camera Lucida*: 'What! a whole book (even a short one) to discover something I know at first glance?' (p. 115). And yet, moving the analysis of television away from the traditional political questions of bias and ideology to face the obvious is more difficult than one might imagine.

second nature to our viewing expectations.[35] But figuring time as a linear sequence of 'happenings' carries inevitable risks. The release of Nelson Mandela from prison in 1991 provided a striking example. Despite the fact that many networks, including the US majors, wanted to show Mandela's 'first steps to freedom', the event was unusual for its lack of co-ordination with the media (this in itself revealed the extent to which the South African government was out of touch with 'world opinion'). In the end, Mandela's release ran behind schedule; the networks were forced to fill-in, crossing between impatient on-the-spot reporters and experts in domestic studios who quickly ran out of things to say. As the minutes dragged on, new calculations were made; some abandoned the scene, others persisted, revealing what is always an undercurrent of television: a profound dis-ease when confronted by the stare of empty time.[36]

While the particular example was uncommon, the trajectory it indicates is not: television displays 'history-making' events live on a daily, if not hourly or up-to-the-minute basis. What it does highlight is the problem created by overinvestment in the present moment. For Heidegger:

> In the ordinary interpretation of time as a sequence of 'nows', both datability and significance are *missing*. These two structures are not permitted to 'come to the fore' when time is characterized as a pure succession. The ordinary interpretation of time *covers them up*. When these are covered up, the ecstatico-horizonal constitution of temporality, in which the datability and the significance of the 'now' are grounded, gets *levelled off*. The 'nows' get shorn of these relations, as it were, and, as thus shorn, they simply range themselves along one after another so as to make up the succession.[37]

Television's attempts to pursue the present moment within a linear economy of time brings what Heidegger called levelled-off time 'to the fore'. When time becomes indifferent, every event becomes the same. We experience television, not as the horizon of the unexpected which interrupts us and radically redefines our bounds, but as a radical interchangeability of channels, images and events, an image-world in which significance wanes and meaning flees. In this mode, television exemplifies the empty time of commodity culture in which, as Benjamin observed: 'monotony is nourished by the new'.[38] This is the crux of our ambivalence to the screen. As much as television watching is experienced as pleasure, keeping us in touch, up to date and informed, distilling the particular and the transient with uncanny

35 Television's temporal economy always tries to present a marked contrast to films in which 'nothing happens', particularly extreme experiments in pure duration such as Andy Warhol's *Empire* (1964) which lasted 485 minutes with no conventional action.

36 This touches television's unique possibilities for evoking what Blanchot terms the 'dead present'. For Blanchot: 'The dead present is the impossibility of making any presence real – an impossibility which is present, which is there as the present's double, the shadow of the present which the present bears and hides in itself.' Blanchot, *Space of Literature*, p. 31. It is hard to imagine a better description of the way in which television symptomatically exposes the absence at the heart of every presence.

37 Heidegger, *Being and Time* (trans. J. Macquarie and E. Robinson), Oxford, Basil Blackwell, 1973, p. 474.

38 Benjamin quoted in Buck-Morss, *Dialectics of Seeing*, p. 104.

clarity and endless fascination, its other visage is boredom: the sensation that time has ceased, the world is absent, the chattering, smiling faces are masks, the viewer is alone, adrift in a lost zone which belongs only to television. The dead time belonging to a TV set left on in an empty room, a million empty rooms. This experience shouldn't be ascribed simply to 'bad' television, but belongs to the ambivalence of the spatio-temporal relations sustained in the scene of watching. Tele-presence opens the line of time to its own paradox: the more we insist on occupying the instant, the more decisively it eludes us.[39]

*

Virilio has argued that, in the quarrel between theology and scientific teleology, science has never renounced the demand for a homogeneous origin:

> Ever since the time of Galileo, it was simply displaced from increasingly precise measurements of time and space onto the immeasurable excesses of an instant without duration and without dimension. An instant in which constructive reason finds its destiny.[40]

The theory of the 'Big Bang' (like the search for elementary particles) displays the resilience of scientific concern for that unique event which would – by the sheer force of its uniqueness – start the universe's clock. Everything could proceed smoothly once the beginning could be determined.

In the waning of theology, speed became a new catechism. The Enlightenment wanted to accelerate knowledge–production so as to achieve faster progress; modernity pursued the future with obsessive fervour; even today, the desire to go faster, to produce more rapidly, to accelerate social processes through technological innovation, remain capitalism's grounding values. Television maps this state of permanent overexposure in which immediacy, simultaneity, transparency and ubiquity have achieved unprecedented prominence as perceptual, epistemological and existential frames: the total spectacle of objects and events in a global milieu where relevance is defined by the guillotine of the instant. The fundamental 'problem' of tele-presence is precisely what produces its seductive power: it leaves no time for the other, for the otherness of time, the memory of what resists being seen or shown. (What is not seen or shown on television – what Kluge terms the deliberate non-publicity given to situations which cannot be legitimated – passes unacknowledged.)

At the beginning of this century, confidence in the linear time of progress seemed unbounded. Today, under the shadow of an uncertain future,

---

39 Heine suggests: 'The more insistent that *Dasein* is that something be done "now" at this "instant", expecting more time while realizing there is less and less, the more it refuses to confront its finitude.' *Existential and Ontological Dimensions of Time in Heidegger and Dogen*, Albany, State University of New York Press, 1985, p. 45.
40 Virilio, *Lost Dimension*, p. 68.

television reveals a social form which perhaps believes itself to be running out of time. Might this presage the exhaustion of the culture of speed? (This does not mean termination: refinements of the present system, from videophones which 'connect' people along domestic circuits to Imax and Omnimax cinemas, high-definition TV screens and virtual reality 'home entertainment' suites, all seem utterly predictable.)

A different heading, one which might make television more capable of fulfilling the fairytale promise bound up in its name, demands the displacement of the linear time which drives its current economy (the economy of current affairs and the hyper-presence of the real). Acknowledging the heterogeneity of time, paying attention to other times, the times of other cultures, the time of those irreducible absences which telematics both conceals and reveals: would this still belong to what we have hitherto called time? Given the hysteria of the now which directs so many forces in the contemporary world, one of the most radical changes imaginable would undoubtedly be a collective deceleration in which the pressure of time is released. Marx once described revolutions as 'the locomotives of world history'. Walter Benjamin's speculative response seems apt: 'Perhaps it is totally different. Perhaps revolutions are the reaching of humanity travelling in this train for the emergency brake.'[41]

41 Benjamin quoted in Buck-Morss, *Dialectics of Seeing*, p. 92.

Sources for Epigraphs

Page 1   William Henry Fox Talbot, *Literary Gazette* (14 February 1841), quoted in Buckland, *Fox Talbot and the Invention of Photography*, p. 60.

Page 11   Walter Benjamin, *Illuminations*, p. 224.

Page 11   Marcel Duchamp, *MSS* no. 4 (December 1922), quoted in Hambourg, *New Vision*, p. 74.

Page 13   André Bazin, *What is Cinema?* vol. 1, pp. 13–14.

Page 18   E.H. Gombrich, *Art and Illusion*, p. 9.

Page 27   L.J.M Daguerre, quoted in Coe et al., *Techniques of the World's Great Photographers*, p. 22.

Page 27   Jacques Derrida, *Of Grammatology*, p. 9.

Page 33   Alfred Donné, quoted in Darius, *Beyond Vision*, p. 22.

Page 44   Paul Strand quoted in Tompkins, 'Look to the things around you', p. 54.

Page 44   Jean Baudrillard, *Simulations*, p. 10.

Page 64   René Clair, quoted in Kracauer, *Theory of Film*, p. 34.

Page 70   Luigi Pirandello, *Shoot: The Notebooks of Serafino Gubbio, Cinematograph Operator*, quoted in Kern, *Culture of Time and Space*, p. 119.

Page 70   Jean-Luc Godard, *Godard on Godard*, pp. 214–15.

Page 92   *Videodrome*, written and directed by David Cronenberg, Canada, 1982.

Page 92   Maurice Blanchot, *Space of Literature*, p. 262.

Page 105   Roland Barthes, *Camera Lucida*, pp. 87–8.

Page 107   Hart Crane, letter to Alfred Stieglitz (15 April 1923), quoted in Hambourg, *New Vision*, p. 279, note 107.

Page 112   Walter Benjamin, *Illuminations*, p. 269.

Page 119   Susan Sontag, *On Photography*, p. 10.

Page 127   Christa Wolf, *A Model Childhood*, p. 3.

Page 132   Abel Gance quoted in Benjamin, *Illuminations*, p. 224.

Page 132   Trinh T. Minh-Ha, 'Documentary is/not a name', p. 77.

Page 132   *Medium Cool*, H. and J. Pictures, written and directed by Haskell Wexler, Paramount, 1969.

Page 151   Jean-François Lyotard, *Heidegger and 'the jews'*, p. 23.

Page 164   Theodor W. Adorno, *Negative Dialectics*, p. 361.

Page 181   El Lissitsky, 'The film of El's life till 1926', quoted in Berger, *Sense of Sight*, p. 167.

Page 183   Umberto Boccioni, 'Absolute + relative motion = dynamism' (1914), reprinted in Apollonio, *Futurist Manifestos*, p. 152.

Page 183   Nam June Paik, quoted in Virilio, *War and Cinema*, p. 11.

Page 191   Dietmar Kamper and Christoph Wulf, *Looking Back on the End of the World*, p. 1

Page 200   Gertrude Stein, quoted in Niven, *Bring on the Empty Horses*, p. 15.

Page 208   Alexander Kluge, 'Assault of the present', p. 21.

Page 218   Homi Bhabha, *Location of Culture*, p. 5.

Page 233   Paul Virilio, 'The overexposed city', p. 16.

Page 233   Advertisement for Network MCI, 1994.

Page 246   Martin Heidegger, *On Time and Being*, p. 4.

Select Bibliography

Ades, D., *Photomontage*, London, Thames and Hudson, 1976.

Adorno, T.W., *Negative Dialectics* (trans. E.B. Ashton), New York, Seabury Press, 1973.

Adorno, T.W., 'Transparencies on film' (trans. T.Y. Levin), *New German Critique*, 24/25 (1981–2), pp. 199–205.

Adorno, T.W. and Horkheimer, M., *Dialectic of Enlightenment* (trans. J. Cumming), London, Allen Lane, 1973.

Alloula, M., *The Colonial Harem* (trans. M. and W. Godzich), Minneapolis, University of Minnesota Press, 1986.

Anderson, B., *Imagined Communities: Reflections on the Origins and Spread of Nationalism*, London, Verso, 1983.

Ang, I., *Watching Dallas*, London, Methuen, 1985.

Apollonio, U. (ed.), *Futurist Manifestos* (trans. R. Brain et al.), London, Thames and Hudson, 1973.

Aristotle, *Physics*, Book IV (trans. E. Hussey), Oxford, Clarendon Press, 1983.

Augustine, *Confessions* (1631) (trans. W. Watts), London, Heinemann, 1913.

Avisar, I., *Screening the Holocaust*, Bloomington, Indiana University Press, 1988.

Balio, T. (ed.), *The American Film Industry*, Madison, University of Wisconsin Press, 1985.

Banham, R., *The Architecture of the Well-Tempered Environment*, London, Architectural Press, 1969.

Bann, S. (ed.), *The Tradition of Constructivism*, New York, Viking, 1974.

Barfield, O., *Saving the Appearance: A Study in Idolatry*, New York, Harcourt Brace Jovanovich, 1965.

Barnouw, E., *Documentary: A History of the Non-Fiction Film*, Oxford, Oxford University Press, 1983.

Barthes, R., *Barthes: Selected Writings*, London, Fontana, 1983.

Barthes, R., *Camera Lucida* (trans. R. Howard), London, Fontana, 1984.

Barthes, R., *Empire of Signs* (trans. R. Howard), New York, Hill and Wang, 1982.

Barthes, R., *The Responsibility of Forms* (trans. R. Howard). New York, Hill and Wang, 1985.

Barthes, R., *Sade Fourier Loyola* (trans. R. Miller), New York, Hill and Wang, 1976.

Baudrillard, J., *Simulations* (trans. P. Foss et al.), New York, Semiotext(e), 1983.

Baudrillard, J., *In The Shadow of the Silent Majorities*, New York, Semiotext(e), 1983.

Baudrillard, J., *The Evil Demon of Images* (trans. P. Patton and P. Foss), Sydney, Power Institute, 1984.

Baudrillard, J., *America* (trans. C. Turner), London, Verso, 1988.

Baxandall, M., *Painting and Experience in Fifteenth Century Italy*, Oxford, Oxford University Press, 1972

Bazin, A., *What is Cinema?* (trans. H. Gray), Berkeley, University of California Press, 1967.

Benjamin, W., *Charles Baudelaire: A Lyric Poet in an Era of High Capitalism* (trans. H. Zohn), London, New Left Books, 1973.

Benjamin, W., *Illuminations* (trans. H. Zohn), London, Fontana, 1973.

Benjamin, W., *One Way Street and Other Writings* (trans. E. Jephcott and K. Shorter), London, Verso, 1985.

Berg, A.S., *Goldwyn*, London, Hamish Hamilton, 1989.

Berger, J., *The Moment of Cubism and Other Essays*, London, Weidenfeld and Nicolson, 1969.

Berger, J., *Ways of Seeing*, London, BBC and Harmondsworth, Penguin, 1972.

Berger, J., *About Looking*, London, Writers and Readers, 1984.

Berger, J., *And Our Faces, My Heart, Brief as Photos*, London, Writers and Readers, 1984.

Berger, J., *The Sense of Sight*, New York, Pantheon, 1985.

Berger, J. and Mohr, J., *Another Way of Telling*, New York, Pantheon, 1982.

Bergson, H., *Creative Evolution* (trans. A. Mitchell), London, Macmillan, 1912.

Bergson, H., *Matter and Memory* (trans. N.M. Paul and W.S. Palmer), New York, Zone Books, 1988.

Bhabha, H., 'The other question', *Screen*, 24, 6 (November–December 1983), pp. 18–36.

Bhabha, H., 'Freedom's basis in the indeterminate', *October*, 61 (Summer 1992), pp. 46–57.

Bhabha, H., *The Location of Culture*, London, Routledge, 1994.

Bhabha, H. (ed.), *Nation and Narration*, London, Routledge, 1990.

Blanchot, M., *The Space of Literature* (trans. A. Smock), Lincoln and London, University of Nebraska Press, 1982.

Blanchot, M., *The Writing of the Disaster* (trans. A. Smock), Lincoln and London, University of Nebraska Press, 1986.

Bordo, S., *The Flight to Objectivity*, Albany, State University of New York, 1987.

Borges, J.-L., *Labyrinths* (trans. D.A. Yates et al.), Harmondsworth, Penguin, 1970.

Borges, J.-L., *Seven Nights* (trans. E. Weinberger), New York, New Directions, 1984.

Bourdieu, P., Castel, R., Shambouredon, J.-C. and Schapper, D., *Photography: A Middle Brow Art* (1965) (trans. S. Whiteside), Cambridge, Polity Press, 1990.

Brownlow, K., *The Parade's Gone By . . .* , London, Abacus, 1968.

Buckland, G., *Fox Talbot and the Invention of Photography*, Boston, David R. Godine, 1980.

Buck-Morss, S., *The Dialectics of Seeing: Walter Benjamin and the Arcades Project*, Cambridge, MA and London, MIT Press, 1991.

Buck-Morss, S., 'Aesthetics and anaesthetics: Walter Benjamin's artwork essay reconsidered', *October*, 62 (Fall 1992), pp. 3–41.

Burch, N., *Theory of Film Practice* (trans. H.R. Lane), London, Secker and Warburg, 1973.

Burgin, V. (ed.), *Thinking Photography*, London, Macmillan, 1982.

Cartwright, L., ' "Experiments of destruction": cinematic inscriptions of physiology', *Representations*, 40 (Fall 1992), pp. 129–52.

Cassirer, E., *The Philosophy of the Enlightenment* (trans. F.C.A. Koelln and J.P. Pettegrove), Boston, Beacon Press, 1951.

Ceram, C.W., *Archaeology of the Cinema* (trans. R. Winston), London, Thames and Hudson, 1965.

Chamberlain, E.R., *Everyday Life in Renaissance Times*, New York, Capricorn, 1965.

Coe, B. et al., *Techniques of the World's Great Photographers*, New Jersey, Chartwell Books, 1981.

Collins, R., 'Wall-to-wall *Dallas*: the US–UK trade in television', *Screen*, 27, 3/4 (1986), pp. 66–77.

Commission of the European Communities, *Television Without Frontiers*, Brussels, 1984.

Crary, J., 'Techniques of the observer', *October*, 45 (Summer 1988), pp. 3–35.

Crary, J., 'Spectacle, attention, counter-memory', *October*, 50 (Fall 1989), pp. 97–107.

Crary, J., *Techniques of the Observer: On Vision and Modernity in the Nineteenth Century*, Cambridge, MA, October/MIT Press, 1990.

Cripps, T., *Making Movies Black: The Hollywood Message Movie from World War Two to the Civil Rights Era*, New York and Oxford, Oxford University Press, 1993.

Crofts, S. and Enzensberger M., 'Medvedkin: investigation of a citizen above suspicion', *Screen*, 19, 1 (Spring 1978), pp. 71–89.

Dagognet, F., *A Passion for the Trace* (trans. R. Galeta and J. Herman), New York, Zone Books, 1992.

Darius, J., *Beyond Vision*, Oxford, Oxford University Press, 1984.

Daston, L. and Galison, P., 'The image of objectivity', *Representations*, 40 (Fall 1992), pp. 81–124.
Dayan, D., 'The tutor code of classical cinema', *Film Quarterly* (Fall 1974), pp. 22–31.
Debord, G., *Society of the Spectacle* (revised edition), Detroit, Black and Red, 1977.
Deleuze, G., *Cinema 1: The Movement-Image* (trans. H. Tomlinson and B. Hammerjam), London, Athlone Press, 1986.
Deleuze, G., *Cinema 2: The Time-Image* (trans. H. Tomlinson and R. Galeta), London, Athlone Press, 1989.
de Man, P., *Blindness and Insight*, Minneapolis, University of Minnesota Press, 1983.
Derrida, J., *Of Grammatology* (trans. G.C. Spivak), Baltimore, Johns Hopkins University Press, 1976.
Derrida, J., *Writing and Difference* (trans. A. Bass), London and Henley, Routledge and Kegan Paul, 1978.
Derrida, J., *Spurs: Nietzsche's Styles* (trans. B. Harlow), Chicago and London, University of Chicago Press, 1979.
Derrida, J., 'The Parergon' (trans. C. Owens), *October*, 9 (1979), pp. 3–40.
Derrida, J., *Dissemination* (trans. B. Johnson), Chicago, University of Chicago Press, 1981.
Derrida, J., *Margins of Philosophy* (trans. A. Bass), Brighton, Harvester Press, 1982.
Derrida, J., 'Sending: on representation' (trans. P. and M.A. Caws), *Social Research*, 49, 2 (Summer 1982), pp. 294–326.
Derrida, J., *Memoires: For Paul De Man* (trans. C. Lindsay et al.), New York, Columbia University Press, 1986.
Derrida, J., 'Like the sound of the sea deep within a shell: Paul De Man's war' (trans. P. Kamuf), *Critical Inquiry*, 14 (Spring 1988), pp. 591–652.
Derrida, J., 'Biodegradables: seven diary fragments' (trans. P. Kamuf), *Critical Inquiry*, 15 (Summer 1989), pp. 812–73.
Derrida, J., 'Right of inspection' (trans. D. Wills), *Art & Text*, 32 (Autumn 1989), pp. 20–97.
Derrida, J., *The Other Heading: Reflections on Today's Europe* (trans. P.A. Brault and M.B. Naas), Bloomington, Indiana University Press, 1992.
Derrida, J., 'The deconstruction of actuality' (trans. J. Rée), *Radical Philosophy*, 68 (Autumn 1994), pp. 28–41.
Descartes, R., *Discourse on Method* (1637) (trans. P.J. Olscamp), Indianapolis, Bobbs-Merril, 1965.
Descartes, R., *The Philosophical Works of Descartes*, vol. 1 (trans. E. Haldane and G.R.T. Ross), Cambridge, Cambridge University Press, 1970.
Eco, U., 'A guide to the neo-television of the '80s' (trans. B. Lumley), *Framework*, 25 (1984), pp. 19–27.
Edwards, E. (ed.), *Anthropology and Photography*, New Haven, Yale University Press and London, Royal Anthropological Institute, 1992.
Einstein, A., *Relativity: The Special and General Theories* (1916) (trans. R.W. Lawson), New York, Crown, 1961.
Eisenstein, S., *Film Form: Essays in Film Theory* (trans. J. Leyda), London, Harcourt Brace Jovanovich, 1949.
Eisenstein, S., *The Film Sense* (trans. J. Leyda), London, Faber and Faber, 1963.
Eisenstein, S., *Immoral Memories: An Autobiography* (trans. H. Marshall), Boston, Houghton Mifflin, 1983.
Elsaesser, T., 'Cinema – the irresponsible signifier or "the gamble with history": film theory or cinema theory', *New German Critique*, 40 (Winter 1987), pp. 65–89.
Elsaesser, T., 'Memory, home and Hollywood', *Monthly Film Bulletin*, 52, 13 (February 1985), p. 64.
Elsaesser, T., *New German Cinema: A History*, London, Macmillan, 1989.
Elsaesser, T. (ed.), *Early Cinema: Space, Frame, Narrative*, London, British Film Institute, 1990.

Fabb, N. et al. (eds), *The Linguistics of Writing: Arguments Between Language and Literature*, New York, Methuen, 1987.

Fabian, J., *Time and the Other: How Anthropology Makes its Object*, New York, Columbia University Press, 1983.

Feldman, S.R., *Dziga Vertov: A Guide To References and Sources*, Boston, MA, G.K. Hall, 1978.

Fell, J. (ed.), *Film Before Griffith*, Berkeley, University of California Press, 1983.

Ferguson, R., Olander, W., Tucker, M. and Fiss, K. (eds), *Discourses: Conversations in Postmodern Art and Culture*, New York, New Museum of Contemporary Art and Cambridge, MA, MIT Press, 1990.

Fisher, J., 'The health of the people is the highest law', *Third Text*, 2 (Winter 1987/88), pp. 67–75.

Foster, H. (ed.), *Postmodern Culture*, London, Pluto Press, 1983.

Foster, H. (ed.), *Vision and Visuality*, Seattle, Bay Press, 1988.

Foucault, M., *The Archaeology of Knowledge* (trans. A.M. Sheridan Smith), London, Tavistock, 1972.

Foucault, M., *Madness and Civilization*, New York, Vintage Books, 1973.

Foucault, M., *The Order of Things*, New York, Random House, 1973.

Foucault, M., *The Birth of the Clinic* (trans. A.M. Sheridan Smith), New York, Vintage Books, 1975.

Foucault, M., *Discipline and Punish: The Birth of the Prison* (trans. A. Sheridan), Harmondsworth, Penguin, 1977.

Foucault, M., 'Michel Foucault: interview', *Edinburgh '77 Magazine* (History/Production/Memory), 2 (1977), pp. 20–5.

Foucault, M., 'The subject and power', *Critical Inquiry*, 8 (Summer 1982), pp. 777–95.

Foucault, M., 'What is enlightenment?', in P. Rabinow (ed.), *Foucault Reader*, New York, Pantheon Books, 1984.

Foucault, M. and Blanchot, M., *Foucault/Blanchot* (trans. J. Mehlman and B. Massumi), New York, Zone Books, 1987.

Fox Talbot, H., *The Pencil of Nature* (1844), New York, Hans P. Krauss, 1989.

Frampton, H., *Circles of Confusion*, New York, Visual Studies Workshop Press, 1983.

Freud, S., *The Interpretation of Dreams* (1900), vols. 4 and 5 of *The Standard Edition of the Complete Psychological Works of Sigmund Freud* (translated under the general editorship of J. Strachey), London, Hogarth Press, 1953.

Freud, S., *The Paths to the Formation of Symptoms*, vol. 16 of *The Standard Edition of the Complete Psychological Works of Sigmund Freud* (translated under the general editorship of J. Strachey), London, Hogarth Press, 1963.

Freud, S., *A Project for a Scientific Psychology* (1895), vol. 1 of *The Standard Edition of the Complete Psychological Works of Sigmund Freud* (translated under the general editorship of J. Strachey), London, Hogarth Press, 1966, pp. 295-397.

Freud, S., 'Beyond the pleasure principle', *On Metapsychology: The Theory of Psychoanalysis* (Pelican Freud Library vol. 11), Harmondsworth, Penguin, 1984.

Freud, S., 'A note upon the "mystic writing pad" ' (1925), *On Metapsychology: The Theory of Psychoanalysis* (Pelican Freud Library vol. 11), Harmondsworth, Penguin, 1984.

Freud, S. and Breuer, J., 'Studies in Hysteria' (1893–95), in vol. 2 of *The Standard Edition of the Complete Psychological Works of Sigmund Freud* (translated under the general editorship of J. Strachey), London, Hogarth Press, 1955.

Fusco, C., *English is Broken Here*, New York, New Press, 1995.

Gernsheim, H. and A., *L.J.M. Daguerre: The History of the Diorama and Daguerreotype*, London, Dover, 1968.

Gidal, P. (ed.), *Structural Film Anthology*, London, British Film Industry, 1976.

Gilman, S.L. (ed.), *The Face of Madness: Hugh W. Diamond and the Origin of Psychiatric Photography*, New Jersey, Brunner Mazel, 1976.

Gish, L., *The Movies, Mr. Griffith and Me*, London, W.H. Allen, 1969.

Gitlin, T. (ed.), *Watching Television*, New York, Pantheon, 1986.

Godard, J.-L., *Godard on Godard* (trans. and ed. T. Milne), London, Martin Secker and Warburg, 1972.

Gombrich, E.H., *Art and Illusion*, New York, Pantheon, 1960.

Grierson, J., *Grierson on Documentary* (ed. F. Hardy), London and Boston, Faber and Faber, 1979.

Guattari, F., *Molecular Revolution* (trans. R. Sheed), Harmondsworth, Penguin, 1984.

Gunning, T., 'An aesthetic of astonishment: early film and the (in)credulous spectator', *Art & Text*, 34 (Spring 1989), pp. 31–45.

Gunning, T., 'The cinema of attractions: early film, its spectator and the avant-garde', *Wide Angle*, 8, 3/4 (1986), pp. 63–70.

Hambourg, M. (ed.), *The New Vision (Photography Between the Wars)*, New York, Metropolitan Museum of Art, 1989.

Hansen, M., 'Benjamin, cinema and experience: "the blue flower in the land of technology" ', *New German Critique*, 40 (Winter 1987), pp. 179–224.

d'Harnoncourt, A. (ed.), *Futurism and the International Avant-Garde*, Philadelphia, Philadelphia Museum of Art, 1980.

Haworth-Booth, M. (ed.), *The Golden Age of British Photography 1839–1900*, New York, Aperture, 1984.

Heath, S., 'Difference', *Screen*, 19, 3 (Autumn 1978), pp. 51–112.

Heath, S., *Questions of Cinema*, London, Macmillan, 1981

Heath, S. and De Lauretis, T. (eds), *The Cinematic Apparatus*, London, Macmillan, 1980.

Hegel, G.W.F., *The Philosophy of History* (trans. J. Sibree), New York, Dover, 1956.

Hegel, G.W.F., *Hegel's Philosophy of Nature (Encyclopaedia Part Two)* (trans A.V. Miller), Oxford, Clarendon Press, 1970.

Heidegger, M., *An Introduction to Metaphysics* (trans. R. Mannheim), New York, Anchor Books, 1961.

Heidegger, M., *Kant and the Problem of Metaphysics* (trans T.S. Churchill), Bloomington, Indiana University Press, 1962.

Heidegger, M., *Poetry, Language, Thought* (trans. A. Hofstadter), New York, Harper and Row, 1971.

Heidegger, M., *On Time and Being* (trans. J. Stambaugh), New York, Harper and Row, 1972.

Heidegger, M., *Being and Time* (trans. J. Macquarie and E. Robinson), Oxford, Basil Blackwell, 1973.

Heidegger, M., *The Question Concerning Technology and Other Essays* (trans. W. Lovitt), New York, Harper and Row, 1977.

Heisenberg, W., *Physics and Philosophy*, London, Allen and Unwin, 1959.

Hobsbawm, E. and Ranger, T. (eds), *The Invention of Tradition*, Cambridge, Cambridge University Press, 1983.

Hoskins, C. and Mirus, R., 'Reasons for US dominance in international trade in television programs', *Media, Culture and Society*, 10, 4 (1988), pp. 499–515.

Hughes, R., *The Shock of the New*, New York, Alfred A. Knopf, 1981.

Illich, I. and Sanders, B., *The Alphabetization of the Popular Mind*, San Francisco, North Point Press, 1988.

Ivins, W.M., *Art and Geometry*, New York, Dover, 1964.

Jameson, F., *The Geopolitical Aesthetic: Cinema and Space in the World System*, Bloomington, Indiana University Press and London, British Film Institute, 1992.

Kaes, A., *From Hitler to Heimat*, Cambridge, MA, Harvard University Press, 1989.

Kaes, A., Jay, M. and Dimendberg, E. (eds), *The Weimar Republic Sourcebook*, Berkeley, University of California Press, 1994.

Kamper, D. and Wulf, C. (eds), *Looking Back on the End of the World* (trans. D. Antal), New York, Semiotext(e), 1989.

Kant, I., *Critique of Pure Reason* (trans. N.K. Smith), New York, St Martin's Press, 1965.

Keller, E.F., *Reflections on Gender and Science*, New Haven, Yale University Press, 1985.

Kern, S., *The Culture of Time and Space 1880–1918*, Cambridge, MA, Harvard University Press, 1983.

Khan-Magomedov, S.O., *Rodchenko: The Complete Work* (trans. H. Evans), London, Thames and Hudson, 1986.

Kluge, A., 'The assault of the present on the rest of time' (trans. T. Evans and S. Liebman), *New German Critique*, 49 (Winter 1990), pp. 11–22.

Kluge, A. and Negt, O., 'The public sphere and experience' (trans. P. Labanyi), *October*, 46 (Fall 1988), pp. 60–82.

Kracauer, S., *From Caligari to Hitler: A Psychological History of the German Film* (1947), Princeton, Princeton University Press, 1974.

Kracauer, S., *Theory of Film: The Redemption of Physical Reality*, Oxford, Oxford University Press, 1960.

Kracauer, S., *History, the Last Things Before the Last*, New York, Oxford University Press, 1969.

Kracauer, S., 'The mass ornament' (1927), *New German Critique*, 5 (Spring 1975), pp. 67–76.

Kracauer, S., 'Cult of distraction: on Berlin's picture palaces' (1926) (trans. T.Y. Levin), *New German Critique*, 40 (Winter 1987), pp. 91–7.

Kracauer, S., *The Mass Ornament* (trans. and ed. T.Y. Levin), Cambridge, MA and London, Harvard University Press, 1995.

Kristeva, J., *Tales of Love* (trans. L.S. Roudiez), New York, Columbia University Press, 1987.

Kuleshov, L., *Kuleshov on Film: Writings of Lev Kuleshov* (trans. R. Levaco), Berkeley, University of California Press, 1974.

Kundera, M., *The Book of Laughter and Forgetting* (trans. M.H. Heim), Harmondsworth, Penguin, 1983.

Kwinter, S., 'La citta nuova: modernity and continuity', *Zone* 1/2 (1986), pp. 81–121.

Lanzmann, C., 'Why Spielberg has distorted the truth', *Guardian Weekly*, 3 April 1994.

Lacan, J., *Écrits: A Selection* (trans. A. Sheridan), London, Tavistock, 1977.

Lacan, J., *The Four Fundamental Concepts of Psycho-analysis* (trans. A. Sheridan), Harmondsworth, Penguin, 1979.

Lacoue-Labarthes, P., *Heidegger, Art and Politics: The Fiction of the Political* (trans. C. Turner), Oxford, Basil Blackwell, 1990.

Léger, F., *Functions of Painting* (trans. A. Anderson), New York, Viking, 1973.

Levi, P., *The Drowned and the Saved* (trans. R. Rosenthal), New York, Vintage, 1989.

Levin, G.R., *Documentary Explorations: Fifteen Interviews with Film-Makers*, New York, Doubleday, 1971.

Leyda, J. (ed.), *Voices of Film Experience 1894 to the Present*, New York, Macmillan, 1977.

Leyda, J. and Voynow, Z., *Eisenstein at Work*, London, Methuen, 1982.

Lyotard, J.-F., *Driftworks* (trans. R. McKeon), New York, Semiotext(e), 1984.

Lyotard, J.-F., *The Postmodern Condition* (trans. G. Bennington and B. Massumi), Manchester, Manchester University Press, 1984.

Lyotard, J.-F., *The Differend: Phases in Dispute* (trans. G. Van Den Abbeele), Minneapolis, University of Minnesota Press, 1988.

Lyotard, J.-F., *Heidegger and 'the jews'* (trans. A. Michel and M.S. Roberts), Minneapolis, University of Minnesota Press, 1990.

Lyssiotis, P., *Journey of a Wise Electron and Other Stories*, Prahran, Champion Books, 1981.

McCabe, C. (ed.), *High Theory/Low Culture*, Manchester, Manchester University Press, 1986.

Mackie, F., *The Status of Everyday Life*, London, Routledge and Kegan Paul, 1985.

McLuhan, M., *Understanding Media: The Extensions of Man*, London, Abacus, 1974.

Mamber, S., *Cinema Verite in America: Studies in Uncontrolled Cinema*, Massachusetts, MIT Press, 1974.

Marx, K., *The Eighteenth Brumaire of Louis Bonaparte* (1852), New York, International Publishers, 1963.

Marx, K., *Grundrisse: Foundations of the Critique of Political Economy* (trans. M. Nicolaus), London, Allen Lane/NLR, 1973.

Marx, K. and Engels, F., *Manifesto of the Communist Party* (1848) (trans. S. Moore), Moscow, Progress Publishers, 1977.

Merleau-Ponty, M., *The Primacy of Perception* (trans. J.M. Edie et al.), Evanston, IL, Northwestern University Press, 1964.

Merleau-Ponty, M., *Sense and Non-Sense* (trans. H.L. and P.A. Dreyfus), Evanston, IL, Northwestern University Press, 1964.

Metz, C., *Psychoanalysis and the Cinema: The Imaginary Signifier* (trans. B. Brewster et al.), London, Macmillan, 1982.

Meyerowitz, J., *No Sense of Place: The Impact of Electronic Media on Social Behaviour*, New York and Oxford, Oxford University Press, 1985.

Michaels, E., *For a Cultural Future: Francis Jupurrurla Makes TV at Yuendumu*, Melbourne, Art & Criticism Monograph Series, 1987.

Michaels, E., 'Bad Aboriginal art', *Art & Text*, 28 (March–May 1988), pp. 59–73.

Miller, D., *The Reason of Metaphor: A Study in Politics*, New Delhi, Sage, 1992.

Miller, J.A., 'Suture' (trans. J. Rose), *Screen*, 18, 4 (Winter 1977–8), pp. 24–34.

Misterlich, A. and M., *The Inability to Mourn*, London, Tavistock, 1975.

Mitchell, W.T.J. (ed.), *On Narrative*, Chicago, Chicago University Press, 1981.

Monaco, J., *Alan Resnais*, New York, Oxford University Press, 1979.

Morley, D., *Family Viewing: Culture, Power and Domestic Leisure*, London, Comedia, 1986.

Morley, D. and Robins, K., *Spaces of Identity: Global Media, Electronic Landscapes and Cultural Boundaries*, London and New York, Routledge, 1995.

Mulvey, L., 'Visual pleasure and narrative cinema', *Screen*, 16, 3 (Autumn 1975), pp. 6–18.

Niven, D., *Bring on the Empty Horses*, London, Coronet Books, 1975.

Nowotny, H., *Time: The Modern and Postmodern Experience* (trans. N. Plaice), London, Polity Press, 1996.

Ong, W., *Orality and Literacy: The Technologising of the Word*, London, Methuen, 1982.

O'Regan, T. and Shoesmith, B. (eds), *History on/and/in Film*, Perth, History and Film Association of Australia, 1987.

Oudart, J.-P., 'Cinema and suture' (trans. K. Hanet), *Screen* 18, 4 (Winter 1977–8), pp. 35–47.

Panofsky, E., *Renaissance and Renascences in Western Art*, New York, Harper and Row, 1969.

Papastergiadis, N., *Modernity as Exile: The Stranger in John Berger's Writing*, Manchester, Manchester University Press, 1993.

Passuth, K., *Moholy-Nagy* (trans. E. Grusz et al.), London, Thames and Hudson, 1985.

Penny, S., 'Virtual bodybuilding', *Media Information Australia*, 69 (1993), pp. 17–22.

Petley, J., *Capital and Culture: German Cinema 1933–45*, London, British Film Institute, 1979.

Rawlence, C. (ed.), *About Time*, London, Jonathan Cape, 1985.

Robinson, R., Gallagher, J. and Denny, A., *Africa and the Victorians: The Official Mind of Imperialism*, London, Macmillan, 1972.

Rogin, M., *'Ronald Reagan' The Movie and Other Episodes in Political Demonology*, Berkeley, University of California Press, 1988.

Rorty, R., *Philosophy and the Mirror of Nature*, Oxford, Blackwell, 1980.

Rosemount, F. (ed.), *What is Surrealism?*, London, Pluto Press, 1978.

Rothman, W., 'Against the system of suture', *Film Quarterly* (Fall 1975), pp. 45–50.

Roud, R. (ed.), *Cinema: A Critical Dictionary*, New York, Viking, 1980.

Said, E., *Orientalism*, New York, Pantheon, 1978.

Sartre, J.-P., *Being and Nothingness* (trans. H.E. Barnes), London, Methuen, 1969.

Scharf, A., *Art and Photography*, London, Penguin, 1979.

Schiller, H., *Mass Communications and American Empire*, New York, Beacon Press, 1971

Schiller, H., *Communication and Cultural Domination*, New York, International Arts and Sciences Press, 1976.

Schneider, C. and Wallis, B. (eds), *Global Television*, New York, Wedge Press and Cambridge, MA, MIT Press, 1988.

Schor, N., '*Cartes Postales*: representing Paris 1900', *Critical Inquiry*, 18 (Winter 1992), pp. 188–241.

Sekula, A., 'The body and the archive', *October*, 39 (1986), pp. 3–65.

Sinclair, J., 'Television in the post-colonial world', *Arena*, 96 (1991), pp. 127–134

Sontag, S., *On Photography*, Harmondsworth, Penguin, 1979.

Sontag, S. *Under the Sign of Saturn*, New York, Farrar Strauss and Giroux, 1980.

Sorlin, P., *The Film in History: Restaging the Past*, Oxford, Basil Blackwell, 1980.

Spengler, O., *Decline of the West* (trans. C.F. Atkinson), London, Allen and Unwin, 1926.

Spivak, G.C., 'Three women's texts and a critique of imperialism', *Critical Inquiry*, 12 (Autumn 1985), pp. 243–61.

Spivak, G.C., *The Postcolonial Critic: Interviews, Strategies, Dialogues* (ed. S. Harasym), New York and London, Routledge, 1990.

Stanton, G., 'The oriental city: a North African itinerary', *Third Text*, 3/4 (Spring/Summer 1988), pp. 3–38.

Stern, F. (ed.), *The Varieties of History: From Voltaire to the Present*, New York, Vintage, 1973.

Syberberg, H.J., *Hitler: A Film from Germany* (trans. J. Neugroschel), New York, Farrar Srauss and Giroux, 1982.

Tagg, J., *The Burden of Representation*, Macmillan, London, 1988.

Tarkovsky, A., *Sculpting in Time: Reflections on the Cinema* (trans. K. Hunter-Blair), London, Bodley Head, 1986.

Terdiman, R., *Discourse/Counter-Discourse: The Theory and Practice of Symbolic Resistance in Nineteenth Century France*, Ithaca, Cornell University Press, 1985.

Terdiman, R., 'Deconstructing memory: on representing the past and theorizing culture in France since the Revolution', *Diacritics*, 15, 4 (Winter 1985–6), pp. 13–36.

Thompson, E.P., 'Time, work discipline and industrial capitalism', *Past and Present*, 38 (1967), pp. 56–97.

Tompkins, C., 'Look to the things around you: Paul Strand', *New Yorker*, 16 September 1974.

Toulmin, S. and Goodfield, J., *The Discovery of Time*, Harmondsworth, Penguin, 1967.

Trinh T. Minh-Ha, 'Documentary is/not a name', *October*, 52 (Spring 1990), pp. 76–97.

Trinh T. Minh-Ha, *Framer Framed*, New York and London, Routledge, 1992.

Urrichio, W., 'Rituals of reception, patterns of neglect: Nazi television and its postwar representation', *Wide Angle*, 11, 1 (1989), pp. 48–66.

Veeser, H.A. (ed.), *The New Historicism*, New York and London, Routledge, 1989.

Varis, T., 'Trends in international television flow', *International Political Science Review*, 7, 3 (July 1986), pp. 235–49.

Virilio, P., 'The over-exposed city' (trans. A. Hustvedt), *Zone*, 1/2 (1986), pp. 14–31.

Virilio, P., *Speed and Politics* (trans. M. Polizzotti), New York, Semiotext(e), 1986.

Virilio, P., *War and Cinema: The Logistics of Perception* (trans. P. Camiller), London and New York, Verso, 1989.

Virilio, P., *The Aesthetics of Disappearance* (trans. P. Beitchmann), New York, Semiotext(e), 1991.

Virilio, P., *The Lost Dimension* (trans. D. Moshenberg), New York, Semiotext(e), 1991.

Virilio, P., *The Vision Machine* (trans. J. Rose), Bloomington and Indianapolis, Indiana University Press and London, British Film Institute, 1994.

Wallis, B. (ed.), *Blasted Allegories: An Anthology of Contemporary Artists' Writings*, New York, New Museum of Contemporary Art and Cambridge, MA, MIT Press, 1987.

Walvin, J., *Victorian Values*, London, Cardinal, 1988.

Williams, L., *Hardcore: Power, Pleasure and the 'Frenzy of the Visible'*, Berkeley, University of California Press, 1989.

Wolf, C., *A Model Childhood* (trans. U. Molinaro and H. Rappolt), London, Virago, 1983.
Yates, F., *The Art of Memory*, London, Routledge, 1966.
Youngblood, D.J., *Soviet Cinema in the Silent Era 1918–1935*, Michigan, UMI Research Press, 1980.
Zerubavel, E., 'The standardisation of time: a sociohistorical perspective', *American Journal of Sociology*, 88, 1 (1988), pp. 1–23.

Index